AMERICA FIRSTHAND

*READINGS
IN
AMERICAN
HISTORY*

*A*MERICA *FIRSTHAND*

Volume I *FROM SETTLEMENT TO
RECONSTRUCTION*

ROBERT D. MARCUS

State University of New York College at Brockport

and

DAVID BURNER

State University of New York at Stony Brook

ST. MARTIN'S PRESS
New York

Editor: Don Reisman
Project Management: Susan Hunsberger/Editing, Design & Production, Inc.
Cover Design: Darby Downey
Cover Art: *The Cornell Farm* by Edward Hicks. National Gallery of Art, Washington;
Gift of Edgar William and Bernice Chrysler Garbisch.

Library of Congress Catalog Card Number: 87–60518

Copyright © 1989 by St. Martin's Press, Inc.

Manufactured in the United States of America.
32109
fedcba

For information, write:
St. Martin's Press, Inc.
175 Fifth Avenue
New York, NY 10010

ISBN: 0-312-00305-6

Preface

The two volumes of *America Firsthand* are a response to the growing difficulty of teaching and learning American history. While virtually no one uses the term "relevant" anymore, the old issue of the usability of the past continues to torment teachers and writers of history. Historians wonder who is listening to them besides other historians; students question why they must study what is past and gone. In recent years, this problem has increased. With the vast expansion of subject matter, historians have less and less of either a shared language or an implied synthesis or consensus around which to argue. Not long ago any American historian could expect to be able to read and understand the writing of almost any other American historian. Today many of the languages are technical, employing terms either created to express new sensibilities, or borrowed from the language of statistics or other social sciences.

And learning, of course, is always harder than teaching. Students understandably object to synthesizing a field in fragments (less understandable are objections to reading and to writing). Like their professors, however, students must draw *their own* threads through the past, whatever color these threads may be. Otherwise, it is all gray on gray.

Students need to find exemplars of themselves in the past, and *America Firsthand* is an effort to help them discover how the diversities of recent scholarship can respond to that need. The focus is on people, mostly real people, but occasionally fictional characters who speak directly of the experiences of their creators. Included are memoirs, letters, diaries, oral histories, speeches, testimonies, and pieces of fiction, the rich store that historians of the last quarter of a century have learned to find, read, and interpret. Individuals are presented insofar as possible in their own words and in selections long enough to be memorable, personal, and immediate. The accounts of indentured servants, runaway slaves, cowboys, factory workers, civil rights activists, business people, and many others offer students possible identifications while providing teachers with entries for the diverse kinds of analyses that have flourished in recent decades in American historical writing. They can also serve as occasions for student essays and research projects.

We have included enough political documents to maintain the traditional markers of United States history, which continue to provide a useful political and narrative spine. While the readings convey the experiences and forces of specific personalities, they include observations on the debates in the first meetings of the United States Senate, on the war of 1812, and on the style and policy of President John F. Kennedy. All teachers and students must struggle with the problem of connecting traditional chronology with the new materials of social history, and no formula for doing that is without its problems. We have, however, offered a set of connections that will be workable for many courses. Careful headnotes and questions at the end of each section help make the essential links.

America Firsthand explores the many ways of being an American and the many minds and personalities that make up a diverse history and nation. We see the American experience through the eyes of varied people who have in common the fact that, in some form, they have left behind vivid records of the times in which they lived. These personal eyewitness recollections serve as fertile ground in which students can begin to root their interest in history.

Acknowledgments

The authors wish to thank the following individuals who reviewed *America Firsthand* for St. Martin's Press: John Barnard, Oakland University; Virginia Bernhard, University of St. Thomas; Leonard Dinnerstein, University of Arizona; Henry C. Ferrell, Jr., East Carolina University; Patrick J. Furlong, Indiana University at South Bend; Maurine Greenwald, University of Pittsburgh; Patrick F. Palermo, University of Dayton; Nancy Rachels, Hillsborough Community College; James E. Sefton, California State University, Northridge; G. L. Seligmann, Jr., University of North Texas; Curtis Solberg, Santa Barbara City College.

Contents

AMERICA FIRSTHAND

PART I | DISCOVERY AND EARLY SETTLEMENT

The age of exploration combined the ambitions of science and humanism emerging from the Renaissance with older hopes of discovering the lost tribes of Israel and of reaching the trade of the Orient by sailing west. After Christopher Columbus discovered the "New World," he and other explorers sent reports back to Europe that were as much a product of their own age's mixed dreams as they were of America's realities. The letter from Columbus to his European supporter is representative.

The people in this new land were named Indians by explorers who mistook the Americas for the East Indies or the Orient. These American Indians had their own complex culture, which rapidly came into conflict with that of the white settlers. Chief Johnson's account of the Indian chief Hiawatha presents an Indian legend of building a nation among the Iroquois and associated tribes of upstate New York. William Apes offers an Indian view of the arrival of white settlers and the conflicts that quickly began to develop. And Father Le Jeune's account of his experience in Canada suggests how little understanding existed even between friendly whites and receptive Indians.

The New World's wilderness brought reality to the Old World's visions in strange and surprising ways. Men lusted for El Dorado but found their gold in Virginia tobacco fields or on the Grand Banks of Newfoundland. Many even found new freedoms for themselves—although black slavery and race warfare also developed at this time. Religion flourished in the colonies, as it did throughout the seventeenth-century world, but the new American environment altered society so that the churches found themselves in a losing competition with the more mundane interests required for adapting to the harshness of the colonial frontier and its economic life.

In both Virginia and New England the tremendous difficulties of making a settlement required that the new settlers have a firm belief in their mission.

1

Religious motives played a role in both settlements but were far stronger in New England. William Bradford kept a careful account of life in Plymouth, which consists of a series of reckonings over whether the colony had kept its faith with the deity, while John Smith was more concerned to sell his Virginia to prospective investors and settlers. Some of the brutal realities of life in the colonies are recounted by the early settlers Richard Frethorne and the son of William Pond.

The settlement of the middle colonies, which came later and which could be supported by the older colonies, was less dramatic and less often punctuated with tragedy. Most of the writings from these new colonies are promotional literature concentrating on opportunities for plain folk. The account of early Pennsylvania by Gabriel Thomas is representative of an important pamphlet literature that conveyed the good news about the colonies, which was somewhat embellished by the pamphleteers' imagination.

CHRISTOPHER COLUMBUS

1 | Letter to Luis de Sant' Angel

The idea of sailing west to reach the riches of the East Indies and the Asian mainland was much in vogue with literate Europeans during the late fifteenth century. Learned people agreed that the earth was round; their only question was how long and how dangerous would be a trip to reach the Orient.

Christopher Columbus, the son of an obscure Genoan weaver, and himself a weaver of ambitious dreams, made his historic voyage to the New World in 1492. Sailing with a tiny fleet of three ships and a crew of ninety sailors, he found the thirty-three-day crossing simpler than was his nearly decade long effort to find royal patrons willing to support it. The trip drew not only on his own skills as an expert ship's captain, but also on his ability to plan such an expedition, obtain governmental approval and financing, and, finally, to demonstrate (or advertise) its success so that such explorations could continue. (Columbus himself was to make a total of four voyages to the New World.)

The explorations that followed Columbus—those of Cabot, Verrazano, Cartier, and many others—benefited from a new maritime technology borrowed from Arab sailors and from a variety of new vessels such as the light-weight caravels employed by Columbus. Mariners also perfected sails and various types of riggings that gave ships added stability and greater maneuverability on the open seas. And when leaving sight of the coast, new navigational aids—charts, compasses, and astrolabes—permitted them to determine their position with some, though not perfect, accuracy.

Although Columbus himself never realized he had stumbled upon a new continent, letters such as the following, written in early 1493 to a leading supporter and a high official in the court of the Kingdom of Aragon, helped establish in the European mind the image of a brave new world.

Sir,
As I know that you will have pleasure of the great victory which our Lord hath given me in my voyage, I write you this, by which you shall know that in [thirty-three] days I passed over to the Indies with the fleet

Spanish Letter of Columbus to Luis de Sant' Angel, Escribano de Racion of the Kingdom of Aragon, Dated 15 February 1493, Reprinted in Facsimile, Translated and Edited from the Unique Copy of the Original Edition. *(London, 1891), pp. 22–27. (Translator unknown; reprinted in 1891 from a copy in the possesion of Bernard Quaritch)*

3

which the most illustrious King and Queen, our Lords, gave me: where I found very many islands peopled with inhabitants beyond number. And, of them all, I have taken possession for their Highnesses, with proclamation and the royal standard displayed; and I was not gainsaid. On the first which I found, I put the name Sant Salvador, in commemoration of His High Majesty, who marvellously hath given all this: the Indians call it [Guanhani]. The second I named the Island of Santa Maria de Concepcion, the third Ferrandina, the fourth *Fair Island*, the fifth La Isla Juana; and so for each one a new name. When I reached Juana, I followed its coast westwardly, and found it so large that I thought it might be the mainland province of Cathay. And as I did not thus find any towns and villages on the sea-coast, save small hamlets with the people whereof I could not get speech, because they all fled away forthwith, I went on further in the same direction, thinking I should not miss of great cities or towns. And at the end of many leagues, seeing that there was no change, and that the coast was bearing me northwards, whereunto my desire was contrary since the winter was already confronting us, I formed the purpose of making from thence to the South, and as the wind also blew against me, I determined not to wait for other weather and turned back as far as a port agreed upon; from which I sent two men into the country to learn if there were a king, or any great cities. They traveled for three days, and found interminable small villages and a numberless population, but nought of ruling authority; wherefore they returned. I understood sufficiently from other Indians whom I had already taken, that this land, in its continuousness, was an island; and so I followed its coast eastwardly for a hundred and seven leagues as far as where it terminated; from which headland I saw another island to the east [eighteen] leagues distant from this, to which I at once gave the name La Spañola. And I proceeded thither, and followed the northern coast, as with La Juana, eastwardly for a hundred and [eighty-eight] great leagues in a direct easterly course, as with La Juana. The which, and all the others, are more [fertile] to an excessive degree, and this extremely so. In it, there are many havens on the sea-coast, incomparable with any others that I know in Christendom, and plenty of rivers so good and great that it is a marvel. The lands thereof are high, and in it are very many ranges of hills, and most lofty mountains incomparably beyond the Island of [Tenerife]; all most beautiful in a thousand shapes, and all accessible, and full of trees of a thousand kinds, so lofty that they seem to reach the sky. And I am assured that they never lose their foliage; as may be imagined, since I saw them as green and as beautiful as they are in Spain during May. And some of them were in flower, some in fruit, some in another stage according to their kind. And the nightingale was singing, and other birds of a thousand sorts, in the month of November, round about the way that I was going. There are palm-trees of six or eight species, wondrous to see for their beautiful variety; but so are the other trees, and fruits, and plants therein. There are wonderful pine-groves, and very large plains of verdure, and there is honey, and many kinds of birds, and many various fruits. In the earth there are many mines of metals; and there is a population of incalculable number. Spañola is a marvel; the mountains and hills, and plains, and fields, and land, so beautiful and rich for planting and sowing, for breeding cattle of all sorts, for building of towns and villages. There could be no believing, without seeing, such harbours as are here, as well as the many and great rivers, and excellent waters, most of which contain gold. In the trees and fruits and plants, there are great differences from those of Juana. In [La Spañola], there are many spiceries, and great mines of gold and other metals. The people of this island, and of all the others that I have found and seen, or not seen, all go naked, men and women, just as their mothers bring them forth; although some women cover a single place with the leaf of a plant, or a cotton something which they make for that purpose. They have no iron or steel, nor any weapons; nor are they fit thereunto; not because they be not a well-formed people and of fair stature, but that they are most wondrously timorous. They have no other weapons than the stems of reeds in their seeding state, on the end of which they fix little sharpened stakes. Even these, they dare not use; for many times has it happened that I sent two or three men ashore to some village to parley, and countless numbers of them sallied forth, but as soon as they saw those approach, they fled away in such wise that even a father would not wait for his son. And this was not because any hurt had ever done to any of them:— on the contrary, at every headland where I have gone and been able to hold speech with them, I gave them of everything which I had, as well cloth as many other things, without accepting aught therefor—; but such they are, incurably timid. It is true that since they have become more assured, and are losing that terror, they are artless and generous with what they have, to such a degree as no one would believe but him who had seen it. Of anything they have, if it be asked for, they never say no, but do rather invite the person to accept it, and show as much loving-ness as though they would give their hearts. And whether it be a thing of value, or one of little worth, they are straightways content with what-soever trifle of whatsoever kind may be given them in return for it. I forbade that anything so worthless as fragments of broken platters, and pieces of broken glass, and strap-buckles, should be given them; al-though when they were able to get such things, they seemed to think they had the best jewel in the world, for it was the hap of a sailor to get, in exchange for a strap, gold to the weight of two and a half castellanos, and others much more for other things of far less value; while for new blancas[1] they gave everything they had even though it were [the worth of] two or three gold castellanos, or one or two arrobas[2] of spun cotton.

1. Copper-coins.
2. An arroba = 25 lbs.

They took even pieces of broken barrel-hoops, and gave whatever they had, like senseless brutes; insomuch that it seemed to me ill. I forbade it and I gave gratuitously a thousand useful things that I carried, in order that they may conceive affection, and furthermore may be made Christians; for they are inclined to the love and service of their Highnesses and of all the Castilian nation, and they strive to combine in giving us things which they have in abundance, and of which we are in need. And they knew no sect, nor idolatry; save that they all believe that power and goodness are in the sky, and they believed very firmly that I, with these ships and crew, came from the sky; and in such opinion, they received me at every place were I landed, after they had lost their terror. And this comes not because they are ignorant: on the contrary, they are men of very subtle wit, who navigate all those seas, and who give a marvellously good account of everything—but because they never saw men wearing clothes nor the like of our ships. And as soon as I arrived in the Indies, in the first island that I found, I took some of them by force to the intent that they should learn [our speech] and give me information of what there was in those parts. And so it was, that very soon they understood [us] and we them, what by speech or what by signs; and those [Indians] have been of much service. To this day I carry them [with me] who are still of the opinion that I come from heaven [as appears] from much conversation which they have had with me. And they were the first to proclaim it wherever I arrived; and the others went running from house to house and to the neighbouring villages, with loud cries of "Come! come to see the people from heaven!" Then, as soon as their minds were reassured about us, every one came, men as well as women, so that there remained none behind, big or little; and they all brought something to eat and drink, which they gave with wondrous lovingness. They have in all the islands very many canoes, after the manner of rowing-galleys, some larger, some smaller; and a good many are larger than a galley of eighteen benches: but a galley could not keep up with them in rowing, for their motion is a thing beyond belief. And with these, they navigate through all those islands which are numberless, and ply their traffic. I have seen some of those canoes with seventy, and eighty, men in them, each one with his oar. In all those islands, I saw not much diversity in the looks of the people, nor in their manners and language; but they all understand each other, which is a thing of singular towardness for what I hope their Highnesses will determine, as to making them conversant with our holy faith, unto which they are well disposed. I have already told how I had gone a hundred and seven leagues, in a straight line from West to East, along the sea-coast of the Island of Juana; according to which itinerary, I can declare that that island is larger than England and Scotland combined; as, over and above those hundred and seven leagues, there remains for me, on the western side, two provinces whereto I did not go—one of which they call Avan, where the people are born with tails—which provinces cannot be less in length than fifty or sixty leagues, according to what may be understood from the Indians with me, who know all the islands. This other, Española, has a greater circumference than the whole of Spain from Co*libre in Catal*unya, by the sea-coast, as far as Fuente Ravia in Biscay; since, along one of its four sides, I went for a hundred and eighty-eight great leagues in a straight line from West to East. This is [a land] to be desired,—and once seen, never to be relinquished—in which (—although, indeed, I have taken possession of them all for their Highnesses, and all are more richly endowed than I have skill and power to say, and I hold them all in the name of their Highnesses who can dispose thereof as much and as completely as of the kingdoms of Castile—) in this Española, in the place most suitable and best for its proximity to the gold mines, and for traffic with the continent, as well on this side as on the further side of the Great Can, where there will be great commerce and profit,—I took possession of a large town which I named the city of Navidad.[3] And I have made fortification there, and a fort (which by this time will have been completely finished) and I have left therein men enough for such a purpose, with arms and artillery, and provisions for more than a year, and a boat, and a [man who is] master of all seacraft for making others; and great friendship with the King of that land, to such a degree that he prided himself on calling and holding me as his brother. And even though his mind might change towards attacking those men, neither he nor his people know what arms are, and go naked. As I have already said, they are the most timorous creatures there are in the world, so that the men who remain there are alone sufficient to destroy all that land, and the island is without personal danger for them if they know how to behave themselves. It seems to me that in all those islands, the men are all content with a single wife; and to their chief or king they give as many as twenty. The women, it appears to me, do more work than the men. Nor have I been able to learn whether they held personal property, for it seemed to me that whatever one had, they all took share of, especially of eatable things. Down to the present, I have not found in those islands any monstrous men, as many expected, but on the contrary all the people are very comely; nor are they black like those in Guinea, but have flowing hair; and they are not begotten where there is an excessive violence of the rays of the sun. It is true that the sun is there very strong, notwithstanding that it is twenty-six degrees distant from the equinoctial line. In those islands, where there are lofty mountains, the cold was very keen there, this winter; but they endure it by being accustomed thereto, and by the help of the meats which they eat with many and inordinately hot spices. Thus I have not found, nor had any information of monsters, except of an island which is here the second in the approach to the Indies, which is inhabited by a people whom, in all the islands, they regard as very fero-

3. *Navidad* is the same as *Natividad:* he reached the spot on Christmas-day, 1492.

cious, who eat human flesh. Amongst those other tribes who are excessively cowardly, these are ferocious; but I hold them as nothing more than the others. These are they who have to do with the women of [Matinino]—which is the first island that is encountered in the passage from Spain to the Indies—in which there are no men. Those women practise no female usages, but have bows and arrows of reed such as above mentioned; and they arm and cover themselves with plates of copper of which they have much. In another island, which they assure me is larger than Española, the people have no hair. In this, there is incalculable gold; and concerning these and the rest I bring Indians with me as witnesses. And in conclusion, to speak only of what has been done in this voyage, which has been so hastily performed, their Highnesses may see that I shall give them as much gold as they may need, with very little aid which their Highnesses will give me; spices and cotton at once, as much as their Highnesses will order to be shipped, and as much as they shall order to be shipped of mastic,—which till now has never been found except in Greece, in the island of [Chios], and the Seignory [of Genoa] sells it for what it likes; and aloe-wood as much as they shall order to be shipped; and slaves as many as they shall order to be shipped,—and these shall be from idolators. And I believe that I have discovered rhubarb and cinnamon, and I shall find that the men whom I am leaving there will have discovered a thousand other things of value; as I made no delay at any point, so long as the wind gave me an opportunity of sailing, except only in the town of Navidad till I had left things safely arranged and well established. And in truth I should have done much more if the ships had served me as well as might reasonably have been expected. This is enough; and [thanks to] eternal God our Lord who gives to all those who walk His way, victory over things which seem impossible; and this was signally one such, for although men have talked or written of those lands, it was all by conjecture, without confirmation from eyesight, importing just so much that the hearers for the most part listened and judged that there was more fable in it than anything actual, however trifling. Since thus our Redeemer has given to our most illustrious King and Queen, and to their famous kingdoms, this victory in so high a matter, Christendom should take gladness therein and make great festivals, and give solemn thanks to the Holy Trinity for the great exaltation they shall have by the conversion of so many peoples to our holy faith; and next for the temporal benefit which will bring hither refreshment and profit, not only to Spain, but to all Christians. This briefly, in accordance with the facts. Dated, on the caravel, off the Canary Islands, the 15 February of the year 1493.

At your command,

THE ADMIRAL.

CHIEF ELIAS JOHNSON

2 | On the Founding of the Indian Nations

When the first European settlers reached North America, they encountered people who themselves had complex values and traditions. For over two hundred years after its organization in about 1570, the Iroquois Confederacy, also known as the Five Indian Nations (later the Tuscarora joined as the sixth nation), dominated upstate New York and blocked the way west for British settlers in New England and the Hudson Valley. Richly embroidered Indian legend attributed the founding of the Confederacy to Hiawatha, a leader of the Mohawks—one of the five tribes—whom Indian lore eventually transformed into a wise and powerful god. Hiawatha, according to the legend, saw common ground among the five tribes that enabled them to create an effective confederacy without sacrificing the autonomy of the tribes. The American republic would wrestle with a similar problem, as Benjamin Franklin foresaw. Franklin, in fact, was so impressed with the structure of the Iroquois Confederacy that he recommended its government as a model for the colonies to join separate sovereign states into a powerful nation.

We learn of Hiawatha from Chief Elias Johnson, whose tribe, the Tuscarora, had migrated from North Carolina in the early eighteenth century to join the Iroquois Confederacy in New York. He collected the oral traditions of the Iroquois tribes, many of which had passed from generation to generation for centuries. His book, Legends, Traditions, and Laws of the Iroquois, or Six Nations, and History of the Tuscarora Indians, *published in 1881, is a standard reference on the history of the Iroquois.*

When another day had expired, the council again met. Hiawatha entered the assembly with even more than ordinary attention, and every eye was fixed upon him, when he began to address the council in the following words:

"Friends and Brothers:—You being members of many tribes, you have come from a great distance; the voice of war has aroused you up; you are afraid of your homes, your wives and your children; you trembled for your safety. Believe me, I am with you. My heart beats with

Elias Johnson (A Native Tuscarora Chief), Legends, Traditions and Laws of the Iroquois, or Six Nations, and History of the Tuscarora Indians. (Lockport, N.Y., Union Printing and Publishing Company, 1881), pp 50–53.

your hearts. We are one. We have one common object. We come to promote our common interest, and to determine how this can be best done.

"To oppose those hordes of northern tribes, singly and alone, would prove certain destruction. We can make no progress in that way. We must unite ourselves into one common band of brothers. We must have but one voice. Many voices makes confusion. We must have one fire, one pipe and one war club. This will give us strength. If our warriors are united they can defeat the enemy and drive them from our land; if we do this, we are safe.

"Onondaga, you are the people sitting under the shadow of the *Great Tree*, whose branches spread far and wide, and whose roots sink deep into the earth. You shall be the first nation, because you are warlike and mighty.

"Oneida, and you, the people who recline your bodies against the *Everlasting Stone*, that cannot be moved, shall be the second nation, because you always give good counsel.

"Seneca, and you, the people who have your habitation at the foot of the *Great Mountain*, and are overshadowed by its crags, shall be the third nation, because you are all greatly gifted in speech.

"Cayuga, you, whose dwelling is in the *Dark Forest*, and whose home is everywhere, shall be the fourth nation, because of your superior cunning in hunting.

"Mohawk, and you, the people who live in the open country, and possess much wisdom, shall be the fifth nation, because you understand better the art of raising corn and beans and making cabins.

"You five great and powerful nations, with your tribes, must unite and have one common interest, and no foe shall disturb or subdue you.

"And you of the different nations of the south, and you of the west, may place yourselves and our protection, and we will protect you. We earnestly desire the alliance and friendship of you all. . . .

"If we unite in one band the Great Spirit will smile upon us, and we shall be free, prosperous and happy; but if we shall remain as we are we shall incur his displeasure. We shall be enslaved, and perhaps annihilated forever.

"Brothers, these are the words of Hiawatha. Let them sink deep into your hearts. I have done."

A deep and impressive silence followed the delivery of this speech. On the following day the council again assembled to act on it. High wisdom recommended this deliberation.

The union of the tribes into one confederacy was discussed and unanimously adopted. To denote the character and intimacy of the union they employed the figure of a single council-house, or lodge, whose boundaries be co-extensive with their territories. Hence the name of Ako-no-shu-ne, who were called the Iroquois. . . .

Hiawatha, the guardian and founder of the league, having now accomplished the will of the Great Spirit, immediately prepared to make his final departure. Before the great council, which had adopted his advice just before dispersing, he arose, with a dignified air, and addressed them in the following manner:

"Friends and Brothers:—I have now fulfilled my mission here below; I have furnished you seeds and grains for your gardens; I have removed obstructions from your waters, and made the forest habitable by teaching you how to expel its monsters; I have given you fishing places and hunting grounds; I have instructed you in the making and using of war implements; I have taught you how to cultivate corn, and many other arts and gifts. I have been allowed by the Great Spirit to communicate to you. Last of all, I have aided you to form a league of friendship and union. If you preserve this, and admit no foreign element of power by the admission of other nations, you will always be free, numerous and happy. If other tribes and nations are admitted to your councils, they will sow the seed of jealousy and discord, and you will become few, feeble and enslaved.

"Friends and brothers, these are the last words you will hear from the lips of Hiawatha. The Great Creator of our bodies calls me to go; I have patiently awaited his summons; I am ready to go. Farewell."

As the voice of the wise man ceased, sweet strains of music from the air burst on the ears of the multitide. The whole sky appeared to be filled with melody; and while all eyes were directed to catch glimpses of the sights, and enjoy strains of the celestial music that filled the sky, Hiawatha was seen, seated in his snow-white canoe, amid the air, *rising, rising* with every choral chant that burst out. As he rose the sound of the music became more soft and faint, until he vanished amid the summer clouds, and the melody ceased. . . .

3 | Encounter with the Indians

The society of Jesus of the Roman Catholic Church, known usually as the Jesuits, in the sixteenth and seventeenth century energetically proselytized in virtually every Portuguese, Spanish, and French colony. Coming from a world and culture apart from their new clientele, the first Jesuit missionaries arrived in French Canada in 1632 determined to bring Christianity to the Indians by living with them, learning their languages, educating their children, and demonstrating (sometimes at the cost of their lives) that they were as brave as the Indian warriors. The Jesuits played a major role in cementing French alliance with many Indian tribes across Canada and into the Ohio Valley. This gave France a strategic position in the New World, hemming the colonies of British North America against the eastern seaboard until French power was destroyed in the mid-eighteenth century. The Jesuits in Canada reported regularly on their ministry. These reports form an important account of Indian life and greatly influenced the European perception of the New World.

Father Paul Le Jeune, born in France in 1591, became a Jesuit in 1613; he had been a professor of rhetoric as well as Superior of the Jesuit House at Dieppe before he radically changed his activities by going to French North America in 1632. Le Jeune worked with the Indians until 1649. He died in Paris in 1664.

Le Jeune found much to admire in the Indians, as well as much that he could neither understand nor accept. The reports below, written from Quebec in August 1634, indicate how little whites and Indians could undertand one another, even when they shared common hardships.

CHAPTER IV. ON THE BELIEF, SUPERSTITIONS, AND ERRORS OF THE MONTAGNAIS SAVAGES.

I have already reported that the Savages believe that a certain one named Atachocam had created the world, and that one named Messou had restored it. I have questioned upon this subject the famous Sorcerer and the old man with whom I passed the Winter; they answered

Reuben Gold Thwaites (editor), The Jesuit Relations and Allied Documents: Travels and Explorations of the Jesuit Missionaries in New France, 1610–1791. (Cleveland, The Burrows Brothers Company, 1897) From Volume VI: pp. 157, 159, 161, 201, 203, 205, 225, 229, 231, 233, 243, 245, 247. From Volume VII: pp. 35, 37, 39, 41, 43.

that they did not know who was the first Author of the world,—that it was perhaps Atahocham, but that was not certain; that they only spoke of Atahocam as one speaks of a thing so far distant that nothing sure can be known about it; . . .

As to the Messou, they hold that he restored the world, which was destroyed in the flood; whence it appears that they have some tradition of that great universal deluge which happened in the time of Noë. . .

They also say that all animals, of every species, have an elder brother, who is, as it were, the source and origin of all individuals, and this elder brother is wonderfully great and powerful. . . . Now these elders of all the animals are the juniors of the Messou. Behold him well related, this worthy restorer of the Universe, he is elder brother to all beasts. If any one, when asleep, sees the elder or progenitor of some animals, he will have a fortunate chase; if he sees the elder of the Beavers, he will take Beavers; if he sees the elder of the Elks, he will take Elks, possessing the juniors through the favor of their senior whom he has seen in the dream. . . .

Their Religion, or rather their superstition, consists besides in praying; but O, my God, what prayers they make! In the morning, when the little children come out from their Cabins, they shout, *Cacouakhi, Pakhais Amiscouakhi, Pakhais Mousouakhi, Pakhais*, "Come, Porcupines; come, Beavers; come, Elk;" and this is all of their prayers.

When the Savages sneeze, and sometimes even at other times, during the Winter, they cry out in a loud voice, *Etouctaian miraouinam an Mirouscamikhi*, "I shall be very glad to see the Spring."

At other times, I have heard them pray for the Spring, or for deliverance from evils and other similar things; and they express all these things in the form of desires, crying out as loudly as they can, "I would be very glad if this day would continue, if the wind would change," etc. I could not say to whom these wishes are addressed, for they themselves do not know, at least those whom I have asked have not been able to enlighten me. . . .

These are some of their superstitions. How much dust there is in their eyes, and how much trouble there will be to remove it that they may see the beautiful light of truth! I believe, nevertheless, that any one who knew their language perfectly, in order to give them good reasons promptly, would soon make them laugh at their own stupidity; for sometimes I have made them ashamed and confused, although I speak almost entirely by my hands, I mean by signs. . . .

CHAPTER V. ON THE GOOD THINGS WHICH ARE FOUND AMONG THE SAVAGES.

If we begin with physical advantages, I will say that they possess these in abundance. They are tall, erect, strong, well proportioned, agile; and there is nothing effeminate in their appearance. Those little Fops that are seen elsewhere are only caricatures of men, compared with our Savages. I almost believed, heretofore, that the Pictures of the Roman Emperors represented the ideal of the painters rather than men who had ever existed, so strong and powerful are their heads; but I see here upon the shoulders of these people the heads of Julius Cæsar, of Pompey, of Augustus, of Otho, and of others, that I have seen in France, drawn upon paper, or in relief on medallions.

As to the mind of the Savage, it is of good quality. I believe that souls are all made from the same stock, and that they do not materially differ; hence, these barbarians having well formed bodies, and organs well regulated and well arranged, their minds ought to work with ease. Education and instruction alone are lacking. Their soul is a soil which is naturally good, but loaded down with all the evils that a land abandoned since the birth of the world can produce. I naturally compare our Savages with certain villagers, because both are usually without education, though our Peasants are superior in this regard; and yet I have not seen any one thus far, of those who have come to this country, who does not confess and frankly admit that the Savages are more intelligent than our ordinary peasants.

Moreover, if it is a great blessing to be free from a great evil, our Savages are happy; for the two tyrants who provide hell and torture for many of our Europeans, do not reign in their great forests,—I mean ambition and avarice. As they have neither political organization, nor offices, nor dignities, nor any authority, for they only obey their Chief through good will toward him, therefore they never kill each other to acquire these honors. Also, as they are contented with a mere living, not one of them gives himself to the Devil to acquire wealth.

They make a pretence of never getting angry, not because of the beauty of this virtue, for which they have not even a name, but for their own contentment and happiness, I mean, to avoid the bitterness caused by anger. The Sorcerer said to me one day, speaking of one of our Frenchmen, "He has no sense, he gets angry; as for me, nothing can disturb me; let hunger oppress me, let my nearest relation pass to the other life, let the Hiroquois, our enemies, massacre our people, I never get angry." What he says is not an article of faith; for, as he is more haughty than any other Savage, so I have seen him oftener out of humor than any of them; it is true also that he often restrains and governs himself by force, especially when I expose his foolishness. I have only heard one Savage pronounce this word, *Ninichcatihin*, "I am angry," and he only said it once. But I noticed that they kept their eyes on him, for when these Barbarians are angry, they are dangerous and unrestrained.

Whoever professes not to get angry, ought also to make a profession of patience; the Savages surpass us to such an extent, in this respect, that we ought to be ashamed. I saw them, in their hardships and in their labors, suffer with cheerfulness. My host, wondering at the great number of people who I told him were in France, asked me if the men were good, if they did not become angry, if they were patient. I have never seen such patience as is shown by a sick Savage. You may yell, storm, jump, dance, and he will scarcely ever complain. I found myself, with them, threatened with great suffering; they said to me, "We shall be sometimes two days, sometimes three, without eating, for lack of food; take courage, *Chihiné*, let thy soul be strong to endure suffering and hardship; keep thyself from being sad, otherwise thou wilt be sick; see how we do not cease to laugh, although we have little to eat." One thing alone casts them down,—it is when they see death, for they fear this beyond measure; take away this apprehension from the Savages, and they will endure all kinds of degradation and discomfort, and all kinds of trials and suffering very patiently. . . .

They are very much attached to each other, and agree admirably. You do not see any disputes, quarrels, enmities, or reproaches among them. Men leave the arrangement of the household to the women, without interfering with them; they cut, and decide, and give away as they please, without making the husband angry. . . .

CHAPTER VI. ON THEIR VICES AND THEIR IMPERFECTIONS.

The Savages, being filled with errors, are also haughty and proud. Humility is born of truth, vanity of error and falsehood. They are void of the knowledge of truth, and are in consequence, mainly occupied with thought of themselves. They imagine that they ought by right of birth, to enjoy the liberty of Wild ass colts, rendering no homage to any one whomsoever, except when they like. They have reproached me a hundred times because we fear our Captains, while they laugh at and make sport of theirs. All the authority of their chief is in his tongue's end; for he is powerful in so far as he is eloquent; and, even if he kills himself talking and haranguing, he will not be obeyed unless he pleases the Savages. . . .

I have shown in my former letters how vindictive the Savages are toward their enemies, with what fury and cruelty they treat them, eating them after they have made them suffer all that an incarnate fiend could invent. This fury is common to the women as well as to the men, and they even surpass the latter in this respect. I have said that they eat the lice they find upon themselves, not that they like the taste of them, but because they want to bite those that bite them.

These people are very little moved by compassion. When any one is sick in their Cabins, they ordinarily do not cease to cry and storm, and make as much noise as if everybody were in good health. They do not know what it is to take care of a poor invalid, and to give him the food which is good for him; if he asks for something to drink, it is given to him, if he asks for something to eat, it is given to him, but otherwise he is neglected; to coax him with love and gentleness, is a language which they do not understand. As long as a patient can eat, they will carry or drag him with them; if he stops eating, they believe that it is all over with him and kill him, as much to free him from the sufferings that he is enduring, as to relieve themselves of the trouble of taking him with them when they go to some other place. I have both admired and pitied the patience of the invalids whom I have seen among them.

The Savages are slanderous beyond all belief; I say, also among themselves, for they do not even spare their nearest relations, and with it all they are deceitful. For, if one speaks ill of another, they all jeer with loud laughter; if the other appears upon the scene, the first one will show him as much affection and treat him with as much love, as if he had elevated him to the third heaven by his praise. The reason of this is, it seems to me, that their slanders and derision do not come from malicious hearts or from infected mouths, but from a mind which says what it thinks in order to give itself free scope, and which seeks gratification from everything, even from slander and mockery. Hence they are not troubled even if they are told that others are making sport of them, or have injured their reputation. All they usually answer to such talk is, *mama irinisiou*, "He has no sense, he does not know what he is talking about;" and at the first opportunity they will pay their slanderer in the same coin, returning him the like.

Lying is as natural to Savages as talking, not among themselves, but to strangers. Hence it can be said that fear and hope, in one word, interest, is the measure of their fidelity. I would not be willing to trust them, except as they would fear to be punished if they failed in their duty, or hoped to be rewarded if they were faithful to it. They do not know what it is to keep a secret, to keep their word, and to love with constancy,— especially those who are not of their nation, for they are harmonious among themselves, and their slanders and raillery do not disturb their peace and friendly intercourse. . . .

CHAPTER XII. WHAT ONE MUST SUFFER IN WINTERING WITH THE SAVAGES.

In order to have some conception of the beauty of this edifice, its construction must be described. I shall speak from knowledge, for I have often helped to build it. Now, when we arrived at the place where we were to camp, the women, armed with axes, went here and there in the great forests, cutting the framework of the hostelry where we were to lodge; meantime the men, having drawn the plan thereof, cleared away the snow with their snowshoes, or with shovels which they make and carry expressly for this purpose. Imagine now a great ring or square in the snow, two, three or four feet deep, according to the weather or the place where they encamp. This depth of snow makes a white wall for us, which surrounds us on all sides, except the end where it is broken through to form the door. The framework having been brought, which consists of twenty or thirty poles, more or less, according to the size of the cabin, it is planted, not upon the ground but upon the snow; then they throw upon these poles, which converge a little at the top, two or three rolls of bark sewed together, beginning at the bottom, and behold, the house is made. The ground inside, as well as the wall of snow which extends all around the cabin, is covered with little branches of fir; and, as a finishing touch, a wretched skin is fastened to two poles to serve as a door, the doorposts being the snow itself. . . .

You cannot stand upright in this house, as much on account of its low roof as the suffocating smoke; and consequently you must always lie down, or sit flat upon the ground, the usual posture of the Savages. When you go out, the cold, the snow, and the danger of getting lost in these great woods drive you in again more quickly than the wind, and keep you a prisoner in a dungeon which has neither lock nor key.

This prison, in addition to the uncomfortable position that one must occupy upon a bed of earth, has four other great discomforts,—cold, heat, smoke, and dogs. As to the cold, you have the snow at your head with only a pine branch between, often nothing but your hat, and the winds are free to enter in a thousand places. . . . When I lay down at night I could study through this opening both the Stars and the Moon as easily as if I had been in the open fields.

Nevertheless, the cold did not annoy me as much as the heat from the fire. A little place like their cabins is easily heated by a good fire, which sometimes roasted and broiled me on all sides, for the cabin was so narrow that I could not protect myself against the heat. You cannot move to right or left, for the Savages, your neighbors, are at your elbows; you cannot withdraw to the rear, for you encounter the wall of snow, or the bark of the cabin which shuts you in. I did not know what position to take. Had I stretched myself out, the place was so narrow that my legs would have been halfway in the fire; to roll myself up in a ball, and crouch down in their way, was a position I could not retain as long as they could; my clothes were all scorched and burned. You will ask me perhaps if the snow at our backs did not melt under so much heat. I answer, "no;" that if sometimes the heat softened it in the least, the cold immediately turned it into ice. I will say, however, that both the cold and the heat are endurable, and that some remedy may be found for these two evils.

But, as to the smoke, I confess to you that it is martyrdom. It almost killed me, and made me weep continually, although I had neither grief nor sadness in my heart. It sometimes grounded all of us who were in the cabin; that is, it caused us to place our mouths against the earth in order to breathe. For, although the Savages were accustomed to this torment, yet occasionally it became so dense that they, as well as I, were compelled to prostrate themselves, and as it were to eat the earth, so as not to drink the smoke. I have sometimes remained several hours in this position, especially during the most severe cold and when it snowed; for it was then the smoke assailed us with the greatest fury, seizing us by the throat, nose, and eyes. . . .

As to the dogs, which I have mentioned as one of the discomforts of the Savages' houses, I do not know that I ought to blame them, for they have sometimes rendered me good service. . . . These poor beasts, not being able to live outdoors, came and lay down sometimes upon my shoulders, sometimes upon my feet, and as I only had one blanket to serve both as covering and mattress, I was not sorry for this protection, willingly restoring to them a part of the heat which I drew from them. It is true that, as they were large and numerous, they occasionally crowded and annoyed me so much, that in giving me a little heat they robbed me of my sleep, so that I very often drove them away. . . .

WILLIAM APES

4 | Eulogy on King Philip,
Wampanoag Chief

*William Apes, an ordained Methodist minister, was a direct descendant of the
Wampanoag chief King Philip, who fought and lost New England's greatest
Indian War in 1675. The first selection that follows is an account by Apes of
early Indian-white relations in Massachusetts. The second is a eulogy of King
Philip, delivered by Apes in Boston in 1836. Apes mysteriously disappeared
soon after making the eulogy of King Philip.*

*As with the reading on the Iroquois, in the absence of first-hand Indian
testimony from the seventeenth century, one must turn to a source like the following—a remembrance, handed down orally from one generation to another—
to try to understand the Indian perspective on events.*

THE PILGRIM INVASION

December, 1620, the pilgrims landed at Plymouth; and without asking
liberty from any one, they possessed themselves of a portion of the
country, and built themselves houses, and then made a treaty, and commanded them [the Indians] to accede to it. This, if now done, would be
called an insult, and every white man would be called to go out and act
the part of a patriot, to defend their country's rights; and if every in-
truder were butchered, it would be sung upon every hilltop in the
Union, that victory and patriotism was the order of the day. And yet
the Indians, (though many were dissatisfied), without the shedding of
blood, or imprisoning any one, bore it. And yet for their kindness and
resignation towards the whites, they were called savages, and made by
God on purpose for them to destroy. . . . It appears that a treaty was
made by the pilgrims and the Indians, which treaty was kept during
forty years; the young chiefs during this time, was showing the pilgrims
how to live in their country, and find support for their wives and little
ones; and for all this, they were receiving the applauses of being savages. The two gentlemen chiefs were Squanto and Samoset, that were
so good to the pilgrims.

The next we present before you are things very appalling. We turn
our attention to dates, 1623, January and March, when Mr. Weston['s]

William Apes, Eulogy on King Philip as Pronounced at the Odeon in Federal Street, Boston, by the Reverand William Apes, An Indian. *(Boston, published by the author, 1837) pp.*
10–14, 27–31, 36–40.

19

Colony, came very near starving to death; some of them were obliged to hire themselves to the Indians, to become their servants, in order that they might live. Their principal work was to bring wood and water; but not being contented with this, many of the whites sought to steal the Indian's corn; and because the Indians complained of it, and through their complaint, some one of their number being punished, as they say, to appease the savages. Now let us see who the greatest savages were; the person that stole the corn was a stout athletic man, and because of this, they wished to spare him, and take an old man who was lame and sickly, and that used to get his living by weaving; and because they thought he would not be of so much use to them, he was, although innocent of the crime, hung in his stead. Oh, savage! where art thou, to weep over the Christian's crimes! Another act of humanity for Christians, as they call themselves, that one Captain Standish, gathering some fruit and provisions, goes forward with a black and hypocritical heart, and pretends to prepare a feast for the Indians; and when they sit down to eat, they seize the Indian's knives hanging about their necks, and stab them to the heart. The white people call this stabbing, feasting the savages. We suppose it might well mean themselves, their conduct being more like savages than Christians. They took one Wittu-mumet, the Chief's head, and put it upon a pole in their fort; and for aught we know, gave praise to God for success in murdering a poor Indian; for we know it was their usual course to give praise to God for this kind of victory, believing it was God's will and command, for them to do so. . . .

But we have more to present; and that is, the violation of a treaty that the pilgrims proposed for the Indians to subscribe to, and they the first to break it. The pilgrims promised to deliver up every transgressor of the Indian treaty, to them, to be punished according to their laws, and the Indians were to do likewise. Now it appears that an Indian had committed treason, by conspiring against the king's life, which is punishable with death, and Massasoit makes demand for the transgressor, and the pilgrims refuse to give him up, although by their oath of alliance they had promised to do so. Their reasons were, he was beneficial to them. This shows how grateful they were to their former safeguard, and ancient protector. Now, who would have blamed this venerable old chief if he had declared war at once, and swept the whole colonies away? It was certainly in his power to do it, if he pleased; but no, he forbore, and forgave the whites. But where is there a people, called civilized, that would do it? we presume, none; and we doubt not but the pilgrims would have exerted all their powers to be avenged, and to appease their ungodly passions. But it will be seen that this good old chief exercised more Christian forbearance than any of the governors of that age, or since. It might well be said he was a pattern for the Christians themselves; but by the Pilgrims he is denounced, as being a savage.

The history of New England writers say, that our tribes were large and respectable. How then, could it be otherwise, but their safety rested in the hands of friendly Indians and this would ever have remained so, had they been treated kindly.

KING PHILIP'S WAR

At council it appears that Philip made the following speech to his chiefs, counsellors and warriors.

Brothers,—You see this vast country before us, which the Great Spirit gave to our fathers and us; you see the buffalo and deer that now are our support.—Brothers, you see these little ones, our wives and children, who are looking to us for food and raiment; and you now see the foe before you, that they have grown insolent and bold; that all our ancient customs are disregarded; the treaties made by our fathers and us are broken, and all of us insulted; our council fires put out, our brothers murdered before our eyes, and their spirits cry to us for revenge. Brothers, these people from the unknown world will cut down our groves, spoil our hunting and planting grounds, and drive us and our children from the graves of our fathers, and our women and children will be enslaved.

This famous speech of Philip was calculated to arouse them to arms, to do the best they could in protecting and defending their rights. . . . Philip's young men were eager to do exploits, and to lead captive their haughty lords. It does appear that every Indian heart had been lighted up at the council fires, at Philip's speech, and that the forest was literally alive with this injured race. And now town after town fell before them. The Pilgrims with their forces were ever marching in one direction, while Philip and his forces were marching in another, burning all before them, until Middleborough, Taunton and Dartmouth were laid in ruins, and forsaken by its inhabitants.

At the great fight at Pocasset, Philip commanded in person, where he also was discovered with his host in a dismal swamp. He had retired here with his army to secure a safe retreat from the pilgrims, who were in close pursuit of him, and their numbers were so powerful they thought the fate of Philip was sealed. They surrounded the swamp, in hopes to destroy him and his army. At the edge of the swamp Philip had secreted a few of his men to draw them into ambush, upon which the pilgrims showed fight; Philip's men retreating and the whites pursuing them till they were surrounded by Philip, and nearly all cut off. This was a sorry time to them; the pilgrims, however, reinforced, but ordered a retreat, supposing it impossible for Philip to escape, and knowing his forces to be great, it was conjectured by some to build a fort to starve him out, as he had lost but few men in the fight. The situation of Philip was rather peculiar, as there was but one outlet to the swamp, and a river before him nearly seven miles to descend. The pilgrims placed a guard around the swamp for thirteen days, which gave Philip and his men time to prepare canoes to make good his retreat; in which he did, to the Connecticut river, and in his retreat lost but fourteen men. We may look upon this move of Philip's to be equal, if not superior to that of Washington crossing the Delaware. For while Washington was assisted by all the knowledge that art and science could give, together with the instruments of defence, and edged tools to prepare rafts, and the like helps for safety across the river, Philip was naked as to any of these thing[s], possessing only what nature, his mother, had bestowed upon him; and yet makes his escape with equal praise. . . .

Philip having now taken possession of the back settlements of Massachusetts, one town after another was swept off. A garrison being established at Northfield by the pilgrims, and while endeavoring to reinforce it with thirty-six armed, twenty out of their number was killed, and one taken prisoner. At the same time Philip so managed it as to cut off their retreat, and take their ammunition from them.

About the month of August, they [the Indians] took a young lad about fourteen years of age, whom they intended to make merry with the next day; but the pilgrims said God touched the Indians' heart, and they let him go. About the same time, the whites took an old man of Philip's, whom they found alone; and because he would not turn traitor, and inform them where Philip was, they pronounced him worthy of death; and by them was executed, cutting off first his arms and then his head. We wonder why God did not touch the pilgrims' heart, and save them from cruelty, as well as the Indians. . . .

But we have another dark and corrupt deed for the sons of the pilgrims to look at; and that is the fight and capture of Philip's son and wife, and many of his warriors, in which Philip lost about 130 men killed and wounded; this was in August 1676. But the most horrid act was in taking Philip's son, about ten years of age, and selling them [Philip's son and wife] to be slaves in foreign lands. While I am writing, I can hardly restrain my feelings, to think a people calling themselves Christians, should conduct so scandalous, so outrageous, making themselves appear so despicable in the eyes of the Indians; and even now in this audience I doubt not but there are men honorable enough to despise the conduct of those pretended Christians. And surely none but such as believe they did right, will ever go and undertake to celebrate that day of their landing, the 22d of December. . . .

Philip's forces had now become very small, so many having been duped away by the whites, and killed, that it was now easy surrounding him. Therefore, upon the 12th of August, Captain Church surrounded the swamp where Philip and his men had encamped, early in the morning, before they had risen, doubtless led on by an Indian who was either compelled or hired to turn traitor. Church had now placed his guard so that it was impossible for Philip to escape without being shot. It is doubtful, however, whether they would have taken him if he had not been surprised. Suffice it to say, however, this was the case. A sorrowful morning to the poor Indians, to lose such a valuable man. When coming out of the swamp, he was fired upon by an Indian, and killed dead upon the spot.

I rejoice that it was even so, that the pilgrims did not have the pleasure of tormenting him. The white man's gun missing fire, he lost the honor of killing the truly great man, Philip. The place where Philip fell was very muddy. Upon this news, the pilgrims gave three cheers; then Church ordering his body to be pulled out of the mud, while one of those tender-hearted Christians exclaims, what a dirty creature he looks like. And we have also Church's speech upon that subject, as follows: For as much as he has caused many a pilgrim to lie above ground unburied, to rot, not one of his bones shall be buried. With him fell five of his best and most trusty men; one the son of a chief, who fired the first gun in the war.

Captain Church now orders him to be cut up. Accordingly, he was quartered and hung up upon four trees; his head and one hand given to the Indian who shot him, to carry about to show. At which sight it so overjoyed the pilgrims, that they would give him money for it; and in this way obtained a considerable sum. After which, his head was sent to Plymouth, and exposed upon a gibbet for twenty years; and his hand to Boston, where it was exhibited in savage triumph; and his mangled body denied a resting place in the tomb. . . .

I think that as a matter of honor, that I can rejoice that no such evil conduct is recorded of the Indians; that they never hung up any of the white warriors, who were head men. And we add the famous speech of Dr. Increase Mather: he says, during the bloody contest, the pious fathers wrestled hard and long with their God, in prayer, that he would prosper their arms, and deliver their enemies into their hands. . . . The Doctor closes thus: Nor could they, the Pilgrims, cease crying to the Lord against Philip, until they had prayed the bullet through his heart. However, if this is the way they pray, that is bullets through people's hearts, I hope they will not pray for me; I should rather be excused.

5 | Description of Virginia

Captain John Smith (1580–1631) fought the Turks in eastern Europe before his adventures in Virginia began. His life was full of high adventure and the exploration of unknown lands, but his writing is a bit more colorful than it is truthful.

Smith was one of the original settlers of Jamestown, Virginia, in 1607, and he took part in governing the colony and managing relations with the Indians. According to legend, he was saved from death at the Indians' hands by the friendly intervention of the chief's daughter, Pocahontas (most historians doubt the veracity of this and many other Smith anecdotes).

Smith returned with Pocahontas to England in 1609. His later years were given over to promoting both himself and the settlement of the New World he had helped to colonize. His description of Virginia as a land of opportunity, like Columbus's description of the Americas, is an early example of the boosterism and exaggerated advertising that can be found throughout American history. Smith's description of the Indians, with its mixture of admiration, distrust, and contempt for their failure to behave like Europeans, also set a pattern that continued for centuries.

THE COMMODITIES IN VIRGINIA OR THAT MAY BE HAD BY INDUSTRIE.

The mildnesse of the aire, the fertilitie of the soile, and the situation of the rivers are so propitious to the nature and use of man as no place is more convenient for pleasure, profit, and mans sustenance. Under that latitude or climat, here will live any beasts, as horses, goats, sheep, asses, hens, &c. as appeared by them that were carried thither. The waters, Isles, and shoales, are full of safe harbours for ships of warre or marchandize, for boats of all sortes, for transportation or fishing, &c.

The Bay and rivers have much marchandable fish and places fit for Salt coats, building of ships, making of iron, &c.

Muscovia and *Polonia* doe yearely receave many thousands, for pitch,

Captain John Smith of Willoughby by Alford, Lincolnshire; President of Virginia, and Admiral of New England. Works: 1608–1631. *Edited by Edward Arber, The English Scholar's Library, No. 16. Birmingham, 1884, pp. 63–67.*

tarre, sope ashes, Rosen, Flax, Cordage, Sturgeon, masts, yards, wain-scot, Firres, glasse, and such like; also *Swethland* for iron and copper. *France* in like manner, for Wine, Canvas, and Salt, *Spaine* asmuch for Iron, Steele, Figges, Reasons, and Sackes. *Italy* with Silkes and Velvets, consumes our chiefe commodities. *Hol[l]and* maintaines it selfe by fish-ing and trading at our owne doores. All these temporize with other for necessities, but all as uncertaine as peace or warres: besides the charge, travell, and danger in transporting them, by seas, lands, stormes, and Pyrats. Then how much hath Virginia the prerogative of all those florish-ing kingdomes for the benefit of our land, whenas within one hundred miles all those are to bee had, either ready provided by nature, or else to bee prepared, were there but industrious men to labour. Only of Cop-per wee may doubt is wanting, but there is good probabilitie that both copper and better munerals are there to be had for their labor. Other Countries have it. So then here is a place a nurse for souldiers, a practise for marriners, a trade for marchants, a reward for the good, and that which is most of all, a businesse (most acceptable to God) to bring such poore infidels to the true knowledge of God and his holy Gospell.

OF THE NATURALL INHABITANTS OF VIRGINIA.

The land is not populous, for the men be fewe; their far greater number is of women and children. Within 60 miles of *James* Towne there are about some 5000 people, but of able men fit for their warres scarse 1500. To nourish so many together they have yet no means, because they make so small a benefit of their land, be it never so fertill.

6 or 700 have beene the most [that] hath beene seene together, when they gathered themselves to have surprised *Captaine Smyth at Pamaunke*, having but 15 to withstand the worst of their furie. As small as the pro-portion of ground that hath yet beene discoverd, is in comparison of that yet unknowne. The people differ very much in stature, especially in language, as before is expressed.

Some being very great as the *Sesquesahamocks*, others very little as the *Wighcocomocoes:* but generally tall and straight, of a comely propor-tion, and of a colour browne, when they are of any age, but they are borne white. Their haire is generally black; but few have any beards. The men weare halfe their heads shaven, the other halfe long. For Bar-bers they use their women, who with 2 shels will grate away the haire, of any fashion they please. The women are cut in many fashions agree-able to their yeares, but ever some part remaineth long.

They are very strong, of an able body and full of agilitie, able to endure to lie in the woods under a tree by the fire, in the worst of winter, or in the weedes and grasse, in *Ambuscado* in the Sommer.

They are inconstant in everie thing, but what feare constraineth them to keepe. Craftie, timerous, quicke of apprehension and very ingenuous. Some are of disposition feareful, some bold, most cautelous, all *Savage*. Generally covetous of copper, beads, and such like trash. They are soone moved to anger, and so malitious, that they seldome forget an injury: they seldome steale one from another, least their conjurors should reveale it, and so they be pursued and punished. That they are thus feared is certaine, but that any can reveale their offences by conjuration I am doubtful. Their women are carefull not to bee suspected of dishonesty without the leave of their husbands.

Each household knoweth their owne lands and gardens, and most live of their owne labours.

For their apparell, they are some time covered with the skinnes of wilde beasts, which in winter are dressed with the haire, but in sommer without. The better sort use large mantels of deare skins not much differing in fashion from the Irish mantels. Some imbrodered with white beads, some with copper, other painted after their manner. But the common sort have scarce to cover their nakednesse but with grasse, the leaves of trees, or such like. We have seen some use mantels made of Turkey feathers, so prettily wrought and woven with threeds that nothing could bee discerned but the feathers, that was exceeding warme and very handsome. But the women are alwaies covered about their midles with a skin and very shamefast to be seene bare.

They adorne themselves most with copper beads and paintings. Their women some have their legs, hands, breasts and face cunningly imbrodered with diverse workes, as beasts, serpentes, artificially wrought into their flesh with blacke spots. In each eare commonly they have 3 great holes, whereat they hange chaines, bracelets, or copper. Some of their men weare in those holes, a smal greene and yellow coloured snake, neare halfe a yard in length, which crawling and lapping her selfe about his necke often times familiarly would kiss his lips. Others wear a dead Rat tied by the tail. Some on their heads weare the wing of a bird or some large feather, with a Rattell. Those Rattels are somewhat like the chape of a Rapier but lesse, which they take from the taile of a snake. Many have the whole skinne of a hawke or some strange fowle, stuffed with the wings abroad. Others a broad peece of copper, and some the hand of their enemy dryed. Their heads and shoulders are painted red with the roote *Pocone* braied to powder mixed with oyle; this they hold in somer to preserve them from the heate, and in winter from the cold. Many other formes of paintings they use, but he is the most gallant that is the most monstrous to behould.

Their buildings and habitations are for the most part by the rivers or not farre distant from some fresh spring. Their houses are built like our Arbors of small young springs bowed and tyed, and so close covered with mats or the barkes of trees very handsomely, that notwithstanding either winde raine or weather, they are as warme as stooves, but very smoaky, yet at the toppe of the house there is a hole made for the smoake to goe into right over the fire.

Against the fire they lie on little hurdles of Reedes covered with a mat, borne from the ground a foote and more by a hurdle of wood. On these round about the house, they lie heads and points one by thother against the fire: some covered with mats, some with skins, and some starke naked lie on the ground, from 6 to 20 in a house.

Their houses are in the midst of their fields or gardens; which are smal plots of ground, some 20, some 40, some 100. some 200. some more, some lesse. Some times from 2 to 100 of these houses [are] togither, or but a little separated by groves of trees. Neare their habitations is little small wood, or old trees on the ground, by reason of their burning of them for fire. So that a man may gallop a horse amongst these woods any waie, but where the creekes or Rivers shall hinder.

Men women and children have their severall names according to the severall humor of their Parents. Their women (they say) are easilie delivered of childe, yet doe they love children verie dearly. To make them hardy, in the coldest mornings they wash them in the rivers, and by painting and ointments so tanne their skins, that after year or two, no weather will hurt them.

The men bestowe their times in fishing, hunting, wars, and such manlike exercises, scorning to be seene in any woman like exercise, which is the cause that the women be verie painefull and the men often idle. The women and children do the rest of the worke. They make mats, baskets, pots, morters, pound their corne, make their bread, prepare their victuals, plant their corne, gather their corne, beare all kind of burdens, and such like. . . . .

6 | Letter from Jamestown

Richard Frethorne was an indentured servant who lived during the difficult, early days of the Jamestown colony. He wrote the following letter to his parents in England in 1623. It contrasts strikingly with John Smith's glowing account of Virginia, suggesting that one's view of the colony depended on socioeconomic position.

It is not known what response, if any, was produced as a result of Frethorne's complaints. It is entirely possible that Richard Frethorne died not long after he sent his pleas to his parents in Europe. Nothing is known of his life beyond what is revealed in the contents of this letter, which survives in government records in London, and which has been reprinted in collections published in the United States.

Even one of his early seventeenth-century contemporaries might have had trouble understanding Frethorne's barely literate English. While it remains as true in tone and structure to the original as possible, the following version of Frethorne's 1623 letter contains modernized spellings and additional editorial notes.

Loving and kind father and mother, my most humble duty remembered to you, hoping in God of your good health, as I my self at the making hereof. This is to let you understand that I, your child, am in a most heavy case, by reason of the nature of the country [which] is such that it causeth me much sickness, as [for example] the scurvy and the bloody flux, and diverse other diseases, which make the body very poor, and weak. And when we are sick, there is nothing to comfort us; for since I came out of the ship, I never ate anything but peas, and loblollie (that is, water gruel[1]). As for deer or venison, I never saw any since I came into this land; there is indeed some fowl, but we are not allowed to go, and get it, but must work hard both early and late for a mess of water gruel, and a mouthful of bread, and beef. A mouthful of bread for a

Richard Frethorne, "Letter to His Father and Mother, March 20, April 2 and 3, 1623," In Susan M. Kingsbury (editor) The Records of the Virignia Company of London. Volume IV (Washington, D.C., Government Printing Office, 1935) pp. 58–60. Spelling modernized.

1. Flour (sometimes cornmeal or oatmeal) mixed with water

penny loaf must serve 4 men, which is most pitiful, if you did know as much as I, when people cry out day, and night. Oh that they were in England without their limbs and would not care to loose any limbs to be in England again, yea though they beg from door to door. For we live in fear of the enemy [Indians] every hour, yet we have had a combat with them on the Sunday before Shrovetide,[2] and we took two alive and make slaves of them. But it [this] was by policy, for we are in great danger, for our plantation is very weak, by reason of death and sickness of our company. For we came but twenty for the merchants, and they are half dead just; and we look every hour when two more should go, yet there came for some other men yet to live with us, of which there is but one alive, and our lieutenant is dead, and his father, and his brother, and there was some 5 or 6 of the last year's 20 of which there is but 3 left, so that we are fain to get other men to plant with us, and yet we are but 32 to fight against 3000 if they should come, and the nighest help that we have is ten miles of us. And when the rogues overcame this place last, they slew 80 persons. How then shall we do for we lie even with their teeth? They may easily take us but that God is merciful and can save with few as with many; as he showed to Gilead,[3] and like Gilead's soldiers if they lapped water, we drink water which is but weak.[4] And I have nothing to comfort me, nor is there nothing to be gotten here but sickness and death, except [in the case] that one had money to lay out in some things for profit. But I have nothing at all, no, not a shirt on my back, but two rags, nor no clothes, but one poor suit, nor but one pair of shoes, but one pair of stockings, but one cap, but two bands. My cloak was stolen by one of my own fellows, and to his dying hour he would not tell me what he did with it, but some of my fellows saw him have butter and beef out of a ship, which my cloak I [do not] doubt paid for, so that I have not a penny, nor a penny worth to help me to either spice, or sugar, or strong waters, without the which one cannot live here.

For as strong beer in England doth fatten and strengthen thee, so water doth wash and weaken [a person] here, [but it] only keeps life and soul together. But I am not half a quarter as strong as I was in England, and all is for want of victuals, for I do protest unto you, that I have eaten more in [a] day at home then I have allowed me here for a week. You have given more than my day's allowance to a beggar at the door. And, if Mr. Jackson had not relieved me, I should be in a poor case, but he like a father and she like a loving mother doth still help me, for when we go up to James Towne that is 10 miles of us, there lie all the ships that come to the land, and there they must deliver their goods. And

2. The three day period immediately preceding Ash Wednesday
3. A region in the Middle East in what is now Jordan
4. Without alcohol or nourishment

when we went up to town as it may be on Monday at noon, and come there by night, then load the next day by noon, and go home in the afternoon, and unload, and then away again in the night, and be up about midnight, then if it rained, or blowed never so hard we must lie in the boat in the water, and have nothing but a little bread, for when we go in the boat we have a loaf allowed to two men, and it is all if we stayed there 2 days, which is hard, and [we] must lie all that while in the boat. But the Goodman Jackson pitied me and made me a cabin to lie in always when I come up, and he would give me some poor jacks to take home with me, which comforted me more than peas, or water gruel. Oh they be very godly folks, and love me very well, and will do anything for me, and he much marveled that you would send me a servant to the company. He said I had been better [would have been better off] knocked on the head, and indeed I find it now to my great grief and misery, and say, that if you love me you will redeem me suddenly [soon], for which I do entreat and beg. And if you cannot get the merchant to redeem me for some little money, then for God's sake get a gathering or entreat some folks to lay out some little sum of money, in meals, and cheese and butter, and beef. Any eating meat will yield great profit, oil and vinegar is [also] very good, but, father, there is great loss in leakings. But, for God's sake, send beef and cheese and butter or more of one sort and none of another, but if you send cheese it must be very old cheese, and at the cheesemongers you may buy very good cheese for twopence farthing or halfpenny that will be liked very well, but if you send cheese you must have a care how you pack it in barrels, and you must put cooper's [packing] chips between every cheese, or else the heat of the hold will rot them, and, whatsoever you send me, be it so much what I make of it. I will deal truly [truthfully] with you before I send it out, and beg the profit to redeem me, and, if I die before it come, I have entrated Goodman Jackson to send you the worth of it, who hath promised he will. If you send, you must direct your letters to Goodman Jackson, at James Towne, a gunsmith. You must set down his freight because there may be more of his name there; good father do not forget me but have mercy and pity my miserable case. I know if you did but see me you would weep to see me, for I have but one suit. But [even though] it is a strange one, it is very well guarded. Wherefore, for God's sake, pity me. I pray you to remember my love to all my friends and kindred. I hope all my brothers and sisters are in good health, and, as for my part, I have set down my resolution that certainly will be: that is, that the answer of this letter will be life or death to me. Therefore, good father, send as soon as you can, and if you send me anything let this be the mark.

ROT

Richard Frethorne
Martin's Hundred

7 | A Letter from Massachusetts Bay

The Massachusetts Bay Colony, begun in 1630, was a far larger undertaking than the earlier English settlements at Jamestown and Plymouth. As a result of harsh and lasting religious strife in England, immigration to the colony remained substantial for a decade after 1630, with perhaps 20,000 settlers arriving in New England.

But as in the prior settlements, the colonists of early Massachusetts Bay experienced intense suffering. The next letter is addressed to William Pond, a well-to-do farmer who lived near Groton Manor in England. Pond had been advanced money from Governor Winthrop of Massachusetts Bay so that he might send two of his sons to the new colony. Unfortunately, we do not know which of the two sons, Robert or John Pond, was responsible for the unsigned letter. Though his letter speaks of continuing dependency on "old England," and an inability to gain access to the many resources available in a sparsely settled land, the junior Pond speaks with less desperation than we witnessed with Richard Frethorne. Even with death all around him, the younger Pond was determined to make a new home in the New World.

Most loving and kind father and mother,—My humble duty remembered unto you, trusting in God you are in good health, and I pray remember my love unto my brother Joseph and thank him for his kindness that I have had at his hand at London . . . My writing unto you is to let you understand what a country this New England is where we live. Here are but a few [Indians], a great part of them died this winter, it was thought a case of the plague. They are a crafty people and will cozen and cheat, and they are a subtle people, and whereas we did expect great store of beaver here is little or none to be found. They are proper men . . . and many of them go naked with a skin about their loins, but now some of them get Englishmen's apparel; and the country

Proceedings of the Massachusetts Historical Society, *Second Series, Volume VIII: 1892–1894.* (Boston, Massachusetts Historical Society, 1894), pp. 471–473. Spelling modernized.

is hilly and rocky and some . . . soil is very flat and here is some good ground and marshy ground, but here is no Myckellmes.[1] Spring cattle thrive well here, but they give small amount of milk. The best cattle for profit is swines . . . Here is timber good store and acorns good store, and here is good store of fish if we had boats to go for and lines to serve to do fishing. Here are a good store of wild fowl, but they are hard to come by. It is harder to get a shoot then it is in old England and people here are subjects to disease, for here [many] have died of scurvy and of burning fever, near two hundred . . . beside as many lay lame and all Sudbury men are dead but three and three women and some children . . . If this ship had not come in when it did we would had been put to a wonderful [terrible] strait but thanks be to God for sending it in. I received from the ship a hogshead of meal, and the Governor told me of a hundred weight of cheese the which I have reserved parts of it. I humbly thank you for it. I did expect two cows, the which I had none, nor did I earnestly desire that you should send me any, because the country is not so as we did expect it. Therefore, loving father, I would entreat you that you would send me . . . butter and a hogshead of malt unground, for we drink nothing but water . . . For the freight, if you of your love will send them I will pay the freight, for here is nothing to be got without commodities to up to the . . . parties amongst the Indians to [trade], for here where we live there is no beaver. Here is no cloth to be had to make no apparel. So I pray, father, send me four or five yards of cloth to make some apparel, and loving father, though I be far distant from you yet I pray you remember me as your child, and we do not know how long we may subsist, for we can not live here without provisions from old England. Therefore, I pray do not put away your shop stuff, for we do not know how long this plantation will stand, for some of the magnates that did uphold it have turned off their men and have given it over. Besides, God had taken away . . . Mr. Johnson and Lady Arabella his wife, which was the chiefest man of estate in the land and the one who could have done the most good.

. . . So here we may live if we have supplies every year from old England, otherwise we can not subsist. I may, as I will, work hard, set an acorn of Eindey wheat . . . So father, I pray, consider my cause, for here will be but a very poor being, no being without, loving father, your help with provisions from old England. I had thought to come home on this ship, for my provisions are almost all spent, but that I humbly thank you for your great love and kindness in sending me some provisions, or else I should . . . have famished, but now I will, if it please God that I have my health, I will plant what corn I have, and if provisions be not cheaper between this and Myckellmes and that I do not hear from you what I was best to do, I propose to come home at Myckellmes.

1. Refers to the old English custom of eating roast goose on Michaelmas, the Feast of St. Michael, on the 29th of September.

My wife remembers her humble duty to you and to my mother, and my love to my brother Joseph and to Sarah Myler. Thus I leave you to the protection of Almighty God.

From Watertown in New England the 15 of March, 1630.[2]

[Unsigned]

We were wonderful sick as we came at sea, with the smallpox. No man thought that I and my little child would have lived. My boy is lame and my girl too, and there died on the ship that I came in 14 persons.

---

2. Pond dated his letter March 15, 1630. However, a portion of the letter (deleted here) refers to an arrival of a ship that, according to other records, arrived in port in 1631.

8 | *Of Plymouth Plantation*

William Bradford (1589/90–1657) lived the entire Pilgrim adventure: persecution in England, migration to Holland from 1609 to 1620, and settlement in Plymouth, Massachusetts, in 1620. He served as governor of the colony almost continuously from 1621 to 1656. His History of Plymouth Plantation, *written during the twenty years before 1650, has fixed the place of the Pilgrims in the American popular mind, defining sharply how their religion dealt with the realities of a new world.*

Because the Pilgrims, like the larger Puritan settlement at Massachusetts Bay, considered themselves a chosen people, they had a special need to understand that everything that took place in their society accorded with their ideals. As part of that effort, Bradford wrote this excellent social history to try to explain the various outbreaks of "wickedness" in his colony.

Out of a dramatic case of bestiality, Bradford drew important insights into the development of the Plymouth colony. He began with theological explanations of that "wickedness," he quickly moved to psychological explanations of the effect of "strict laws," to a sociological explanation of better "reporting" (as we in the present would say) of the evidence of deviance, and to economic explanations involving a shortage of labor and the economic interests of ship captains and merchants.

A KIND OF WICKEDNESS BREAKS FORTH

Marvilous it may be to see and consider how some kind of wickednes did grow and breake forth here, in a land wher the same was so much witnesed against, and so narrowly looked unto, and severly punished when it was knowne; as in no place more, or so much, that I have known or heard of; insomuch as they have been somewhat censured, even by moderate and good men, for their severitie in punishments.[1] And yet all this could not suppress the breaking out of sundrie notorious sins, (as this year, besides other, gives us too many sad presidents and instances,) espetially drunkennes and un[cleanness]; not only in-

William Bradford, History of Plymouth Plantation, 1620–1647, *Volume II. (Massachusetts Historical Society, 1912), pp. 308–310, 328–330.*

continencie betweene persons unmaried, for which many both men and women have been punished sharply enough, but some maried persons allso. But that which is worse, even sodomie and bugerie, (things fearful to name,) have broak forth in this land, oftener then once. I say it may justly be marveled at, and cause us to fear and tremble at the consideration of our corrupte natures, which are so hardly bridled, subdued, and mortified; nay, cannot by any other means but the powerful worke and grace of Gods spirite. But (besides this) one reason may be, that the Divell [Devil] may carrie a greater spite against the churches of Christ and the gospell hear, by how much the more they indea[v]our to preserve holynes and puritie amongst them, and strictly punisheth the contrary when it ariseth either in church or comone wealth; that he might cast a blemishe and staine upon them in the eyes of [the] world, who use to be rash in judgmente. I would rather thinke thus, then that Satane hath more power in these heathen lands, as som have thought, then in more Christian nations, espetially over Gods servants in them.

An other reason may be, that it may be in this case as it is with waters when their streames are stopped or dammed up, when they gett passage they flow with more violence, and make more [noise] and disturbance, then when they are suffered to [run] quietly in their owne chanels. So wikednes being here more stopped by strict laws, and the same more [nearly] looked unto, so as it cannot [run] in a comone road of liberty as it would, and is inclined, it searches every wher, and at last breaks out wher it getts vente.

A third reason may be, hear (as I am verily perswaded) is not more evills in this kind, nor nothing nere so many by proportion, as in other places; but they are here more discovered and seen, and made publick by due serch, inquisision, and due punishment; for the churches looke narrowly to their members, and the magistrates over all, more strictly then in other places. Besides, here the people are but few in comparison of other places, which are full and populous, and lye hid, as it were, in a wood or thickett, and many horrible evills by that means are never seen nor knowne; whereas hear, they are, as it were, brought into the light, and set in the plaine feeld, or rather on a hill, made conspicuous to the view of all. . . .

A CASE OF BESTIALITY

And after the time of the writing of these things befell a very sadd accidente of the like foule nature in this govermente, this very year, which I shall now relate. Ther was a youth whose name was Thomas Granger; he was servant to an honest man of Duxbery,[1] being aboute 16 or 17 years of age. (His father and mother lived at the same time at Sityate.) He was this year detected of buggery (and indicted for the same) with a mare, a cowe, [two] goats, five sheep, [two] calves, and a turkey. Horrible it is to mention, but the truth of the historie requires it. He was first discoverd by one that accidentally saw his lewd practise towards the mare. (I forbear perticulers.) Being upon it examined and committed, in the end he not only confest the fact with that beast at that time, but sundrie times before, and at severall times with all the rest of the forenamed in his indictmente; and this his free-confession was not only in private to the magistrates, (though at first he strived to deney it,) but to sundrie, both ministers and others, and afterwards, upon his indictemente, to the whole court and jury; and confirmed it at his execution. And wheras some of the sheep could not so well be knowne by his description of them, others with them were brought before him, and he declared which were they, and which were not. And accordingly he was cast by the jury, and condemned, and after executed about the 8 of Sept[ember,] 1642.[1] A very sade spectakle it was; for first the mare, and then the cowe, and the rest of the lesser catle, were [killed] before his face, according to the law, Levit: 20 .15. and then he him selfe was executed. The catle were all cast into a great and large pitte that was digged of purpose for them, and no use made of any part of them.

Upon the examenation of this person, and also of a former that had made some sodomiticall attempts upon another, it being demanded of them how they came first to the knowledge and practice of shuch wickednes, the one confessed he had long used it in old England; and this youth last spoaken of said he was taught it by an other that had heard of shuch things from some in England when he was ther, and they kept catle togeather. By which it appears how one wicked person may infecte many; and what care all ought to have what servants they bring into their families.

But it may be demanded how came it to pass that so many wicked persons and profane people should so quickly come over into this land, and mixe them selves amongst them? seeing it was religious men that begane the work, and they came for religions sake. I confess this may be marveilled at, at least in time to come, when the reasons therof should not be knowne; and the more because here was so many hardships and wants mett withall. I shall therfore indeavor to give some answer hereunto. 1. And first, according to that in the gospell, it is ever to be remembered that wher the Lord begins to sow good seed, ther the envious man will endeavore to sow tares. 2. Men being to come over into a wildernes, in which much labour and servise was to be done aboute building and planting, etc., shuch as wanted help in that respecte, when they could not have shuch as they would, were glad to take shuch as they could; and so, many untoward servants, sundry of them proved, that were thus brought over, both men and women kind; who, when their times were expired, became families of them selves,

---

1. The criminal was hanged. He left a wife and children.

which gave increase hereunto. 3. An other and a maine reason hearof was, that men, finding so many godly disposed persons willing to come into these parts, some begane to make a trade of it, to transeport passengers and their goods, and hired ships for that end; and then, to make up their fraight and advance their profite, cared not who the persons were, so they had money to pay them. And by this means the cuntrie became pestered with many unworthy persons, who, being come over, crept into one place or other. 4. Againe, the Lords blesing usually following his people, as well in outward as spirituall things, (though afflictions be mixed withall,) doe make many to adhear to the people of God, as many followed Christ, for the loaves sake, John 6. 26. and a mixed multitud came into the willdernes with the people of God out of Eagipte of old, Exod. 12. 38. 5. So allso many were sente by their friends some under hope that they would be made better; others that they might be eased of shuch burthens, and they kept from shame at home that would necessarily follow their dissolute courses. And thus, by one means or other, in 20 years time, it is a question whether the greater part be not growne the worser?

9 | An Account of Pennsylvania

As early as 1623 settlements had been made in what is today Pennsylvania. Sweden, Holland, and England all claimed the area, and not until 1664 did England establish clear control.

Gabriel Thomas was a Quaker who lived in Pennsylvania and western New Jersey from 1682 until 1697. An Historical and Geographical Account of the Province and Country of Pennsylvania, in America *was first published in London in 1698, seventeen years after William Penn received a royal grant to the territory. Thomas's comments about the opportunities for men, women, farmers, and merchants and for low land prices and high wages struck themes of enduring importance in attracting immigrants to the New World.*

THE HISTORY OF PENSILVANIA, &C.

Pensilvania lies between the Latitude of Forty and Forty five Degrees: *West-Jersey* on the East, *Virginia* on the West, *Mary-Land* South, and *Canada* on the North. In Length three hundred, and in Breadth one hundred and eighty Miles.

The Natives, or first Inhabitants of this Country in their Original, are suppos'd by most People to have been of the Ten Scattered Tribes, for they resemble the *Jews* very much in the *Make* of their *Persons*, and *Tincture* of their *Complexions:* They observe New *Moons*, they offer their *first Fruits* to a *Maneto*, or suppos'd Deity, whereof they have two, one, as they fansie, above (good,) another below (bad,) and have a kind of *Feast* of *Tabernacles*, laying their *Altars* upon *Twelve Stones*, observe a sort of *Mourning* twelve Months, *Customs of Women*, and many other *Rites* to be toucht (here) rather than dwelt upon, because they shall be handled more at large at the latter end of this Treatise.

They are very Charitable to one another, the Lame and the Blind (amongst them) living as well as the best; they are also very kind and obliging to the *Christians*.

/ / /

But it remain'd [following small immigrations of Dutch, Swedes Fins, and English] with very little Imp[r]ovement till the Year 1681, in

Gabriel Thomas, An Account of Pennsylvania and West New Jersey. *(Cleveland, Burrows Brothers Company, 1903), pp. 23–28, 30–51.*

which *William Penn* Esq; had the Country given him by King *Charles* the *Second*, in lieu of Money that was due to (and signal Service done by) his Father, Sir *William Penn*, and from him bor the Name of *Pensilvania*.

Since that time, the Industrious (nay Indefatigable) Inhabitants have built a *Noble* and *Beautiful* City, and called it *Philadelphia*, which contains above two thousand Houses, all Inhabited; and most of them Stately, and of Brick, generally three Stories high, after the Mode in *London*, and as many several Families in each. . . .

It hath in it Three *Fairs* every Year, and Two *Markets* every Week. They kill above Twenty *Fat Bullocks* every Week, in the hottest time in Summer, for their present spending in that City, besides many *Sheep, Calves*, and *Hogs*.

This City is Situated between *Schoolkill-River* and the great River *Delaware*, which derives its Name from Captain *Delaware*, who came there pretty early: Ships of Two or Three Hundred Tuns may come up to this City, by either of these two Rivers. Moreover, in this Province are Four Great *Market-Towns*, viz. *Chester*, the *German Town, New-Castle*, and *Lewis-Town*, which are mightily Enlarged in this latter Improvement. . . .

The *Air* here is very delicate, pleasant, and wholesom; the *Heavens* serene, rarely overcast, bearing mighty resemblance to the better part of *France*; after Rain they have commonly a very clear Sky, the Climate is something Colder in the depth of Winter, and Hotter in the height of Summer; (the cause of which is its being a Main Land or Continent; the Days also are two Hours longer in the shortest Day in Winter, and shorter by two Hours in the longest Day of Summer) than here in *England*, which makes the Fruit so good, and the Earth so fertil.

The Corn-Harvest is ended before the middle of *July*, and most Years they have commonly between Twenty and Thirty Bushels of Wheat for every one they Sow. Their Ground is harrowed with Wooden Tyned Harrows, twice over in a place is sufficient; twice mending of their Plow-Irons in a Years time will serve. Their Horses commonly go without being shod; two Men may clear between Twenty and Thirty Acres of Land in one Year, fit for the Plough, in which Oxen are chiefly us'd, though Horses are not wanting, and of them Good and well shap'd. A Cart or a Wain may go through the middle of the Woods, between the Trees without getting any damage, and of such Land in a convenient place, the Purchase will cost between *Ten* and *Fifteen Pounds* for a Hundred Acres. Here is much Meadow Ground. Poor People both Men and Women, will get near three times more Wages for their Labour in this Country, than they can earn either in *England* or *Wales*.

/ / /

Here is curious Diversion in Hunting, Fishing, and Fowling, especially upon that Great and Famous River *Suskahanah*, which runs down quite through the heart of the Country to *Mary-land*, where it makes the Head of *Chesepeck-Bay*, in which place ther are an Infinite Number of Sea and Land Fowl, of most sorts, *viz. Swans, Ducks, Teal*, (which two are the most Grateful and most Delicious in the World) *Geese, Divers, Brands, Snipe, Curlew;* as also *Eagles, Turkies* (of Forty or Fifty Pound Weight) *Pheasants, Partridges, Pidgeons, Heath-Birds, Black-Birds;* and that Strange and Remarkable Fowl, call'd (in these Parts) the *Mocking-Bird*, that Imitates all sorts of Birds in their various Notes. And for Fish, there are prodigious quantities of most sorts, *viz. Shadds Cats Heads, Sheeps-Heads, Herrings, Smelts, Roach, Eels, Perch.* As also the large sort of Fish, as *Whales* (of which a great deal of Oyl is made) *Salmon, Trout, Sturgeon, Rock, Oysters*, (some six Inches long) *Crabs, Cockles*, (some as big as Stewing *Oysters* of which are made a Choice Soupe or Broth) *Canok* and *Mussels*, with many other sorts of Fish, which would be too tedious to insert.

There are several sorts of wild *Beasts* of great Profit, and good Food; *viz. Panthers, Woolves, Fither, Deer, Beaver, Otter, Hares, Musk-Rats, Minks, Wild Cats, Foxes, Rackoons, Rabits*, and that strange Creature, the *Possam*, she having a false Belly to swallow her Young ones, by which means she preserveth them from danger, when any thing comes to disturb them. There are also *Bears* some *Wolves*, are pretty well destroy'd by the *Indians*, for the sake of the Reward given them by the *Christians* for that Service. Here is also that Remarkable Creature the *Flying-Squirrel*, having a kind of Skinny Wings, almost like those of the *Batt*, though it hath the like Hair and Colour of the Common *Squirrel*, but is much less in Bodily Substance; I have (my self) seen it fly from one Tree to another in the Woods, but how long it can maintain its Flight is not yet exactly known.

There are in the Woods abundance of *Red Deer* (vulgarly called *Stags*) for I have bought of the *Indians* a whole *Buck*, (both Skin and Carcass) for two Gills of Gunpowder. Excellent Food, most delicious, far exceeding that in *Europe*, in the Opinion of most that are Nice and Curious People. There are vast Numbers of other Wild Creatures, as *Elks, Bufalos*, &c. all which as well Beasts, Fowl, and Fish, are free and common to any Person who can shoot or take them, without any lett, hinderance or Opposition whatsoever.

There are among other various sorts of *Frogs*, the *Bull-Frog*, which makes a roaring noise, hardly to be distinguished from that well known of the Beast, from whom it takes its Name: There is another sort of *Frog* that crawls up to the tops of Trees, there seeming to imitate the Notes of several *Birds*, with many other strange and various Creatures, which would take up too much room here to mention.

Next I shall proceed to instance in the several sorts of Wild Fruits, as excellent *Grapes, Red, Black, White, Muscadel*, and *Fox*, which upon frequent Experience have produc'd Choice Wine, being daily Cultivated by skilful *Vinerons;* they will in a short space of time, have very good Liquor of their own, and some to supply their Neighbours, to their great advantage; as these Wines are more pure, so much more wholsom; the Brewing Trade of Sophisticating and Adulterating of Wines, as in *En-*

gland, Holland (especially) and in some other places not being known there yet, nor in all probability will it in many Years. . . .

The common Planting *Fruit-Trees,* are *Apples,* which from a Kernel (without Inoculating) will shoot up to be a large Tree, and produce very delicious, large, and pleasant Fruit, of which much excellent *Cyder* is made, in taste resembling that in *England* press'd from *Pipins* and Pear-mains, sold commonly for between Ten and Fifteen Shillings *per* Barrel. *Pears, Peaches,* &c. of which they distil a Liquor much like the taste of *Rumm* or *Brandy,* which they Yearly make in great quantities: There are *Quinces, Cherries, Goosberries, Currants, Squashes, Pumpkins, Water-Mellons, Muskmellons,* and other *Fruits* in great Numbers, which seldom fail of yielding great plenty. There are also many curious and excellent *Physical Wild Herbs, Roots,* and *Drugs* of great vertue, and very sanative, as the *Sassafras,* and *Sarsaparilla,* so much us'd in Diet-Drinks for the Cure of the Veneral Disease, which makes the *Indians* by a right applica-tion of them, as able *Doctors* and *Surgeons* as any in *Europe,* performing celebrated Cures therewith, and by the use of some particular *Plants* only, find Remedy in all *Swellings, Burnings, Cuts,* &c. There grows also in great plenty the *Black Snake-Root,* (fam'd for its sometimes preserving, but often curing the *Plague,* being infused only in Wine, Brandy or Rumm) *Rattle-Snake-Root, Poke-Root,* called in *England Jallop,* with several other beneficial *Herbs, Plants* and *Roots,* which *Physicians* have approved of, far exceeding in Nature and Vertue, those of other Countries. . . .

Their sorts of *Grain* are, *Wheat, Rye, Pease, Oates, Barley, Buck-Wheat, Rice, Indian-Corn, Indian-Pease,* and *Beans,* with great quantities of *Hemp* and *Flax;* as also several sorts of eating Roots, as *Turnips, Potatoes, Car-rats, Parsnips,* &c. all which are produc'd Yearly in greater quantities than in *England,* those *Roots* being much larger, and altogether as sweet, if not more delicious; *Cucumbers, Coshaws, Artichokes,* with many others; most sorts of Saladings, besides what grows naturally Wild in the Coun-try, and that in great plenty also, as *Mustard, Rue, Sage, Mint, Tanzy, Wormwood, Penny-Royal* and *Purslain,* and most of the Herbs and Roots found in the Gardens in *England.* There are several Husband-Men, who sow Yearly between Seventy and Eighty Acres of *Wheat* each, besides *Barley, Oates, Rye, Pease, Beans,* and other Grain.

They have commonly *Two Harvests* in the Year; First of *English Wheat,* and next of *Buck,* (or *French*) Wheat. They have great Stocks both of *Hogs* and *Horses,* kept in the Woods, out of which, I saw a *Hog* kill'd, of about a Year old, which weigh'd Two Hundred weight; whose Flesh is much sweeter, and even more luscious than that in *England,* because they feed and fatten on the rich (though wild) Fruits, besides those fatned at home by *Peaches, Cherries* and *Apples.* . . . And for *Sheep,* they have consider-able Numbers which are generally from from those infectious Diseases which are incident to those Creatures in *England,* as the *Rot, Scab,* or Maggots; They commonly bring forth two *Lambs* at once, some *twise in one Year,* and the Wooll is very fine, and thick, and also very white.

Bees thrive and multiply exceedingly in those Parts, the *Sweeds* often get great store of them in the Woods, where they are free for any Body. Honey (and choice too) is sold in the Capital City for Five Pence *per* Pound. Wax is also plentiful, cheap, and a considerable Commerce. Tame Fowls, as *Chickens, Hens, Geese, Ducks, Turkeys,* &c. are large, and very plentiful all over this Countrey. . . .

Now the true Reason why this Fruitful Countrey and Florishing City advance so considerably in the Purchase of Lands both in the one and the other, is their great and extended Traffique and Commerce both by Sea and Land, *viz.* to *New-York, New-England, Virgnina, Mary-Land, Carolina, Jamaica, Barbadoes, Nevis, Monserat, Antego,* St. *Cristophers, Barmudoes, New-Found-Land, Maderas, Saltetudeous,* and *Old-England;* besides several other places. Their Merchandize chiefly consists in *Horses, Pipe-Staves, Pork* and *Beef* Salted and Barrelled up, *Bread,* and *Flower,* all sorts of Grain, *Pease, Beans, Skins, Furs, Tobacco,* or *Pot-Ashes, Wax,* &c. which are Barter'd for Rumm, Sugar, Molasses, Silver, Negroes, Salt, Wine, Linen, Household-Goods, &c.

However there still remain Lots of Land both in the aforesaid City and Country, that any may Purchase almost as cheap as they could at the first Laying out or Parcelling of either City or Country; which is, (in the Judgment of most People) the likeliest to turn to account to those that lay their Money out upon it, and in a shorter time than the aforementioned Lots and Lands that are already improved, and for several Reasons. In the first place, the Countrey is now well inhabited by the Christians, who have great Stocks of all sorts of Cattle, that encrease extraordinarily, and upon that account they are oblig'd to go farther up into the Countrey, because there is the chiefest and best place for their Stocks, and for them that go back into the Countrey, they get the richest Land, for the best lies thereabouts.

Secondly, Farther into the Countrey is the Principal Place to Trade wih the *Indians* for all sorts of *Pelt,* as *Skins* and *Furs,* and also *Fat Venison,* of whom People may Purchase cheaper by three Parts in four than they can at the City of *Philadelphia.*

Thirdly, Backwards in the Countrey lies the *Mines* where is *Copper* and *Iron,* besides other *Metals,* and *Minerals,* of which there is some Improvement made already in order to bring them, to greater Perfection; and that will be a means to erect more Inland Market-Towns, which exceedingly promote Traffick.

Fourthly, and lastly, Because the Countrey at the first, laying out, was void of Inhabitants (except the Heathens, or very few Christians not worth naming) and not many People caring to abandon a quiet and easie (at least tolerable) Life in their Native Countrey (usually the most agreeable to all Mankind) to seek out a new hazardous, and careful one in a Foreign Wilderness or Desart Countrey, wholly destitute of Christian Inhabitants, and even to arrive at which they must pass over a vast Ocean, expos'd to some Dangers, and not a few Inconveniencies: But now all those Cares, Fears and Hazards are vanished, for the Countrey is pretty well peopled, and very much Improv'd, and will be more every Day, now the Dove is return'd with the Olive-branch of Peace in her Mouth.

I must needs say, even the present Encouragements are very great and inviting, for Poor People (both Men and Women) of all kinds, can here get three times the Wages for their Labour they can in *England* or *Wales.*

I shall instance in a few, which may serve; nay, and will hold in all the rest. The first was a *Black-Smith,* (my next Neighbour) who himself and one Negro Man he had, got Fifty Shillings in one Day, by working up a Hundred Pound Weight of Iron, which at Six Pence *per* Pound (and that is the common Price in that Countrey) amounts to that Summ.

And for *Carpenters,* both *House* and *Ship, Bricklayers, Masons,* either of these Trades-Men, will get between Five and Six Shillings every Day constantly. As to *Journey-Men Shooe-Makers,* they have Two Shillings *per* Pair both for Men and Womens Shooes: And *Journey-Men Taylors* have Twelve Shillings *per* Week and their Diet. *Sawyers* get between Six and Seven Shillings the Hundred for Cutting of Pine-Boards. And for *Weavers,* they have Ten or Twelve Pence the Yard for Weaving of that which is little more than half a Yard in breadth. *Wooll-Combers,* have for combing Twelve Pence *per* Pound. *Potters* have Sixteen Pence for an Earthen Pot which may be bought in *England* for Four Pence. *Tanners,* may buy their Hides green for Three Half Pence *per* Pound, and sell their Leather for Twelve Pence *per* Pound. And *Curriers* have Three Shillings and Four Pence *per* Hide for Dressing it; they buy their Oyl at Twenty Pence *per* Gallon. *Brick-Makers* have Twenty Shillings *per* Thousand for their Bricks at the Kiln. *Felt-Makers* will have for their Hats Seven Shillings a piece, such as may be bought in *England* for Two Shillings a piece; yet they buy their *Wooll* commonly for Twelve or Fifteen Pence *per* Pound. And as to the *Glaziers,* they will have Five Pence a Quarry for their Glass. The Rule for the *Coopers* I have almost forgot; but this I can affirm of some who went from *Bristol,* (as their Neighbours report) that could hardly get their Livelihoods there, are now reckon'd in *Pensilvania,* by a modest Computation to be worth some Hundreds, (if not Thousands) of Pounds. The *Bakers* make as White Bread as any in *London,* and as for their Rule, it is the same in all Parts of the World that I have been in. The *Butchers* for killing a Beast, have Five Shillings and their Diet; and they may buy a good fat large Cow for Three Pounds, or thereabouts. The *Brewers* sell such Beer as is equal in Strength to that in *London,* half Ale and half Stout for Fifteen Shillings *per* Barrel; and their Beer hath a better Name, that is, is in more esteem than *English Beer* in *Barbadoes,* and is sold for a high Price there. And for *Silver-Smiths,* they have between Half a Crown and Three Shillings an Ounce for working their Silver, and for Gold equivalent. *Plasterers* have commonly Eighteen Pence *per* Yard for *Plastering. Last-Makers* have Sixteen Shillings *per* dozen for their Lasts. And *Heel-Makers* have Two Shillings a dozen for their Heels. *Wheel* and *Mill-Wrights, Joyners, Braziers, Pewterers,*

Dyers, Fullers, Comb-Makers, Wyer-Drawers, Cage-Makers, Card-Makers, Painters, Cutlers, Rope-Makers, Carvers, Block-Makers, Turners, Button-Makers, Hair and *Wood Sieve-Makers, Bodies-Makers, Gun-Smiths, Lock-Smiths, Nailers, File-Cuters, Skinners, Furriers, Glovers, Pattern-Makers, Watch-Makers, Clock-Makers, Sadlers, Coller-Makers, Barbers, Printers, Book-Binders,* and all other *Trades-Men,* their Gains and Wages are about the same proportion as the forementioned Trades in their Advancements, as to what they have in *England.* . . .

Of *Lawyers* and *Physicians* I shall say nothing, because this Countrey is very Peaceable and Healt[h]y; long may it so continue and never have occasion for the Tongue of the one, nor the Pen of the other, both equally destructive to Mens Estates and Lives; besides forsooth, they, Hang-Man like, have a License to Murder and make Mischief. *Labouring-Men* have commonly here, between 14 and 15 Pounds a Year, and their Meat, Drink, Washing and Lodging; and by the Day their Wages is generally between Eighteen Pence and Half a Crown, and Diet also; But in Harvest they have usually between Three and Four Shilling each Day, and Diet. The *Maid Servants Wages* is commonly betwixt Six and Ten Pounds *per Annum,* with very good Accommodation. And for the *Women* who get their Livelihood by their own Industry, their Labour is very dear, for I can buy in *London* a Cheese-Cake for Two Pence, bigger than theirs at that price, when at the same time their Milk is as cheap as we can buy it in *London,* and their Flour cheaper by one half.

Corn and Flesh, and what else serves Man for Drink, Food and Rayment, is much cheaper here than in *England,* or elsewhere; but the chief reason why Wages of Servants of all sorts is much higher here than there, arises from the great Fertility and Produce of the Place; besides, if these large Stipends were refused them, they would quickly set up for themselves, for they can have Provision very cheap, and Land for a very small matter, or next to nothing in comparison of the Purchace of Lands in *England;* and the Farmers there, can better afford to give that great Wages than the Farmers in *England* can, for several Reasons very obvious.

As First, their Land costs them (as I said but just now) little or nothing in comparison, of which the Farmers commonly will get twice the encrease of Corn for every Bushel they sow, that the Farmers in *England* can from the richest Land they have.

In the Second place, they have constantly good price for their Corn, by reason of the great and quick vent into *Barbadoes* and other Islands; through which means *Silver* is become more plentiful than here in *England,* considering the Number of People, and that causes a quick Trade for both Corn and Cattle; and that is the reason that Corn differs now from the Price formerly, else it would be at half the Price it was at then; for a Brother of mine (to my own particular knowledge) sold within the compass of one Week, about One Hundred and Twenty fat Beasts, most of them good handsom large Oxen.

Thirdly, They pay no *Tithes*, and their *Taxes* are inconsiderable; the Place is free for all Persuasions, in a Sober and Civil way; for the Church of *England* and the *Quakers* bear equal Share in the Government. They live Friendly and Well together; there is no Persecution for Religion, nor ever like to be; 'tis this that knocks all Commerce on the Head, together with high Imposts, strict Laws, and cramping Orders. Before I end this Paragraph, I shall add another Reason why Womens Wages are so exorbitant; they are not yet very numerous, which makes them stand upon high Terms for their several Services, in *Sempstering, Washing, Spinning, Knitting, Sewing*, and in all the other parts of their Imployments; for they have for Spinning either Worsted or Linen, Two Shillings a Pound, and commonly for Knitting a very Course pair of Yarn Stockings, they have half a Crown a pair; moreover they are usually marry'd before they are Twenty Years of Age, and when once in that Noose, are for the most part a little uneasie, and make their Husbands so too, till they procure them a Maid Servant to bear the burden of the Work, as also in some measure to wait on them too.

It is now time to return to the City of *Brotherly-Love* (for so much the *Greek* Word or Name *Philadelphia* imports) which though at present so obscure, that neither the *Map-Makers*, nor *Geographers* have taken the least notice of her, tho she far exceeds her Namesake of *Lydia*, (having above Two Thousand Noble Houses for her Five Hundred Ordinary) or *Celisia*, or *Cælesyria*; yet in a very short space of time she will, in all probability, make a fine Figure in the World, and be a most Celebrated *Emporeum*. Here is lately built a Noble *Town-House* or *Guild-Hall*, also a Handsom *Market-House*, and a convenient *Prison*. The Number of Christians both Old and Young Inhabiting in that Countrey, are by a Modest Computation, adjudged to amount to above Twenty Thousand.

The Laws of this Countrey, are the same with those in *England;* our Constitution being on the same Foot: Many Disputes and Differences are determined and composed by Arbitration; and all Causes are decided with great Care and Expedition, being concluded (generally) at furthest at the Second Court, unless they happen to be very Nice and Difficult Cases; under Forty Shillings any one Justice of the Peace has Power to Try the Cause. Thieves of all sorts, are oblig'd to restore four fold after they have been Whipt and Imprison'd, according to the Nature of their Crime; and if they be not of Ability to restore four fold, they must be in Servitude till 'tis satisfied.

They have Curious Wharfs as also several large and fine Timber-Yards, both at *Philadelphia*, and *New-Castle*, especially at the *Metropolis*, before *Robert Turner's* Great and Famous House, where are built Ships of considerable Burthen; they Cart their Goods from that Wharf into the City of *Philadelphia*, under an Arch, over which part of the Street is built, which is called *Chesnut-Street Wharf*, besides other *Wharfs*, as *High-Street Wharf, Mulberry-Street Wharf*, and *Vine-Street Wharf*, and all those are Common Wharfs; and likewise there are very pleasant Stairs, as *Trus* and *Carpenter-Stairs*, besides several others. There are above Thirty Carts belonging to that City, Four or Five Horses to each. There is likewise a very convenient Wharf called *Carpenter's Wharf*, which hath a fine necessary *Crain* belonging to it, with suitable *Granaries*, and *Store-Houses*. A Ship of Two Hundred Tun may load and unload by the side of it, and there are other Wharfs (with *Magazines* and *Ware-Houses*) which front the City all along the River, as also a Curious and Commodious *Dock* with a *Draw-Bridge* to it, for the convenient Reception of Vessels; where have been built some Ships of Two or Three Hundred Tuns each: They have very Stately Oaks to build Ships with, some of which are between Fifty and Sixty Foot long, and clear from Knots, being very straight and well Grain'd. In this famous City of *Philadelphia* there are several *Rope-Makers*, who have large and curious *Rope-Walks* especially one *Joseph Wilcox*. Also Three or Four Spacious *Malt-Houses*, as many large *Brew-Houses*, and many handsom *Bake-Houses* for Publick Use.

In the said City are several good *Schools of Learning* for Youth, in order to the Attainment of *Arts* and *Sciences*, as also *Reading, Writing,* &c. Here is to be had on any Day in the Week, *Tarts, Pies, Cakes,* &c. We have also several *Cooks-Shops*, both *Roasting* and *Boyling*, as in the City of *London; Bread, Beer, Beef,* and *Pork,* are sold at any time much cheaper than in *England* (which arises from their Plenty) our Wheat is very white and clear from Tares, making as good and white Bread as any in *Europe*. Happy Blessings, for which we owe the highest Gratitude to our Plentiful Provider, the great Creator of Heaven and Earth. The *Water-Mills* far exceed those in *England*, both for quickness and grinding good Meal, their being great choice of good Timber, and earlier Corn than in the aforesaid Place. . . .

The *Christian Children* born here are generally *well-favoured*, and *Beautiful* to behold; I never knew any come into the World with the least blemish on any part of its Body, being in the general, observ'd to be *better natur'd, Milder,* and more *tender Hearted* than those born in *England*. . . .

Reader, what I have here written, is not a *Fiction, Flam, Whim,* or any sinister *Design*, either to impose upon the Ignorant, or Credulous, or to curry Favour with the Rich and Mighty, but in meer Pity and pure Compassion to the Numbers of Poor Labouring Men, Women, and Children in *England*, half starv'd, visible in their meagre looks, that are continually wandering up and down looking for Employment without finding any, who here need not lie idle a moment, nor want due Encouragement or Reward for their Work, much less Vagabond or Drone it about. Here are no Beggars to be seen (it is a Shame and Disgrace to the State that there are so many in *England*) nor indeed have any here the least Occasion or Temptation to take up that Scandalous Lazy Life.

Jealousie among Men is here very rare, and Barrenness among Women hardly to be heard of, nor are old Maids to be met with; for all commonly Marry before they are Twenty Years of Age, and seldom any young Married Woman but hath a Child in her Belly, or one upon her Lap.

What I have deliver'd concerning this *Province,* is indisputably true, I was an Eye-Witness to it all, for I went in the first Ship that was bound from *England* for that Countrey, since it received the Name of *Pensilvania,* which was in the Year 1681. The Ship's Name was the *John* and *Sarah* of *London, Henry Smith* Commander. I have declin'd giving any Account of several things which I have only heard others speak of, because I did not see them my self, for I never held that way infallible, to make Reports from *Hear-say.* I saw the first Cellar when it was digging for the use of our Governour *Will. Penn.* . . .

Questions for Part I

1   What was Christopher Columbus's view of the Indians? How did it reflect the European culture from which he came?

2   What cultural values can you find expressed in the legends of the Iroquois Confederacy?

3   How does Father Le Jeune perceive Indian Religion? What does he say about the Indians' character and morality? Do you believe him? Why or why not?

4   How does Apes's account of white and Indian relations compare with our traditional Thanksgiving stories? With whom does Apes compare King Philip?

5   Compare John Smith's view of the Indians with Father Le Jeune's and Columbus's. What do the three views have in common? How do they differ?

6   Compare John Smith's description of Virginia with that of Richard Frethorne.

7   What difficulties does Pond mention in his letter? Are they similar to Frethorne's?

8   What explanations does William Bradford give for the "wickedness" in the Plymouth colony? What sense do you get of the Pilgrims' religion from his writing?

9   According to Thomas, in what ways is Pennsylvania superior to England? Does his description of Pennsylvania sound realistic to you?

PART II | FROM COLONIES TO REPUBLIC

The colonial America of the eighteenth century is the society celebrated by the Daughters of the American Revolution and the illustrators of many American history textbooks. It is the world of Benjamin Franklin, maple furniture, and Mount Vernon.

Colonial America consisted of, in fact, many different societies and many different experiences. Some colonists, including those described by Gottlieb Mittelberger, came to the New World as indentured servants. The status of such persons was difficult and painful, yet some, nonetheless, advanced to higher stations in life. Others, like Benjamin Franklin, were freeborn but experienced the constraints of apprenticeship. Black slaves had no such easy transition to freedom. Venture Smith's journey from Africa offered far fewer hopes than the travels down the coastline that Benjamin Franklin made to Philadelphia and freedom. Smith's eventual success in gaining his freedom was indeed unusual for a black man in colonial America.

Though life did hold some astonishing surprises for Mary Jemison, a white woman who was taken captive and assimilated into Indian culture, white men had considerably more freedom in colonial America than did women and children. Jemison's account of her capitivity provides interesting details about Indian life and the attitude of whites toward Indians. Even though Jemison's experience made for a sensational story, a woman's life as determined by a kidnapping is hardly a tale of independence and free choice.

Children could freely be sold, sent away, or punished by their parents without restriction. Along with society's concern for the raising and educating of children came an overemphasis on their doings, as in the overreaction of otherwise sensible adults to the ill-mannered or sometimes merely inconvenient behavior of children. As if to exempt themselves from having any part in creating a society that did not suit all the dreams of its youthful inhabitants, the adults gave great credence to supernatural explanations of the causes of children's unhappiness or recalcitrance. A misbehaving child was easily seen as a victim or

49

perpetrator of witchcraft. In some cases, the young person became the body through which the Devil operated in the material world, or at least so thought the Puritan divine Cotton Mather.

The generation that guided the nation's destinies through the revolutionary era was welded together, despite the remarkable differences among colonies and their peoples, by a common commitment to American nationality. The French-born Crèvecoeur describes the emergence of the new American out of this complex mixture of people.

This new American was accustomed to considerable self-government. When, after 1763, the English developed restrictive colonial policies to raise revenues for the administration of an enlarged empire that included India and Canada, the colonists almost instantly perceived threats to their traditional liberties. The self-awareness induced by the lengthy constitutional quarrel revealed many stresses in colonial society, which set it on the way to revolt against England. The struggle for independence had many facets. It was part of a radical change in European diplomacy; it was a revolution in national identity, and a challenge to traditional assumptions about the distribution of power within a society and to long-held theories of human nature—for many denied the capacity of human beings rationally to create a new form of government. Most important, the American Revolution ushered in a vast age of democratic revolutions throughout the world. More than any other publicist, Thomas Paine captured all the themes of democratic revolution. In the selections that follow we see a generation of Americans asserting their rights on the streets of Boston, organizing an army, suffering at Valley Forge, and triumphing at Yorktown.

Beyond the victory in war, the revolutionary generation proved itself by organizing a new government. The arguments passing before us in William Maclay's journal of the first session of Congress are part of a half century of defining what a republic might be. We are accustomed to considering the Constitution as the great achievement of the age. But it is more fruitful to see the lengthy process of constitution building: the asssertion of rights in the stamp act crisis and the continental Congresses, the evolution of an American diplomacy, the Articles of Confederation, the Northwest Ordinance, the Constitution itself, the many precedents of the Washington administration, Hamiltonian policy, the rise of political parties, the orderly transition of government in 1801, and the work of the Supreme Court under Justice Marshall. The American Constitution as we have come to know it was not the outcome of one meeting in Philadelphia; it was the experience of the entire revolutionary generation.

COTTON MATHER ET AL.

10 | Children in Colonial America

Any age reflects its best and worst qualities in its treatment of children. Seventeenth-century Englishmen and colonists showed the same range of behaviors as we do today.

Many scholars believe that children were accused of witchcraft for engaging in behaviors that today would be associated with typical adolescent rebellion. Although this close observation of children's behavior focused much attention on their moral development in colonial America, it produced hideous cycles of punishment and retribution among both children and adults.

From the perspective we now have on adolescent growth and social development, it is easier to understand the group hysteria of restless youths than the unbalanced response of their elders who hanged suspects on the evidence of testimony that legal traditions of the era rightly rejected. An examination of the full range of tensions in Massachusetts Bay in the 1690s—the constitutional, political, economic, and religious transition of the colony—puts this overreaction into perspective.

In the seventeenth century, selling children as servants or apprentices, even sending them overseas, was all too common. In modern times there has been considerably more social concern with the exploitation of children. Some parallels, however, still remain: In both past and present, society tends to worry much less about the children of the poor than it does about those of the rich.

The following pages contain selections from many sources about children in Colonial America.

The Puritans believed in the existence of witchcraft and found in it a logical explanation for the strange behavior of children. Following are two readings: The first is a newspaper report about a young girl accused of being a witch. The

51

second is a 1689 account of an entire family of witches, written by the famous Puritan Divine, Cotton Mather. Such tales occasionally led these religious people to overreact. Many of the adults accused of witchcraft were hanged, an action that was quickly regretted.*

It was not many days ere she was hurried again into violent fits after a different manner, being taken again speechless, and using all endeavors to make away with herself, and do mischief unto others: striking those that held her, spitting in their faces, and if at any time she had done any harm or frightened them, she would laugh immediately, which fits held her sometimes longer, sometimes shorter. Few occasions she had of speech, but when she could speak, she complained of a hard heart, counselled some to beware of sin, for that had brought her to this, bewailed that so many prayers had been put up for her, and she still so hard hearted, and no more good wrought upon her. But being asked whether she were willing to repent, shaked her head and said nothing. Thus she continued till the next sabbath in the afternoon, on which day, in the morning, being somewhat better than at other times, she had but little company tarried with her in the afternoon, when the Devil began to make more full discovery of himself. It had been a question before whether she might properly be called a Demoniac, a person possessed of the Devil, but it was then put out of question. He began (as the persons with her testify) by drawing her tongue out of her mouth most frightfully to an extraordinary length and greatness, and many amazing postures of her body; and then by speaking vocally in her. Whereupon her father and another neighbor were called from the meeting, on whom (as soon as they came in), he railed, calling them rogues, charging them for folly in going to hear a black rogue who told them nothing but a parcel of lies, and deceived them, and many like expressions. After exercise I was called, but understood not the occasion till I came and heard the same voice, a grim, low, yet audible voice it was. The first salutation I had was, Oh! You are a great rogue. I was at the first something daunted and amazed, and many reluctances I had upon my spirits, which brought me to a silence and amazement in my spirits, till at last God heard my groans and gave me both refreshment in Christ and courage. I then called for a light to see whether it might not appear a counterfeit, and observed not any of her organs to move. The voice was hollow, as if it issued out of her throat. He then again called me great black rogue. I challenged him to make it appear. But all the answer was, You tell your people a company of lies. I reflected on myself, and could not but magnify the goodness of God not to suffer Satan to bespatter the names of his people with those sins which he himself hath

---

*Samuel Willard, Minister at Groton, to Cotton Mather, 1672, in S.A. Green, Groton in the Witchcraft Times (Groton, Mass., 1883), pp. 17–20.

pardoned in the blood of Christ. I answered, Satan, thou art a liar and deceiver, and God will vindicate his own truth one day. He answered nothing directly, but said, I am not Satan. I am a pretty black boy; this is my pretty girl. I have been here a great while. I sat still and answered nothing to these expressions. But when he directed himself to me again, Oh! You black rogue, I do not love you, I replied through God's grace, I hate thee . . . On Friday in the evening she was taken again violently, and then the former voice . . . was heard in her again, not speaking, but imitating the crowing of a cock, accompanied with many other gestures, some violent, some ridiculous, which occasioned my going to her, where by signs she signified that the Devil threatened to carry her away that night. God was again then sought for her. And when in prayer that expression was used, that God had proved Satan a liar, in preserving her once when he had threatened to carry her away that night, and was entreated so to do again, the same voice, which had ceased two days before, was again heard by the by-standers five times distinctly to cry out, Oh! You are a rogue, and then ceased. But the whole time of prayer, sometimes by violence of fits, sometimes by noises she made, she drowned her own hearing from receiving our petition, as she afterwards confessed. Since that time she hath continued for the most part speechless, her fits coming upon her sometimes often, sometimes with greater intermission, and with great varieties in the manner of them, sometimes by violence, sometimes by making her sick, but (through God's goodness) so abated in violence that now one person can as well rule her as formerly four or five. She is observed always to fall into her fits when any strangers go to visit her, and the more go the more violent are her fits.

COTTON MATHER: WITCHCRAFTS AND POSSESSIONS. THE FIRST EXAMPLE.*

There dwells at this time, in the south part of Boston, a sober and pious man, whose Name is John Goodwin, whose Trade is that of a Mason, and whose Wife (to which a Good Report gives a share with him in all the Characters of Vertue) has made him the Father of six (now living) Children. Of these Children, all but the Eldest, who works with his Father at his Calling, and the Youngest, who lives yet upon the Breast of its mother, have laboured under the direful effects of a . . . stupendous Witchcraft. . . .

The four Children [ages 13, 11, 7, and 5 years old] had enjoyed a Religious Education, and answered it with a very towardly [promise]. They had an observable Affection unto Divine and Sacred things; and those of them that were capable of it, seem'd to have such a [feeling] of

*Cotton Mather, "Memorable Providences." In George Lincoln Burr (editor) Narratives of the Witchcraft Cases: 1648–1706. (New York, Charles Scribner's Sons, 1914), pp. 99–103.

their eternal Concernments as is not altogether usual. Their Parents also kept them to a continual Employment, which did more than deliver them from the Temptations of Idleness, and as young as they were, they took a delight in it, it may be as much as they should have done. In a word, Such was the whole Temper and Carriage of the Children, that there cannot easily be any thing more unreasonable, than to imagine that a Design to Dissemble could cause them to fall into any of their odd Fits; though there should not have happened, as there did, a thousand Things, wherein it was perfectly impossible for any Dissimulation of theirs to produce what scores of spectators were amazed at.

About Midsummer, in the year 1688, the Eldest of these Children, who is a Daughter, saw cause to examine their Washerwoman, upon their missing of some Linnen, which twas fear'd she had stollen from them. . . . This Laundress was the Daughter of an ignorant and a scandalous old Woman in the Neighbourhood; whose miserable Husband before he died, had sometimes complained of her, that she was undoubtedly a Witch. . . . This Woman in her daughters Defence bestow'd very bad Language upon the Girl that put her to the Question; immediatley upon which, the poor child became variously indisposed in her health, and visited with strange Fits, beyond those that attend an Epilepsy, or a Catalepsy, or those that they call The Disease of Astonishment.[1]

It was not long before one of her Sisters, and two of her Brothers, were seized, in Order one after another. . . . Within a few weeks, they were all four tortured every where in a manner so very grievous, that it would have broke an heart of stone to have seen their Agonies. Skilful Physicians were consulted for their Help, and particularly our worthy and prudent Friend Dr. Thoms Oakes, who found himself so [dumbfounded] by the Distempers of the children, tht he concluded nothing but an hellish Witchcraft could be the [origin] of these maladies. And that which yet more confirmed such Apprehension was, That for one good while, the children were tormented just in the same part of their bodies all at the same time together; and tho they saw and heard not one anothers complaints, tho likewise their pains and sprains were swift like Lightening, yet when (suppose) the Neck, or the Hand, or the Back of one was Rack't, so it was at that instant with t'other too.

The variety of their tortures increased continually. . . . Sometimes they would be Deaf, sometimes Dumb, and sometimes Blind, and often, all this at once. One while their Tongues would be drawn down their Throats; another-while they would be pull'd out upon their Chins, to a prodigious length. They would have their Mouths opened unto such a Wideness, that their Jaws went out of joint; and anon they would clap together again with a Force like that of a strong Spring-Lock. The same would happen to their Shoulder-Blades, and their Elbows, and Handwrists, and several of their joints. . . . They would make most pitteous

1. *I.e.*, stupefaction: diseases that rob one of his wits.

out-cries, that they were cut with Knives, and struck with Blows that they could not bear. Their Necks would be broken, so that their Neck-bone would seem dissolved unto them that felt after it; and yet on the sudden, it would become again so stiff that there was no stirring of their Heads; yea, their Heads would be twisted almost round. . . . Thus they lay some weeks most pittiful Spectacles; and this while as a further Demonstration of Witchcraft in these horrid Effects, when I went to Prayer by one of them, that was very desireous to hear what I said, the Child utterly lost her Hearing till our Prayer was over.

It was a Religious Family that these Afflictions happened unto; and none but a Religious Contrivance to obtain Releef, would have been welcome to them. . . . Accordingly they requested the four Ministers of Boston, with the Minister of Charlstown, to keep a Day of Prayer at their thus haunted house; which they did in the Company of some devout people there. Immediately upon this Day, the youngest of the four chil-dren was delivered, and never felt any trouble as afore. But there was yet a greater Effect of these our Applications unto our God!

The Report of the Calamities of the Family for which we were thus concerned, arrived now unto the ears of the magistrats, who presently and prudently apply'd themselves, with a just vigour, to enquire into the story. The Father of the Children complained of his Neighbour, the suspected ill woman, . . . and she being sent for by the Justices, gave such a wretched Account of her self, that they saw cause to commit her unto the Gaolers Custody. Goodwin had no proof that could have done her any Hurt; but the Hag had not power to deny her interest in the Enchantment of the Children; and when she was asked, Whether she believed there was a God? her Answer was too blasphemous and horri-ble for any Pen of mine to mention. An Experiment was made, Whether she could recite the Lords Prayer; and it was found, that tho clause after clause was most carefully repeated unto her, yet when she said it after them that prompted her, she could not possibly avoid making Nonsense of it, with some ridiculous Depravations. This Experiment I had the curi-osity since to see made upon two more, and it had the same Event. Upon the Commitment of this extraordinary Woman, all the Children had some present ease; until one (related unto her) accidentally meeting one or two of them, entertain'd them with her Blessing, that is, Railing; upon which Three of them fell ill again, as they were before. . . .

Children were often sent to the colonies as apprentices. The next selection is a statement of the conditions of the Virginia Company that accepted child apprentices. *

*Susan M. Kingsbury (editor) The Records of the Virginia Company of London, Volume I. (Washington, D.C., Government Printing Office, 1906), pp. 270–271. Spelling modernized.

The Treasurer, Council, and Company of Virginia assembled in their great and general Court the 17th of November 1619 have taken into Consideration the continual great forwardness of his honorable City in advancing the Plantation of Virginia and particularly in furnishing out one hundred Children this last year, which by the goodness of God there safely Arrived, (save such as died in the way) and are well pleased we doubt not for their benefit, for which your bountiful assistance, we in the name of the whole plantation do yield unto you due and deserved thanks.

And forasmuch as we have now resolved to send this next Spring very large supplies for the strength and increasing of the Colony, styled by the name of the London Colony, and find that the sending of those Children to be apprentices has both been very grateful to the people: We pray your Lord and the rest in pursuit of your former so pious Actions to renew your like favors and furnish us again with one hundreth more for the next sprint; Our desire is that we may have them of Twelve years old and upward with allowance of Three pounds apiece for their Transportation and forty shillings apiece for their apparel as was formerly granted. They shall be Apprentices the boys till they come to 21 years of Age; the Girls till the like Age or till they be married and afterwards they shall be placed as Tenants upon the public Land with best Conditions where they shall have houses with stock of Corn and Cattle to begin with, and afterward the moiety of all increase and profit whatsoever. And so we leave this motion to your honorable and grave Consideration.

Sometimes parents actually sold children to entrepreneurs, thereby partially fulfiling the desperate need for labor in the colonies. The following piece protests such practices. *

I have inquired after the child that was lost, and have spoken with the parents. His name was John Brookes. The last night he was after much trouble and charge freed again, and he relates that there are divers other children in the ship crying, that were enticed away from their parents, that are kept and detained in the ship. The name of the ship is the Seven Brothers and as I hear bound for Virginia; and she is now fallen

*George C. [torn away] to Sir Anthony Ashley Cooper, April [?], 1668 British Public Records Office, Cabinet Office 1/22, No. 56.

down to Gravesend, and, if a speedy course be not taken to stop her she will be gone. I heard of two other ships in the river that are at the same work, although the parents of the children see their children in the ship, yet without money they will not let them have them. The woman and child will wait on you, where you approach and when to give you this relation and 'tis believed there are divers people and others carried away that are strangers come from other parts, so that it were good to get the ships searched, and to see who are against their wills carried away. Pray you move it in the House to have a law to make it death. I am confident your mercy to these innocent children will ground a blessing on yourself your own. Pray let not your great affairs put this good work out of your head to stop the ships and discharge the children.

Your most humble servant
George

Many children were sold in transactions that were part of the African slave trade, as evidenced by the following readings.

*I**

Henry Carpenter and Robert Helmes to the Royal African Company, 1681:
    On the 3rd instant in the Evening, Capt. Cope in the *George and Betty* arrived in this Road with 415 Negroes, most women, amongst which [were] about 40 children under the ages of 8 years to our best Judgment, which we told him was contrary to his Charter Party, who answered that they could not buy so many men and women without [also taking] that number of Children, but we believe something else in it which we hope in Little time to discover . . .

Edwin Stede and Stephen Gascoigne to the Royal African Company, 1683:
    And about one third part of those he did bring were very small, most of them no better than sucking children, nay many of them did suck their mothers that were on board . . . some of [the] mothers we

*Elizabeth Donnan, ed., Documents Illustrative of the History of the Slave Trade to America, Volume I (Washington, D.C., Carnegie Institution of Washington, 1930) p. 275.

believe died on board of ship, and the most part of those small ones [were] not worth above £5 per head. We told Agent White we wondered to see so many small children brought by him, for that they were not worth their freight, to which he replied they cost not much, and the ship as good bring them as nothing, she being paid by the month . . .

II*

I also remember that I once, among my several runs along that coast, happened to have aboard a whole family, man, wife, three young boys, and a girl, bought here one after another at several places; and cannot but observe here what mighty satisfaction those poor creatures expressed to be so come together again, though in bondage. For several days successively they could not forbear shedding tears of joy, and continually embracing and caressing one another; which moving me to compassion, I ordered they should be better treated aboard than commonly we can afford to do it, where there are four or five hundred in a ship. And at Martinico, I sold them all together to a considerable planter, at a cheaper rate than I might have expected had they been disposed of severally, being informed of that gentleman's good nature, and having taken his word that he would use that family as well as their circumstances would permit, and settle them in some part by themselves.

*The outlook for children in Europe deeply influenced the Pilgrims' decision to migrate to the New World. William Bradford writes of the Pilgrims' experience in Holland.***

As necessity was a taskmaster over them, so they were forced to be such, not only to their servants (but in a sort) to their dearest children; the which as it did not a little wound the tender hearts of many a loving father and mother, so it produced likewise sundry sad and sorrowful effects. For many of their children that were of best dispositions and

---

*John Barbot, "A Description of the Coasts of North and South Guinea . . . [1682]," in Elizabeth Donnan, ed., Documents of the Slave Trade, I, p. 289.
**William Bradford, History of Plymouth Plantation, 1620–1647 (Boston, 1912), I, pp. 54–55.

gracious inclinations (having learned to bear the yoke in their youth) and willing to bear part of their parents burden, were (often times) so oppressed with their heavy labors, that though their minds were free and willing, yet their bodies bowed under the weight of the same, and became decrepit in their early youth, the vigor of nature being consumed in the very bud as it were. But that which was more lamentable, and of all sorrows most heavy to be borne, was that many of their children, by these occasions, and the great licentiousness of youth in that country, and the manifold temptations of the place, were drawn away by evil examples into extravagant and dangerous courses, getting the reins off their necks and departing from their parents. Some became soldiers, others took upon them far voyages by sea, and others some worse courses, tending to dissoluteness and the danger of their souls, to the great grief of their parents and dishonor of God. So that they saw their posterity would be in danger to degenerate and be corrupted.

Lastly, (and which was not least) a great hope, and inward zeal they had of laying some good foundation, (or at least to make some way thereunto) for the propagating and advancing the gospel of the kingdom of Christ in those remote parts of the world; yea, though they should be but even as stepping-stones unto others for the performing of so great a work.

Advice to parents has never been in short supply. Here Benjamin Wadsworth, a Boston clergyman, prescribes rules for raising children. *

They should love their children and carefully provide for their outward supply and comfort while unable to provide for themselves . . . Parents should nourish in themselves a very tender love and affection to their children, and should manifest it by suitably providing for their outward comforts. Here I might say, as soon as the mother perceives herself with child, she should be careful not to do any thing injurious to herself or to the child God has formed in her. A conscientious regard to the Sixth Commandment (which is, *Thou shalt not kill*) should make her thus careful. If any purposely endeavor to destroy the fruit of their womb (whether

*Benjamin Wadsworth, The Well-Ordered Family or Relative Duties Being the Substance of Several Sermons (Boston, 1719), pp. 44–58.

they actually do it or not) they're guilty of murder in God's account. Further, before the child is born, provision should be made for its comfort when born. Some observe concerning our Saviour's Mother (the Virgin Mary) that though she was very poor and low and far from home when delivered of her Son, yet she had provided swaddling clothes to wrap her Son in. Mothers also, if able, should suckle their children. . . . Those mothers who have milk and are so healthy as to be able to suckle their children, and yet through sloth or niceness neglect to suckle them, seem very criminal and blameworthy. They seem to dislike and reject that method of nourishing their children which God's wise bountiful Providence has provided as most suitable. Having given these hints about mothers, I may say of parents (comprehending both father and mother) they should provide for the outward supply and comfort of their children. They should nourish and bring them up . . . They should endeavor that their children may have food suitable for quality and quantity, suitable *raiment* and *lodging.* In case of sickness, lameness, or other distress on children, parents should do all they can for their health or relief. *He that provides not for his own, especially those of his own house, hath denied the faith, and is worse than an infidel* I Tim. 8 . . . Therefore, if they can help it, they should not suffer their children to want any thing that's really good, comfortable, and suitable for them, even as to their outward man. Yet by way of caution I might say, let wisdom and prudence sway, more than fond indulgent fancy, in feeding and clothing your children. Too much niceness and delicateness in these things is not good; it tends not to make them healthy in their bodies, nor serviceable and useful in their generation, but rather the contrary. Let not your children (especially while young and unable to provide for themselves) want any thing needful for their outward comfort.

/   /   /

Parents should govern their children well, restrain, reprove, correct them, as there is occasion. A Christian householder should rule well his own house . . . Children should not be left to themselves, to a loose end, to do as they please; but should be under tutors and governors, *not being fit to govern* themselves . . . Children being bid to obey their parents in all things . . . plainly implies that parents should give suitable precepts to, and maintain a wise government over their children; so carry it, as their children may both fear and love them. You should restrain your children from sin as much as possible . . . You should reprove them for their faults; yea, if need be, correct them too . . . Divine precepts plainly show that, as there is occasion, you should chasten and correct your children; you dishonor God and hurt them if you neglect it. Yet, on the other hand, a father should pity his children . . . You should by no means carry it ill to them; you should not frown, be harsh, morose, faulting and blaming them when they don't deserve it, but do behave themselves well. If you fault and blame your children, show yourself displeased and discontent when they do their best to please you, this is the way to provoke them to wrath and anger, and to discourage them; therefore you should carefully avoid such ill carriage to them. Nor should you ever correct them upon uncertainties, without sufficient evidence of their fault. Neither should you correct them in a rage or passion, but should deliberately endeavor to convince them of their fault, their sin; and that 'tis out of love to God's honor and their good (if they're capable of considering such things) that you correct them. Again, you should never be cruel nor barbarous in your corrections, and if milder ones will reform them, more severe ones should never be used. Under this head of government I might further say, you should refrain your children from bad company as far as possibly you can . . . If you would not have your sons and daughters destroyed, then keep them from ill company as much as may be . . . You should not suffer your children needlessly to frequent taverns, nor to be abroad unseasonably on nights, lest they're drawn into numberless hazards and mischiefs thereby. You can't be too careful in these matters.

/   /   /

In Puritan Massachusetts Bay, respect for parents was legally enforced as was the obligation of the parents for the nurture and education of their children.

I*

[1646]. If any child[ren] above sixteen years old and of sufficient understanding shall curse or smite their natural father or mother, they shall be put to death, unless it can be sufficiently testified that the parents have been very unchristianly negligent in the education of such children, or so provoked them by extreme and cruel correction that they have been forced thereunto to preserve themselves from death or maiming. . . .

If a man have a stubborn or rebellious son of sufficient years of understanding, viz. sixteen, which will not obey the voice of his father or the voice of his mother, and that when they have chastened him will not harken unto them, then shall his father and mother, being his natural parents, lay hold on him and bring him to the magistrates assembled in Court, and testify to them by sufficient evidence that this their son is stubborn and rebellious and will not obey their voice and chastisement, but lives in sundry notorious crimes. Such a son shall be put to death.

*Mass. Records, III (1854), p. 101.

II*

[1670]. Ordered that John Edy, Senior, shall go to John Fisk's house and to George Lawrence's and Wiliam Priest's houses to inquire about their children, whether they be learned to read the English tongue and in case they be defective to warn in the said John, George, and William to the next meeting of the Selectmen.

/   /   /

William Priest, John Fisk, and George Lawrence, being warned to a meeting of the Selectmen at John Bigulah's house, they making their appearance and being found defective, were admonished for not learning their children to read the English tongue: were convinced, did acknowledge their neglects, and did promise amendment.

/   /   /

[1674]. Agreed that Thomas Fleg, John Whitney, and Joseph Bemus should go about the town to see that children were taught to read the English tongue and that they were taught some orthodox catechism and to see that each man has in his house a copy of the capital laws. For which end the Selectmen agreed there should be copies procured by Captain Mason at the printers and they to be paid for out of the town rate and the men above mentioned to carry them along with them to such of the inhabitants as have none.

/   /   /

Thomas Fleg, John Whitney, and Joseph Bemus gave in an account of what they had found concerning children's education and John Fisk being found wholly negligent of educating his children as to reading or catechizing, the Selectmen agreed that Joseph Bemus should warn him into answer for his neglect at the next meeting of the Selectmen.

/   /   /

[1676]. Ordered that Captain Mason and Simon Stone shall go to John Fisk to see if his children be taught to read English and their catechism.

III**

[1675]. William Scant of Braintree being bound over to this court to answer for his not ordering and disposing of his children as may be for

*Watertown Records . . . , I (Watertown, Mass., 1894), pp. 102–103, 121–122, 128.
**Samuel Eliot Morison, ed., "Records of the Suffolk County Court, 1671–1680," CSM Publications. XXX (1933), pp. 599, 915.

their good education, and for refusing to consent to the Selectmen of Braintree in the putting of them forth to service as the law directs; the court having duly weighed and considered what was alleged by him and the state of his family do[th] leave it to the prudence of the Select-men of Braintree to dispose of his children to service so far forth as the necessity of his family will give leave.

[1678]. Robert Styles of Dorchester presented for not attending the public worship of God, negligence in his calling, and not submitting to authority, testified upon the oaths of Thomas Davenport and Isaac Jones, grandjurymen. Sentenced to be admonished, and order[ed] that he put forth his children, or otherwise the selectmen are hereby empowered to do it according to Law.

11 | Captured by the Indians

Captivity narratives were popular during the entire period in which Indians were thought to constitute a danger to white settlers on the frontier. Mary Jemison's narrative is perhaps the most famous, having gone through dozens of printings since its initial publication in 1824. Although it is written in the first person, it is not really an autobiography. Mrs. Jemison was eighty years old and illiterate when James E. Seaver interviewed her and wrote the Narrative. *By then she was long famous in western New York as the "white woman of the Genesee" who had lived her entire life since her abduction—probably in 1758 at the age of 15—among the Seneca Indians. The* Narrative *is an important source for descriptions of New York Indian life and culture as well as a fascinating account of a white American who was assimilated into Indian culture.*

CHAPTER III.

The night was spent in gloomy forebodings. What the result of our captivity would be, it was out of our power to determine, or even imagine. At times, we could almost realize the approach of our masters to butcher and scalp us; again, we could nearly see the pile of wood kindled on which we were to be roasted; and then we would imagine ourselves at liberty, alone and defenseless in the forest, surrounded by wild beasts that were ready to devour us. The anxiety of our minds drove sleep from our eyelids; and it was with a dreadful hope and painful impatience that we waited for the morning to determine our fate.

The morning at length arrived, and our masters came early and let us out of the house, and gave the young man and boy to the French, who immediately took them away. Their fate I never learned, as I have not seen nor heard of them since.

I was now left alone in the fort, deprived of my former companions, and of every thing that was near or dear to me but life. But it was not long before I was in some measure relieved by the appearance of two pleasant-looking squaws, of the Seneca tribe, who came and examined

James E. Seaver, A Narrative of the Life of Mary Jemison; Deh-He-Wa-Mis. *Fourth edition.* (New York, Miller, Orton, and Mulligan, 1856), pp. 52, 55–63, 67–70, 72–74.

me attentively for a short time, and then went out. After a few minutes' absence, they returned in company with my former masters, who gave me to the squaws to dispose of as they pleased.

The Indians by whom I was taken were a party of Shawnees, if I remember right, that lived, when at home, a long distance down the Ohio.

My former Indian masters and the two squaws were soon ready to leave the fort, and accordingly embarked—the Indians in a large canoe, and the two squaws and myself in a small one—and went down to Ohio. When we set off, an Indian in the forward canoe took the scalps of my former friends, strung them on a pole that he placed upon his shoulder, and in that manner carried them, standing in the stern of the canoe directly before us, as we sailed down the river, to the town where the two squaws resided.

On the way we passed a Shawnee town, where I saw a number of heads, arms, legs, and other fragments of the bodies of some white people who had just been burned. The parts that remained were hanging on a pole, which was supported at each end by a crotch stuck in the ground, and were roasted or burnt black as a coal. The fire was yet burning; and the whole appearance afforded a spectacle so shocking that even to this day the blood almost curdles in my veins when I think of them.

At night we arrived at a small Seneca Indian town, at the mouth of a small river that was called by the Indians, in the Seneca language, She-nan-jee, about eighty miles by water from the fort, where the two squaws to whom I belonged resided. There we landed, and the Indians went on; which was the last I ever saw of them.

Having made fast to the shore, the squaws left me in the canoe while they went to their wigwam or house in the town, and returned with a suit of Indian clothing, all new, and very clean and nice. My clothes, though whole and good when I was taken, were now torn in pieces, so that I was almost naked. They first undressed me, and threw my rags into the river; then washed me clean and dressed me in the new suit they had just brought, in complete Indian style; and then led me home and seated me in the center of their wigwam.

I had been in that situation but a few minutes before all the squaws in the town came in to see me. I was soon surrounded by them, and they immediately set up a most dismal howling, crying bitterly, and wringing their hands in all the agonies of grief for a deceased relative.

Their tears flowed freely, and they exhibited all the signs of real mourning. At the commencement of this scene, one of their number began, in a voice somewhat between speaking and singing, to recite some words to the following purport, and continued the recitation till the ceremony was ended; the company at the same time varying the appearance of their countenances, gestures, and tone of voice, so as to correspond with the sentiments expressed by their leader.

"Oh, our brother! alas! he is dead—he has gone; he will never return! Friendless he died on the field of the slain, where his bones are yet
lying unburied! Oh! who will not mourn his sad fate? No tears dropped
around him: oh, no! No tears of his sisters were there! He fell in his
prime, when his arm was most needed to keep us from danger! Alas!
he has gone, and left us in sorrow, his loss to bewail! Oh, where is his
spirit? His spirit went naked, and hungry it wanders, and thirsty and
wounded, it groans to return! Oh, helpless and wretched, our brother
has gone! No blanket nor food to nourish and warm him; nor candles
to light him, nor weapons of war! Oh, none of those comforts had he!
But well we remember his deeds! The deer he could take on the chase!
The panther shrunk back at the sight of his strength! His enemies fell
at his feet! He was brave and courageous in war! As the fawn, he was
harmless; his friendship was ardent; his temper was gentle; his pity was
great! Oh! our friend, our companion, is dead! Our brother, our brother!
alas, he is gone! But why do we grieve for his loss? In the strength of a
warrior, undaunted he left us, to fight by the side of the chiefs! His
warwhoop was shrill! His rifle well aimed laid his enemies low: his tomahawk drank of their blood: and his knife flayed their scalps while yet
covered with gore! And why do we mourn? Though he fell on the field
of the slain, with glory he fell; and his spirit went up to the land of his
fathers in war! They why do we mourn? With transports of joy, they
received him, and fed him, and clothed him, and welcomed him there!
Oh, friends, he is happy; then dry up your tears! His spirit has seen our
distress, and sent us a helper whom with pleasure we greet. Deh-he-
wä-mis has come: then let us receive her with joy!—she is handsome
and pleasant! Oh! she is our sister, and gladly we welcome her here. In
the place of our brother she stands in our tribe. With care we will guard
her from trouble; and may she be happy till her spirit shall leave us."

In the course of that ceremony, from mourning they became serene,—joy sparkled in their countenances, and they seemed to rejoice
over me as over a long-lost child. I was made welcome among them as
a sister to the two squaws before mentioned, and was called Deh-he-
wä-mis; which, being interpreted, signifies a pretty girl, a handsome
girl, or a pleasant, good thing. That is the name by which I have ever
since been called by the Indians.

I afterward learned that the ceremony I at that time passed through
was that of adoption. The two squaws had lost a brother in Washington's war, sometime in the year before, and in consequence of his death
went up to Fort Du Quesne on the day on which I arrived there, in order
to receive a prisoner, or an enemy's scalp, to supply their loss. It is a
custom of the Indians, when one of their number is slain or taken prisoner in battle, to give to the nearest relative of the dead or absent a
prisoner, if they have chanced to take one; and if not, to give him the
scalp of an enemy. On the return of the Indians from the conquest,
which is always announced by peculiar shoutings, demonstrations of joy,

and the exhibition of some trophy of victory, the mourners come forward and make their claims. If they receive a prisoner, it is at their option either to satiate their vengeance by taking his life in the most cruel manner they can conceive of, or to receive and adopt him into the family, in the place of him whom they have lost. All the prisoners that are taken in battle and carried to the encampment or town by the Indians are given to the bereaved families, till their number is good. And unless the mourners have but just received the news of their bereavement, and are under the operation of a paroxysm of grief, anger, or revenge; or, unless the prisoner is very old, sickly, or homely, they generally save them, and treat them kindly. But if their mental wound is fresh, their loss so great that they deem it irreparable, or if their prisoner or prisoners do not meet their approbation, no torture, let it be ever so cruel, seems sufficient to make them satisfaction. It is family and not national sacrifices among the Indians, that has given them an indelible stamp as barbarians, and identified their character with the idea which is generally formed of unfeeling ferocity and the most barbarous cruelty.

It was my happy lot to be accepted for adoption. At the time of the ceremony I was received by the two squaws to supply the place of their brother in the family; and I was ever considered and treated by them as a real sister, the same as though I had been born of their mother.

During the ceremony of my adoption, I sat motionless, nearly terrified to death at the appearance and actions of the company, expecting every moment to feel their vengeance, and suffer death on the spot. I was, however, happily disappointed; when at the close of the ceremony the company retired, and my sisters commenced employing every means for my consolation and comfort.

Being now settled and provided with a home, I was employed in nursing the children, and doing light work about the house. Occasionally, I was sent out with the Indian hunters, when they went but a short distance, to help them carry their game. My situation was easy; I had no particular hardships to endure. But still, the recollection of my parents, my brothers and sisters, my home, and my own captivity, destroyed my happiness, and made me constantly solitary, lonesome, and gloomy.

My sisters would not allow me to speak English in their hearing; but remembering the charge that my dear mother gave me at the time I left her, whenever I chanced to be alone I made a business of repeating my prayer, catechism, or something I had learned, in order that I might not forget my own language. By practicing in that way, I retained it till I came to Genesee flats, where I soon became acquainted with English people, with whom I have been almost daily in the habit of conversing.

My sisters were very diligent in teaching me their language; and to their great satisfaction, I soon learned so that I could understand it readily, and speak it fluently. I was very fortunte in falling into their hands; for they were kind, good-natured women; peaceable and mild in their dispositions; temperate and decent in their habits, and very tender and gentle toward me. I have great reason to respect them, though they have been dead a great number of years.

/   /   /

In the second summer of my living at Wiishto, I had a child, at the time that the kernels of corn first appeared on the cob. When I was taken sick, Sheninjee was absent, and I was sent to a small shed on the bank of the river, which was made of boughs, where I was obliged to stay till my husband returned. My two sisters, who were my only companions, attended me; and on the second day of my confinement my child was born; but it lived only two days. It was a girl; and notwithstanding the shortness of the time that I possessed it, it was a great grief to me to lose it.

After the birth of my child I was very sick, but was not allowed to go into the house for two weeks; when, to my great joy, Sheninjee returned, and I was taken in, and as comfortably provided for as our situation would admit. My disease continued to increase for a number of days; and I became so far reduced that my recovery was despaired of by my friends, and I concluded that my troubles would soon be finished. At length, however, my complaint took a favorable turn, and by the time the corn was ripe I was able to get about. I continued to gain my health, and in the fall was able to go to our winter quarters, on the Saratoga, with the Indians.

From that time nothing remarkable occurred to me till the fourth winter of my captivity, when I had a son born, while I was at Sciota. I had a quick recovery, and my child was healthy. To commemorate the name of my much-lamented father, I called my son Thomas Jemison.

CHAPTER IV.

In the spring, when Thomas was three or four moons (months) old, we returned from Sciota to Wiishto, and soon after set out to go to Fort Pitt, to dispose of our furs and our skins that we had taken in the winter, and procure some necessary articles for the use of our family.

I had then been with the Indians four summers and four winters, and had become so far accustomed to their mode of living, habits, and dispositions, that my anxiety to get away, to be set at liberty and leave them, had almost subsided. With them was my home; my family was there, and there I had many friends to whom I was warmly attached in consideration of the favors, affection, and friendship with which they had uniformily treated me from the time of my adoption. Our labor was not severe; and that of one year was exactly similar in almost every respect to that of the others, without that endless variety that is to be observed in the common labor of the white people. Notwithstanding the Indian women have all the fuel and bread to procure, and the cooking to perform, their task is probably not harder than that of white women, who have those articles provided for them; and their cares certainly are not half as numerous, nor as great. In the summer season, we planted, tended, and harvested our corn, and generally had all our children with us; but had no master to oversee or drive us, so that we could work as leisurely as we pleased. We had no plows on the Ohio, but performed the whole process of planting and hoeing with a small tool that resembled, in some respect, a hoe with a very short handle.

/   /   /

Our cooking consisted in pounding our corn into samp or hominy, boiling the hominy, making now and then a cake and baking it in the ashes, and in boiling or roasting our venison. As our cooking and eating utensils consisted of a hominy block and pestle, a small kettle, a knife or two, and a few vessels of bark or wood, it required but little time to keep them in order for use.

Spinning, weaving, sewing, stocking knitting, and the like, are arts which have never been practiced in the Indian tribes generally. After the revolutionary war, I learned to sew, so that I could make my own clothing after a poor fashion; but I have been wholly ignorant of the application of the other domestic arts since my captivity. In the season of hunting, it was our business, in addition to our cooking, to bring home the game that was taken by the Indians, dress it, and carefully preserve the eatable meat, and prepare or dress the skins. Our clothing was fastened together with strings of deerskin, and tied on with the same.

In that manner we lived, without any of those jealousies, quarrels, and revengeful battles between families and individuals, which have been common in the Indian tribes since the introduction of ardent spirits among them.

The use of ardent spirits among the Indians, and a majority of the attempts which have been made to civilize them by the white people, have constantly made them worse and worse; increased their vices, and robbed them of many of their virtues, and will ultimately produce their extermination. I have seen, in a number of instances, the effects of education upon some of our Indians, who were taken, when young, from their families, and placed at school before they had had an opportunity to contract many Indian habits, and there kept till they arrived to manhood; but I have never seen one of those but was an Indian in every respect after he returned. Indians must and will be Indians, in spite of all the means that can be used to instruct them in the arts and sciences.

One thing only marred my happiness while I lived with them on the Ohio, and that was the recollection that I once had tender parents, and a home that I loved. Aside from that recollection, which could not have existed had I been taken in my infancy, I should have been contented in my situation. Notwithstanding all that has been said against the Indians, in consequence of their cruelties to their enemies—cruelties that I have witnessed and had abundant proof of—it is a fact that they are naturally kind, tender, and peaceable toward their friends, and strictly honest; and that those cruelties have been practiced only upon their enemies, according to their idea of justice.

/   /   /

GOTTLIEB MITTELBERGER

12 | On the Misfortune of Indentured Servants

Indentured, or bonded, servants were an important source of labor in seventeenth-and eighteenth-century America. The term generally refers to immigrants who, in return for passage from Europe to America, had bound themselves to work in America for a number of years, after which time they would become completely free. The practice was closely related to the tradition of apprenticeship, in which a youth was assigned to work for a master in a certain trade and in return was taught the skills of the trade. (See the selection by Benjamin Franklin, reading 13.) Convicts were another important source of colonial labor; thousands of English criminals were sentenced to labor in the colonies for a specified period, after which time they were freed.

Gottlieb Mittelberger came to Pennsylvania from Germany in 1750. He returned to Europe four years later. Mittelberger's own fortunes were not so bleak as those of his shipmates. Mittelberger served as a schoolmaster and organist in Philadelphia for three years. He returned to Germany in 1754.

Both in Rotterdam and in Amsterdam the people are packed densely, like herrings so to say, in the large sea-vessels. One person receives a place of scarcely 2 feet width and 6 feet length in the bedstead, while many a ship carries four to six hundred souls; not to mention the innumerable implements, tools, provisions, water-barrels and other things which likewise occupy much space.

On account of contrary winds it takes the ships sometimes 2, 3 and 4 weeks to make the trip from Holland to . . . England. But when the wind is good, they get there in 8 days or even sooner. Everything is examined there and the custom-duties paid, whence it comes that the ships ride there 8, 10 to 14 days and even longer at anchor, till they have taken in their full cargoes. During that time every one is compelled to spend his last remaining money and to consume his little stock of provisions which had been reserved for the sea; so that most passengers,

Gottlieb Mittelberger's Journey to Pennsylvania in the Year 1750 and Return to Germany in the Year 1754. *Translated from the German by Carl Theo. Eben. (Philadelphia, John Jos. McVey, 1898), pp. 19–29.*

finding themselves on the ocean where they would be in greater need of them, must greatly suffer from hunger and want. Many suffer want already on the water between Holland and Old England.

When the ships have for the last time weighed their anchors near the city of Kaupp [Cowes] in Old England, the real misery begins with the long voyage. For from there the ships, unless they have good wind, must often sail 8, 9, 10 to 12 weeks before they reach Philadelphia. But even with the best wind the voyage lasts 7 weeks.

But during the voyage there is on board these ships terrible misery, stench, fumes, horror, vomiting, many kinds of sea-sickness, fever, dysentery, headache, heat, constipation, boils, scurvy, cancer, mouth-rot, and the like, all of which come from old and sharply salted food and meat, also from very bad and foul water, so that many die miserably.

Add to this want of provisions, hunger, thirst, frost, heat, dampness, anxiety, want, afflictions and lamentations, together with other trouble, as . . . the lice abound so frightfully, especially on sick people, that they can be scraped off the body. The misery reaches the climax when a gale rages for 2 or 3 nights and days, so that every one believes that the ship will go to the bottom with all human beings on board. In such a visitation the people cry and pray most piteously.

When in such a gale the sea rages and surges, so that the waves rise often like high mountains one above the other, and often tumble over the ship, so that one fears to go down with the ship; when the ship is constantly tossed from side to side by the storm and waves, so that no one can either walk, or sit, or lie, and the closely packed people in the berths are thereby tumbled over each other, both the sick and the well— it will be readily understood that many of these people, none of whom had been prepared for hardships, suffer so terribly from them that they do not survive it.

I myself had to pass through a severe illness at sea, and I best know how I felt at the time. These poor people often long for consolation, and I often entertained and comforted them with singing, praying and exhorting; and whenever it was possible and the winds and waves permitted it, I kept daily prayer-meetings with them on deck. Besides, I baptized five children in distress, because we had no ordained minister on board. I also held divine service every Sunday by reading sermons to the people; and when the dead were sunk in the water, I commended them and our souls to the mercy of God.

Among the healthy, impatience sometimes grows so great and cruel that one curses the other, or himself and the day of his birth, and sometimes come near killing each other. Misery and malice join each other, so that they cheat and rob one another. One always reproaches the other with having persuaded him to undertake the journey. Frequently children cry out against their parents, husbands against their wives and wives against their husbands, brothers and sisters, friends and acquaintances against each other. But most against the soul-traffickers.

Many sigh and cry: "Oh, that I were at home again, and if I had to lie in my pig-sty!" Or they say: "O God, if I only had a piece of good bread, or a good fresh drop of water." Many people whimper, sigh and cry piteously for their homes; most of them get home-sick. Many hundred people necessarily die and perish in such misery, and must be cast into the sea, which drives their relatives, or those who persuaded them to undertake the journey, to such despair that it is almost impossible to pacify and console them. . . .

No one can have an idea of the sufferings which women in confinement have to bear with their innocent children on board these ships. Few of this class escape with their lives; many a mother is cast into the water with her child as soon as she is dead. One day, just as we had a heavy gale, a woman in our ship, who was to give birth and could not give birth under the circumstances, was pushed through a loop-hole [port-hole] in the ship and dropped into the sea, because she was far in the rear of the ship and could not be brought forward.

Children from 1 to 7 years rarely survive the voyage. I witnessed . . . misery in no less than 32 children in our ship, all of whom were thrown into the sea. The parents grieve all the more since their children find no resting-place in the earth, but are devoured by the monsters of the sea.

/   /   /

That most of the people get sick is not surprising, because, in addition to all other trials and hardships, warm food is served only three times a week, the rations being very poor and very little. Such meals can hardly be eaten, on account of being so unclean. The water which is served out on the ships is often very black, thick and full of worms, so that one cannot drink it without loathing, even with the greatest thirst. Toward the end we were compelled to eat the ship's biscuit which had been spoiled long ago; though in a whole biscuit there was scarcely a piece the size of a dollar that had not been full of red worms and spiders' nests . . .

At length, when, after a long and tedious voyage, the ships come in sight of land, so that the promontories can be seen, which the people were so eager and anxious to see, all creep from below on deck to see the land from afar, and they weep for joy, and pray and sing, thanking and praising God. The sight of the land makes the people on board the ship, especially the sick and the half dead, alive again, so that their hearts leap within them; they shout and rejoice, and are content to bear their misery in patience, in the hope that they may soon reach the land in safety. But alas!

When the ships have landed at Philadelphia after their long voyage, no one is permitted to leave them except those who pay for their passage or can give good security; the others, who cannot pay, must remain on board the ships till they are purchased, and are released from the ships by their purchasers. The sick always fare the worst, for the healthy are naturally preferred and purchased first; and so the sick and wretched must often remain on board in front of the city for 2 or 3 weeks, and frequently die, whereas many a one, if he could pay his debt and were permitted to leave the ship immediately, might recover and remain alive.

/   /   /

The sale of human beings in the market on board the ship is carried on thus: Every day Englishmen, Dutchmen and High-German people come from the city of Philadelphia and other places, in part from a great distance, say 20, 30, or 40 hours away, and go on board the newly arrived ship that has brought and offers for sale passengers from Europe, and select among the healthy persons such as they deem suitable for their business, and bargain with them how long they will serve for their passage money, which most of them are still in debt for. When they have come to an agreement, it happens that adult persons bind themselves in writing to serve 3, 4, 5 or 6 years for the amount due by them, according to their age and strength. But very young people, from 10 to 15 years, must serve till they are 21 years old.

Many parents must sell and trade away their children like so many head of cattle; for if their children take the debt upon themselves, the parents can leave the ship free and unrestrained; but as the parents often do not know where and to what people their children are going, it often happens that such parents and children, after leaving the ship, do not see each other again for many years, perhaps no more in all their lives.

/   /   /

It often happens that whole families, husband, wife, and children, are separated by being sold to different purchasers, especially when they have not paid any part of their passage money.

When a husband or wife has died at sea, when the ship has made more than half of her trip, the survivor must pay or serve not only for himself or herself, but also for the deceased.

When both parents have died over half-way at sea, their children, especially when they are young and have nothing to pawn or to pay, must stand for their own and their parents' passage, and serve till they are 21 years old. When one has served his or her term, he or she is entitled to a new suit of clothes at parting; and if it has been so stipulated, a man gets in addition a horse, a woman, a cow.

When a serf has an opportunity to marry in this country, he or she must pay for each year which he or she would have yet to serve, 5 to 6 pounds. But many a one who has thus purchased and paid for his bride, has subsequently repented his bargain, so that he would gladly have returned his exorbitantly dear ware, and lost the money besides.

If some one in this country runs away from his master, who has treated him harshly, he cannot get far. Good provision has been made for such cases, so that a runaway is soon recovered. He who detains or returns a deserter receives a good reward.

If such a runaway has been away from his master one day, he must serve for it as a punishment a week, for a week a month, and for a month half a year.

/ / /

13 | A Slave's Capture and His Purchase of Freedom

The first African slaves came to the American colonies in 1619, to Jamestown, Virginia. Many of the African slaves, as this reading tells, were first captured in battle by other Africans and then sold to white slave traders. In the course of the eighteenth century, the black slaves who worked on the tobacco and rice plantations of the South began to outnumber white indentured servants. To a lesser extent, slaves also worked on the farms and in the mercantile pursuits of the northern colonies. Venture Smith's account suggests why even defenders of slavery in the eighteenth and nineteenth centuries were embarrassed by the trade that brought them their slaves.

Venture Smith was born in 1729. Enslaved when he was six-and-a-half years old, he became a man of remarkable moral and physical strength. He performed gargantuan feats of labor in the many years he spent working as a slave before, while still a young man, he managed to purchase his and his family's freedom. It was unusual but far from unknown for a slave to purchase his freedom. This was particularly likely among urban slaves and those in some areas of the North who could "hire out" for wages to purchase their freedom over time.

Smith's account of his experiences was published in 1798. Whether he wrote or dictated the account is uncertain. It should be noted that Venture Smith's passage to the colonies was more gentle than what was usual. In most cases, there was overcrowding and poor sanitation. Casualties among the prospective slaves ran high.

CHAPTER I. CONTAINING AN ACCOUNT OF HIS LIFE, FROM HIS BIRTH TO THE TIME OF HIS LEAVING HIS NATIVE COUNTRY.

I was born at Dukandarra, in Guinea, about the year 1729. My father's name was Saungm Furro, Prince of the tribe of Dukandarra. My father had three wives. Polygamy was not uncommon in that country, espe-

Venture Smith, A Narrative of the Life and Adventures of Venture, A Native of Africa, But Resident Above Sixty Years in the United States of America. (Middletown, CT, J.S. Stewart, Printer and Bookbinder, 1897), p. 5, 7–15, 17–19, 21–22.

cially among the rich, as every man was allowed to keep as many wives as he could maintain. By his first wife he had three children. The eldest of them was myself, named by my father, Broteer. The other two were named Cundazo and Soozaduka. My father had two children by his second wife, and one by his third. I descended from a very large, tall and stout race of beings, much larger than the generality of people in other parts of the globe, being commonly considerable above six feet in height, and every way well proportioned.

/ / /

   Before I dismiss [my] country, I must first inform my reader what I remember concerning this place. A large river runs through this country in a westerly course. The land for a great way on each side is flat and level, hedged in by a considerable rise in the country at a great distance from it. It scarce ever rains there, yet the land is fertile; great dews fall in the night which refresh the soil. About the latter end of June or first of July, the river begins to rise, and gradually increases until it has inundated the country for a great distance, to the height of seven or eight feet. This brings on a slime which enriches the land surprisingly. When the river has subsided, the natives begin to sow and plant, and the vegetation is exceeding rapid. Near this rich river my guardian's* land lay. He possessed, I cannot exactly tell how much, yet this I am certain of respecting it, that he owned an immense tract. He possessed likewise a great many cattle and goats. During my stay with him I was kindly used, and with as much tenderness, for what I saw, as his only son, although I was an entire stranger to him, remote from friends and relatives. The principal occupations of the inhabitants there were the cultivation of the soil and the care of their flocks. They were a people pretty similar in every respect to that of mine, except in their persons, which were not so tall and stout. They appeared to be very kind and friendly. I will now return to my departure from that place.

   My father sent a man and horse after me. After settling with my guardian for keeping me, he took me away and went for home. It was then about one year since my mother brought me here. Nothing remarkable occurred to us on our journey until we arrived safe home. I found then that the difference between my parents had been made up previous to their sending for me. On my return, I was received both by my father and mother with great joy and affection, and was once more restored to my paternal dwelling in peace and happiness. I was then about six years old.

   Not more than six weeks had passed after my return, before a mes-

---

*It is not clear from Smith's narrative why he had been placed with a "guardian," but it would seem that the "difference" between his parents has something to do with it.

sage was brought by an inhabitant of the place where I lived the preceding year to my father, that that place had been invaded by a numerous army, from a nation not far distant, furnished with musical instruments, and all kinds of arms then in use; that they were instigated by some white nation who equipped and sent them to subdue and possess the country; that his nation had made no preparation for war, having been for a long time in profound peace; that they could not defend themselves against such a formidable train of invaders, and must, therefore, necessarily evacuate their lands to the fierce enemy, and fly to the protection of some chief; and that if he would permit them they would come under his rule and protection when they had to retreat from their own possessions. He was a kind and merciful prince, and therefore consented to these proposals.

He had scarcely returned to his nation with the message before the whole of his people were obliged to retreat from their country and come to my father's dominions. He gave them every privilege and all the protection his government could afford. But they had not been there longer than four days before news came to them that the invaders had laid waste their country, and were coming speedily to destroy them in my father's territories. This affrighted them, and therefore they immediately pushed off to the southward, into the unknown countries there, and were never more heard of.

Two days after their retreat, the report turned out to be but too true. A detachment from the enemy came to my father and informed him that the whole army was encamped not far from his dominions, and would invade the territory and deprive his people of their liberties and rights, if he did not comply with the following terms. These were, to pay them a large sum of money, three hundred fat cattle, and a great number of goats, sheep, asses, etc.

My father told the messenger he would comply rather than that his subjects should be deprived of their rights and privileges, which he was not then in circumstances to defend from so sudden an invasion. Upon turning out those articles, the enemy pledged their faith and honor that they would not attack him. On these he relied, and therefore thought it unnecessary to be on his guard against the enemy. But their pledges of faith and honor proved no better than those of other unprincipled hostile nations, for a few days after, a certain relation of the king came and informed him that the enemy who sent terms of accommodation to him, and received tribute to their satisfaction, yet meditated an attack upon his subjects by surprise, and that probably they would commence their attack in less than one day, and concluded with advising him, as he was not prepared for war, to order a speedy retreat of his family and subjects. He complied with this advice.

The same night which was fixed upon to retreat, my father and his family set off about the break of day. The king and his two younger wives went in one company, and my mother and her children in another. We left our dwellings in succession, and my father's company went on first. We directed our course for a large shrub plain, some distance off, where we intended to conceal ourselves from the approaching enemy, until we could refresh ourselves a little. But we presently found that our retreat was not secure. For having struck up a little fire for the purpose of cooking victuals, the enemy, who happened to be encamped a little distance off, had sent out a scouting party who discovered us by the smoke of the fire, just as we were extinguishing it and about to eat. As soon as we had finished eating, my father discoverd the party and immediately began to discharge arrows at them. This was what I first saw, and it alarmed both me and the women, who, being unable to make any resistance, immediately betook ourselves to the tall, thick reeds not far off, and left the old king to fight alone. For some time I beheld him from the reeds defending himself with great courage and firmness, till at last he was obliged to surrender himself into their hands.

They then came to us in the reeds, and the very first salute I had from them was a violent blow on the head with the fore part of a gun, and at the same time a grasp round the neck. I then had a rope put about my neck, as had all the women in the thicket with me, and were immediately led to my father, who was likewise pinioned and haltered for leading. In this condition we were all led to the camp. The women and myself, being submissive, had tolerable treatment from the enemy, while my father was closely interrogated respecting his money, which they knew he must have. But as he gave them no account of it, he was instantly cut and pounded on his body with great inhumanity, that he might be induced by the torture he suffered to make the discovery. All this availed not in the least to make him give up his money, but he despised all the tortures which they inflicted, until the continued exercise and increase of torment obliged him to sink and expire. He thus died without informing his enemies where his money lay. I saw him while he was thus tortured to death. The shocking scene is to this day fresh in my memory, and I have often been overcome while thinking on it. He was a man of remarkable stature. I should judge as much as six feet and six or seven inches high, two feet across the shoulders, and every way well proportioned. He was a man of remarkable strength and resolution, affable, kind and gentle, ruling with equity and moderation.

The army of the enemy was large, I should suppose consisting of about six thousand men. Their leader was called Baukurre. After destroying the old prince, they decamped and immediately marched towards the sea, lying to the west, taking with them myself and the women prisoners. In the march, a scouting party was detached from the main army. To the leader of this party I was made waiter, having to carry his gun, etc. As we were a-scouting, we came across a herd of fat cattle consisting of about thirty in number. These we set upon and immediately wrested from their keepers, and afterwards converted them into food for the army. The enemy had remarkable success in de-

stroying the country wherever they went. For as far as they had pene-
trated they laid the habitations waste and captured the people. The distance they had now brought me was about four hundred miles. All the
march I had very hard tasks imposed on me, which I must perform on
pain of punishment. I was obliged to carry on my head a large flat stone
used for grinding our corn, weighing, as I should suppose, as much as
twenty-five pounds; besides victuals, mat and cooking utensils. Though
I was pretty large and stout of my age, yet these burdens were very
grievous to me, being only six years and a half old.

We were then come to a place called Malagasco. When we entered
the place, we could not see the least appearance of either houses or
inhabitants, but on stricter search found that instead of houses above
ground they had dens in the sides of hillocks, contiguous to ponds and
streams of water. In these we perceived they had all hid themselves, as
I suppose they usually did on such occasions. In order to compel them
to surrender, the enemy contrived to smoke them out with faggots.
These they put to the entrance of the caves and set them on fire. While
they were engaged in this business, to their great surprise some of them
were desperately wounded with arrows which fell from above on them.
This mystery they soon found out. They perceived that the enemy discharged these arrows through holes on the top of the dens directly into
the air. Their weight brought them back, point downwards, on their
enemies' heads, whilst they were smoking the inhabitants out. The
points of their arrows were poisoned, but their enemy had an antidote
for it which they instantly applied to the wounded part. The smoke at
last obliged the people to give themselves up. They came out of their
caves, first spatting the palms of their hands together, and immediately
after extended their arms, crossed at their wrists, ready to be bound and
pinioned. I should judge that the dens above mentioned were extended
about eight feet horizontally into the earth, six feet in height, and as
many wide. They were arched overhead and lined with earth, which
was of the clay kind and made the surface of their walls firm and
smooth.

The invaders then pinioned the prisoners of all ages and sexes indiscriminately, took their flocks and all their effects, and moved on their
way towards the sea. On the march, the prisoners were treated with
clemency, on account of their being submissive and humble. Having
come to the next tribe, the enemy laid siege and immediately took men,
women, children, flocks, and all their valuable effects. They then went
on to the next district, which was contiguous to the sea, called in Africa,
Anamaboo. The enemies' provisions were then almost spent, as well as
their strength. The inhabitants, knowing what conduct they had pursued, and what were their present intentions, improved the favorable
opportunity, attacked them, and took enemy, prisoners, flocks and all
their effects. I was then taken a second time. All of us were then put
into the castle and kept for market. On a certain time, I and other pris-

oners were put on board a canoe, under our master, and rowed away to a vessel belonging to Rhode Island, commanded by Captain Collingwood, and the mate, Thomas Mumford. While we were going to the vessel, our master told us to appear to the best possible advantage for sale. I was bought on board by one Robertson Mumford, steward of said vessel, for four gallons of rum and a piece of calico, and called VENTURE, on account of his having purchased me with his own private venture. Thus I came by my name. All the slaves that were bought for that vessel's cargo were two hundred and sixty.

CHAPTER II. CONTAINING AN ACCOUNT OF HIS LIFE FROM THE TIME OF HIS LEAVING AFRICA TO THAT OF HIS BECOMING FREE.

The first of the time of living at my master's own place, I was pretty much employed in the house, carding wool and other household business. In this situation I continued for some years, after which my master put me to work out of doors. After many proofs of my faithfulness and honesty, my master began to put great confidence in me. My behavior had as yet been submissive and obedient. I then began to have hard tasks imposed on me. Some of these were to pound four bushels of ears of corn every night in a barrel for the poultry, or be rigorously punished. At other seasons of the year, I had to card wool until a very late hour. These tasks I had to perform when only about nine years old. Some time after, I had another difficulty and oppression which was greater than any I had ever experienced since I came into this country. This was to serve two masters. James Mumford, my master's son, when his father had gone from home in the morning and given me a stint to perform that day, would order me to do *this* and *that* business different from what my master had directed me. One day in particular, the authority which my master's son had set up had like to have produced melancholy effects. For my master having set me off my business to perform that day and then left me to perform it, his son came up to me in the course of the day, big with authority, and commanded me very arrogantly to quit my present business and go directly about what he should order me. I replied to him that my master had given me so much to perform that day, and that I must faithfully complete it in that time. He then broke out into a great rage, snatched a pitchfork and went to lay me over the head therewith, but I as soon got another and defended myself with it, or otherwise he might have murdered me in his outrage. He immediately called some people who were within hearing at work for him, and ordered them to take his hair rope and come and bind me with it. They all tried to bind me, but in vain, though there were three assistants in number. My upstart master then desisted, put his pocket handkerchief before his eyes and went home with a design to tell his

mother of the struggle with young VENTURE. He told that their young
VENTURE had become so stubborn that he could not control him, and
asked her what he should do with him. In the meantime I recovered my
temper, voluntarily caused myself to be bound by the same men who
tried in vain before, and carried before my young master, that he might
do what he pleased with me. He took me to a gallows made for the
purpose of hanging cattle on, and suspended me on it. Afterwards he
ordered one of his hands to go to the peach orchard and cut him three
dozen of whips to punish me with. These were brought to him, and
that was all that was done with them, as I was released and went to
work after hanging on the gallows about an hour.

/   /   /

Not a long time passed after that before Heddy* was sent by my
master to New London [jail]. At the close of that year I was sold to a
Thomas Stanton, and had to be separated from my wife and one daughter, who was about one month old. He resided at Stonington Point. To
this place I brought with me from my late master's, two johannes, three
old Spanish dollars, and two thousand of coppers, besides five pounds
of my wife's money. This money I got by cleaning gentlemen's shoes
and drawing-boots, by catching muskrats and minks, raising potatoes
and carrots, etc., and by fishing in the night, and at odd spells.

/   /   /

Towards the close of the time that I resided with this master, I had
a falling out with my mistress. This happened one time when my master
was gone to Long Island a-gunning. At first the quarrel began between
my wife and her mistress. I was then at work in the barn, and hearing
a racket in the house, induced me to run there and see what had broken
out. When I entered the house, I found my mistress in a violent passion
with my wife, for what she informed me was a mere trifle—such a small
affair that I forbear to put my mistress to the shame of having it known.
I earnestly requested my wife to beg pardon of her mistress for the sake
of peace, even if she had given no just occasion for offence. But whilst
I was thus saying, my mistress turned the blows which she was repeating on my wife to me. She took down her horse whip, and while she
was glutting her fury with it, I reached out my great black hand, raised
it up and received the blows of the whip on it which were designed for
my head. Then I immediately committed the whip to the devouring fire.
     When my master returned from the island, his wife told him of the
affair, but for the present he seemed to take no notice of it, and men-

*Venture's wife, who he met when they were both owned by the Mumfords.

tioned not a word of it to me. Some days after his return, in the morning as I was putting on a log in the fireplace, not suspecting harm from any one, I received a most violent stroke on the crown of my head with a club two feet long and as large around as a chair post. This blow very badly wounded my head, and the scar of it remains to this day. The first blow made me have my wits about me you may suppose, for as soon as he went to renew it I snatched the club out of his hands and dragged him out of the door. He then sent for his brother to come and assist him, but I presently left my master, took the club he wounded me with, carried it to a neighboring justice of the peace, and complained of my master. He finally advised me to return to my master and live contented with him till he abused me again, and then complain. I consented to do accordingly. But before I set out for my master's, up he came and his brother Robert after me. The Justice improved this convenient opportunity to caution my master. He asked him for what he treated his slave thus hastily and unjustly, and told him what would be the consequence if he continued the same treatment towards me. After the justice had ended his discourse with my master, he and his brother set out with me for home, one before and the other behind me. When they had come to a by-place, they both dismounted their respective horses and fell to beating me with great violence. I became enraged at this and immediately turned them both under me, laid one of them across the other, and stamped them both with my feet what I would.

This occasioned my master's brother to advise him to put me off. A short time after this, I was taken by a constable and two men. They carried me to a blacksmith's shop and had me handcuffed. When I returned home my mistress enquired much of her waiters whether VENTURE was handcuffed. When she was informed that I was, she appeared to be very contented and was much transported with the news. In the midst of this content and joy, I presented myself before my mistress, showed her my handcuffs, and gave her thanks for my gold rings. For this my master commanded a negro of his to fetch him a large ox chain. This my master locked on my legs with two padlocks. I continued to wear the chain peaceably for two or three days, when my master asked me with contemptuous hard names whether I had not better be freed from my chains and go to work. I answered him, "No." "Well, then," said he, "I will send you to the West Indies, or banish you, for I am resolved not to keep you." I answered him, "I crossed the waters to come here and I am willing to cross them to return."

For a day or two after this not anyone said much to me, until one Hempstead Miner of Stonington asked me if I would live with him. I answered that I would. He then requested me to make myself discontented and to appear as unreconciled to my master as I could before that he bargained with him for me, and that in return he would give me a good chance to gain my freedom when I came to live with him. I did as he requested me. Not long after, Hempstead Miner purchased me of my master for fifty-six pounds lawful. He took the chain and padlocks from off me immediately after.

At age 31, Venture is sold to Colonel Smith.

As I never had an opportunity of redeeming myself whilst I was owned by Miner, though he promised to give me a chance, I was then very ambitious of obtaining it. I asked my master one time if he would consent to have me purchase my freedom. He replied that he would.

/   /   /

The next summer I again desired he would give me a chance of going to work. But he refused and answered that he must have my labor this summer, as he did not have it the past winter. I replied that I considered it as hard that I could not have a chance to work out when the season became advantageous, and that I must only be permitted to hire myself out in the poorest season of the year. He asked me after this what I would give him for the privilege per month. I replied that I would leave it wholly to his own generosity to determine what I should return him a month. Well then, said he, if so, two pounds a month. I answered him that if that was the least he would take I would be contented.

Accordingly I hired myself out at Fisher's Island, earning twenty pounds; thirteen pounds six shillings of which my master drew for the privilege and the remainder I paid for my freedom. This made fifty-one pounds two shillings which I paid him. In October following I went and wrought six months at Long Island. In that six month's time I cut and corded four hundred cords of wood, besides threshing out seventy-five bushels of grain, and received of my wages down only twenty pounds, which left remaining a larger sum. Whilst I was out that time, I took up on my wages only one pair of shoes. At night I lay on the hearth, with one coverlet over and another under me. I returned to my master and gave him what I received of my six months' labor. This left only thirteen pounds eighteen shillings to make up the full sum of my redemption. My master liberated me, saying that I might pay what was behind if I could ever make it convenient, otherwise it would be well. The amount of the money which I had paid my master towards redeeming my time, was seventy-one pounds two shillings. The reason of my master for asking such an unreasonable price, was, he said, to secure himself in case I should ever come to want. Being thirty-six years old, I left Colonel Smith once more for all. I had already been sold three different times, made considerable money with seemingly nothing to derive it from, had been cheated out of a large sum of money, lost much by misfortunes, and paid an enormous sum for my freedom.

14 | How I Became a Printer in Philadelphia

Although Benjamin Franklin's (1706–1790) autobiography breaks off in 1757, it is an invaluable document for understanding both colonial life and the eighteenth-century American mind. In this excerpt Franklin gives an excellent picture of the important eighteenth-century institution of apprenticeship and offers some clues as to why in America it inevitably became a looser arrangement than it was in the old world. Franklin, one of the nation's founding fathers, exhibited a versatility that ranged from a capacity to conduct scientific experiment to service as a diplomat in the court at Paris. His self-made background, illustrated in this selection, fitted him for a range of activities almost unparalleled in the revolutionary period.

My elder brothers were all put apprentices to different trades. I was put to the grammar-school at eight years of age, my father intending to devote me, as the tithe of his sons, to the service of the Church. My early readiness in learning to read (which must have been very early, as I do not remember when I could not read), and the opinion of all his friends, that I should certainly make a good scholar, encouraged him in this purpose of his. My uncle Benjamin, too, approved of it, and proposed to give me all his short-hand volumes of sermons, I suppose as a stock to set up with, if I would learn his character. I continued, however, at the grammar-school not quite one year, though in that time I had risen gradually from the middle of the class of that year to be the head of it, and farther was removed into the next class above it, in order to go with that into the third at the end of the year. But my father, in the mean time, from a view of the expense of a college education, which having so large a family he could not well afford, and the mean living many so educated were afterwards able to obtain—reasons that he gave to his friends in my hearing—altered his first intention, took me from the grammar-school, and sent me to a school for writing and arithmetic, kept by a then famous man, Mr. George Brownell, very successful in his profession generally, and that by mild, encouraging methods. Under

John Bigelow (editor), Autobiography of Benjamin Franklin. *(Philadelphia, J. B. Lippincott and Company, 1868), pp. 85–86, 90–93, 103–107, 114.*

him I acquired fair writing pretty soon, but I failed in the arithmetic, and made no progress in it. At ten years old I was taken home to assist my father in his business, which was that of a tallow-chandler and sope-boiler; a business he was not bred to, but had assumed on his arrival in New England, and on finding his dying trade would not maintain his family, being in little request. Accordingly, I was employed in cutting wick for the candles, filling the dipping mold and the molds for cast candles, attending the shop, going of errands, etc.

I disliked the trade, and had a strong inclination for the sea, but my father declared against it; however, living near the water, I was much in and about it, learnt early to swim well, and to manage boats; and when in a boat or canoe with other boys, I was commonly allowed to govern, especially in any case of difficulty; and upon other occasions I was generally a leader among the boys, and sometimes led them into scrapes.

/   /   /

To return: I continued thus employed in my father's business for two years, that is, till I was twelve years old; and my brother John, who was bred to that business, having left my father, married, and set up for himself at Rhode Island, there was all appearance that I was destined to supply his place, and become a tallow-chandler. But my dislike to the trade continuing, my father was under apprehensions that if he did not find one for me more aggreeable, I should break away and get to sea, as his son Josiah had done, to his great vexation. He therefore sometimes took me to walk with him, and see joiners, bricklayers, turners, braziers, etc., at their work, that he might observe my inclination, and endeavor to fix it on some trade or other on land. It has ever since been a pleasure to me to see good workmen handle their tools; and it has been useful to me, having learnt so much by it as to be able to do little jobs myself in my house when a workman could not readily be got, and to construct little machines for my experiments, while the intention of making the experiment was fresh and warm in my mind. My father at last fixed upon the cutler's trade, and my uncle Benjamin's son Samuel, who was bred to that business in London, being about that time established in Boston, I was sent to be with him some time on liking. But his expectations of a fee with me displeasing my father, I was taken home again.

From a child I was fond of reading, and all the little money that came into my hands was ever laid out in books. Pleased with the Pilgrim's Progress, my first collection was of John Bunyan's works in separate little volumes. I afterward sold them to enable me to buy R. Burton's Historical Collections; they were small chapmen's books, and cheap, 40 or 50 in all.

/   /   /

This bookish inclination at length determined my father to make me a printer, though he had already one son (James) of that profession. In 1717 my brother James returned from England with a press and letters to set up his business in Boston. I liked it much better than that of my father, but still had a hankering for the sea. To prevent the apprehended effect of such an inclination, my father was impatient to have me bound to my brother. I stood out some time, but at last was persuaded, and signed the indentures when I was yet but twelve years old. I was to serve as an apprentice till I was twenty-one years of age, only I was to be allowed journeyman's wages during the last year. In a little time I made great proficiency in the business, and became a useful hand to my brother.

/   /   /

Though a brother, he considered himself as my master, and me as his apprentice, and, accordingly, expected the same services from me as he would from another, while I thought he demean'd me too much in some he requir'd of me, who from a brother expected more indulgence. Our disputes were often brought before our father, and I fancy I was either generally in the right, or else a better pleader, because the judgment was generally in my favor. But my brother was passionate, and had often beaten me, which I took extreamly amiss; and, thinking my apprenticeship very tedious, I was continually wishing for some opportunity of shortening it, which at length offered in a manner unexpected.[1]

One of the pieces in our newspaper on some political point, which I have now forgotten, gave offense to the Assembly. He [James] was taken up, censur'd, and imprison'd for a month, by the speaker's warrant, I suppose, because he would not discover [reveal] his author. I too was taken up and examin'd before the council; but, tho' I did not give them any satisfaction, they content'd themselves with admonishing me, and dismissed me, considering me, perhaps, as an apprentice, who was bound to keep his master's secrets.

During my brother's confinement, which I resented a good deal, notwithstanding our private differences, I had the management of the paper; and I made bold to give our rulers some rubs in it, which my brother took very kindly, while others began to consider me in an unfavorable light, as a young genius that had a turn for libelling and satyr. My brother's discharge was accompany'd with an order of the House (a very odd one), that *"James Franklin should no longer print the paper called the New England Courant."*

---

1. I fancy his harsh and tyrannical treatment of me might be a means of impressing me with that aversion to arbitrary power that has stuck to me through my whole life.

There was a consultation held in our printing-house among his friends, what he should do in this case. Some proposed to evade the order by changing the name of the paper; but my brother, seeing inconveniences in that, it was finally concluded on as a better way, to let it be printed for the future under the name of BENJAMIN FRANKLIN; and to avoid the censure of the Assembly, that might fall on him as still printing it by his apprentice, the contrivance was that my old indenture should be return'd to me, with a full discharge on the back of it, to be shown on occasion, but to secure to him the benefit of my service, I was to sign new indentures for the remainder of the term, which were to be kept private. A very flimsy scheme it was; however, it was immediately executed, and the paper went on accordingly, under my name for several months.

At length, a fresh difference arising between my brother and me, I took upon me to assert my freedom, presuming that he would not venture to produce the new indentures. It was not fair in me to take this advantage, and this I therefore reckon one of the first errata of my life; but the unfairness of it weighed little with me, when under the impressions of resentment for the blows his passion too often urged him to bestow upon me, though he was otherwise not an ill-natur'd man: perhaps I was too saucy and provoking.

When he found I would leave him, he took care to prevent my getting employment in any other printing-house of the town, by going round and speaking to every master, who accordingly refus'd to give me work. I then thought of going to New York, as the nearest place where there was a printer; and I was rather inclin'd to leave Boston when I reflected that I had already made myself a little obnoxious to the governing party, and, from the arbitrary proceedings of the Assembly in my brother's case, it was likely I might, if I stay'd, soon bring myself into scrapes; and farther, that my indiscrete disputations about religion began to make me pointed at with horror by good people as an infidel or atheist. I determin'd on the point, but my father now siding with my brother, I was sensible that, if I attempted to go openly, means would be used to prevent me. My friend Collins, therefore, undertook to manage a little for me. He agreed with the captain of a New York sloop for my passage, under the notion of my being a young acquaintance of his, that had got a naughty girl with child, whose friends would compel me to marry her, and therefore I could not appear or come away publicly. So I sold some of my books to raise a little money, was taken on board privately, and as we had a fair wind, in three days I found myself in New York, near 300 miles from home, a boy of but 17,[2] without the least recommendation to, or knowledge of any person in the place, and with very little money in my pocket.

---

2. This was in October, 1723.—B.

My inclinations for the sea were by this time worne out, or I might now have gratify'd them. But, having a trade, and supposing myself a pretty good workman, I offer'd my service to the printer in the place, old Mr. William Bradford, who had been the first printer in Pennsylvania, but removed from thence upon the quarrel of George Keith. He could give me no employment, having little to do, and help enough already; but says he, "My son at Philadelphia has lately lost his principal hand, Aquila Rose, by death; if you go thither, I believe he may employ you." Philadelphia was a hundred miles further; I set out, however, in a boat for Amboy, leaving my chest and things to follow me round by sea.

/   /   /

Then I made myself as tidy as I could, and went to Andrew Bradford the printer's. I found in the shop the old man his father whom I had seen at New York, and who, traveling on horseback, had got to Philadelphia before me. He introduc'd me to his son, who receiv'd me civilly, gave me a breakfast, but told me he did not at present want a hand, being lately suppli'd with one; but there was another printer in town, lately set up, one Keimer, who, perhaps, might employ me; if not, I should be welcome to lodge at his house, and he would give me a little work to do now and then till fuller business should offer.

/   /   /

15 | What Is an American?

Michel Crèvecoeur's Letters from an American Farmer *was first published in London in 1782. Crèvecoeur was certainly an unusual American farmer. Born in France in 1735, he served with the French against the British in the French and Indian War and from 1783 to 1790 was the French consul in New York City, but he lived as an "American farmer" in Orange County, New York, from 1769 to 1780.*

It has been an article of faith for three centuries that moving from Europe to America is a transforming experience, creating a new person from the old. What is American about America is one of the continuing subjects of our history and literature. Few writers have given so persuasive or influential a response as Crèvecoeur to the question, "What is the American, this new man?" Crèvecoeur died in France in 1813. He published his book using an Americanized name: J. Hector St. John.

LETTER III. WHAT IS AN AMERICAN.

I wish I could be acquainted with the feelings and thoughts which must agitate the heart and present themselves to the mind of an enlightened Englishman, when he first lands on this continent. He must greatly rejoice that he lived at a time to see this fair country discovered and settled; he must necessarily feel a share of national pride, when he views the chain of settlements which embellishes these extended shores. When he says to himself, this is the work of my countrymen, who, when convulsed by factions, afflicted by a variety of miseries and wants, restless and impatient, took refuge here. They brought along with them their national genius, to which they principally owe what liberty they enjoy, and what substance they possess. Here he sees the industry of his native country displayed in a new manner, and traces in their works the embrios of all the arts, sciences, and ingenuity which flourish in Europe. Here he beholds fair cities, substantial villages, extensive fields,

J. Hector St. John (Michel-Guillaume-Jean de Crèvecoeur), Letters from an American Farmer; Describing Certain Provincial Situations, Manners and Customs Not Generally Known. (London, Thomas Davies, 1782), pp. 48–49, 51, 54–68, 71.

an immense country filled with decent houses, good roads, orchards, meadows, and bridges, where an hundred years ago all was wild, woody and uncultivated! What a train of pleasing ideas this fair spectacle must suggest; it is a prospect which must inspire a good citizen with the most heartfelt pleasure. The difficulty consists in the manner of viewing so extensive a scene. He is arrived on a new continent; a modern society offers itself to his contemplation, different from what he had hitherto seen. It is not composed, as in Europe, of great lords who possess every thing, and of a herd of people who have nothing. Here are no aristocratical families, no courts, no kings, no bishops, no ecclesiastical dominion, no invisible power giving to a few a very visible one; no great manufacturers employing thousands, no great refinements of luxury. The rich and the poor are not so far removed from each other as they are in Europe.

/ / /

The next wish of this traveller will be to know whence came all these people? they are a mixture of English, Scotch, Irish, French, Dutch, Germans, and Swedes. From this promiscuous breed, that race now called Americans have arisen. . . .

/ / /

What attachment can a poor European emigrant have for a country where he had nothing? The knowledge of the language, the love of a few kindred as poor as himself, were the only cords that tied him: his country is now that which gives him land, bread, protection, and consequence: *Ubi panis ibi patria* [where I have bread, there is my homeland], is the motto of all emigrants. What then is the American, this new man? He is either an European, or the descendant of an European, hence that strange mixture of blood, which you will find in no other country. I could point out to you a family whose grandfather was an Englishman, whose wife was Dutch, whose son married a French woman, and whose present four sons have now four wives of different nations. *He* is an American, who leaving behind him all his ancient prejudices and manners, receives new ones from the new mode of life he has embraced, the new government he obeys, and the new rank he holds. He becomes an American by being received in the broad lap of our great *Alma Mater.* Here individuals of all nations are melted into a new race of men, whose labours and posterity will one day cause great changes in the world. Americans are the western pilgrims, who are carrying along with them that great mass of arts, sciences, vigour, and industry which began long since in the east; they will finish the great circle. The Americans were once scattered all over Europe; here they are incorporated into one of the finest systems of population which has ever appeared, and which will hereafter become distinct by the power of the different climates they inhabit. The American ought therefore to love this country much better than that wherein either he or his forefathers were born. Here the rewards of his industry follow with equal steps the progress of his labour; his labour is founded on the basis of nature, *self-interest;* can it want a stronger allurement? Wives and children, who before in vain demanded of him a morsel of bread, now, fat and frolicsome, gladly help their father to clear those fields whence exuberant crops are to arise to feed and to clothe them all; without any part being claimed, either by a despotic prince, a rich abbot, or a mighty lord. Here religion demands but little of him; a small voluntary salary to the minister, and gratitude to God; can he refuse these? The American is a new man, who acts upon new principles; he must therefore entertain new ideas, and form new opinions. From involuntary idleness, servile dependence, penury, and useless labour, he has passed to toils of a very different nature, rewarded by ample subsistence.—This is an American.

British America is divided into many provinces, forming a large association, scattered along a coast 1500 miles extent and about 200 wide. This society I would fain examine, at least such as it appears in the middle provinces; if it does not afford that variety of tinges and gradations which may be observed in Europe, we have colours peculiar to ourselves. For instance, it is natural to conceive that those who live near the sea, must be very different from those who live in the woods; the intermediate space will afford a separate and distinct class.

Men are like plants; the goodness and flavour of the fruit proceeds from the peculiar soil and exposition in which they grow. We are nothing but what we derive from the air we breathe, the climate we inhabit, the goverment we obey, the system of religion we profess, and the nature of our employment. Here you will find but few crimes; these have acquired as yet no root among us. I wish I were able to trace all my ideas; if my ignorance prevents me from describing them properly, I hope I shall be able to delineate a few of the outlines, which are all I propose.

Those who live near the sea, feed more on fish than on flesh, and often encounter that boisterous element. This renders them more bold and enterprising; this leads them to neglect the confined occupations of the land. They see and converse with a variety of people; their intercourse with mankind becomes extensive. The sea inspires them with a love of traffic, a desire of transporting produce from one place to another; and leads them to a variety of resources which supply the place of labour. Those who inhabit the middle settlements, by far the most numerous, must be very different; the simple cultivation of the earth purifies them, but the indulgences of the government, the soft remonstrances of religion, the rank of independent freeholders, must necessarily inspire them with sentiments, very little known in Europe among people of the same class. What do I say? Europe has no such class of men; the early knowledge they acquire, the early bargains they make, give them a great degree of sagacity. As freemen they will be litigious; pride and obstinacy are often the cause of law suits; the nature of our laws and governments may be another. As citizens it is easy to imagine, that they will carefully read the newspapers, enter into every political disquisition, freely blame or censure governors and others. As farmers they will be carful and anxious to get as much as they can, because what they get is their own. As northern men they will love the chearful cup. As Christians, religion curbs them not in their opinions; the general indulgence leaves every one to think for themselves in spiritual matters; the laws inspect our actions, our thoughts are left to God. Industry, good living, selfishness, litigiousness, country politics, the pride of freemen, religious indifference, are their characteristics. If you recede still farther from the sea, you will come into more modern settlements; they exhibit the same strong lineaments, in a ruder appearance. Religion seems to have still less influence, and their manners are less improved.

Now we arrive near the great woods, near the last inhabited districts; there men seem to be placed still farther beyond the reach of government, which in some measure leaves them to themselves. How can it pervade every corner; as they were driven there by misfortunes, necessity of beginnings, desire of acquiring large tracks of land, idleness, frequent want of economy, ancient debts; the re-union of such people does not afford a very pleasing spectacle. When discord, want of unity and friendship; when either drunkenness or idleness prevail in such remote districts; contention, inactivity, and wretchedness must ensue. There are not the same remedies to these evils as in a long established community. The few magistrates they have, are in general little better than the rest; they are often in a perfect state of war; that of man against man, sometimes decided by blows, sometimes by means of the law; that of man against every wild inhabitant of these venerable woods, of which they are come to dispossess them. There men appear to be no beter than carnivorous animals of a superior rank, living on the flesh of wild animals when they can catch them, and when they are not able, they subsist on grain. He who would wish to see America in its proper light, and have a true idea of its feeble beginnings and barbarous rudiments, must visit our extended line of frontiers where the last settlers dwell, and where he may see the first labours of settlement, the mode of clearing the earth, in all their different appearances; where men are wholly left dependent on their native tempers, and on the spur of uncertain industry, which often fails when not sanctified by the efficacy of a few moral rules. There, remote from the power of example, and check of shame, many families exhibit the most hideous parts of our society. They are a kind of forlorn hope, preceding by ten or twelve years the most respectable army of veterans which come after them. In that space, prosperity will polish some, vice and the law will drive off the rest, who uniting again with others like themselves will recede still farther; making room for more industrious people, who will finish their improvements, convert the loghouse into a convenient habitation, and rejoicing that the first heavy labours are finished, will change in a few years that hitherto barbarous country into a fine fertile, well regulated district. Such is our progress, such is the march of the Europeans toward the interior parts of this continent. In all societies there are off-casts; this impure part serves as our precursors or pioneers; my father himself was one of that class, but he came upon honest principles, and was therefore one of the few who held fast; by good conduct and temperance, he transmitted to me his fair inheritance, when not above one in fourteen of his contemporaries had the same good fortune.

Forty years ago this smiling country was thus inhabited; it is now purged, a general decency of manners prevails throughout, and such has been the fate of our best countries.

Exclusive of those general characteristics, each province has its own, founded on the government, climate, mode of husbandry, customs, and peculiarity of circumstances. Europeans submit insensibly to these great powers, and become, in the course of a few generations, not only Americans in general, but either Pensylvanians, Virginians, or provincials under some other name. Whoever traverses the continent must easily observe those strong differences, which will grow more evident in time. The inhabitants of Canada, Massachuset, the middle provinces, the southern ones will be as different as their climates; their only points of unity will be those of religion and language.

As I have endeavoured to shew you how Europeans become Americans; it may not be disagreable to shew you likewise how the various Christian sects introduced, wear out, and how religious indifference becomes prevalent. When any considerable number of a particular sect happen to dwell contiguous to each other, they immediately erect a temple, and there worship the Divinity agreeably to their own peculiar ideas. Nobody disturbs them. If any new sect springs up in Europe, it may happen that many of its professors will come and settle in America. As they bring their zeal with them, they are at liberty to make proselytes if they can, and to build a meeting and to follow the dictates of their consciences; for neither the government nor any other power interferes. If they are peaceable subjects, and are industrious, what is it to their neighbours how and in what manner they think fit to address their prayers to the Supreme Being? But if the sectaries are not settled close together, if they are mixed with other denominations, their zeal will cool for want of fuel, and will be extinguished in a little time. Then the Americans become as to religion, what they are as to country, allied to all. In them the name of Englishman, Frenchman, and European is lost, and in like manner, the strict modes of Christianity as practised in Europe are lost also. This effect will extend itself still farther hereafter, and though this may appear to you as a strange idea, yet it is a very true one. I shall be able perhaps hereafter to explain myself better, in the meanwhile, let the following example serve as my first justification.

Let us suppose you and I to be travelling; we observe that in this house, to the right, lives a Catholic, who prays to God as he has been taught, and believes in transubstantion; he works and raises wheat, he has a large family of children, all hale and robust; his belief, his prayers offend nobody. About one mile farther on the same road, his next neighbour may be a good honest plodding German Lutheran, who addresses himself to the same God, the God of all, aggreably to the modes he has been educated in, and believes in consubstantiation; by so doing he scandalizes nobody; he also works in his fields, embellishes the earth, clears swamps, &c. What has the world to do with his Lutheran principles? He persecutes nobody, and nobody persecutes him, he visits his neighbours, and his neighbours visit him. Next to him lives a seceder, the most enthusiastic of all sectaries; his zeal is hot and fiery, but separated as he is from others of the same complexion, he has no congregation of his own to resort to, where he might cabal and mingle religious pride with worldly obstinacy. He likewise raises good crops, his house is handsomely painted, his orchard is one of the fairest in the neighbourhood. How does it concern the welfare of the country, or of the province at large, what this man's religious sentiments are, or really whether he has any at all? He is a good farmer, he is a sober, peaceable, good citizen: William Penn himself would not wish for more. This is the visible character, the invisible one is only guessed at, and is nobody's business. Next again lives a Low Dutchman, who implicitly believes the rules laid down by the synod of Dort. He conceives no other idea of a clergyman than that of an hired man; if he does his work well he will pay him the stipulated sum; if not he will dismiss him, and do without his sermons, and let his church be shut up for years. But notwithstanding this coarse idea, you will find his house and farm to be the neatest in all the country; and you will judge by his waggon and fat horses, that he thinks more of the affairs of this world than of those of the next. He is sober and laborious, therefore he is all he ought to be as to the affairs of this life; as for those of the next, he must trust to the great Creator. Each of these people instruct their children as well as they can, but these instructions are feeble compared to those which are given to the youth of the poorest class in Europe. Their children will therefore grow up less zealous and more indifferent in matters of religion than their parents. The foolish vanity, or rather the fury of making Proselytes, is unknown here; they have no time, the seasons call for all their attention, and thus in a few years, this mixed neighbourhood will exhibit a strange religious medley, that will be neither pure Catholicism nor pure Calvinism. A very perceptible indifference even in the first generation, will become apparent; and it may happen that the daughter of the Catholic will marry the son of the seceder, and settle by themselves at a distance from their parents. What religious education will they give their children? A very imperfect one. If there happens to be in the neighbourhood any place of worship, we will suppose a Quaker's meeting; rather than not shew their fine clothes, they will go to it, and some of them may perhaps attach themselves to that society. Others will remain in a perfect state of indifference; the children of these zealous parents will not be able to tell what their religious principles are, and their grandchildren still less. The neighbourhood of a place of worship generally leads them to it, and the action of going thither, is the strongest evidence they can give of their attachment to any sect. The Quakers are the only people who retain a fondness for their own mode of worship; for be they ever so far separated from each other, they hold a sort of communion with the society, and seldom depart from its rules, at least in this country. Thus all sects are mixed as well as all nations; thus religious indifference is imperceptibly disseminated from one end of the continent to the other; which is at present one of the strongest characteristics of the Americans. Where this will reach no one can tell, perhaps it may leave a vacuum fit to receive other systems. Persecution, religious pride, the love of contradiction, are the food of what the world commonly calls religion. These motives have ceased here: zeal in Europe is confined; here it evaporates in the great distance it has to travel; there it is a grain of powder inclosed, here it burns away in the open air, and consumes without effect.

But to return to our back settlers. I must tell you, that there is something in the proximity of the woods, which is very singular. It is with men as it is with the plants and animals that grow and live in the forests; they are entirely different from those that live in the plains. I will candidly tell you all my thoughts but you are not to expect that I shall advance any reasons. By living in or near the woods, their actions are regulated by the wildness of the neighbourhood. The deer often come to eat their grain, the wolves to destroy their sheep, the bears to kill their hogs, the foxes to catch their poultry. This surrounding hostility, immediately puts the gun into their hands; they watch these animals, they kill some; and thus by defending their property, they soon become professed hunters; this is the progress; once hunters, farewell to the plough. The chase renders them ferocious, gloomy, and unsociable; a hunter wants no neighbour, he rather hates them, because he dreads the competition. In a little time their success in the woods makes them neglect their tillage. They trust to the natural fecundity of the earth, and therefore do little; carelessness in fencing, often exposes what little they sow to destruction; they are not at home to watch; in order therefore to make up the deficiency, they go oftener to the woods. That new mode of life brings along with it a new set of manners, which I cannot easily describe. These new manners being grafted on the old stock, produce a strange sort of lawless profligacy, the impressions of which are indelible. The manners of the Indian natives are respectable, compared with this European medley. Their wives and children live in sloth and inactivity; and having no proper pursuits, you may judge what education the latter receive. Their tender minds have nothing else to contemplate but the example of their parents; like them they grow up a mongrel breed, half civilized, half savage, except nature stamps on them some constitutional propensities. That rich, that voluptuous sentiment is gone that struck them so forcibly; the possesson of their freeholds no longer conveys to their minds the same pleasure and pride. To all these reasons you must add, their lonely situation, and you cannot imagine what an effect on manners the great distances they live from each other has! Consider one of the last settlements in it's first view: of what is it composed? Europeans who have not that sufficient share of knowledge they ought to have, in order to prosper; people who have suddenly passed from oppression, dread of government, and fear of laws, into the unlimited freedom of the woods. This sudden change must have a very great effect on most men, and on that class particularly. Eating of wild meat, whatever you may think, tends to alter their temper: though all the proof I can adduce, is, that I have seen it: and having no place of worship to resort to, what little society this might afford, is denied them.

/ / /

It is in consequence of this straggling situation, and the astonishing power it has on manners, that the back-settlers of both the Carolinas, Virginia, and many other parts, have been long a set of lawless people; it has been even dangerous to travel among them. Government can do nothing in so extensive a country, better it should wink at these irregularities, than that it should use means inconsistent with its usual mildness.

/ / /

16 | Two Accounts of the Boston Massacre

Historians in recent years have stressed the role of the "crowd" in the coming of the American Revolution. Anonymous colonists taking to the streets in the years after 1763 were an important part of the dynamic of revolution.

First hand accounts of an event do not necessarily make it easy to determine precisely what occurred. In early 1770 British troops were quartered in Boston. Many townspeople resented their presence, and on March 5 a mob of about sixty attacked a small group of soldiers. In the ensuing disturbance, some soldiers, without orders, fired on the mob, killing five people and wounding eight. The incident was taken up and exaggerated by anti-British radicals—the "Patriots" —in Boston, who called it the Boston Massacre. In the following reading, two contemporary accounts of the incident are presented: the first by a British soldier, Captain Preston, who along with several other soldiers was tried for manslaughter; the second by an anonymous Patriot pamphleteer. All but two of the accused soldiers were acquitted (John Adams took part in their defense), but the "Massacre" served to inflame anti-British sentiment throughout the colonies.

CAPTAIN THOMAS PRESTON'S ACCOUNT OF THE BOSTON MASSACRE (13 MARCH 1770)

It is [a] matter of too great notoriety to need any proofs that the arrival of his Majesty's troops in Boston was extremely obnoxious to its inhabitants. They have ever used all means in their power to weaken the regiments, and to bring them into contempt by promoting and aiding desertions, and with impunity, even where there has been the clearest evidence of the fact, and by grossly and falsely propagating untruths concerning them. On the arrival of the 64th and 65th their ardour seemingly began to abate; it being too expensive to buy off so many, and attempts of that kind rendered too dangerous from the numbers

/   /   /

Captain Thomas Preston's Account of the Boston Massacre (13 march 1770), from British Public Records Office, C.O. 5/759. Reprinted in Merrill Jensen (editor) English Historical Documents, *Volume IX. (London, 1964) pp. 750–53.*

And has ever since their departure been breaking out with greater violence after their embarkation. One of their justices, most thoroughly acquainted with the people and their intentions, on the trial of a man of the 14th Regiment, openly and publicly in the hearing of great numbers of people and from the seat of justice, declared "that the soldiers must now take care of themselves, *nor trust too much to their arms*, for they were but a handful; that the inhabitants carried weapons concealed under their clothes, and would destroy them in a moment, *if they pleased*". This, considering the malicious temper of the people, was an alarming circumstance to the soldiery. Since which several disputes have happened between the townspeople and the soldiers of both regiments, the former being encouraged thereto by the countenance of even some of the magistrates, and by the protection of all the party against government. In general such disputes have been kept too secret from the officers. On the 2d instant two of the 29th going through one Gray's ropewalk, the rope-makers insultingly asked them if they would empty a vault. This unfortunately had the desired effect by provoking the soldiers, and from words they went to blows. Both parties suffered in this affray, and finally the soldiers retired to their quarters. The officers, on the first knowledge of this transaction, took every precaution in their power to prevent any ill consequence. Notwithstanding which, single quarrels could not be prevented, the inhabitants constantly provoking and abusing the soldiery. The insolence as well as utter hatred of the inhabitants to the troops increased daily, insomuch that Monday and Tuesday, the 5th and 6th instant, were privately agreed on for a general engagement, in consequence of which several of the militia came from the country armed to join their friends, menacing to destroy any who should oppose them. This plan has since been discovered.

On Monday night about 8 o'clock two soldiers were attacked and beat. But the party of the townspeople in order to carry matters to the utmost length, broke into two meeting houses and rang the alarm bells, which I supposed was for fire as usual, but was soon undeceived. About 9 some of the guard came to and informed me the town inhabitants were assembling to attack the troops, and that the bells were ringing as the signal for that purpose and not for fire, and the beacon intended to be fired to bring in the distant people of the country. This, as I was captain of the day, occasioned my repairing immediately to the main guard. In my way there I saw the people in great commotion, and heard them use the most cruel and horrid threats against the troops. In a few minutes after I reached the guard, about 100 people passed it and went towards the custom house where the king's money is lodged. They immediately surrounded the sentry posted there, and with clubs and other weapons threatened to execute their vengeance on him. I was soon informed by a townsman their intention was to carry off the soldier from his post and probably murder him. On which I desired him to return for further intelligence, and he soon came back and assured me he heard

the mob declare they would murder him. This I feared might be a prelude to their plundering the king's chest. I immediately sent a non-
commissioned officer and 12 men to protect both the sentry and the
king's money, and very soon followed myself to prevent, if possible, all
disorder, fearing lest the officer and soldiers, by the insults and provocations of the rioters, should be thrown off their guard and commit some
rash act. They soon rushed through the people, and by charging their
bayonets in half-circles, kept them at a little distance. Nay, so far was I
from intending the death of any person that I suffered the troops to go
to the spot where the unhappy affair took place without any loading in
their pieces; nor did I ever give orders for loading them. This remiss
conduct in me perhaps merits censure; yet it is evidence, resulting from
the nature of things, which is the best and surest that can be offered,
that my intention was not to act offensively, but the contrary part, and
that not without compulsion. The mob still increased and were more
outrageous, striking their clubs or bludgeons one against another, and
calling out, come on you rascals, you bloody backs, you lobster scoun-
drels, fire if you dare, G-d damn you, fire and be damned, we know
you dare not, and much more such language was used. At this time I
was between the soldiers and the mob, parleying with, and endeavour-
ing all in my power to persuade them to retire peaceably, but to no
purpose. They advanced to the points of the bayonets, struck some of
them and even the muzzles of the pieces, and seemed to be endeavour-
ing to close with the soldiers. On which some well behaved persons
asked me if the guns were charged. I replied yes. They then asked me
if I intended to order the men to fire. I answered no, by no means,
observing to them that I was advanced before the muzzles of the men's
pieces, and must fall a sacrifice if they fired; that the soldiers were upon
the half cock and charged bayonets, and my giving the word fire under
those circumstances would prove me to be no officer. While I was thus
speaking, one of the soldiers having received a severe blow with a stick,
stepped a little on one side and instantly fired, on which turning to and
asking him why he fired without orders, I was struck with a club on my
arm, which for some time deprived me of the use of it, which blow had
it been placed on my head, most probably would have destroyed me.
On this a general attack was made on the men by a great number of
heavy clubs and snowballs being thrown at them, by which all our lives
were in imminent danger, some persons at the same time from behind
calling out, damn your bloods–why don't you fire. Instantly three or
four of the soldiers fired, one after another, and directly after three more
in the same confusion and hurry. The mob then ran away, except three
unhappy men who instantly expired, in which number was Mr. Gray
at whose rope-walk the prior quarrels took place; one more is since
dead, three others are dangerously, and four slightly wounded. The
whole of this melancholy affair was transacted in almost 20 minutes. On
my asking the soldiers why they fired without orders, they said they

heard the word fire and supposed it came from me. This might be the case as many of the mob called out fire, fire, but I assured the men that I gave no such order; that my words were, don't fire, stop your firing. In short, it was scarcely possible for the soldiers to know who said fire, or don't fire, or stop your firing. On the people's assembling again to take away the dead bodies, the soldiers supposing them coming to attack them, were making ready to fire again, which I prevented by striking up their firelocks with my hand. Immediately after a townsman came and told me that 4 or 5000 people were assembled in the next street, and had sworn to take my life with every man's with me. On which I judged it unsafe to remain there any longer, and therefore sent the party and sentry to the main guard, where the street is narrow and short, there telling them off into street firings, divided and planted them at each end of the street to secure their rear, momently expecting an attack, as there was a constant cry of the inhabitants to arms, to arms, turn out with your guns; and the town drums beating to arms, I ordered my drums to beat to arms, and being soon after joined by the different companies of the 29th regiment, I formed them as the guard into street firings. The 14th regiment also got under arms but remained at their barracks. I immediately sent a sergeant with a party to Colonel Dalrymple, the commanding officer, to acquaint him with every particular. Several officers going to join their regiment were knocked down by the mob, one very much wounded and his sword taken from him. The lieutenant-governor and Colonel Carr soon after met at the head of the 29th regiment and agreed that the regiment should retire to their barracks, and the people to their houses, but I kept the picket to strengthen the guard. It was with great difficulty that the lieutenant-governor prevailed on the people to be quiet and retire. At last they all went off, excepting about a hundred.

A Council was immediately called, on the breaking up of which three justices met and issued a warrant to apprehend me and eight soldiers. On hearing of this procedure I instantly went to the sheriff and surrendered myself, though for the space of 4 hours I had it in my power to have made my escape, which I most undoubtedly should have attempted and could easily executed, had I been the least conscious of any guilt. On the examination before the justices, two witnesses swore that I gave the men orders to fire. The one testified he was within two feet of me; the other that I swore at the men for not firing at the first word. Others swore they heard me use the word "fire," but whether do or do not fire, they could not say; others that they heard the word fire, but could not say if it came from me. The next day they got 5 or 6 more to swear I gave the word to fire. So bitter and inveterate are many of the malcontents here that they are industriously using every method to fish out evidence to prove it was a concerted scheme to murder the inhabitants. Others are infusing the utmost malice and revenge into the minds of the people who are to be my jurors by false publications, votes of towns, and all other artifices. That so from a settled rancour against the officers and troops in general, the suddenness of my trial after the affair while the people's minds are all greatly inflamed, I am, though perfectly innocent, under most unhappy circumstances, having nothing in reason to expect but the loss of life in a very ignominous manner, without the interposition of his Majesty's royal goodness.

/   /   /

THE HORRID MASSACRE IN BOSTON, PERPETRATED IN THE EVENING OF THE FIFTH DAY OF MARCH, 1770, BY SOLDIERS OF THE TWENTY-NINTH REGIMENT, WHICH WITH THE FOURTEENTH REGIMENT WERE THEN QUARTERED THERE; WITH SOME OBSERVATIONS ON THE STATE OF THINGS PRIOR TO THAT CATASTROPHE

It may be a proper introduction to this narrative, briefly to represent the state of things for some time previous to the said Massacre; and this seems necessary in order to the forming a just idea of the causes of it.

At the end of the late [French and Indian] war, in which this province bore so distinguished a part, a happy union subsisted between Great Britain and the colonies. This was unfortunately interrupted by the Stamp Act; but it was in some measure restored by the repeal of it.[1] It was again interrupted by other acts of parliament for taxing America; and by the appointment of a Board of Commissioners, in pursuance of an act, which by the face of it was made for the relief and encouragement of commerce, but which in its operation, it was apprehended, would have, and it has in fact had, a contrary effect. By the said act the said Commissioners were "to be resident in some convenient part of his Majesty's dominions in America." This must be understood to be in some part convenient for the whole. But it does not appear that, in fixing the place of their residence, the convenience of the whole was at all consulted, for Boston, being very far from the centre of the colonies, could not be the place most convenient for the whole. Judging by the act, it may seem this town was intended to be favored, by the Commissioners being appointed to reside here; and that the consequence of that residence would be the relief and encouragement of commerce; but the reverse has been the constant and uniform effect of it; so that the commerce of the town, from the embarrassments in which it has been lately involved, is greatly reduced.

/   /   /

A Short Narrative of the Horrid Massacre in Boston. *Printed by Order of the Town of Boston. Re-published with Notes and Illustrations by John Doggett, Jr., (New York, 1849), pp. 13–19; 21–22; 28–30.*

1. The stamp act was passed 22d of March, 1765; and repealed 18th of March, 1766. D.

The residence of the Commissioners here has been detrimental, not only to the commerce, but to the political interests of the town and province; and not only so, but we can trace from it the causes of the late horrid massacre. Soon after their arrival here in November, 1767, instead of confining themselves to the proper business of their office, they became partizans of Governor Bernard in his political schemes; and had the weakness and temerity to infringe upon one of the most essential rights of the house of commons of this province—that of giving their votes with freedom, and not being accountable therefor but to their constituents. One of the members of that house, Capt. Timothy Folgier, having voted in some affair contrary to the mind of the said Commissioners, was for so doing dismissed from the office he held under them.

These proceedings of theirs, the difficulty of access to them on office-business, and a supercilious behavior, rendered them disgustful to people in general, who in consequence thereof treated them with neglect. This probably stimulated them to resent it; and to make their resentment felt, they and their coadjutor, Governor Bernard, made such representations to his Majesty's ministers as they thought best calculated to bring the displeasure of the nation upon the town and province; and in order that those representations might have the more weight, they are said to have contrived and executed plans for exciting disturbances and tumults, which otherwise would probably never have existed; and, when excited, to have transmitted to the ministry the most exaggerated accounts of them.

/　　　　/　　　　/

Unfortunately for us, they have been too successful in their said representations, which, in conjunction with Governor Bernard's, have occasioned his Majesty's faithful subjects of this town and province to be treated as enemies and rebels, by an invasion of the town by sea and land; to which the approaches were made with all the circumspection usual where a vigorous opposition is expected. While the town was surrounded by a considerable number of his Majesty's ships of war, two regiments landed and took possession of it; and to support these, two other regiments arrived some time after from Ireland; one of which landed at Castle Island, and the other in the town.

Thus were we, in aggravation of our other embarrassments, embarrassed with troops, forced upon us contrary to our inclination—contrary to the spirit of Magna Charta—contrary to the very letter of the Bill of Rights, in which it is declared, that the raising or keeping a standing army within the kingdom in time of peace, unless it be with the consent of parliament, is against law, and without the desire of the civil magistrates, to aid whom was the pretence for sending the troops hither; who were quartered in the town in direct violation of an act of parliament for quartering troops in America; and all this in consequence of the representations of the said Commissioners and the said Governor, as appears by their memorials and letters lately published.

As they were the procuring cause of troops being sent hither, they must therefore be the remote and a blameable cause of all the disturbances and bloodshed that have taken place in consequence of that measure.

/　　　　　　/　　　　　　/

We shall next attend to the conduct of the troops, and to some circumstances relative to them. Governor Bernard without consulting the Council, having given up the State House to the troops at their landing, they took possession of the chambers, where the representatives of the province and the courts of law held their meetings; and (except the council-chamber) of all other parts of that house; in which they continued a considerable time, to the great annoyance of those courts while they sat, and of the merchants and gentlemen of the town, who had always made the lower floor of it their exchange. They [the merchants] had a right so to do, as the property of it was in the town; but they were deprived of that right by mere power. The said Governor soon after, by every stratagem and by every method but a forcibly entry, endeavored to get possession of the manufactory-house, to make a barrack of it for the troops; and for that purpose caused it to be besieged by the troops, and the people in it to be used very cruelly;

/　　　　　　/　　　　　　/

The General Court, at the first session after the arrival of the troops, viewed it in this light, and applied to Governor Bernard to cause such a nuisance to be removed; but to no purpose.

/　　　　　　/　　　　　　/

the challenging the inhabitants by sentinels posted in all parts of the town before the lodgings of officers, which (for about six months, while it lasted), occasioned many quarrels and uneasiness.[2]

Capt. Wilson, of the 59th, exciting the negroes of the town to take away their masters' lives and property, and repair to the army for protection, which was fully proved against him. The attack of a party of soldiers on some of the magistrates of the town—the repeated rescues of soldiers from peace officers—the firing of a loaded musket in a public

---

2. While the British troops were in Boston, the citizens, whenever it was necessary to be out in the evening, generally went armed with walking-sticks, clubs, &c., to protect themselves from insult.

street, to the endangering a great number of peaceable inhabitants—the frequent wounding of persons by their bayonets and cutlasses, and the numerous instances of bad behavior in the soldiery, made us early sensible that the troops were not sent here for any benefit to the town or province, and that we had no good to expect from such conservators of the peace.

It was not expected, however, that such an outrage and massacre, as happened here on the evening of the fifth instant, would have been perpetrated. There were then killed and wounded, by a discharge of musketry, eleven of his Majesty's subjects, viz.:

Mr. Samuel Gray, killed on the spot by a ball entering his head.

Crispus Attucks, a mulatto, killed on the spot, two balls entering his breast.

Mr. James Caldwell, killed on the spot, by two balls entering his back.

Mr. Samuel Maverick, a youth of seventeen years of age, mortally wounded; he died the next morning.

Mr. Patrick Carr mortally wounded; he died the 14th instant.

Christopher Monk and John Clark, youths about seventeen years of age, dangerously wounded. It is apprehended they will die.

Mr. Edward Payne, merchant, standing at his door; wounded.

Messrs. John Green, Robert Patterson, and David Parker; all dangerously wounded.

The actors in this dreadful tragedy were a party of soldiers commanded by Capt. Preston of the 29th regiment. This party, including the Captain, consisted of eight, who are all committed to jail.

There are depositions in this affair which mention, that several guns were fired at the same time from the Custom-house; before which this shocking scene was exhibited. Into this matter inquisition is now making. In the meantime it may be proper to insert here the substance of some of those depositions.

Benjamin Frizell, on the evening of the 5th of March, having taken his station near the west corner of the Custom-house in King street, before and at the time of the soldiers firing their guns, declares (among other things) that the first discharge was only of one gun, the next of two guns, upon which he the deponent thinks he saw a man stumble; the third discharge was of three guns, upon which he thinks he saw two men fall; and immediately after were discharged five guns, two of which were by soldiers on his right hand; the other three, as appeared to the deponent, were discharged from the balcony, or the chamber window of the Custom-house, the flashes appearing on the left hand, and higher than the right hand flashes appeared to be, and of which the deponent was very sensible, although his eyes were much turned to the soldiers, who were all on his right hand.

/   /   /

What gave occasion to the melancholy event of that evening seems to have been this. A difference having happened near Mr. Grays rope-walk, between a soldier and a man belonging to it, the soldier challenged the ropemakers to a boxing match. The challenge was accepted by one of them, and the soldier worsted. He ran to the barrack in the neighborhood, and returned with several of his companions. The fray was renewed, and the soldiers were driven off. They soon returned with recruits and were again worsted. This happened several times, till at length a considerable body of soldiers was collected, and they also were driven off, the ropemakers having been joined by their brethren of the contiguous ropewalks. By this time Mr. Gray being alarmed interposed, and with the assistance of some gentlemen prevented any further disturbance. To satisfy the soldiers and punish the man who had been the occasion of the first difference, and as an example to the rest, he turned him out of his service; and waited on Col. Dalrymple, the commanding officer of the troops, and with him concerted measures for preventing further mischief. Though this affair ended thus, it made a strong impression on the minds of the soldiers in general, who thought the honor of the regiment concerned to revenge those repeated repulses. For this purpose they seem to have formed a combination to commit some outrage upon the inhabitants of the town indiscriminately; and this was to be done on the evening of the 5th instant or soon after; as appears by the depositions of the following persons, viz.:

William Newhall declares, that on Thursday night the 1st of March instant, he met four soldiers of the 29th regiment, and that he heard them say, "there were a great many that would eat their dinners on Monday next, that should not eat any on Tuesday."

Daniel Calfe declares, that on Saturday evening the 3d of March, a camp-woman, wife to James McDeed, a grenadier of the 29th, came into his father's shop, and the people talking about the affrays at the ropewalks, and blaming the soldiers for the part they had acted in it, the woman said, "the soldiers were in the right;" adding, "that before Tuesday or Wednesday night they would wet their swords or bayonets in New England people's blood."

/   /   /

Samuel Drowne declares that, about nine o'clock of the evening of the fifth of March current, standing at his own door in Cornhill, he saw about fourteen or fifteen soldiers of the 29th regiment, who came from Murray's barracks, armed with naked cutlasses, swords, &c., and came upon the inhabitants of the town, then standing or walking in Cornhill, and abused some, and violently assaulted others as they met them; most of whom were without so much as a stick in their hand to defend themselves, as he very clearly could discern, it being moonlight, and himself being one of the assaulted persons. All or most of the said soldiers he saw go into King street (some of them through Royal Exchange lane), and there followed them, and soon discovered them to be quarrelling and fighting with the people whom they saw there, which he thinks were not more than a dozen, when the soldiers came first, armed as aforesaid. Of those dozen people, the most of them were gentlemen, standing together a little below the Town House, upon the Exchange. At the appearance of those soldiers so armed, the most of the twelve persons went off, some of them being first assaulted.

The violent proceedings of this party, and their going into King street, "quarrelling and fighting with the people whom they saw there" (mentioned in Mr. Drowne's deposition), was immediately introductory to the grand catastrophe.

These assailants, who issued from Murray's barracks (so called), after attacking and wounding divers persons in Cornhill, as above-mentioned, being armed, proceeded (most of them) up the Royal Exchange lane into King street; where, making a short stop, and after assaulting and driving away the few they met there, they brandished their arms and cried out, "Where are the boogers! where are the cowards!" At this time there were very few persons in the street beside themselves. This party in proceeding from Exchange lane into King street, must pass the sentry posted at the westerly corner of the Custom House, which butts on that lane and fronts on that street. This is needful to be mentioned, as near that spot and in that street the bloody tragedy was acted, and the street actors in it were stationed: their station being but a few feet from the front side of the said Custom House. The outrageous behavior and the threats of the said party occasioned the ringing of the meeting-house bell near the head of King street, which bell ringing quick, as for fire, it presently brought out a number of inhabitants, who being soon sensible of the occasion of it, were naturally led to King street, where the said party had made a stop but a little while before, and where their stopping had drawn together a number of boys, round the sentry at the Custom House. Whether the boys mistook the sentry for one of the said party, and thence took occasion to differ with him, or whether he first affronted them, which is affirmed in several depositions,—however that may be, there was much foul language between them, and some of them, in consequence of his pushing at them with his bayonet, threw snowballs at him, which occasioned him to knock hastily at the door of the Custom House. From hence two persons thereupon proceeded immediately to the main-guard, which was posted opposite to the State House, at a small distance, near the head of the said street. The officer on guard was Capt. Preston, who with seven or eight soldiers, with fire-arms and charged bayonets, issued from the guardhouse, and in great haste posted himself and his soldiers in front of the Custom House, near the corner aforesaid. In passing to this station the soldiers pushed several persons with their bayonets, driving through the people in so rough a manner that it appeared they intended to create a disturbance. This occasioned some snowballs to be thrown at them, which seems to have been the only provocation that was given. Mr. Knox (between whom and Capt. Preston there was some conversation on the spot) declares, that while he was talking with Capt. Preston, the soldiers of his detachment had attacked the people with their bayonets; and that there was not the least provocation given to Capt. Preston or his party; the backs of the people being toward them when the people were attacked. He also declares, that Capt. Preston seemed to be in great haste and much agitated, and that, according to his opinion, there were not then present in King street above seventy or eighty persons at the extent.

The said party was formed into a half circle; and within a short time after they had been posted at the Custom House, began to fire upon the people.

Captain Preston is said to have ordered them to fire, and to have repeated that order. One gun was fired first; then others in succession, and with deliberation, till ten or a dozen guns were fired; or till that number of discharges were made from the guns that were fired. By which means eleven persons were killed and wounded, as above represented.

/   /   /

THOMAS PAINE

17 | On the Colonial Army's Retreat from New York

Thomas Paine (1737–1809) was an international revolutionary who saw the American Revolution as the beginning of an era of republican revolutions. Born in England, he came to America in 1774. An incomparable publicist, he wrote pamphlets that rallied American public opinion around the patriot cause and articulated an emerging ideology of republicanism that contributed greatly to the willingness to rebel against a king. His widely circulated pamphlet Common Sense, *published in January 1776, helped prepare American opinion for independence. The first "issue" of* The Crisis—*excerpted below—appeared in late December of 1776 when the patriot army was in retreat from the battle of New York. Fifteen more such pamphlets contributed to the revolutionary cause throughout the lengthy war. Later, Paine returned to England and supported the French Revolution. During that upheaval he was imprisoned in France for a year. Tainted by his support for a violent revolution, Paine died in poverty in the United States, rejected in the very country whose birth he had helped to oversee.*

These are the times that try men's souls. The summer soldier and the sunshine patriot will, in this crisis, shrink from the service of their country; but he that stands it now, deserves the love and thanks of man and woman. Tyranny, like hell, is not easily conquered; yet we have this consolation with us, that the harder the conflict, the more glorious the triumph. What we obtain too cheap, we esteem too lightly: it is dearness only that gives every thing its value. Heaven knows how to put a proper price upon its goods; and it would be strange indeed if so celestial an article as FREEDOM should not be highly rated. Britain, with an army to enforce her tyranny, has declared that she has a right (*not only to* TAX) but "to BIND *us in* ALL CASES WHATSOEVER," and if being *bound in that manner*, is not slavery, then is there not such a thing as slavery upon earth. Even the expression is impious; for so unlimited a power can belong only to God.

Whether the independence of the continent was declared too soon,

Thomas Paine, The Crisis: Being a Series of Pamphlets in Sixteen Numbers. *(Reprinted in New York by D.M. Bennett, Liberal and Scientific Publishing House, 1877), pp. 3–11.*

or delayed too long, I will not now enter into as an argument; my own simple opinion is, that had it been eight months earlier, it would have been much better. We did not make a proper use of last winter, neither could we, while we were in a dependant state. However, the fault, if it were one, was all our own; we have none to blame but ourselves. But no great deal is lost yet. All that [British General] Howe has been doing for this month past, is rather a ravage than a conquest, which the spirit of the Jerseys, a year ago, would have quickly repulsed, and which time and a little resolution will soon recover.

I have as little superstition in me as any man living, but my secret opinion has ever been, and still is, that God Almighty will not give up a people to military destruction, or leave them unsupportedly to perish, who have so earnestly and so repeatedly sought to avoid the calamities of war, by every decent method which wisdom could invent. Neither have I so much of the infidel in me, as to suppose that He has relinquished the government of the world, and given us up to the care of devils; and as I do not, I cannot see on what grounds the king of Britain can look up to heaven for help against us: a common murderer, a highwayman, or a house-breaker, has as good a pretence as he.

'Tis surprising to see how rapidly a panic will sometimes run through a country. All nations and ages have been subject to them: Britain has trembled like an ague at the report of a French fleet of flat bottomed boats; and in the fourteenth [fifteenth] century the whole English army, after ravaging the kingdom of France, was driven back like men petrified with fear; and this brave exploit was performed by a few broken forces collected and headed by a woman, Joan of Arc. Would that heaven might inspire some Jersey maid to spirit up her countrymen, and save her fair fellow sufferers from ravage and ravishment! Yet panics, in some cases, have their uses; they produce as much good as hurt. Their duration is always short; the mind soon grows through them, and acquires a firmer habit than before. But their peculiar advantage is, that they are the touchstones of sincerity and hypocrisy, and bring things and men to light, which might otherwise have lain forever undiscovered. In fact, they have the same effect on secret traitors, which an imaginary apparition would have upon a private murderer. They sift out the hidden thoughts of man, and hold them up in public to the world. Many a disguised tory has lately shown his head, that shall penitentially solemnize with curses the day on which Howe arrived upon the Delaware.

As I was with the troops at Fort Lee, and marched with them to the edge of Pennsylvania, I am well acquainted with many circumstances, which those who live at a distance know but little or nothing of. Our situation there was exceedingly cramped, the place being a narrow neck of land between the North River and the Hackensack. Our force was inconsiderable, being not one fourth so great as Howe could bring against us. We had no army at hand to have relieved the garrison, had we shut ourselves up and stood on our defence. Our ammunition, light artillery, and the best part of our stores, had been removed, on the apprehension that Howe would endeavor to penetrate the Jerseys, in which case Fort Lee could be of no use to us; for it must occur to every thinking man, whether in the army or not, that these kind of field forts are only for temporary purposes, and last in use no longer than the enemy directs his force against the particular object, which such forts are raised to defend. Such was our situation and condition at Fort Lee on the morning of the 20th of November, when an officer arrived with information that the enemy with 200 boats had landed about seven miles above: Major General [Nathaniel] Green, who commanded the garrison, immediately ordered them under arms, and sent express to General Washington at the town of Hackensack, distant by the way of the ferry, six miles. Our first object was to secure the bridge over the Hackensack, which laid up the river between the enemy and us, about six miles from us, and three from them. General Washington arrived in about three quarters of an hour, and marched at the head of the troops towards the bridge, which place I expected we should have a brush for; however, they did not choose to dispute it with us, and the greatest part of our troops went over the bridge, the rest over the ferry, except some which passed at a mill on a small creek, between the bridge and the ferry, and made their way through some marshy grounds up to the town of Hackensack, and there passed the river. We brought off as much baggage as the wagons could contain, the rest was lost. The simple object was to bring off the garrison, and march them on till they could be strengthened by the Jersey or Pennsylvania militia, so as to be enabled to make a stand. We staid four days at Newark, collected our out-posts with some of the Jersey militia, and marched out twice to meet the enemy, on being informed that they were advancing, though our numbers were greatly inferior to theirs. Howe, in my little opinion, committed a great error in generalship in not throwing a body of forces off from Staten Island through Amboy, by which means he might have seized all our stores at Brunswick, and intercepted our march into Pennsylvania; but if we believe the power of hell to be limited, we must likewise believe that their agents are under some providential controul.

I shall not now attempt to give all the particulars of our retreat to the Delaware; suffice it for the present to say, that both officers and men, though greatly harassed and fatigued, frequently without rest, covering, or provision, the inevitable consequences of a long retreat, bore it with a manly and martial spirit. All their wishes centred in one, which was, that the country would turn out and help them to drive the enemy back. Voltaire has remarked that king William never appeared to full advantage but in difficulties and in action; the same remark may be made on General Washington, for the character fits him. There is a natural firmness in some minds which cannot be unlocked by trifles, but which, when unlocked, discovers a cabinet of fortitude; and I reckon it among those kind of public blessings, which we do not immediately see, that God hath blessed him with uninterrupted health, and given him a mind that can even flourish upon care.

I shall conclude this paper with some miscellaneous remarks on the state of our affairs; and shall begin with asking the following question, Why is it that the enemy have left the New-England provinces, and made these middle ones the seat of war? The answer is easy: New-England is not infested with tories, and we are. I have been tender in raising the cry against these men, and used numberless arguments to show them their danger, but it will not do to sacrifice a word either to their folly or their baseness. The period is now arrived, in which either they or we must change our sentiments, or one or both must fall. And what is a tory? Good God! what is he? I should not be afraid to go with a hundred whigs against a thousand tories, were they to attempt to get into arms. Every tory is a coward; for servile, slavish, self-interested fear is the foundation of toryism; and a man under such influence, though he may be cruel, never can be brave.

But, before the line of irrecoverable separation be drawn between us, let us reason the matter together: Your conduct is an invitation to the enemy, yet not one in a thousand of you has heart enough to join him. Howe is as much deceived by you as the American cause is injured by you. He expects you will all take up arms, and flock to his standard, with muskets on your shoulders. Your opinions are of no use to him, unless you support him personally, for 'tis soldiers, and not tories, that he wants.

I once felt all that kind of anger, which a man ought to feel, against the mean principles that are held by the tories: a noted one, who kept a tavern at Amboy, was standing at his door, with as pretty a child in his hand, about eight or nine years old, as I ever saw, and after speaking his mind as freely as he thought was prudent, finished with this unfatherly expression, *"Well! give me peace in my day."* Not a man lives on the continent but fully believes that a separation must some time or other finally take place, and a generous parent should have said, *"If there must be trouble, let it be in my day, that my child may have peace;"* and this single reflection, well applied, is sufficient to awaken every man to duty. Not a place upon earth might be so happy as America. Her situation is remote from all the wrangling world, and she has nothing to do but to trade with them. A man can distinguish himself between temper and principle, and I am as confident, as I am that God governs the world, that America will never be happy till she gets clear of foreign dominion. Wars, without ceasing, will break out till that period arrives, and the continent must in the end be conqueror; for though the flame of liberty may sometimes cease to shine, the coal can never expire.

America did not, nor does not want force; but she wanted a proper application of that force. Wisdom is not the purchase of a day, and it is no wonder that we should err at the first setting off. From an excess of tenderness, we were unwilling to raise an army, and trusted our cause to the temporary defence of a well-meaning militia. A summer's experience has now taught us better; yet with those troops, while they were collected, we were able to set bounds to the progress of the enemy, and, thank God! they are again assembling. I always considered militia as the best troops in the world for a sudden exertion, but they will not do for a long campaign. Howe, it is probable, will make an attempt on this city; should he fail on this side the Delaware, he is ruined: if he succeeds, our cause is not ruined. He stakes all on his side against a part on ours; admitting he succeeds, the consequence will be, that armies from both ends of the continent will march to assist their suffering friends in the middle states; for he cannot go everywhere, it is impossible. I consider Howe as the greatest enemy the tories have; he is bringing a war into their country, which, had it not been for him and partly for themselves, they had been clear of. Should he now be expelled, I wish with all the devotion of a Christian, that the names of whig and tory may never more be mentioned; but should the tories give him encouragement to come, or assistance if he come, I as sincerely wish that our next year's arms may expel them from the continent, and the congress appropriate their possessions to the relief of those who have suffered in well-doing. A single successful battle next year will settle the whole. America could carry on a two years war by the confiscation of the property of disaffected persons, and be made happy by their expulsion. Say not that this is revenge, call it rather the soft resentment of a suffering people, who, having no object in view but the *good of all*, have staked their *own all* upon a seemingly doubtful event. Yet it is folly to argue against determined hardness; eloquence may strike the ear, and the language of sorrow draw forth the tear of compassion, but nothing can reach the heart that is steeled with prejudice.

Quitting this class of men, I turn with the warm ardor of a friend to those who have nobly stood, and are yet determined to stand the matter out: I call not upon a few, but upon all: not on *this* state or *that* state, but on *every* state: up and help us; lay your shoulders to the wheel; better have too much force than too little, when so great an object is at stake. Let it be told to the future world, that in the depth of winter, when nothing but hope and virtue could survive, that the city and the country, alarmed at one common danger, came forth to meet and to repulse it. Say not that thousands are gone, turn out your tens of thousands; throw not the burden of the day upon Providence, but "*show your faith by your works*," that God may bless you. It matters not where you live, or what rank of life you hold, the evil or the blessing will reach you all. The far and the near, the home counties and the back, the rich and the poor, will suffer or rejoice alike. The heart that feels not now, is dead: the blood of his children will curse his cowardice, who shrinks back at a time when a little might have saved the whole, and made *them* happy. I love the man that can smile in trouble, that can gather strength from distress, and grow brave by reflection. 'Tis the business of little minds to shrink; but he whose heart is firm, and whose conscience approves his conduct, will pursue his principles unto death. My own line of reasoning is to myself as straight and clear as a ray of light. Not all the treasures of the world, so far as I believe, could have induced me to support an offensive war, for I think it murder; but if a thief breaks into my house, burns and destroys my property, and kills or threatens to kill me, or those that are in it, and to *"bind me in all cases whatsoever"* to his absolute will, am I to suffer it? What signifies it to me, whether he who does it is a king or a common man; my countryman or not my countryman; whether it be done by an individual villain, or an army of them? If we reason to the root of things we shall find no difference; neither can any just cause be assigned why we should punish in the one case and pardon in other. Let them call me rebel, and welcome, I feel no concern from it; but I should suffer the misery of devils, were I to make a whore of my soul by swearing allegiance to one whose character is that of a sottish, stupid, stubborn, worthless, brutish man. I conceive likewise a horrid idea in receiving mercy from a being, who at the last day shall be shrieking to the rocks and mountains to cover him, and fleeing with terror from the orphan, the widow, and the slain of America.

There are cases which cannot be overdone by language, and this is one. There are persons, too, who see not the full extent of the evil which threatens them; they solace themselves with hopes that the enemy, if he succeed, will be merciful. It is the madness of folly, to expect mercy from those who have refused to do justice; and even mercy, where conquest is the object, is only a trick of war; the cunning of the fox is as murderous as the violence of the world, and we ought to guard equally against both. Howe's first object is, partly by threats and partly by promises, to terrify or seduce the people to deliver up their arms and receive mercy. The ministry recommended the same plan to Gage, and this is what the tories call making their peace, *"a peace which passeth all understanding"* indeed! A peace which would be the immediate forerunner of a worse ruin than any we have yet thought of. Ye men of Pennsylvania, do reason upon these things! Were the back counties to give up their arms, they would fall an easy prey to the Indians, who are all armed: this perhaps is what some tories would not be sorry for. Were the home counties to deliver up their arms, they would be exposed to the resentment of the back counties, who would then have it in their power to chastise their defection at pleasure. And were any one state to give up its arms, *that* state must be garrisoned by all Howe's army of Britons and Hessians to preserve it from the anger of the rest. Mutual fear is the principal link in the chain of mutual love, and woe be to that state that breaks the compact. Howe is mercifully inviting you to barbarous destruction, and men must be either rogues or fools that will not see it. I dwell not upon the vapours of imagination: I bring reason to your ears, and, in language as plan as A, B, C, hold up truth to your eyes.

I thank God, that I fear not. I see no real cause for fear. I know our situation well, and can see the way out of it. While our army was collected, Howe dared not risk a battle; and it is no credit to him that he decamped from the White Plains, and waited a mean opportunity to ravage the defenceless Jerseys; but it is great credit to us, that, with a handful of men, we sustained an orderly retreat for near an hundred miles, brought off our ammunition, all our field pieces, the greatest part of our stores, and had four rivers to pass. None can say that our retreat was precipitate, for we were near three weeks in performing it, that the country might have time to come in. Twice we marched back to meet the enemy, and remained out till dark. The sign of fear was not seen in our camp, and had not some of the cowardly and disaffected inhabitants spread false alarms through the country, the Jerseys had never been ravaged. Once more we are again collected and collecting; our new army at both ends of the continent is recruiting fast, and we shall be able to open the next campaign with sixty thousand men, well armed and clothed. This is our situation, and who will may know it. By perserverance and fortitude we have the prospect of a glorious issue; by cowardice and submission, the sad choice of a variety of evils—a ravaged country—a depopulated city—habitations without safety, and slavery without hope—our homes turned into barracks and bawdy-houses for Hessians, and a future race to provide for, whose fathers we shall doubt of. Look on this picture and weep over it! and if there yet remains one thoughtless wretch who believes it not, let him suffer it unlamented.

18 | Recruiting and Maintaining an Army

Part of the mythology of the American Revolution is that patriot farmers, "Min-utemen," left their plows in the field and joined the cause to defeat the British. Something like that may have happened in 1775 and at the important Battle of Saratoga in 1777, but at other times the truth was less glamorous. General George Washington wrote to John Hancock, the president of the Continental Congress, in September 1776, and discussed the condition of the Continental Army. The "Militia" that Washington refers to were untrained forces raised by the states to serve for a sharply limited period.

TO THE PRESIDENT OF CONGRESS, *Colonel Morris's,
on the Heights of Harlem, September 24, 1776.*

Sir: From the hours allotted to Sleep, I will borrow a few Moments to convey my thoughts on sundry important matters to Congress. I shall offer them, with that sincerity which ought to characterize a man of candour; and with the freedom which may be used in giving useful information, without incurring the imputation of presumption.

We are now as it were, upon the eve of another dissolution of our Army; the remembrance of the difficulties which happened upon that occasion last year, the consequences which might have followed the change, if proper advantages had been taken by the Enemy; added to a knowledge of the present temper and Situation of the Troops, reflect but a very gloomy prospect upon the appearance of things now, and satisfie me, beyond the possibility of doubt, that unless some speedy, and effectual measures are adopted by Congress, our cause will be lost.

It is in vain to expect, that any (or more than a trifling) part of this Army will again engage in the Service on the encouragement offered by Congress. When Men find that their Townsmen and Companions are receiving 20, 30, and more Dollars, for a few Months Service, (which is truely the case) it cannot be expected; without using compulsion; and

John C. Fitzpatrick (editor), The Writings of George Washington from the Original Manuscript Sources: 1745–1799, Volume 6 (September, 1776–January, 1777). (Washington, D.C., Government Printing Office, 1932), pp. 106–112, 114–115.

to force them into the Service would answer no valuable purpose. When Men are irritated, and the Passions inflamed, they fly hastely and chearfully to Arms; but after the first emotions are over, to expect, among such People, as compose the bulk of an Army, that they are influenced by any other principles than those of Interest, is to look for what never did, and I fear never will happen; the Congress will deceive themselves therefore if they expect it.

A Soldier reasoned with upon the goodness of the cause he is engaged in, and the inestimable rights he is contending for, hears you with patience, and acknowledges the truth of your observations, but adds, that it is of no more Importance to him than others. The Officer makes you the same reply, with this further remark, that his pay will not support him, and he cannot ruin himself and Family to serve his Country, when every Member of the community is equally Interested and benefitted by his Labours. The few therefore, who act upon Principles of disinterestedness, are, comparatively speaking, no more than a drop in the Ocean. It becomes evidently clear then, that as this Contest is not likely to be the Work of a day; as the War must be carried on systematically, and to do it, you must have good Officers, there are, in my Judgment, no other possible means to obtain them but by establishing your Army upon a permanent footing; and giving your Officers good pay; this will induce Gentlemen, and Men of Character to engage; and till the bulk of your Officers are composed of such persons as are actuated by Principles of honour, and a spirit of enterprize, you have little to expect from them.—They ought to have such allowances as will enable them to live like, and support the Characters of Gentlemen; and not be driven by a scanty pittance to the low, and dirty arts which many of them practice, to filch the Public of more than the difference of pay would amount to upon an ample allowe. Besides, something is due to the Man who puts his life in his hands, hazards his health, and forsakes the Sweets of domestic enjoyments. Why a Captn. in the Continental Service should receive no more than 5/. Curry per day, for performing the same duties that an officer of the same Rank in the British Service receives 10/. Sterlg. for, I never could conceive; especially when the latter is provided with every necessary he requires, upon the best terms, and the former can scarce procure them, at any Rate. There is nothing that gives a Man consequence, and renders him fit for Command, like a support that renders him Independant of every body but the State he Serves.

With respect to the Men, nothing but a good bounty can obtain them upon a permanent establishment; and for no shorter time than the continuance of the War, ought they to be engaged; as Facts incontestibly prove, that the difficulty, and cost of Inlistments, increase with time. When the Army was first raised at Cambridge, I am persuaded the Men might have been got without a bounty for the War: after this, they began to see that the Contest was not likely to end so speedily as was immagined, and to feel their consequence, by remarking, that to get the Militia

In, in the course of last year, many Towns were induced to give them a bounty. Foreseeing the Evils resulting from this, and the destructive consequences which unavoidably would follow short Inlistments, I took the Liberty in a long Letter, written by myself (date not now recollected, as my Letter Book is not here) to recommend the Inlistments for and during the War; assigning such Reasons for it, as experience has since convinced me were well founded. At that time twenty Dollars would, I am persuaded, have engaged the Men for this term. But it will not do to look back, and if the present opportunity is slip'd, I am perswaded that twelve months more will Increase our difficulties fourfold. I shall therefore take the freedom of giving it as my opinion, that a good Bounty be immediately offered, aided by the proffer of at least 100, or 150 Acres of Land and a suit of Cloaths and Blankt, to each non-Comd. Officer and Soldier; as I have good authority for saying, that however high the Men's pay may appear, it is barely sufficient in the present scarcity and dearness of all kinds of goods, to keep them in Cloaths, much less afford support to their Families. If this encouragement then is given to the Men, and such Pay allowed the Officers as will induce Gentlemen of Character and liberal Sentiments to engage; and proper care and precaution are used in the nomination (having more regard to the Characters of Persons, than the Number of Men they can Inlist) we should in a little time have an Army able to cope with any that can be opposed to it, as there are excellent Materials to form one out of: but while the only merit an Officer possesses is his ability to raise Men; while those Men consider, and treat him as an equal; and (in the Character of an Officer) regard him no more than a broomstick, being mixed together as one common herd; no order, nor no discipline can prevail; nor will the Officer ever meet with that respect which is essentially necessary to due subordination.

To place any dependance upon Militia, is, assuredly, resting upon a broken staff. Men just dragged from the tender Scenes of domestick life; unaccustomed to the din of Arms; totally unacquainted with every kind of Military skill, which being followed by a want of confidence in themselves, when opposed to Troops regulary train'd, disciplined, and appointed, superior in knowledge, and superior in Arms, makes them timid, and ready to fly from their own shadows. Besides, the sudden change in their manner of living, (particularly in the lodging) brings on sickness in many; impatience in all, and such an unconquerable desire of returning to their respective homes that it not only produces shameful, and scandalous Desertions among themselves, but infuses the like spirit in others. Again, Men accustomed to unbounded freedom, and no controul, cannot brook the Restraint which is indispensably necessary to the good order and Government of an Army; without which, licentiousness, and every kind of disorder triumpantly reign. To bring Men to a proper degree of Subordination, is not the work of a day, a Month or even a year; and unhappily for us, and the cause we are Engaged in, the little discipline I have been labouring to establish in the Army under my immediate Command, is in a manner done away by having such a mixture of Troops as have been called together within these few Months.

Relaxed, and unfit, as our Rules and Regulations of War are, for the Government of an Army, the Militia (those properly so called, for of these we have two sorts, the Six Months Men and those sent in as a temporary aid) do not think themselves subject to 'em, and therefore take liberties, which the Soldier is punished for; this creates jealousy; jealousy begets dissatisfaction, and these by degrees ripen into Mutiny; keeping the whole Army in a confused, and disordered State; rendering the time of those who wish to see regularity and good Order prevail more unhappy than Words can describe. Besides this, such repeated changes take place, that all arrangement is set at nought, and the constant fluctuation of things, deranges every plan, as fast as adopted.

These Sir, Congress may be assured, are but a small part of the Inconveniences which might be enumerated and attributed to Militia; but there is one that merits particular attention, and that is the expence. Certain I am, that it would be cheaper to keep 50, or 100,000 Men in constant pay than to depend upon half the number, and supply the other half occasionally by Militia. The time the latter is in pay before and after they are in Camp, assembling and Marching; the waste of Ammunition; the consumption of Stores, which in spite of every Resolution, and requisition of Congress they must be furnished with, or sent home, added to other incidental expences consequent upon their coming, and conduct in Camp, surpasses all Idea, and destroys every kind of regularity and œconomy which you could establish among fixed and Settled Troops; and will, in my opinion prove (if the scheme is adhered to) the Ruin of our Cause.

The Jealousies of a standing Army, and the Evils to be apprehended from one, are remote; and in my judgment, situated and circumstanced as we are, not at all to be dreaded; but the consequence of wanting one, according to my Ideas, formed from the present view of things, is certain, and inevitable Ruin; for if I was called upon to declare upon Oath, whether the Militia have been most serviceable or hurtful upon the whole; I should subscribe to the latter. I do not mean by this however to arraign the Conduct of Congress, in so doing I should equally condemn my own measures, (if I did not my judgment); but experience, which is the best criterion to work by, so fully, clearly, and decisively reprobates the practice of trusting to Militia, that no Man who regards order, regularity, and [e]conomy; or who has any regard for his own honour, Character, or peace of Mind, will risk them upon this Issue.

. . .

Another matter highly worthy of attention, is, that other Rules and Regulation's may be adopted for the Government of the Army than those now in existence, otherwise the Army, but for the name, might as

well be disbanded. For the most attrocious offences, (one or two Instances only excepted) a Man receives no more than 39 Lashes; and
these perhaps (thro' the collusion of the Officer who is to see it inflicted), are given in such a manner as to become rather a matter of sport
than punishment; but when inflicted as they ought, many hardend fellows who have been the Subjects, have declared that for a bottle of Rum
they would undergo a Second operation; it is evident therefore that this
punishment is inadequate to many Crimes it is assigned to, as a proof
of it, thirty and 40 Soldiers will desert at a time; and of late, a practice
prevails, (as you will see by my Letter of the 22d) of the most alarming
nature; and which will, if it cannot be checked, prove fatal both to the
Country and Army; I mean the infamous practice of Plundering, for
under the Idea of Tory property, or property which may fall into the
hands of the Enemy, no Man is secure in his effects, and scarcely in his
Person; for in order to get at them, we have several Instances of People
being frightened out of their Houses under pretence of those Houses
being ordered to be burnt, and this is done with a view of siezing the
Goods; nay, in order that the villany may be more effectually concealed,
some Houses have actually been burnt to cover the theft.

I have with some others, used my utmost endeavours to stop this
horrid practice, but under the present lust after plunder, and want of
Laws to punish Offenders, I might almost as well attempt to remove
Mouth Atlas.—I have ordered instant corporal Punishment upon every
Man who passes our Lines, or is seen with Plunder, that the Offenders
might be punished for disobedience of Orders; and Inclose you the proceedings of a Court Martial held upon an Officer, who with a Party of
Men had robbd a House a little beyond our Lines of a Number of valuable Goods; among which (to shew that nothing escapes) were four
large Pier looking Glasses, Women's Cloaths, and other Articles which
one would think, could be of no Earthly use to him. He was met by a
Major of Brigade who ordered him to return the Goods, as taken contrary to Genl. Orders, which he not only peremptorily refused to do,
but drew up his Party and swore he would defend them at the hazard
of his Life; on which I ordered him to be arrested, and tryed for Plundering, Disobedience of Orders, and Mutiny

/   /   /

ALBIGENCE WALDO

19 | Diary of a Surgeon at Valley Forge

Washington's army spent the winter of 1777 to 1778 at Valley Forge, Pennsylvania. His army was sorely tested. During the winter Washington was nearly in despair over the incompetence and callousness of those responsible for supplying the army. He reported to Congress at one point that "he had not a single hoof of any kind to slaughter, and not more than 25. barls. of flour!" Washington's army, short on all manner of supplies, shrank daily. The British command, but twenty miles away in Philadelphia, probably could have dispersed the patriots, but never thought to try.

Albigence Waldo, a doctor from Connecticut, describes the conditions under which the army miraculously survived until spring.

December 6.—The Enemy forming a Line from towards our right to the extremity of our left upon an opposite long height to ours in a Wood. Our men were under Arms all Day and this Night also, as our Wise General was determined not to be attack'd Napping. . . .

December 8.—All at our Several Posts. Provisions & Whiskey very scarce. Were Soldiers to have plenty of Food & Rum, I believe they would Storm Tophet . . .

December 11.—At four o'clock the Whole Army were Order'd to March to Swedes Ford on the River Schuylkill, about 9 miles N.W. of Chestnut Hill, and 6 from White Marsh our present Encampment. At sun an hour high the whole were mov'd from the Lines and on their march with baggage. This Night encamped in a Semi circle nigh the Ford. The enemy had march'd up the West side of Schuylkill—Potter's Brigade of Pennsylvania Militia were already there, & had several skirmishes with them with some loss on his side and considerable on the Enemies. . . .

I am prodigious Sick & cannot get any thing comfortable—what in the name of Providence am I to do with a fit of Sickness in this place where nothing appears pleasing to the Sicken'd Eye & nausiating Stom-

The Pennsylvania Magazine of History and Biography. *(Philadelphia: The Historical Society of Pennsylvania)* 1897, Volume 21, pp. 303–311.

ach. But I doubt not Providence will find out a way for my relief. But I cannot eat Beef if I starve, for my stomach positively refuses to entertain such Company, and how can I help that?

December 12.—A Bridge of Waggons made across the Schuylkill last Night consisting of 36 waggons, with a bridge of Rails between each. Some skirmishing over the River. Militia and dragoons brought into Camp several Prisoners. Sun Set—We were order'd to march over the River—It snows—I'm Sick—eat nothing—No Whiskey—No Forage— Lord—Lord—Lord. The Army were 'till Sun Rise crossing the River— some at the Waggon Bridge & some at the Raft Bridge below. Cold & uncomfortable.

December 13.—The Army march'd three miles from the West side of the River and encamp'd near a place call'd the Gulph and not an improper name neither, for this Gulph seems well adapted by its situation to keep us from the pleasures & enjoyments of this World, or being conversant with any body in it. It is an excellent place to raise the Ideas of a Philosopher beyond the glutted thoughts and Reflexions of an Epicurian. His Reflexions will be as different from the Common Reflexions of Mankind as if he were unconnected with the world, and only conversant with immaterial beings. It cannot be that our Superiors are about to hold consultations with Spirits infinitely beneath their Order, by bringing us into these utmost regions of the Terraqueous Sphere. No, it is, upon consideraton for many good purposes since we are to Winter here—1st There is plenty of Wood & Water. 2dly There are but few families for the soldiery to Steal from—tho' far be it from a Soldier to Steal. 4^{ly} There are warm sides of Hills to erect huts on. 5^{ly} They will be heavenly Minded like Jonah when in the Belly of a Great Fish. 6^{ly} They will not become home Sick as is sometimes the Case when Men live in the Open World—since the reflections which will naturally arise from their present habitation, will lead them to the more noble thoughts of employing their leisure hours in filling their knapsacks with such materials as may be necessary on the Journey to another Home.

December 14.—Prisoners & Deserters are continually coming in. The Army which has been surprisingly healthy hitherto, now begins to grow sickly from the continued fatigues they have suffered this Campaign. Yet they still show a spirit of Alacrity & Contentment not to be expected from so young Troops. I am Sick—discontented—and out of humour. Poor food—hard lodging—Cold Weather—fatigue—Nasty Cloaths— nasty Cookery—Vomit half my time—smoak'd out of my senses—the Devil's in't—I can't Endure it—Why are we sent here to starve and Freeze—What sweet Felicities have I left at home; A charming Wife— pretty Children—Good Beds—good food—good Cookery—all aggreable—all harmonious. Here all Confusion—smoke & Cold—hunger & filthyness—A pox on my bad luck. There comes a bowl of beef soup— full of burnt leaves and dirt, sickish enough to make a Hector spue—

away with it Boys—I'll live like the Chameleon upon Air. Poh! Poh! crys Patience within me—you talk like a fool. Your being sick Covers your mind with a Melanchollic Gloom, which makes every thing about you appear gloomy. See the poor Soldier, when in health—with what cheerfulness he meets his foes and encounters every hardship—if barefoot, he labours thro' the Mud & Cold with a Song in his mouth extolling War & Washington—if his food be bad, he eats it notwithstanding with seeming content—blesses God for a good Stomach and Whistles it into digestion. But harkee Patience, a moment—There comes a Soldier, his bare feet are seen thro' his worn out Shoes, his legs nearly naked from the tatter'd remains of an only pair of stockings, his Breeches not sufficient to cover his nakedness, his Shirt hanging in Strings, his hair dishevell'd, his face meagre; his whole appearance pictures a person forsaken & discouraged. He comes, and crys with an air of wretchedness & despair, I am Sick, my feet lame, my legs are sore, my body cover'd with this tormenting Itch—my Cloaths are worn out, my Constitution is broken, my former Activity is exhausted by fatigue, hunger & Cold, I fail fast I shall soon be no more! and all the reward I shall get will be—"Poor Will is dead." People who live at home in Luxury and Ease, quietly possessing their habitations, Enjoying their Wives & families in peace, have but a very faint Idea of the unpleasing sensations, and continual Anxiety the Man endures who is in a Camp, and is the husband and parent of an aggreeable family. These same People are willing we should suffer every thing for their Benefit & advantage, and yet are the first to Condemn us for not doing more!!

December 15.—Quiet. Eat Pessimmens, found myself better for their Lenient Opperation. Went to a house, poor & small, but good food within—eat too much from being so long Abstemious, thro' want of palatables. Mankind are never truly thankfull for the Benefits of life, until they have experienc'd the want of them. The Man who has seen misery knows best how to enjoy good. He who is always at ease & has enough of the Blessings of common life is an Impotent Judge of the feelings of the unfortunate. . . .

December 16.—Cold Rainy Day, Baggage ordered over the Gulph of our Division, which were to march at Ten, but the baggage was order'd back and for the first time since we have been here the Tents were pitch'd, to keep the men more comfortable. Good morning Brother Soldier (says one to another) how are you? All wet I thank'e, hope you are so (says the other). The Enemy have been at Chestnut Hill Opposite to us near our last encampment the other side Schuylkill, made some Ravages, kill'd two of our Horsemen, taken some prisoners. We have done the like by them. . . .

December 18.—Universal Thanksgiving—a Roasted pig at Night. God be thanked for my health which I have pretty well recovered. How much better should I feel, were I assured my family were in health. But the same good Being who graciously preserves me, is able to preserve them & bring me to the ardently wish'd for enjoyment of them again

/   /   /

December 21.—[Valley Forge.] Preparations made for hutts. Provisions Scarce. Mr. Ellis went homeward—sent a Letter to my Wife. Heartily wish myself at home, my Skin & eyes are almost spoil'd with continual smoke. A general cry thro' the Camp this Evening among the Soldiers, "No Meat! No Meat!"—the Distant vales Echo'd back the mel-ancholly sound—"No Meat! No Meat!" Immitaing the noise of Crows & Owls, also, made a part of the confused Musick.

What have you for your Dinners Boys? "Nothing but Fire Cake & Water, Sir." At night, "Gentlemen the Supper is ready." What is your Supper Lads? "Fire Cake & Water, Sir." Very poor beef has been drawn in our Camp the greater part of this season. A Butcher bringing a Quarter of this kind of Beef into Camp one day who had white Buttons on the knees of his breeches, a Soldier cries out—"There, there Tom is some more of your fat Beef, by my soul I can see the Butcher's breeches buttons through it."

December 22.—Lay excessive Cold & uncomfortable last Night—my eyes are started out from their Orbits like a Rabbit's eyes, occasion'd by a great Cold & Smoke.

/   /   /

Our Division are under Marching Orders this morning. I am ashamed to say it, but I am tempted to steal Fowls if I could find them, or even a whole Hog, for I feel as if I could eat one. But the Impoverish'd Country about us, affords but little matter to employ a Thief, or keep a Clever Fellow in good humour. But why do I talk of hunger & hard usage, when so many in the World have not even fire Cake & Water to eat. . . .

It is not in the power of Philosphy . . . to convince a man he may be happy and Contented if he will, with a *Hungry Belly.* Give me Food, Cloaths, Wife & Children, kind Heaven! and I'll be as contented as my Nature will permit me to be.

This Evening a Party with two field pieces were order'd out. At 12 of the Clock at Night, Providence sent us a little Mutton, with which we immediately had some Broth made, & a fine Stomach for same. Ye who Eat Pumkin Pie and Roast Turkies, and yet Curse fortune for using you ill, Curse her no more, least she reduce your Allowance of her favours to a bit of Fire Cake, & a draught of Cold Water, & in Cold Weather too.

/   /   /

20 | *Victory at Yorktown*

Ebenezer Denny of Pennsylvania was a major in the Continental Army. His journal offers perhaps the best eyewitness account of the capture of British General Cornwallis's army at Yorktown, Virginia, in 1781, which was the last major battle of the war. The American Revolution was won by patience, endurance, and a certain amount of luck. The British were too busy with other interests to long endure the pinpricks of the colonialists, and, as with the battle at Yorktown, help from the French always seemed to arrive (for the revolutionary army) at just the right time.

CARLISLE, *May 1st,* 1781.—The Pennsylvania Line, after the revolt and discharge of the men, last winter, were reduced to six regiments; the officers ordered to different towns within the State to recruit. An appointment of ensign in the 7th had been obtained for me in August last; the 7th and 4th were incorporated, and under command of Lt.-Col. Comt. William Butler, rendezvoused at this place—companies now about half full. The effective men were formed into four companies, and marched to Little York; I was arranged to one of the marching companies, Samuel Montgomery, captain, and George Bluer, lieutenant. All the recruits fit for service, from the different stations, were brought to York, formed into two regiments of eight companies each, destined for the State of Virginia. A few days spent in equipping, &c., and for the trial of soldiers charged with mutiny, General Anthony Wayne, the commanding officer, influenced, no doubt, by experience of the revolt last winter, expresses a determination to punish, with the utmost rigor, every case of mutiny or disobedience. A general court martial continued sitting several days; twenty odd prisoners brought before them; seven were sentenced to die. The regiments paraded in the evening earlier than usual; orders passed to the officers along the line to put to death instantly any man who stirred from his rank. In front of the parade the ground rose and descended again, and at the distance of about three

The Record of the Court at Upland, in Pennsylvania, 1676 to 1681, and A Military Journal Kept by Major E. Denny, 1781 to 1795. *(Philadelphia, J.B. Lippincott and Company, 1860), pp. 237–249.*

hundred yards over this rising ground, the prisoners were escorted by a captain's guard; heard the fire of one platoon and immediately a smaller one, when the regiments wheeled by companies and marched round by the place of execution. This was an awful exhibition. The seven objects were seen by the troops just as they had sunk or fell under the fire. The sight must have made an impression on the men; it was designed with that view.

YORK, *May* 15th.—Provision for transporting baggage, &c., and other necessary preparation. Commenced our march for Virginia; the weather pleasant and roads tolerably good. Passed through Frederick Town (Maryland), where were some British prisoners quartered; they turned out to see us. Next day reached the Potomac; here we were detained for want of craft—boats few and in bad condition. The artillery passed over first (a battalion of artillery accompanied the brigade). The second flat-boat had left the shore about forty yards, when the whole sunk. Several women were on board; but as hundreds of men were on the bank, relief soon reached them; none were lost—got all over. Proceeded a few miles and encamped. Struck our tents every morning before day. About eight or nine o'clock, as we found water, a short halt was made, the water-call beat; parties, six or eight from each company, conducted by a non-commissioned officer, with canteens, fetched water. Seldom allowed to eat until twelve o'clock, when the arms were stacked, knapsacks taken off, and water sent for by parties as before. Officers of a company generally messed together, sometimes more; one of their servants carried cooked provisions for the day; no cooking until night. Not acquainted with the country on our route, but understood that we were marching much about—very circuitous—keeping off the Blue Ridge close on our right. This to avoid the enemy and secure our junction with the Marquis Lafayette.

June 18th.—Joined the troops under command of Lafayette. The Marquis had marched two or three days to meet us. His men look as if they were fit for business. They are chiefly all light infantry, dressed in frocks and over-alls of linen. One day spent in washing and refreshing—in fixing arms, carriages, &c., and served out ammunition. Move toward Richmond, where Lord Cornwallis with the British army lay. Heard that his lordship was employed burning and destroying warehouses of tobacco, all the public store-houses, &c. Passed through Richmond toward Williamsburg after the enemy—joined by Baron Steuben with some new levies. Near Bacon's Bridge the British turned upon us; our advance pressed them too close. The army was formed for a fight—they did not come on. General Wayne very anxious to do something. Colonel Simcoe, who commands the British legion (horse and mounted infantry), is constantly committing some depredation abroad, and foraging for their army. Wayne hears of him—our brigade leave their tents and baggage, march at dark, with piece of white paper in each man's hat—flints taken out. At day-light reach place called the Bowling Green, where Simcoe had been the evening before. This was a severe march for me—found myself asleep more than once on the route. Returned and met the baggage. A detachment from the brigade put under command of Colonel Richard Butler. After a variety of marching and counter-marching, Butler at length intercepts Simcoe; a smart skirmish takes place; Wayne supports Butler, and Simcoe retreats. Here for the first time saw wounded men; feelings not very agreeable; endeavor to conquer this disposition or weakness; the sight sickened me. This little engagement within six miles of Williamsburg, where the enemy were encamped. Pennsylvania troops retreat—advance again. See the Marquis' light troops but seldom—know they are not far off. Kept constantly on the move. Hear that the enemy have decamped and preparing to cross James river at Jamestown. Our brigade move down; lay on arms all night about nine miles from the enemy. At day-light move on; middle of the afternoon of the 6th of July firing ahead. Our advance drove in the enemy's pickets, marching at this time by companies, in open order. My captain (Montgomery) fell behind his company where my place was, talked with me; gives me a lesson useful to me. When perhaps within one hundred and fifty yards of the enemy, we closed column and displayed; advanced in battalion until the firing commenced, and ran along the whole line. A regiment or more of the light infantry and three pieces of artillery were in the line. Saw the British light infantry, distinctly, advancing at arm's-length distance, and their second line in close order, with shouldered musket, just in front of their camp—their infantry only engaged. The main body were discovered filing off to the right and left, when orders were given us to retreat. My captain, Montgomery, received a shot in his foot and had hopped back in the rear; Lieutenant Bluer being absent, the charge of the company devolved on me; young and inexperienced, exhausted with hunger and fatigue, had like to have disgraced myself—had eat nothing all day but a few blackberries—was faint, and with difficulty kept my place; once or twice was about to throw away my arms (a very heavy espontoon). The company were almost all old soldiers. Kept compact and close to our leading company, and continued running until out of reach of the fire. The enemy advanced no farther than to the ground we left. We could not have been engaged longer than about three or four minutes, but at the distance of sixty yards only. Our loss is said to be upward of one hundred killed and wounded; among the latter twelve officers, one of whom, Lieutenant Herbert, taken prisoner; a few of the wounded not able to get off, were also taken. The artillery horses all killed; two pieces were lost. Retreated two miles to very commanding ground, where we met the Marquis with our main body; halted and had some Indian meal served out, the wounded dressed, &c., and before day changed our ground and encamped about five miles from the field.

July 7th.—An officer, surgeon, and a few men sent with flag to bury the dead, &c. This was done in company with an equal number of the enemy. Our wounded who were prisoners, had been properly treated. The British moved from Jamestown. About a fortnight after the action, visited the field; could trace plainly the ground occupied by both, from the tops of the cartridges which lay in a line; the distance between about sixty paces. The army marched and crossed James river at Westover, the seat of Colonel Bird, said to have been once the most wealthy planter in the State; the improvements superb, saw nothing like them before. Kept at a respectful distance from the enemy; rather between them and the route to North Carolina. Some idea of their design to return to the southward. Report going of a French fleet below. This news confirmed— great joy—army on the alert.

Sept. 1*st.*—Army encamped on the bank of James river—part of French fleet, with troops on board, in view. Recrossed James river and encamped at Williamsburg. Army in high spirits—reinforcements coming on.

14*th.*—General Washington arrived; our brigade was paraded to receive him; he rode along the line—quarters in Williamsburg.

15*th.*—Officers all pay their respects to the Commander-in-chief; go in a body; those who are not personally known, their names given by General Hand and General Wayne. He stands in the door, takes every man by the hand—the officers all pass in, receiving his salute and shake. This the first time I had seen the General. We have an elegant encampment close to town, behind William and Mary College. This building occupied as an hospital. Williamsburg a very handsome place, not so populous as Richmond, but situate on evenly, pretty ground; streets and lots spacious—does not appear to be a place of much business, rather the residence of gentlemen of fortune; formerly it was the seat of government and Dunmore's late residence. A neat public building, called the capitol, fronts the principal street; upon the first floor is a handsome marble statue of William Pitt.

The presence of so many general officers, and the arrival of new corps, seem to give additional life to everything; discipline the order of the day. In all directions troops seen exercising and manœuvring. Baron Steuben, our great military oracle. The guards attend the grand parade at an early hour, where the Baron is always found waiting with one or two aids on horseback. These men are exercised and put through various evolutions and military experiments for two hours—many officers and spectators present; excellent school, this. At length the duty of the parade comes on. The guards are told off; officers take their posts, wheel by platoons to the right; fine corps of music detailed for this duty, which strikes up; the whole march off, saluting the Baron and field officer of the day, as they pass. Pennsylvania brigade almost all old soldiers, and well disciplined when compared with those of Maryland and Virginia. But the troops from the eastward far superior to either.

25*th.*—Joined by the last of the troops from the eastward. French encamped a few miles on the right; busy in getting cannon and military stores from on board the vessels.

28th.—The whole army moved in three divisions toward the enemy, who were strongly posted at York, about twelve miles distant. Their pickets and light troops retire. We encamped about three miles off—change ground and take a position within one mile of York; rising ground (covered with tall handsome pines) called Pigeon Hill, separates us from a view of the town. Enemy keep possession of Pigeon Hill. York on a high, sandy plain, on a deep navigable river of same name. Americans on the right; French on the left, extending on both sides of the river; preparations for a siege. One-third of the army on fatigue every day, engaged in various duties, making gabions, fascines, saucissons, &c., and great exertions and labor in getting on the heavy artillery. Strong covering parties (whole regiments) moved from camp as soon as dark, and lay all night upon their arms between us and the enemy. Our regiment, when on this duty, were under cover, and secured from the shot by Pigeon Hill; now and then a heavy shot from the enemy's works reached our camp. Our patrols, and those of the British, met occasionally in the dark, sometimes a few shot were exchanged—would generally retire. Colonel Schamel, adjutant-general to the army, with two or three attendants, on a party of observation, ventured rather close; they were seen and intercepted by a few smart horsemen from the British. Schamel forced his way through, and got back to camp, but received a wound, of which he died next day. His death was lamented, and noticed by the Commander-in-chief in his orders. Possession taken of Pigeon Hill, and temporary work erected. Generals and engineers, in viewing and surveying the ground, are always fired upon and sometimes pursued. Escorts and covering parties stationed at convenient distances under cover of wood, rising ground, &c., afford support. This business reminds me of a play among the boys, called Prison-base.

At length, everything in readiness, a division of the army broke ground on the night of the 6th of October, and opened the first parallel about six hundred yards from the works of the enemy. Every exertion to annoy our men, who were necessarily obliged to be exposed about the works; however, the business went on, and on the 9th our cannon and mortars began to play. The scene viewed from the camp now was grand, particularly after dark—a number of shells from the works of both parties passing high in the air, and descending in a curve, each with a long train of fire, exhibited a brilliant spectacle. Troops in three divisions manned the lines alternately. We were two nights in camp and one in the lines; relieved about ten o'clock. Passed and repassed by a covert way leading to the parallel.

Oct. 11th.—Second parallel thrown up within three hundred yards of the main works of the enemy; new batteries erected, and additional number of cannon brought forward—some twenty-four pounders and heavy mortars and howitzers. A tremendous fire now opened from all the new works, French and American. The heavy cannon directed against the embrasures and guns of the enemy. Their pieces were soon silenced, broke and dismantled. Shells from behind their works still kept up. Two redoubts advanced of their lines, and within rifle shot of our second parallel, much in the way. These forts or redoubts were well secured by a ditch and picket, sufficiently high parapet, and within were divisions made by rows of casks ranged upon end and filled with earth and sand. On tops of parapet were ranged bags filled with sand—a deep narrow ditch communicating with their main lines. On the night of the 14th, shortly after dark, these redoubts were taken by storm; the one on our right, by the Marquis, with part of his light infantry—the other, more to our left, but partly opposite the centre of the British lines, by the French. Our batteries had kept a constant fire upon the redoubts through the day. Belonged this evening to a command detailed for the purpose of supporting the Marquis. The night was dark and favorable. Our batteries had ceased—there appeared to be a dead calm; we followed the infantry and halted about half way—kept a few minutes in suspense, when we were ordered to advance. The business was over, not a gun was fired by the assailants; the bayonet only was used; ten or twelve of the infantry were killed. French had to contend with a post of more force—their loss was considerable. Colonel Hamilton led the Marquis' advance; the British sentries hailed them—no answer made. They also hailed the French, "Who comes there?" were answered, "French grenadiers." Colonel Walter Stewart commanded the regiment of reserve which accompanied the Marquis; they were immediately employed in connecting, by a ditch and parapet, the two redoubts, and completing and connecting the same with our second parallel. The British were soon alarmed; some from each of the redoubts made their escape. The whole enemy were under arms—much firing round all their lines, but particularly toward our regiment, where the men were at work; the shot passed over. In about three quarters of an hour we were under cover. Easy digging; light sandy ground.

15th.—Heavy fire from our batteries all day. A shell from one of the French mortars set fire to a British frigate; she burnt to the water's edge, and blew up—made the earth shake. Shot and shell raked the town in every direction. Bomb-proofs the only place of safety.

16th.—Just before day the enemy made a sortie, spiked the guns in two batteries and retired. Our troops in the parallel scarcely knew of their approach until they were off; the thing was done silently and in an instant. The batteries stood in advance of the lines, and none within but artillery. This day, the 16th, our division manned the lines—firing continued without intermission. Pretty strong detachments posted in each battery over night.

17th.—In the morning, before relief came, had the pleasure of seeing a drummer mount the enemy's parapet, and beat a parley, and immediately an officer, holding up a white handkerchief, made his appearance outside their works; the drummer accompanied him, beating. Our batteries ceased. An officer from our lines ran and met the other, and tied the handkerchief over his eyes. The drummer sent back, and the British officer conducted to a house in rear of our lines. Firing ceased totally.

18th.—Several flags pass and repass now even without the drum. Had we not seen the drummer in his red coat when he first mounted, he might have beat away till doomsday. The constant firing was too much for the sound of a single drum; but when the firing ceased, I thought I never heard a drum equal to it—the most delightful music to us all.

19th.—Our division man the lines again. All is quiet. Articles of capitulation signed; detachments of French and Americans take possession of British forts. Major Hamilton commanded a battalion which took possession of a fort immediately opposite our right and on the bank of York river. I carried the standard of our regiment on this occasion. On entering the fort, Baron Steuben, who accompanied us, took the standard from me and planted it himself. The British army parade and march out with their colors furled; drums beat as if they did not care how. Grounded their arms and returned to town. Much confusion and riot among the British through the day; many of the soldiers were intoxicated; several attempts in course of the night to break open stores; an American sentinel killed by a British soldier with a bayonet; our patrols kept busy. Glad to be relieved from this disagreeable station. Negroes lie about, sick and dying, in every stage of the small pox. Never was in so filthy a place—some handsome houses, but prodigiously shattered. Vast heaps of shot and shells lying about in every quarter, which came from our works. The shells did not burst, as was expected. Returns of British soldiers, prisoners six thousand, and seamen about one thousand. Lord Cornwallis excused himself from marching out with the troops; they were conducted by General O'Hara. Our loss said to be about three hundred; that of the enemy said not more than five hundred and fifty. Fine supply of stores and merchandise had; articles suitable for clothing were taken for the use of the army. A portion furnished each officer to the amount of sixty dollars.

21 | Titles and Ceremonials in the New Senate

First published in 1890, the journal of Senator William Maclay of Pennsylvania is the most complete record we have of the 1789 debates in the first session of the United States Senate after the Constitution. Suspicious, democratic, and ably representing a rural constituency, this Scotch-Irish Pennsylvanian opposed Hamilton's financial plan, disliked urban speculators, and detested the conservative hunger for aristocracy that he saw still alive after so many years of revolution. His account of the discussion of titles and ceremonies at the very beginning of the Washington administration suggests how uncertain the tradition of republicanism was and how many issues had to be defined before the government sketched in the Constitution took definite form.

30th April, Thursday.—This is a great, important day. Goddess of etiquette, assist me while I describe it. The Senate stood adjourned to half after eleven o'clock. About ten dressed in my best clothes; went for Mr. Morris' lodgings, but met his son, who told me that his father would not be in town until Saturday. Turned into the Hall. The crowd already great. The Senate met. The Vice-President [John Adams] rose in the most solemn manner. This son of *Adam* seemed impressed with deeper gravity, yet what shall I think of him? He often, in the midst of his most important airs—I believe when he is at loss for expressions (and this he often is, wrapped up, I suppose, in the contemplation of his own importance)—suffers an unmeaning kind of vacant laugh to escape him. This was the case to-day, and really to me bore the air of ridiculing the farce he was acting. "Gentlemen, I wish for the direction of the Senate. The President will, I suppose, address the Congress. How shall I behave? How shall we receive it? Shall it be standing or sitting?"

Here followed a considerable deal of talk from him which I could make nothing of. Mr. Lee began with the House of Commons (as is usual with him), then the House of Lords, then the King, and then back again. The result of his information was, that the Lords sat and the Com-

Edgar S. Maclay (editor), Journal of William Maclay, United States Senator from Pennsylvania, 1789-1791. *(New York, D. Appleton and Company, 1890), pp. 7-13.*

mons stood on the delivery of the King's speech. Mr. Izard got up and told how often he had been in the Houses of Parliament. He said a great deal of what he had seen there. [He] made, however, this sagacious discovery, that the Commons stood because they had no seats to sit on, being arrived at the bar of the House of Lords. It was discovered after some time that the King sat, too, and had his robes and crown on.

Mr. Adams got up again and said he had been very often indeed at the Parliament on those occasions, but there always was such a crowd, and *ladies along*, that for his part he could not say how it was. Mr. Carrol got up to declare that he thought it of no consequence how it was in Great Britain; they were no rule to us, etc. But all at once the Secretary, who had been out, whispered to the Chair that the Clerk from the Representatives was at the door with a communication. Gentlemen of the Senate, how shall he be received? A silly kind of resolution of the committee on that business had been laid on the table some days ago. The amount of it was that each House should communicate to the other what and how they chose; it concluded, however, something in this way: That everything should be done with all the *propriety* that was *proper.* The question was, Shall this be adopted, that we may know how to receive the Clerk? It was objected [that] this will throw no light on the subject; it will leave you where you are. Mr. Lee brought the House of Commons before us again. He reprobated the rule; declared that the Clerk should not come within the bar of the House; that the proper mode was for the Sergeant-at-Arms, with the mace on his shoulder, to meet the Clerk at the door and receive his communication; we are not, however, provided for this ceremonious way of doing business, having neither mace nor sergeant nor Masters in Chancery, who carry down bills from the English Lords.

Mr. Izard got up and labored unintelligible to show the great distinction between a communication and a delivery of a thing, but he was not minded. Mr. Elsworth showed plainly enough that if the Clerk was not permitted to deliver the communication, the Speaker might as well send it inclosed. Repeated accounts came [that] the Speaker and Representatives were at the door. Confusion ensued; the members left their seats. Mr. Read rose and called the attention of the Senate to the neglect that had been shown Mr. Thompson, late Secretary. Mr. Lee rose to answer him, but I could not hear one word he said. The Speaker was introduced, followed by the Representatives. Here we sat an hour and ten minutes before the President arrived—this delay was owing to Lee, Izard, and Dalton, who had stayed with us while the Speaker came in, instead of going to attend the President. The President advanced between the Senate and Representatives, bowing to each. He was placed in the chair by the Vice-President; the Senate with their president on the right, the Speaker and the Representatives on his left. The Vice-President rose and addressed a short sentence to him. The import of it was that he should now take the oath of office as President. He seemed to have forgot half what he was to say, for he made a dead pause and stood for some time, to appearance, in a vacant mood. He finished with a formal bow, and the President was conducted out of the middle window into the gallery, and the oath was administered by the Chancellor. Notice that the business done was communicated to the crowd by proclamation, etc., who gave three cheers, and repeated it on the President's bowing to them.

As the company returned into the Senate chamber, the President took the chair and the Senators and Representatives their seats. He rose, and all arose also and addressed them (see the address). This great man was agitated and embarrassed more than ever he was by the leveled cannon or pointed musket. He trembled, and several times could scarce make out to read, though it must be supposed he had often read it before. He put part of the fingers of his left hand into the side of what I think the tailors call the fall of the breeches [corresponding to the modern side-pocket], changing the paper into his left [right] hand. After some time he then did the same with some of the fingers of his right hand. When he came to the words *all the world*, he made a flourish with his right hand, which left rather an ungainly impression. I sincerely, for my part, wished all set ceremony in the hands of the dancing-masters, and that this first of men had read off his address in the plainest manner, without ever taking his eyes from the paper, for I felt hurt that he was not first in everything. He was dressed in deep brown, with metal buttons, with an eagle on them, white stockings, a bag, and sword.

From the hall there was a grand procession to Saint Paul's Church, where prayers were said by the Bishop. The procession was well conducted and without accident, as far as I have heard. The militia were all under arms, lined the street near the church, made a good figure, and behaved well.

The Senate returned to their chamber after service, formed, and took up the address. Our Vice-President called it *his most gracious speech*. I can not approve of this. A committee was appointed on it—Johnson, Carrol, Patterson. Adjourned. In the evening there were grand fireworks. The Spanish Ambassador's house was adorned with transparent paintings; the French Minister's house was illuminated, and had some transparent pieces; the Hall was grandly illuminated, and after all this the people went to bed.

May 1st.—Attended at the Hall at eleven. The prayers were over and the minutes reading. When we came to the minute of the speech it stood, *His most gracious speech.* I looked all around the Senate. Every countenance seemed to wear a blank. The Secretary was going on: I must speak or nobody would. "Mr. President, we have lately had a hard struggle for our liberty against kingly authority. The minds of men are still heated: everything related to that species of government is odious to the people. The words prefixed to the President's speech are the same that are usually placed before the speech of his Britannic Majesty. I know they will give offense. I consider them as improper. I therefore move that they be struck out, and that it stand simply address or speech, as may be judged most suitable."

Mr. Adams rose in his chair and expressed the greatest surprise that anything should be objected to on account of its being taken from the practice of that Government under which we had lived so long and happily formerly; that he was for a dignified and respectable government, and as far as he knew the sentiments of people they thought as he did; that for his part he was one of the first in the late contest [the Revolution], and, if *he could have thought of this, he never would have drawn his sword.*

Painful as it was, I had to contend with the Chair. I admitted that the people of the colonies (now States) had enjoyed formerly great happiness under that species of government, but the abuses of that Government under which they had smarted had taught them what they had to fear from that kind of government; that there had been a revolution in the sentiments of people respecting government equally great as that which had happened in the Government itself; that even the modes of it were now abhorred; that the enemies of the Constitution had objected to it the facility there would be of transition from it to kingly government and all the trappings and splendor of royalty; that if such a thing as this appeared on our minutes, they would not fail to represent it as the first step of the ladder in the ascent to royalty. The Vice-President rose a second time, and declared that he had mentioned it to the Secretary; that he could not possibly conceive that any person could take offense at it. I had to get up again and declare that, although I knew of it being mentioned from the Chair, yet my opposition did not proceed from any motive of contempt; that, although it was a painful task, it was solely a sense of duty that raised me.

The Vice-President stood during this time; said he had been long abroad, and did not know how the temper of people might be now. Up now rose Mr. Read, and declared for the paragraph. He saw no reason to object to it because the British speeches were styled *most gracious.* If we chose to object to words because they had been used in the same sense in Britain, we should soon be at a loss to do business. I had to reply. "It is time enough to submit to necessity when it exists. At present we are at no loss for words. The words speech or address without any addition will suit us well enough." The first time I was up Mr. Lee followed me with a word or two by way of seconding me; but when the Vice-President, on being last up, declared that he was the person from whom the words were taken, Mr. Lee got up and informed the Chair that he did not know that circumstance, as he had been absent when it happened. The question was put and carried for erasing the words without a division.

After the House adjourned the Vice-President took me to one side, declared how much he was for an efficient Government, how much he respected General Washington, and much of that kind. I told him I would yield to no person in respect to General Washington; that our common friends would perhaps one day inform him that I was not wanting in respect to himself [Adams]; that my wishes for an efficient Government were as high as any man's, and begged him to believe that I did myself great violence when I opposed him in the chair, and nothing but a sense of duty could force me to it. He got on the subject of checks to government and the balances of power. His tale was long. He seemed to expect some answer. I caught at the last word, and said undoubtedly without a balance there could be no equilibrium, and so left him hanging in geometry.

The unequivocal declaration tht he would never have drawn his sword, etc., has drawn my mind to the following remarks: That the motives of the actors in the late Revolution were various can not be doubted. The abolishing of royalty, the extinguishment of patronage and dependencies attached to that form of government, were the exalted motives of many revolutionists, and these were the improvements meant by them to be made of the war which was forced on us by British aggression—in fine, the amelioration of government and bettering the condition of mankind. These ends and none other were publicly avowed, and all our constitutions and public acts were formed in this spirit. Yet there were not wanting a party whose motives were different. They wished for the loaves and fishes of government, and cared for nothing else but a translation of the diadem and scepter from London to Boston, New York, or Philadelphia; or, in other words, the creation of a new monarchy in America, and to form niches for themselves in the temple of royalty.

This spirit manifested itself strongly among the officers at the close of the war, and I have been afraid the army would not have been disbanded if the common soldiers could have been kept together. This spirit they developed in the Order of Cincinnati, where I trust it will spend itself in a harmless flame and soon become extinguished. That Mr. Adams should, however, so unequivocally avow this motive, at a time when a republican form of government is secured to every State in the Union, appears to me a mark of extreme folly.*

[Memorandum], *1790.*—It is worthy of remark that about this time a spirit of reformation broke out in France which finally abolished all titles and every trace of the feudal system. Strange, indeed, that in that very country [America], where the flame of freedom had been kindled, an attempt should be made to introduce these absurdities and humiliating distinctions which the hand of reason, aided by our example, was prostrating in the heart of Europe. I, however, will endeavor (as I have

---

* "John Adams was included by Jefferson among the believers in monarchy."—Randall's Life of Jefferson, vol. i, p. 586.

hitherto done) to use the resentment of the Representatives to defeat Mr. Adams and others on the subject of titles. The pompous and lordly distinctions which the Senate have manifested a disposition to establish between the two Houses have nettled the Representatives, and this business of titles may be considered as part of the same tune. While we are debating on titles I will, through the Speaker, Mr. Muhlenberg, and other friends, get the idea suggested of answering the President's address without any title, in contempt of our deliberations, which still continue on that subject. This once effected, will confound them [the Senators] completely, and establish a precedent they will not dare to violate.

/   /   /

Questions for Part II

1 Why do you think the adults in Salem believed the young women's stories about witchcraft? What does it suggest about their religion and society?

2 Why do you think the people described by Gottlieb Mittelberger agreed to come to America as indentured servants?

3 What in Venture Smith's account suggests that even defenders of slavery should have been embarrassed by the slave trade?

4 What differences do you see between the place of children in today's society compared with that in colonial society? Discuss the differences among the varying status of eighteenth century colonials: indentured servants, slaves and apprentices.

5 Summarize how Franklin got into the printing business. Can you suggest why apprenticeship in America was more open than in Europe?

6 Benjamin Franklin's pursuit of moral perfection has offended many of his twentieth-century readers. How does his search for improvement compare with the modern efforts at "self help" with which you are familiar?

7 Explain the Indian custom of adoption as Mary Jemison tells it. How does Jemison describe her Indian husband? Why do you think captivity narratives were popular?

8 Briefly summarize Crèvecoeur's answer to the question, "What then is the American, this new man?" How does Crèvecoeur contrast America with Europe? Be specific. What does he say about the frontiersmen, the "backsettlers?"

9 Which account of the Boston Massacre sounds more believable to you? Why?

10 What problems does Washington discuss in his letter? What solutions does he propose?

11 What is the main objective of Paine's pamphlet? Are there any phrases in it that you have heard before? What is a "summer soldier" and a "sunshine patriot?" Who were the "Hessians" he refers to?

12 Imagine what it was like to be at Valley Forge in the winter of 1777–1778. Why do you think men were willing to endure those conditions?

13 Compare Denny's account with Waldo's Valley Forge diary. How do they differ?

14 Why did Maclay think the choice of titles for officials was so important? What do his views reflect of his understanding of why the Revolutionary War was fought?

PART III | THE GROWTH OF
A NEW NATION

The early republic developed a vigorous economic and political life as the young nation established its independent place in the world, extended its borders through the Louisiana Purchase, and began a rapid movement westward led by explorers such as Lewis and Clark. With the vast territory far beyond the Mississippi to exploit, its national identity and governmental structure largely set, and its relations with foreign powers on a calm course (after the War of 1812), the minds and energies of Americans were engaged in settling the West, creating wealth, and building religious and cultural institutions in an expanding nation.

In the selections that follow, restless Americans who fascinated European travelers are seen wasting their natural resources in the James Fenimore Cooper reading, having their souls saved by preachers such as Peter Cartwright, fighting with Indians such as Black Hawk, living through the boom and bust of a growing economy such as the one that James Flint depicts, founding new industries such as the Lowell Textile Mills, and moving relentlessly westward as did Jane Voorhees Lewis and her family. There is a selection that details the transportation revolution of the era, starting with the Pony Express, which linked California with the rest of the nation. However, amid the growth and change that marked early nineteenth century America, some of the institutions that prevail in more established societies were neglected. This is demonstrated in Caleb Bingham's satirical dialogue about education.

MERIWETHER LEWIS AND
WILLIAM CLARK

22 | Crossing the Great Divide

*The most famous expedition in American history was the brainchild of Thomas
Jefferson. For years Jefferson had dreamed that a party of explorers could search
out a passage to the Pacific, win the Indians to the new republic to the east,
and study the geography, plants, animals, and minerals of a vast and unknown
territory.*

*Meriwether Lewis and William Clark were two young men willing to follow
Jefferson's dream. Their expedition from St. Louis to the mouth of the Columbia
River and back is one of the great adventure stories of our history. The journals
and notebooks that members of the party kept have been used by historians,
geographers, anthropologists, botanists, and zoologists.*

*The selections here present Lewis and Clark crossing the Great Divide. In one
of the most difficult parts of their journey. The reader can see their firm Indian
diplomacy, their careful search for information about the best way west, and
their careful observation of Indian ways. The reader will also glimpse the most
famous single drama of the expedition: the extraordinary moment when Sacajawea, wife of one of their interpreters, meets a party of Shoshonee, her native
tribe, headed by a chief who is the brother she has not seen since she was a small
child. The first excerpt was written by Nicholas Biddle, who was later head of
the Bank of the United States. Biddle's descriptions are taken from the notes of
various participants in the expedition. They have frequently been published as
part of the actual journal of Lewis and Clark.*

[Biddle]   Saturday, August 17th, 1805.

Captain Lewis rose very early and despatched Drewyer and the Indian
down the river in quest of the boats. Shields was sent out at the same
time to hunt, while M'Neal prepared a breakfast out of the remainder
of the meat. Drewyer had been gone about two hours, and the Indians
were all anxiously waiting for some news, when an Indian who had
straggled a short distance down the river, returned with a report that

The Journals of Lewis and Clark *by Barnard DeVoto, pp. 202–206, 207–211, 213–214. Copyright 1953 by Bernard DeVoto. Copyright © renewed 1981 by Avis DeVoto. Reprinted by permission of Houghton Mifflin Company.*

he had seen the white men, who were only a short distance below, and were coming on. The Indians were all transported with joy, and the chief in the warmth of his satisfaction renewed his embrace to Capt. Lewis, who was quite as much delighted as the Indians themselves; the report proved most aggreeably true.

On setting out at seven o'clock, Captain Clarke with Chaboneau and his wife walked on shore, but they had not gone more than a mile before Clarke saw Sacajawea, who was with her husband 100 yards ahead, began to dance and show every mark of the most extravagant joy, turning round him and pointing to several Indians, whom he now saw advancing on horseback, sucking her fingers at the same time to indicate that they were of her native tribe. As they advanced, Captain Clarke discovered among them Drewyer dressed like an Indian, from whom he learnt the situation of the party. While the boats were performing the circuit, he went towards the forks with the Indians, who as they went along, sang aloud with the greatest appearance of delight.

We soon drew near to the camp, and just as we approached it a woman made her way through the crowd towards Sacajawea, and recognising each other, they embraced with the most tender affection. The meeting of these two young women had in it something peculiarly touching, not only in the ardent manner in which their feelings were expressed, but from the real interest of their situation. They had been companions in childhood, in the war with the Minetarees they had both been taken prisoners in the same battle, they had shared and softened the rigours of their captivity, till one of them had escaped from the Minnetarees, with scarce a hope of ever seeing her friend relieved from the hands of her enemies. While Sacajawea was renewing among the women the friendships of former days, Captain Clarke went on, and was received by Captain Lewis and the chief, who after the first embraces and salutations were over, conducted him to a sort of circular tent or shade of willows. Here he was seated on a white robe; and the chief immediately tied in his hair six small shells resembling pearls, an ornament highly valued by these people, who procure them in the course of trade from the sea-coast. The moccasins of the whole party were then taken off, and after much ceremony the smoking began. After this the conference was to be opened, and glad of an opportunity of being able to converse more intelligibly, Sacajawea was sent for; she came into the tent, sat down, and was beginning to interpret, when in the person of Cameahwait she recognised her brother: She instantly jummped up, and ran and embraced him, throwing over him her blanket and weeping profusely: The chief was himself moved, though not in the same degree. After some conversation between them she resumed her seat, and attempted to interpret for us, but her new situation seemed to overpower her, and she was frequently interrupted by her tears. After the council was finished the unfortunate woman learnt that all her family were dead except two brothers, one of whom was absent, and a son of her eldest sister, a small boy, who was immediatley adopted by her.

[Lewis]   SATURDAY AUGUST 17TH 1806.—

we made them [the Indians] sensible of their dependance on the will of our government for every species of merchandize as well for their defence & comfort; and apprized them of the strength of our government and it's friendly dispositions towards them. we also gave them as a reason why we wished to pe[ne]trate the country as far as the ocean to the west of them was to examine and find out a more direct way to bring merchandize to them. that as no trade could be carryed on with them before our return to our homes that it was mutually advantageous to them as well as to ourselves that they should render us such aids as they had in their power to furnish in order to haisten our voyage and of course our return home. that such were their horses to transport our baggage without which we could not subsist, and that a pilot to conduct us through the mountains was also necessary if we could not decend the river by water. but that we did not ask either their horses or their services without giving a satisfactory compensation in return. that at present we wished them to collect as many horses as were necessary to transport our baggage to their village on the Columbia where we would then trade with them at our leasure for such horses as they could spare us.

the chief thanked us for friendship towards himself and nation & declared his wish to serve us in every rispect. that he was sorry to find that it must yet be some time before they could be furnished with firearms but said they could live as they had done heretofore untill we brought them as we had promised. he said they had not horses enough with them at present to remove our baggage to their village over the mountain, but that he would return tomorrow and encourage his people to come over with their horses and that he would bring his own and assist us. this was complying with all we wished at present.

we next enquired who were chiefs among them.   Cameahwait pointed out two others whom he said were Chiefs. we gave him a medal of the small size with the likeness of Mr. Jefferson the President of the U' States in releif on one side and clasp hands with a pipe and tomahawk in the other,   to the other Chiefs we gave each a small medal which were struck in the Presidency of George Washing[ton] Esqr. we also gave small medals of the last discription to two young men whom the 1st Chief informed us wer good young men and much rispected among them. we gave the 1st Chief an uniform coat shirt a pair of scarlet legings a carrot of tobacco and some small articles   to each of the others we gave a shi[r]t leging[s] handkerchief a knife some tobacco and a few small articles   we also distributed a good quantity paint mockerson awles knives beads looking-glasses &c among the other Indians and gave them a plentifull meal of lyed corn which was the first they had ever eaten in their lives. they were much pleased with it. every article about us appeared to excite astonishment in there minds; the appearance of the men, their arms, the canoes, our manner of working them, the b[l]ack man york and the sagacity of my dog were equally objects of admiration. I also shot my air-gun which was so perfectly incomprehensible that they immediately denominated it the great medicine.

Capt. Clark and myself now concerted measures for our future operations, and it was mutually agreed that he should set out tomorrow morning with eleven men furnished with axes and other necessary tools for making canoes, their arms accoutrements and as much of their baggage as they could carry. also to take the indians, C[h]arbono and the indian woman with him; that on his arrival at the Shoshone camp he was to leave Charbono and the Indian woman to haisten the return of the Indians with their horses to this place, and to proceede himself with the eleven men down the Columbia in order to examine the river and if he found it navigable and could obtain timber to set about making canoes immediately. In the mean time I was to bring the party and baggage to the Shoshone Camp, calculating that by the time I should reach that place that he would have sufficiently informed himself with rispect to the state of the river &c. as to determine us whether to prosicute our journey from thence by land or water. in the former case we should want all the horses which we could perchase, and in the latter only to hire the Indians to transport our baggage to the place at which we made the canoes.

SUNDAY AUGUST 18TH 1805.

This morning while Capt Clark was busily engaged in preparing for his rout, I exposed some articles to barter with the Indians for horses as I wished a few at this moment to releive the men who were going with Capt Clark from the labour of carrying their baggage, and also one to keep here in order to pack the meat to camp which the hunters might kill. I soon obtained three very good horses. for which I gave an uniform coat, a pair of legings, a few handkerchiefs, three knives and some other small articles the whole of which did not cost more than about 20$ in the U' States. the Indians seemed quite as well pleased with their bargin as I was. the men also purchased one for an old checked shirt a pair of old legings and a knife. two of those I purchased Capt. C. took on with him. at 10 A.M. Capt. Clark departed with his detachment and all the Indians except 2 men and 2 women who remained with us.

after there departure this morning I had all the stores and baggage of every discription opened and aired. and began the operation of forming the packages in proper parsels for the purpose of transporting them on horseback. the rain in the evening compelled me to desist from my operations. I had the raw hides put in the water in order to cut them in throngs proper for lashing the packages and forming the necessary geer for pack horses, a business which I fortunately had not to learn on this occasion. I had the net arranged and set this evening to catch some trout which we could see in great abundance at the bottom of the river.

MONDAY AUGUST 19TH 1805

The Shoshonees may be estimated at about 100 warriors, and about three times that number of woomen and children.[1] they have more children among them that I expected to have seen among a people who procure subsistence with such difficulty. there are but few very old persons, nor did they appear to treat those with much tenderness or rispect. The man is the sole propryetor of his wives and daughters, and can barter or dispose of either as he thinks proper. a plurality of wives is common among them, but these are not generally sisters as with the Minnitares & Mandans but are purchased of different fathers. The father frequently disposes of his infant daughters in marriage to men who are grown or to men who have sons for whom they think proper to provide wives. the compensation given in such cases usually consists of horses or mules which the father receives at the time of contract and converts to his own uce. the girl remains with her parents untill she is conceived to have obtained the age of puberty which with them is considered to be about the age of 13 or 14 years. the female at this age is surrendered to her soveriegn lord and husband agreeably to contract, and with her is frequently restored by the father quite as much as he received in the first instance in payment for his daughter; but this is discretionary with the father. Sah-car-gar-we-ah had been thus disposed of before she was taken by the Minnetares, or had arrived to the years of puberty. the husband was yet living with this band. he was more than double her age and had two other wives. he claimed her as his wife but said that as she had had a child by another man, who was Charbono, that he did not want her.

They seldom correct their children particularly the boys who soon become masters of their own acts. they give as a reason that it cows and breaks the sperit of the boy to whip him, and that he never recovers his independence of mind after he is grown. They treat their women but with little rispect, and compel them to perform every species of drudgery. they collect the wild fruits and roots, attend to the horses or assist in that duty, cook, dress the skins and make all their apparel, collect wood and make their fires, arrange and form their lodges, and when they travel pack the horses and take charge of all the baggage; in short the man dose little else except attend his horses hunt and fish. the man

1. Lewis's figures refer to this band only.

considers himself degraded if he is compelled to walk any distance; and if he is so unfortunately poor as only to possess two horses he rides the best himself and leavs the woman or women if he has more than one, to transport their baggage and children on the other, and to walk if the horse is unable to carry the additional weight of their persons. the chastity of their women is not held in high estimation, and the husband will for a trifle barter the companion of his bead for a night or longer if he conceives the reward adiquate; tho' they are not so importunate that we should caress their women as the siouxs were. and some of their women appear to be held more sacred than in any nation we have seen. I have requested the men to give them no cause of jealousy by having connection with their women without their knowledge, which with them, strange as it may seem is considered as disgracefull to the husband as clandestine connections of a similar kind are among civilized nations. to prevent this mutual exchange of good officies altogether I know it impossible to effect, particularly on the part of our young men whom some months abstanence have made very polite to those tawney damsels. no evil has yet resulted and I hope will not from these connections.

notwithstanding the late loss of horses which this people sustained by the Minnetares the stock of the band may be very safely estimated at seven hundred of which they are perhaps about 40 coalts and half that number of mules. their arms offensive and defensive consist in the bow and arrows shield, some, lances, and a weapon called by the Cippeways who formerly used it, the pog-gar'-mag-gon' [war club]. in fishing they employ wairs, gigs, and fishing hooks. the salmon is the principal object of their pursuit. they snair wolves and foxes.

I was anxious to learn whether these people had the venerial, and made the enquiry through the intrepreter and his wife; the information was that they sometimes had it but I could not learn their remedy; they most usually die with it's effects. this seems a strong proof that these disorders bothe ganaræhah and Louis Veneræ* are native disorders of America. tho' these people have suffered much by the small pox which is known to be imported and perhaps those other disorders might have been contracted from other indian tribes who by a round of communications might have obtained from the Europeans since it was introduced into that quarter of the globe. but so much detatched on the other ha[n]d from all communication with the whites that I think it most probable that those disorders are original with them.

from the middle of May to the first of September these people reside on the waters of the Columbia where they consider themselves in perfect security from their enemies as they have not as yet ever found their way to this retreat; during this season the salmon furnish the principal part of their subsistence and as this fish either perishes or returns about the 1st of September they are compelled at this season in surch of sub-

---

* Gonorrhea and syphilis.

sistence to resort to the Missouri, in the vallies of which, there is more game even [than] within the mountains. here they move slowly down the river in order to collect and join other bands either of their own nation or the Flatheads, and having become sufficiently strong as they conceive venture on the Eastern side of the Rockey mountains into the plains, where the buffaloe abound. but they never leave the interior of the mountains while they can obtain a scanty subsistence, and always return as soon as they have acquired a good stock of dryed meat in the plains; when this stock is consumed they venture again into the plains; thus alternately obtaining their food at the risk of their lives and retiring to the mountains, while they consume it. These people are now on the eve of their departure for the Missouri, and inform us that they expect to be joined at or about the three forks by several bands of their own nation, and a band of the Flatheads.

[Clark]   AUGUST 19TH MONDAY 1805.

A very Cold morning Frost to be seen   we Set out a 7 oClock and proceeded on thro a wide leavel Vallie   this Vallie Continues 5 miles & then becoms narrow,   we proceeded on up the main branch with a gradial assent to the head and passed over a low mountain and Decended a Steep Decent to a butifull Stream, passed over a Second hill of a verry Steep assent & thro' a hilley Countrey for 8 miles an[d] Encamped on a Small Stream, the Indians with us we wer oblige[d] to feed. one man met me with a mule & Spanish Saddle to ride, I gave him a westcoat   a mule is considered of great value among those people   we proceeded on over a verry mountainous Countrey across the head of hollows & Springs

[Lewis]   TUESDAY AUGUST 20TH 1805.

I walked down the river about ¾ of a mile and selected a place near the river bank unperceived by the Indians for a cash [cache], which I set three men to make, and directed the centinel to discharge his gun if he perceived any of the Indians going down in that direction which was to be the signal for the men at work on the cash to desist and seperate, least these people should discover our deposit and rob us of the baggage we intend leaving here. by evening the cash was completed unperceived by the Indians, and all our packages made up. the Pack-saddles and harnes is not yet complete. in this operation we find ourselves at a loss for nails and boards; for the first we substitute throngs of raw hide which answer verry well, and for the last [had] to cut off the blades of our oars and use the plank of some boxes which have heretofore held other articles and put those articles into sacks of raw hide which I have had made for the purpose. by this means I have obtained as many boards as will make 20 saddles which I suppose will be sufficient for our present exegencies. I made up a small assortment of medicines, together with the specemines of plants, minerals, seeds &c, which, I have collected betwen this place and the falls of the Missouri which I shall deposit here.

I now prevailed on the Chief to instruct me with rispect to the geography of his country. this he undertook very cheerfully, by delineating the rivers on the ground. but I soon found that his information fell far short of my expectaton or wishes. he drew the river on which we now are [the Lemhi] to which he placed two branches just above us, which he shewed me from the openings of the mountains were in view; he next made it discharge itself into a large river which flowed from the S.W. about ten miles below us [the Salmon], then continued this joint stream in the same direction of this valley or N.W. for one days march and then enclined it to the West for 2 more days march. here he placed a number of heaps of sand on each side which he informed me represented the vast mountains of rock eternally covered with snow through which the river passed. that the perpendicular and even juting rocks so closely hemned in the river that there was no possibil[it]y of passing along the shore; that the bed of the river was obstructed by sharp pointed rocks and the rapidity of the stream such that the whole surface of the river was beat into perfect foam as far as the eye could reach. that the mountains were also inaccessible to man or horse. he said that this being the state of the country in that direction that himself nor none of his nation had ever been further down the river than these mountains.

I then enquired the state of the country on either side of the river but he could not inform me. . . . I now asked Cameahwait by what rout the Pierced nosed [Nez Percé] indians, who he informed me inhabited this river below the mountains, came over to the Missouri; this he informed me was to the north, but added that the road was a very bad one as he had been informed by them and that they had suffered excessively with hunger on the rout being obliged to subsist for many days on berries alone as there was no game in that part of the mountains which were broken rockey and so thickly covered with timber that they could scarcely pass. however knowing that Indians had passed, and did pass, at this season on that side of this river to the same below the mountains, my rout was instantly settled in my own mind, p[r]ovided the account of this river should prove true on an investigation of it, which I was determined should be made before we would undertake the rout by land in any direction. I felt perfectly satisfyed, that if the Indians could pass these mountains with their women and Children, that we could also pass them; and that if the nations on this river below the mountains were as numerous as they were stated to be that they must have some means of subsistence which it would be equally in our power to procure in the same country. they informed me that there was no buffaloe on the West side of the mountains; that the game consisted of a few Elk deer and Antelopes, and that the natives subsisted on fish and roots principally.

in this manner I spent the day smoking with them and acquiring what information I could with respect to their country. they informed me that they could pass to the Spaniards by the way of the yellowstone river in 10 days. I can discover that these people are by no means friendly to the Spaniards. their complaint is, that the Spaniards will not let them have fire arms and amunition, that they put them off by telling them that if they suffer them to have guns they will kill each other, thus leaving them defenceless and an easy prey to their bloodthirsty neighbours to the East of them, who being in possession of fire arms hunt them up and murder them without rispect to sex or age and plunder them of their horses on all occasions. they told me that to avoid their enemies who were eternally harrassing them that they were obliged to remain in the interior of these mountains at least two thirds of the year where the[y] suffered as we then saw great heardships for the want of food sometimes living for weeks without meat and only a little fish roots and berries. but this added Câmeahwait, with his ferce eyes and lank jaws grown meager for the want of food, would not be the case if we had guns, we could then live in the country of buffaloe and eat as our enimies do and not be compelled to hide ourselves in these mountains and live on roots and berries as the bear do. we do not fear our enimies when placed on an equal footing with them. I told them that the Minnetares Mandans & recares of the Missouri had promised us to desist from making war on them & that we would indevour to find the means of making the Minnetares of fort d[e] Prarie or as they call them Pahkees desist from waging war aginst them also. that after our finally returning to our homes towards the rising sun whitemen would come to them with an abundance of guns and every other article necessary to their defence and comfort, and that they would be enabled to supply themselves with these articles on reasonable terms in exchange for the skins of the beaver Otter and Ermin so abundant in their country. they expressed great pleasure at this information and said they had been long anxious to see the whitemen that traded guns; and that we might rest assured of their friendship and that they would do whatever we wished them.

CALEB BINGHAM

23 | Dialogue between a Schoolmaster
 | and a School Committee

*In the early 1800s, as in the 1980s, commentators observed that the status and
salary of school teachers was low. Public leaders from seventeenth-century Massachusetts leaders to Thomas Jefferson to members of today's presidential com-
missions have emphasized the central role of public education in an open democratic society. At the same time, most people have generally considered teaching
school a labor of love that should carry compensation not quite adequate to support a middle-class family. Teaching school was frequently the temporary voca-
tion of young men. Not until the twentieth century did teaching become a "profession" to which both men and women might equally aspire. As our sense of
the importance of education, particularly its role in our economic competition
with other countries, has grown, the nation's attitudes have changed somewhat.*

*In this self-published piece from 1807, Caleb Bingham, a Connecticut-born
author of textbooks and advocate of free public schools, satirizes American attitudes toward the support of education.*

[N.B. *The Author is happy in believing, that the following Dialogue is
applicable to but few towns and few teachers in this country; but, so long as
there are any remaining to whom it may apply, he thinks a sufficient apology
exists for its publication.*]

SCENE, *a Public House in the Town of* ———.

Enter School-Master, *with a pack on his back.*

Schoolmaster. How fare you, landlord? what have you got that's good
to drink?

Landlord. I have gin, West-India, genuine New-England, whiskey,
and cider brandy.

Schoolm. Make us a stiff mug of sling. Put in a gill and a half of your
New-England; and sweeten it well with lasses.

Land. It shall be done, sir, to your liking.

Schoolm. Do you know of any vacancy in a school in your part of the
country, landlord?

Caleb Bingham, "Dialog Between a School-Master, and School-Committee," In The Columbian
Orator by Caleb Bingham, 7th Troy Edition. (Tory, Printed and Sold by William S. Parker, 1821),
pp. 158–165.

Land. There is a vacancy in our district; and I expect the parson, with our three school-committee men will be at my house directly, to consult upon matters relative to the school.

Schoolm. Well, here's the lad that will serve them as *cheap* as any man in America; and I believe I may venture to say as *well* too; for I profess no small share of skill in that business. I have kept school eleven winters, and have often had matter of fifty scholars at a time. I have teach'd a child its letters in a day, and to read in the Psalter in a fortnight: and I always feel very much ashamed, if I use more than one quire of paper in larnin a boy to write as well as his master. As for government, I'll turn my back to no man. I never flog my scholars; for that monstrous doctrine of whippin children, which has been so long preached and practiced by our rigid and superstitious forefathers. I have long since exploded. I have a rare knack of *flattering* them into their duty. And this according to a celebrated Doctor at Philadelphia,[1] whose works I have heard of, though I never read them, is the grand criterion of school government. It is, landlord, it is the very philosopher's stone. I am told, likewise, that this same great Doctor does not believe that Solomon and others really meant *licken,* in the proper sense of the word, when they talked so much about using the rod, &c. He supposes that they meant confining them in dungeons; starving them for three or four days at a time; and then giving them a portion of tatromattucks, and such kinds of mild punishment. And, zounds, landlord, I believe he's above half right.

Land. (*Giving the cup to the master.*) Master—— What may I call your name, Sir, if I may be so bold?

Schoolm. Ignoramus, at your service, Sir.

Land. Master Ignoramus, I am glad to see you. You are the very man we wish for. Our committee won't hesitate a moment to employ you, when they become acquainted with your talents. Your sentiments on government I know will suit our people to a nicety. Our last master was a tyrant of a fellow, and very extravagant in his price. He grew so important, the latter part of his time, that he had the frontery to demand *ten dollars* a month and his board. And he might truly be said to rule with a rod of iron; for he kept an *ironwood* cudgel in his school, four feet long; and it was enough to chill one's blood to hear the shrieks of the little innocents, which were caused by his barbarity. I have heard my wife say, that Sue Gossip told her, that she has seen the marks of his lashes on the back of her neighbour Rymple's son Darling, for twelve hours after the drubbing. At least, the boy told her with his own mouth, that they *might* be seen, if they would only take the trouble to strip his shirt off. And, besides, Master Ignoramus, he was the most niggardly of all the human race. I don't suppose that my bar-room was one dollar

1. A reference to Dr. Benjamin Rush whose writings on education argued against corporal punishment.

the richer for him, in the course of the whole time which he tarried with us. While the young people of the town were recreating themselves, and taking a social glass, of an evening, at my house, the stupid blockhead was eternally in his chamber, poring over his musty books. But finally he did the job for himself, and I am rejoiced. The wretch had the dacity to box little Sammy Puney's ears at such an intolerable rate, that his parents fear the poor child will be an idiot all the days of his life. And all this, for nothing more, than partly by design, and partly through mere accident, he happened to spit in his master's face. The child being nephew to the 'squire, you may well suppose, that the whole neighbourhood was soon in an uproar. The indignation of the mother, father, aunts, uncles, cousins, and indeed the whole circle of acquaintance, was roused; and the poor fellow was hooted out of town in less than twenty-four hours.

Schoolm. (*Drinking off his liquor.*) This is a rare dose. Believe me, landlord, I have not tasted a drop before, since six o'clock this morning. (*Enter Parson and Commitee Men.*) Your humble sarvant, gentlemen. I understand you are in want of a school-master.

Parson. Yes Sir; that is the occasion of our present meeting. We have been so unfortuate as to lose one good man; and we should be very glad to find another.

1st Commitee Man. Pray don't say *unfortunate,* Parson. I think we may consider ourselves as very *fortunate,* in having rid the town of an extravagant coxcomb, who was draining us of all the money we could earn, to fill his purse, and rig himself out with fine clothes.

2d Com. Ten dollars a month, and board, for a man whose task is so easy, is no small sum.

3d Com. I am bold to affirm, that we can procure a better man for half the money.

Schoolm. That I believe, friend; for, though I esteem myself as good as the best; that is to say, in the common way; yet I never ax'd but five dollars a month in all my life.

Par. For my own part, whatever these gentlemen's opinion may be, I must tell you that I am much less concerned about the wages we are to give, than I am about the character and abilities of the man with whom we intrust the education of our children. I had much rather you had said you had received forty dollars a month, than five.

1st. Com. Dear Sir, you are beside yourself. You will encourage the man to *rise* in his price; whereas I was in hopes he would have *fallen,* at least one dollar.

Par. Before we talk any further about the price, it is necessary that we examine the gentleman according to law, in order to satisfy ourselves of his capability to serve us. Friend, will you be so obliging as to inform us where you received your education, and what your pretensions are, with respect to your profession?

Schoolm. Law, Sir! I never went to college in my life.

Par. I did not ask you whether you had been to college or not. We wish to know what education you have had; and whether your abilities are such, as that you can do yourself honor in taking the charge of a common English school.

Schoolm. Gentlemen, I will give you a short history of my life. From seven, to fifteen years of age, I went to school perhaps as much as one year. In which time, I went through Dilworth's Spelling-Book, the Psalter, the New-Testament: and could read the newspaper without spelling more than half the words. By this time, feeling a little above the common level, I enlisted a soldier in the army, where I continued six years; and made such proficiency in the military art, that I was frequently talked of for a corporal. I had likewise learn'd to write considerably, and to cypher as fur as Division. The multiplication table I had at my tongue's end, and have not forgot it to this day. At length, receiving a severe flogging for nothing at all, I am not ashamed to own that I deserted, and went into one of the back settlements, and offered myself as a teacher. I was immediately employed in that service; and, though I am obliged to say it myself, I do assure you I soon became very famous. Since that time, which is eleven years, I have followed the business constantly; at least, every winter; for in the summer, it is not customary in the towns in general, to continue a man's school. One thing I would not forget to mention; and that is, I have travelled about the country so much, and been in the army so long (which is allowed to be the best school in the world) that I consider myself as being thoroughly acquainted with mankind. You will not be insensible, gentlemen, of what great importance this last acquisition is, to one who has the care of youth.

3d Com. I admire his conversation. I imagine, by this time, you have cyphered *clear through*; have you not, Sir?

Schoolm. Why, as to that, I have gone so fur that I thought I could *see through*. I can tell how many minutes old my great grandfather was when his first son was born; how many barley corns it would take to measure round the world; and how old the world will be at the end of six thousand years from the creation.

1st Com. It is very strange! You must have studied hard, to learn all these things, and that without a master too.

Schoolm. Indeed I have, Sir; and if I had time, I could tell you things stranger still.

Par. Can you tell in what part of the world you were born; whether in the torrid, frigid, or temperate zone?

Schoolm. I was not born in the *zoon*, Sir, nor in any other of the West-India Islands; but I was born in New-England, in the state of New-Jersey, and Commonwealth of the United States of America.

Par. Do you know how many parts of speech there are in the English language?

Schoolm. How many speeches! Why as many as there are "stars in the sky, leaves on the trees, or sands on the sea shore."

1st Com. Please to let me ask him a question, Parson, How many commandaments are there?

Schoolm. Ten, Sir; and I knew them all before I went into the army.

2d Com. Can you tell when the moon changes, by the almanac?

Schoolm. No! but I'll warrant you, I could soon tell by cyphering.

3d Com. How many varses are there in the 119th Psalm?

Schoolm. Ah! excuse me there, if you please, Sir; I never meddle with psalmody, or metaphysics.

Par. Will you tell me, my friend, what is the difference between the circumference and the diameter of the globe?

Schoolm. There you are to hard for me again. I never larn'd the rule of circumstance nor geometry. I'll tell you what, gentlemen, I make no pretensions to minister larnin, lawyer larnin, or doctor larnin; but put me upon your clear schoolmaster larnin, and there I am even with you.

1st Com. I am satisfied with the gentleman. He has missed but one question, and that was such a metatisical one, that it would have puzzled a Jesuit himself to have answered it. Gentlemen, shall the master withdraw a few minutes, for our further consultation?

(Exit Master.)

2d Com. I am much pleased with the stranger. He appears to be a man of wonderful parts; and I shall cheerfully agree to employ him.

3d Com. For my part, I don't think we shall find a *cheaper* master; and I move for engaging him at once.

Par. Gentlemen, how long will you be blind to your interest? I can say with you, that I am perfectly satisfied—that the man is, in his profession, emphatically what he calls himself by name, an *ignoramus*; and totally incapable of instructing our children. You know not who he is, or what he is; whether he be a thief, a liar, or a drunkard. The very terms, on which he offers himself, ought to operate as a sufficient objection against him. I am sensible that my vote will now be of no avail, since you are all agreed. I have been for years striving to procure a man of abilities and morals, suitable for the employment; and such a one I had obtained; but, alas! we were unworthy of him. We aspersed his character; invented a multitude of falsehoods; magnified every trifling error in his conduct; and even converted his virtues into vices. We refused to give him that pecuniary reward which his services demanded; and he knowing his own worth, and our unworthiness, has left us forever.

1st Com. Come, come, Parson, it is easy for salary men to talk of *liberality,* and to vote away money which they never earned; but it won't do. The new master I dare engage, will do as well or better than the old one. Landlord, call him in for his answer.

Par. I protest against your proceedings, and withdraw myself forever from the committee. But I must tell you, your children will reap the bitter consequences of such injudicious measures. It has always been surprising to me, that people in general are more willing to pay their money for any thing else, than for "the one thing needful," that is, for the education of their children. Their tailor must be a workman, their carpenter, a workman, their hairdresser, a workman, their hostler, a workman; but the instructor of their children must—work *cheap!*

(*Exit Parson.*)

Re-enter School-Master.

1st Com. We have agreed to employ you, Sir; and have only to recommend to you, not to follow the steps of your predecessor. This is an "age of reason"; and we do not imagine our children so stupid, as to need the rod to quicken their ideas, or so vicious, as to require a moral lesson from the ferule. Be gentle and accommodating, and you have nothing to fear.

Land. I'll answer for him. He's as generous and merry a lad as I've had in my house this many a day.

24 | Autobiography of a Circuit Rider

Peter Cartwright was a pioneer Methodist evangelist who contributed to the great work of the Methodists in bringing evangelical Protestantism to new settlements in the West. Born in Virginia in 1785 and raised in Kentucky, Cartwright's "circuit" as an itinerant preacher of enthusiastic religion included parts of Kentucky, Tennessee, Indiana, and Ohio. In 1824, because of his hatred of slavery, Cartwright had his circuit transferred to Illinois. Evidently, however, Cartwright was less persuasive as a politician than as a revivalist; he lost an election for the United States House of Representatives. The winner was Abraham Lincoln.

The circuit riders taught a highly emotional form of religion that emphasized personal morality, civic virtue, and the importance of education. Their contribution to the characteristic culture of the American Middle West quickly came to symbolize all of American life. Cartwright's personal experience of conversion and his subsequent career are highly representative. So, too, was his hatred of slavery; antislavery sentiment in the Middle West was carried powerfully by the moral fervor of the revivals.

Cartwright wrote his autobiography in 1857.

CONVERSION

In 1801, when I was in my sixteenth year, my father, my eldest half brother, and myself, attended a wedding about five miles from home, where there was a great deal of drinking and dancing, which was very common at marriages in those days. I drank little or nothing; my delight was in dancing. After a late hour in the night, we mounted our horses and started for home. I was riding my race-horse.

A few minutes after we had put up the horses, and were sitting by the fire, I began to reflect on the manner in which I had spent the day and evening. I felt guilty and condemned. I rose and walked the floor. My mother was in bed. It seemed to me, all of a sudden, my blood

W.P. Strickland (editor), Autobiography of Peter Cartwright, The Backwoods Preacher. *(New York, Phillips and Hunt, 1856), pp. 34–38, 40–46, 48–53.*

rushed to my head, my heart palpitated, in a few minutes I turned blind; an awful impression rested on my mind that death had come and I was unprepared to die. I fell on my knees and began to ask God to have mercy on me.

My mother sprang from her bed, and was soon on her knees by my side, praying for me, and exhorting me to look to Christ for mercy, and then and there I promised the Lord that if he would spare me, I would seek and serve him; and I never fully broke that promise. My mother prayed for me a long time. At length we lay down, but there was little sleep for me. Next morning I rose, feeling wretched beyond expression. I tried to read in the Testament, and retired many times to secret prayer through the day, but found no relief. I gave up my racehorse to my father, and requested him to sell him. I went and brought my pack of cards, and gave them to mother, who threw them into the fire, and they were consumed. I fasted, watched, and prayed, and engaged in regular reading of the Testament. I was so distressed and miserable, that I was incapable of any regular business.

My father was greatly distressed on my account, thinking I must die, and he would lose his only son. He bade me retire altogether from business, and take care of myself.

Soon it was noised abroad that I was distracted, and many of my associates in wickedness came to see me, to try and divert my mind from those gloomy thoughts of my wretchedness; but all in vain. I exhorted them to desist from the course of wickedness which we had been guilty of together. The class-leader and local preacher were sent for. They tried to point me to the bleeding Lamb, they prayed for me most fervently. Still I found no comfort, and although I had never believed in the doctrine of unconditional election and reprobation, I was sorely tempted to believe I was a reprobate, and doomed, and lost eternally, without any chance of salvation.

At length one day I retired to the horse-lot, and was walking and wringing my hands in great anguish, trying to pray, on the borders of utter dispair. It appeared to me that I heard a voice from heaven, saying, "Peter, look at me." A feeling of relief flashed over me as quick as an electric shock. It gave me hopeful feelings, and some encouragement to seek mercy, but still my load of guilt remained. I repaired to the house, and told my mother what had happened to me in the horse-lot. Instantly she seemed to understand it, and told me the Lord had done this to encourage me to hope for mercy, and exhorted me to take encouragement, and seek on, and God would bless me with the pardon of my sins at another time.

Some days after this, I retired to a cave on my father's farm to pray in secret. My soul was in an agony; I wept, I prayed, and said, "Now, Lord, if there is mercy for me, let me find it," and it really seemed to me that I could almost lay hold of the Saviour, and realize a reconciled God. All of a sudden, such a fear of the devil fell upon me that it really appeared to me that he was surely personally there, to seize and drag me down to hell, soul and body, and such a horror fell on me that I sprang to my feet and ran to my mother at the house. My mother told me that this was a device of Satan to prevent me from finding the blessing then. Three months rolled away, and still I did not find the blessing of the pardon of my sins.

This year, 1801, the Western Conference [of preachers] existed, and I think there was but one presiding elder's district in it, called the Kentucky District. William M'Kendree (afterward bishop) was appointed to the Kentucky District. Cumberland Circuit, which, perhaps, was six hundred miles round, and lying partly in Kentucky and partly in Tennessee, was one of the circuits of this district. John Page and Thomas Wilkerson were appointed to this circuit.

In the spring of this year, Mr. M'Grady, a minister of the Presbyterian Church, who had a congregation and meeting-house, as we then called them, about three miles north of my father's house, appointed a sacramental meeting in this congregation, and invited the Methodist preachers to attend with them, and especially John Page, who was a powerful Gospel minister, and was very popular among the Presbyterians. Accordingly he came, and preached with great power and success.

There were no camp-meetings in regular form at this time, but as there was a great waking up among the Churches, from the revival that had broken out at Cane Ridge, before mentioned, many flocked to those sacramental meetings. The church would not hold the tenth part of the congregation. Accordingly, the officers of the Church erected a stand in a contiguous shady grove, and prepared seats for a large congregation.

The people crowded to this meeting from far and near. They came in their large wagons, with victuals mostly prepared. The women slept in the wagons, and the men under them. Many stayed on the ground night and day for a number of nights and days together. Others were provided for among the neighbors around. The power of God was wonderfully displayed; scores of sinners fell under the preaching, like men slain in mighty battle; Christians shouted aloud for joy.

To this meeting I repaired, a guilty, wretched sinner. On the Saturday evening of said meeting, I went, with weeping multitudes, and bowed before the stand, and earnestly prayed for mercy. In the midst of a solemn struggle of soul, an impression was made on my mind, as though a voice said to me, "Thy sins are all forgiven thee." Divine light flashed all round me, unspeakable joy sprung up in my soul. I rose to my feet, opened my eyes, and it really seemed as if I was in heaven; the trees, the leaves on them, and everything seemed, and I really thought were, praising God. My mother raised the shout, my Christian friends crowded around me and joined me in praising God; and though I have been since then, in many instances, unfaithful, yet I have never, for one moment, doubted that the Lord did, then and there, forgive my sins and give me religion.

Our meeting lasted without intermission all night, and it was believed by those who had a very good right to know, that over eighty souls were converted to God during its continuance. I went on my way rejoicing for many days.

/   /   /

To show the ignorance the early methodist preachers had to contend with in the Western wilds, I will relate an incident or two that occurred to Wilson Lee in Kentucky. He was one of the early pioneer Methodist preachers sent to the West. He was a very solemn and grave minister. At one of his appointments, at a private house on a certain day, they had a motherless pet lamb. The boys of the family had mischievously learned this lamb to butt. They would go near it, and make motions with their heads, and the lamb would back and then dart forward at them, and they would jump out of the way, so that the sheep would miss them.

A man came into the congregation who had been drinking and frolicking all the night before. He came in late, and took his seat on the end of a bench nearly in the door, and, having slept none the night before, presently he began to nod; and as he nodded and bent forward, the pet lamb came along by the door, and seeing this man nodding and bending forward, he took it as a banter, and straightway backed and then sprang forward, and gave the sleeper a severe jolt right on the head, and over he tilted him, to the no small amusement of the congregation, who all burst out into laughter; and grave as the preacher, Mr. Lee, was, it so excited his risibilities that he almost lost his balance. But recovering himself a little, he went on in a most solemn and impressive strain. His subject was the words of our Lord: "Except a man deny himself, and take up his cross, he cannot be my disciple." He urged on his congregation, with melting voices and tearful eyes, to take up the cross, no matter what it was, take it up.

There were in the congregation a very wicked Dutchman and his wife, both of whom were profoundly ignorant of the Scriptures and the plan of salvation. His wife was a notorious scold, and so much was she given to this practice, that she made her husband unhappy, and kept him almost always in a perfect fret, so that he led a most miserable and uncomfortable life. It pleased God that day to cause the preaching of Mr. Lee to reach their guilty souls and break up the great deep of their hearts. They wept aloud, seeing their lost condition, and they, then and there, resolved to do better, and from that time forward to take up the cross and bear it, be it what it might.

The congregation were generally deeply affected. Mr. Lee exhorted them and prayed for them as long as he consistently could, and, having another appointment some distance off that evening, he dismissed the congregation, got a little refreshment, saddled his horse, mounted, and started for his evening appointment. After riding some distance, he saw, a little ahead of him, a man trudging along, carrying a woman on his back. This greatly surprised Mr. Lee. He very naturally supposed that the woman was a cripple, or had hurt herself in some way, so that she could not walk. The traveller was a small man, and the woman large and heavy.

Before he overtook them Mr. Lee began to cast about in his mind how he could render them assistance. When he came up to them, lo and behold, who should it be but the Dutchman and his wife that had been so affected under his sermon at meeting. Mr. Lee rode up and spoke to them, and inquired of the man what had happened, or what was the matter, that he was carrying his wife.

The Dutchman turned to Mr. Lee and said, "Be sure you did tell us in your sarmon dat we must take up de cross and follow de Saviour, or dat we could not be saved or go to heaven, and I does desire to go to heaven so much as any pody; and dish vife is so pad, she scold and scold all de time, and dish woman is de createst cross I have in de whole world, and I does take her up and pare her, for I must save my soul."

You may be sure Mr. Lee was posed for once, but after a few moments' reflection he told the Dutchman to put his wife down, and he dismounted from his horse. He directed them to sit down on a log by the road side. He held the reins of his horse's bridle and sat down by them, took out his Bible, read to them several passages of Scripture, and explained and expounded to them the way of the Lord more perfectly. He opened to them the nature of the cross of Christ, what it is, how it is to be taken up, and how they were to bear that cross; and after teaching and advising them some time, he prayed for them by the road side, left them deeply affected, mounted his horse, and rode on to his evening appointment.

Long before Mr. Lee came around his circuit to his next appointment the Dutchman and his scolding wife were both powerfully converted to God, and when he came round he took them into the Church. The Dutchman's wife was cured of her scolding. Of course he got clear of this cross. They lived together long and happily, adorning their profession, and giving ample evidence that religion could cure a scolding wife, and that God could and did convert poor ignorant Dutch people.

This Dutchman often told his experience in love-feasts, with thrilling effect, and hardly ever failed to melt the whole congregation into a flood of tears; and on one particular occasion which is vividly printed on my recollection, I believe the whole congregation in the love-feast, which lasted beyond the time allotted for such meetings, broke out into a loud shout.

Thus Brother Lee was the honored instrument in the hand of God of planting Methodism, amid clouds of ignorance and opposition, among the early settlers of the far West. Brother Lee witnessed a good confession to the end. At an early period of his ministry he fell from the walls of Zion with the trump of God in his hand, and has gone to his reward in heaven. Peace to his memory.

THE GREAT REVIVAL

From 1801 for years a blessed revival of religion spread through almost the entire inhabited parts of the West, Kentucky, Tennessee, the Carolinas, and many other parts, especially through the Cumberland country, which was so called from the Cumberland River, which headed and mouthed in Kentucky, but in its great bend circled south through Tennessee, near Nashville. The Presbyterians and Methodists in a great measure united in this work, met together, prayed together, and preached together.

In this revival originated our camp-meetings, and in both these denominations they were held every year, and, indeed, have been ever since, more or less. They would erect their camps with logs or frame them, and cover them with clapboards or shingles. They would also erect a shed, sufficiently large to protect five thousand people from wind and rain, and cover it with boards or shingles; build a large stand, seat the shed, and here they would collect together from forty to fifty miles around, sometimes further than that. Ten, twenty, and sometimes thirty ministers, of different denominations, would come together and preach night and day, four or five days together; and, indeed, I have known these camp-meetings to last three or four weeks, and great good resulted from them. I have seen more than a hundred sinners fall like dead men under one powerful sermon, and I have seen and heard more than five hundred Christians all shouting aloud the high praises of God at once; and I will venture to assert that many happy thousands were awakened and converted to God at these camp-meetings. Some sinners mocked, some of the old dry professors opposed, some of the old starched Presbyterian preachers preached against these exercises, but still the work went on and spread almost in every direction, gathering additional force, until our country seemed all coming home to God.

/   /   /

[A] new exercise broke out among us, called the *jerks*, which was overwhelming in its effects upon the bodies and minds of the people. No matter whether they were saints or sinners, they would be taken under a warm song or sermon, and seized with a convulsive jerking all over, which they could not by any possibility avoid, and the more they resisted the more they jerked. If they would not strive against it and pray in good earnest, the jerking would usually abate. I have seen more than five hundred persons jerking at one time in my large congregations. Most usually persons taken with the jerks, to obtain relief, as they said, would rise up and dance. Some would run, but could not get away. Some would resist; on such the jerks were generally very severe.

To see those proud young gentlemen and young ladies, dressed in their silks, jewelry, and prunella, from top to toe, take the *jerks* would often excite my risibilities. The first jerk or so, you would see their fine bonnets, caps, and combs fly; and so sudden would be the jerking of the head that their long loose hair would crack almost as loud as a wagoners whip.

At one of my appointments in 1804 there was a very large congregation turned out to hear the Kentucky boy, as they called me. Among the rest there were two very finely-dressed, fashionable young ladies, attended by two brothers with loaded horsewhips. Although the house was large, it was crowded. The two young ladies, coming in late, took their seats near where I stood, and their two brothers stood in the door. I was a little unwell, and I had a phial of peppermint in my pocket. Before I commenced preaching I took out my phial and swallowed a little of the peppermint. While I was preaching, the congregation was melted into tears. The two young gentlemen moved off to the yard fence, and both the young ladies took the jerks, and they were greatly mortified about it. There was a great stir in the congregation. Some wept, some shouted, and before our meeting closed several were converted.

As I dismissed the assembly a man stepped up to me, and warned me to be on my guard, for he had heard the two brothers swear they would horsewhip me when meeting was out, for giving their sisters the jerks. "Well," said I, "I'll see to that."

I went out and said to the young men that I understood they intended to horsewhip me for giving their sisters the jerks. One replied that he did. I undertook to expostulate with him on the absurdity of the charge against me, but he swore I need not deny it; for he had seen me take out a phial, in which I carried some truck that gave his sisters the jerks. As quick as thought it came into my mind how I would get clear of my whipping, and, jerking out the peppermint phial, said I, "Yes; if I gave your sisters the jerks I'll give them to you." In a moment I saw he was scared. I moved toward him, he backed, I advanced, and he wheeled and ran, warning me not to come near him, or he would kill me. It raised the laugh on him, and I escaped my whipping. I had the pleasure, before the year was out, of seeing all four soundly converted to God, and I took them into the Church.

While I am on this subject I will relate a very serious circumstance which I knew to take place with a man who had the jerks at a camp-meeting, on what was called the Ridge, in William Magee's congregation. There was a great work of religion in the encampment. The jerks were very prevalent. There was a company of drunken rowdies who came to interrupt the meeting. These rowdies were headed by a very large drinking man. They came with their bottles of whisky in their pockets. This large man cursed the jerks, and all religion. Shortly afterward he took the jerks, and he started to run, but he jerked so powerfully he could not get away. He halted among some saplings, and, although he was violently agitated, he took out his bottle of whisky, and swore he would drink the damned jerks to death; but he jerked at such a rate he could not get the bottle to his mouth, though he tried hard. At length he fetched a sudden jerk, and the bottle struck a sapling and was broken to pieces, and pilled his whisky on the ground. There was a great crowd gathered round him, and when he lost his whisky he became very much enraged, and cursed and swore very profanely, his jerks still increasing. At length he fetched a very violent jerk, snapped his neck, fell, and soon expired, with his mouth full of cursing and bitterness.

I always looked upon the jerks as a judgment sent from God, first, to bring sinners to repentance; and, secondly to show professors that God could work with or without means, and that he could work over and above means, and do whatsoever seemeth him good, to the glory of his grace and the salvation of the world.

There is no doubt in my mind that, with weak-minded, ignorant, and superstitious persons, there was a great deal of sympathetic feeling with many that claimed to be under the influence of this jerking exercise; and yet, with many, it was perfectly involuntary. It was, on all occasions, my practice to recommend fervent prayer as a remedy, and it almost universally proved an effectual antidote.

There were many other strange and wild exercises into which the subjects of this revival fell; such, for instance, as what was called the running, jumping, barking exercise. The Methodist preachers generally preached against this extravagant wildness. I did it uniformly in my little ministrations, and sometimes gave great offense; but I feared no consequences when I felt my awful responsibilities to God. From these wild exercises, another great evil arose from the heated and wild imaginations of some. They professed to fall into trances and see visions; they would fall at meetings and sometimes at home, and lay apparently powerless and motionless for days, sometimes for a week at a time, without food or drink; and when they came to, they professed to have seen heaven and hell, to have seen God, angels, the devil and the damned; they would prophesy, and, under the pretense of Divine inspiration, predict the time of the end of the world, and the ushering in of the great millennium.

This was the most troublesome delusion of all; it made such an appeal to the ignorance, superstition, and credulity of the people, even saint as well as sinner. I watched this matter with a vigilant eye. If I opposed it, I would have to meet the clamor of the multitude; and if any one opposed it, these very visionists would single him out, and denounce the dreadful judgments of God against him. They would even set the very day that God was to burn the world, . . . They would prophesy, that if any one did oppose them, God would send fire down from heaven and consume him, like the blasphemous Shakers. They would proclaim that they could heal all manner of diseases, and raise the dead, . . . They progessed to have converse with spirits of the dead in heaven and hell, like the modern spirit rappers. Such a state of things I never saw before, and I hope in God I shall never see again.

I pondered well the whole matter in view of my responsibilities, searched the Bible for the true fulfillment of promise and prophecy, prayed to God for light and Divine aid, and proclaimed open war against these delusions. In the midst of them along came the Shakers, and Mr. Rankin, one of the Presbyterian revival preachers, joined them; Mr. G. Wall, a visionary local preacher among the Methodists, joined them; all the country was in commotion.

I made public appointments and drew multitudes together, and openly showed from the Scriptures that these delusions were false. Some of these visionary men and women prophesied that God would kill me. The Shakers soon pretended to seal my damnation. But nothing daunted, for I knew Him in whom I had believed, I threw my appointments in the midst of them, and proclaimed to listening thousands the more sure word of prophecy. This mode of attack threw a damper on these visionary, self-deluded, false prophets, sobred some, reclaimed others, and stayed the fearful tide of delusion that was sweeping over the country.

/   /   /

25 | The War of 1812

Black Hawk (1767–1838), a leader of the powerful Sauk Indians of the old Northwest, was reputed to be a great warrior. His autobiography, dictated in 1833 to Antoine LeClaire, describes his tribe's role in the War of 1812.

One of the causes of the War of 1812 was a conviction among American westerners like Henry Clay and other "warhawks" that the British were inciting the Indians to violence against the Americans. However, it was almost inevitable that the Indians would side with the British. The American settlers were on the scene pressing for their land while the British were thousands of miles away; the Americans were territorial rivals; the British were diplomatic allies and trading partners.

Soon after our return home, news reached us that a war was going to take place between the British and the Americans. Runners continued to arrive from different tribes, all confirming the reports of the expected war. The British agent, Colonel Dixon, was holding talks with and making presents to the different tribes. I had not made up my mind whether to join the British or remain neutral. I had not discovered yet one good trait in the character of the Americans who had come to the country. They made fair promises, but never fulfilled them, while the British made but few, and we could always rely on their word. . . .

Why did the Great Spirit ever send the whites to this land to drive us from our homes and introduce among us poisonous liquors, disease, and death? They should have remained in the land the Great Spirit allotted them. But I will proceed with my story. My memory, however, is not very good since my late visit to the white people. I have still a buzzing noise in my ears from the noise and bustle incident to travel. I may give some parts of my story out of place, but will make my best endeavors to be correct.

Several of our chiefs were called upon to go to Washington to see our great father (President Madison). They started, and during their ab-

Black Hawk's Autobiography, Through the Interpretation of Antoine LeClaire. *Edited by* J.B. Patterson, *with Introduction and Notes by James D. Rishell. (Rock Island, ILL: American Publishing Company, 1912), pp. 32–39.*

sence I went to Peoria, on the Illinois River, to see my old friend
(Thomas Forsythe, the trader) and get his advice. He was a man who
always told us the truth, and knew everything that was going on. When
I arrived at Peoria he had gone to Chicago, and was not at home. I visited the Pottawattomie villages and then returned to Rock River. Soon
after this, our friends returned from their visit to the great father and
reported what had been said and done. The great father told them that
in the event of a war taking place with England, not to interfere on
either side, but to remain neutral. He did not want our help, but wished
us to hunt and supply our families, and remain at peace. He said that
British traders would not be allowed to come on the Mississippi to furnish goods, but that we would be well supplied by an American trader.
Our chiefs then told him that the British traders always gave us credit
in the fall for guns, powder, and goods, to enable us to hunt and clothe
our families. He replied that the trader at Fort Madison would have
plenty of goods, and if we should go there in the autumn, he would
supply us on credit, as the British traders had done. The party gave a
good account of what they had seen and the kind treatment they had
received. This information pleased us all very much. We all agreed to
follow our great father's advice and not interfere in the war. Our women
were much pleased at the good news. Everything went on cheerfully in
our village. We resumed our pastimes of playing ball, horse racing, and
dancing, which had been laid aside when this great war was first talked
about. We had fine crops of corn which were now ripe, and our women
were busily engaged in gathering it and making caches to contain it.

In a short time we were ready to start to Fort Madison to get our
supply of goods, that we might proceed to our hunting grounds. We
passed merrily down the river, all in high spirits. I had determined to
spend the winter at my old favorite hunting grounds on Skunk River. I
left part of my corn and mats at its mouth to take up as we returned,
and many others did the same.

The next morning we arrived at the fort and made our encampment.
Myself and principal men paid a visit to the war chief at the fort. He
received us kindly, and gave us some tobacco, pipes, and provisions.
The trader came in and we all shook hands with him, for on him all our
dependence was placed, to enable us to hunt and thereby support our
families. We waited a long time, expecting the trader would tell us that
he had orders from our great father to supply us with goods, but he
said nothing on the subject. I got up and told him in a short speech
what we had come for, and hoped he had plenty of goods to supply us.
I told him he should be well paid in the spring, and concluded by informing him that we had decided to follow our great father's advice and
not go to war.

He said that he was happy to hear that we had concluded to remain
at peace. He said that he had a large quantity of goods, and that if we
made a good hunt we should be well supplied; but he remarked that he

had no instructions to furnish us anything on credit, nor could he give us any without receiving the pay for them.

We told him what our great father had said to our chiefs at Washington, and contended that he could supply us if he would, believing that our great father always spoke the truth. The war chief said the trader could not furnish us on credit, and that he had received no such instructions from our great father at Washington.

We left the fort dissatisfied and went to camp. What was now to be done, we knew not. We questioned the party that brought us the news from our great father, that we could get credit for our winter supplies at this place. They still told us the same story and insisted on its truth. Few of us slept that night. All was gloom and discontent.

In the morning a canoe was seen descending the river, bearing an express, who brought intelligence that La Gutrie, a British trader, had landed at Rock Island with two boat-loads of goods. He requested us to come up immediately as he had good news for us, and a variety of presents. The express presented us with tobacco, pipes, and wampum. The news ran through our camp like fire through dry grass on the prairie. Our lodges were soon taken down and we all started for Rock Island. Here ended all hopes of our remaining at peace. We had been forced in to war by being deceived.

Our party were not long in getting to Rock Island. When we came in sight and saw tents pitched, we yelled, fired our guns, and beat our drums. Guns at the island were immediately fired, returning our salute, and a British flag hoisted. We landed, were cordially received by La Gutrie, and then smoked the pipe with him, after which he made a speech to us saying that he had been sent by Colonel Dixon. [This Colonel Dixon had long been a British trader among the Indians, and at the beginning of the war of 1812 had given his services to the British.] He gave us a number of handsome presents, among them a large silk flag and a keg of rum. He then told us to retire, take some refreshments and rest ourselves, as he would have more to say to us next day.

We accordingly retired to our lodges, which in the meantime had been put up, and spent the night. The next morning we called upon him and told him we wanted his two boat loads of goods to divide among our people, for which he should be well paid in the spring in furs and peltries. He consented that we should take them and do as we pleased with them. While our people were dividing the goods, he took me aside and informed me that Colonel Dixon was at Green Bay with twelve boats loaded with goods, guns, and ammunition. He wished to raise a party immediately and go to him. He said our friend, the trader at Peoria, was collecting the Pottawattomies, and would be there before us. I communicated this information to my braves, and a party of two hundred warriors were soon collected and ready to depart. . . . We parted and I soon completed my arrangements and started with my party for Green Bay. On our arrival there we found a large encampment;

were well received by Colonel Dixon and the war chiefs who were with him. He gave us plenty of provisions, tobacco, and pipes, saying that he would hold a council with us the next day. In the encampment I found a great number of Kickapoos, Ottawas, and Winnebagoes. I visited all their camps, and found them in high spirits. They had all received new guns, ammunition, and a variety of clothing.

In the evening a messenger came to visit Colonel Dixon. I went to his tent, in which there were two other war chiefs and an interpreter. He received me with a hearty shake of the hand; presented me to the other chiefs, who treated me cordially, expressing themselves as being much pleased to meet me. After I was seated Colonel Dixon said: "General Black Hawk, I sent for you to explain to you what we are going to do and to give you the reasons for our coming here. Our friend, La Gutrie, informs us in the letter you brought from him, of what has taken place. You will now have to hold us fast by the hand. Your English father has found out that the Americans want to take your country from you and has sent me and my braves to drive them back to their own country. He has, likewise, sent a large quantity of arms and ammunition, and we want all your warriors to join us."

He then placed a medal around my neck and gave me a paper, which I lost in the late war, and a silk flag, saying: "You are to command all the braves that will leave here the day after tomorrow, to join our braves at Detroit."

I told him I was very much disappointed, as I wanted to descend the Mississippi and make war on the settlements. He said that he had been ordered to lay in waste the country around St. Louis; but having been a trader on the Mississippi for many years himself, and always having been treated kindly by the people there, he could not send brave men to murder helpless women and innocent children. There were no soldiers there for us to fight, and where he was going to send us, there were a great many of them. If we defeated them, the Mississippi country should be ours. I was much pleased with this speech, as it was spoken by a brave.

I inquired about my old friend (Forsythe), the trader at Peoria, and said that I had expected that he would have been here before we were.

He shook his head and said: "I have sent express after express for him, and offered him great sums of money to come and bring the Pottawattomies and Kickapoos with him. He has refused, saying that the British father has not money enough to induce him to join us. But I have now laid a trap for him. I have sent Gomo and a party of Indians to take him prisoner and bring him here alive. I expect him in a few days."

The next day, arms and ammunition, knives, tomahawks, and clothing were given to my band. We had a great feast in the evening, and the morning following I started with about five hundred braves to join the British army. We passed Chicago and observed that the fort had been evacuated by the Americans, and their soldiers had gone to Fort

Wayne. They were attacked a short distance from the fort and defeated. They had a considerable quantity of powder in the fort at Chicago, which they had promised to the Indians, but the night before they marched away they destroyed it by throwing it into a well. If they had kept their word to the Indians, they doubtless would have gone to Fort Wayne without molestation. On our arrival, I found that the Indians had several prisoners, and I advised them to treat them well.

We continued our march, joining the British below Detroit, soon after which we had a battle. The Americans fought well, and drove us back with considerable loss. I was greatly surprised at this, as I had been told that the Americans would not fight.

Our next movement was against a fortified place. I was stationed with my braves to prevent any person going to or coming from the fort. I found two men taking care of cattle and took them prisoners. I would not kill them, but delivered them to the British war chief. Soon afterwards, several boats came down the river full of American soldiers. They landed on the opposite side, took the British batteries, and pursued the soldiers that had left them. They went too far without knowing the strength of the British and were defeated. I hurried across the river, anxious for an opportunity to show the courage of my braves, but before we reached the scene of battle, all was over.

The British had taken many prisoners and the Indians were killing them. I immediately put a stop to it, as I never thought it brave, but base and cowardly, to kill an unarmed and helpless foe. We remained here some time. I cannot detail what took place, as I was stationed with my braves in the woods. It appeared, however, that the British could not take this fort, for we marched to another some distance off. When we approached it, I found a small stockade, and concluded that there were not many men in it. The British war chief sent a flag of truce. Colonel Dixon carried it, but soon returned, reporting that the young war chief in command would not give up the fort without fighting. Colonel Dixon came to me and said, ''You will see tomorrow how easily we will take that fort.'' I was of the same opinion, but when the morning came, I was disappointed. The British advance—commenced an attack, and fought like braves; but by braves in the fort, were defeated, and a great number killed! The British army were making preparations to retreat. I was now tired of being with them—our success being bad, and having got no plunder, I determined on leaving them and returning to Rock River, to see what had become of my wife and children, as I had not heard from them since I started. That night, I took about twenty of my braves, and left the British camp for home.

26 | The Panic of 1819

For much of its history, the United States lacked an adequate national banking system. In the nineteenth and early twentieth centuries one consequence of that lack was periodic business booms and busts, or "panics." The first such bust, called the Panic of 1819, actually began in 1818 and continued into 1820. In addition to the irresponsible banking practices of the day, a fundamental economic factor underlay the crisis: the European demand for American agricultural products collapsed as Europe recovered from the Napoleonic Wars. In the following letters, James Flint, a Scotsman traveling at the time in the Ohio Valley, describes and discusses the Panic of 1819.

LETTER IX. CINCINNATI, OHIO, 30TH DEC. 1818.

There is here much trouble with paper money. The notes current in one part, are either refused, or taken at a large discount, in another. Banks that were creditable a few days ago, have refused to redeem their paper in specie [coin, or "hard" money], or in notes of the United States' Bank. In Kentucky, there are two branches of the United States' bank; thirteen of the Kentucky bank, and a list of fifty independent banks, some of which are not in operation. In the state of Ohio, there are thirty chartered banks [that is, chartered by the state], and a few others which have not obtained that pernicious distinction. In Tennessee, the number of banks, including branches, is fourteen. The total number of these establishments in the United States, could not, perhaps, be accurately stated on any given day. The enumeration, like the census of population, might be affected by births and deaths. The creation of this vast host of fabricators, and venders of base money, must form a memorable epoch in the history of the country.—These craftsmen have greatly increased the money capital of the nation; and have, in a corresponding degree, enhanced the *nominal* value of property and labour. By lending, and otherwise emitting, their engravings, they have contrived to mort-

Reuben Gold Thwaites (editor), Early Western Travels, 1748–1846. Volume IX, Flint's Letters From America, 1818–1820. (*Cleveland, Arthur H. Clark Company, 1904*), *pp. 132–132, 219–220, 224–229.*

gage and buy much of the property of their neighbours, and to appropriate to themselves the labour of less moneyed citizens. Proceeding in this manner, they cannot retain specie enough to redeem their bills, admitting the gratuitous assumption that they were once possessed of it. They seem to have calculated that the whole of their paper would not return on them in one day. Small quantities, however, of it have, on various occasions, been sufficient to cause them to suspend specie payments. . . .

Of upwards of a hundred banks that lately figured in Indiana, Ohio, Kentucky, and Tennessee, the money of two is now only received in the land-office, in payment for public lands. Many have perished, and the remainder are struggling for existence. Still giving for their *rags* "bills as *good as their own;*" but, except two, none pay in species, or bills of the United States Bank. Discount varies from thirty to one hundred per cent.

The recent history of banking in these western States, is probably unrivalled. Such a system of knavery could only be developed in a country where avarice and credulity are prominent features of character. About four years ago, the passion for acquiring unearned gains rose to a great height; banking institutions were created in abundance. The designing amongst lawyers, doctors, tavern-keepers, farmers, grocers, shoemakers, tailors, &c. entered into the project, and subscribed for stock. Small moieties [payments] must actually have been advanced to defray the expenses of engraving, and other incidents necessary to putting their schemes in operation. To deposit much capital was out of their power; nor was it any part of their plan. Their main object was to extract it from the community. A common provision in charters, stipulated, that the property of each partner was not liable, in security, to a greater amount than the sum he had subscribed. This exempted the banks from the natural inconveniences that might be occasioned by the insolvencies and elopements of members. Money was accumulated in great abundance, as they bought property; lent on security; and became rich. But their credit was of short duration. When it was found, that a few of them could not redeem their bills, the faith of the people was shaken. A run on the paper shops commenced; and a suspension of specie payments soon became general. Had the people been at liberty to recover a composition, as in the bankrupt concerns of Britain, the evil might have, in some measure, been remedied before this time; but chartered privileges granted by legislators concerned in the fraud, prevented legal recourse. . . .

LETTER XVII. JEFFERSONVILLE, (INDIANA,) MAY 4, 1820.

The accounts given in my last letter of the depredations committed by bankers, will make you suppose that affairs are much deranged here.

. . . Who, it may be asked, would give credit to a people whose laws tolerate the violation of contracts? Mutual credit and confidence are almost torn up by the roots. It is said that in China, knaves are openly commended in courts of law for the adroitness of their management. In the interior of the United States, law has removed the necessity of being either acute or honest.

The money in circulation is puzzling to traders, and more particularly to strangers; for besides the multiplicity of banks, and the diversity in supposed value, fluctuations are so frequent, and so great, that no man who holds it in his possession can be safe for a day. The merchant, when asked the price of an article, instead of making a direct answer, usually puts the question, "What sort of money have you got?" Supposing that a number of bills are shown, and one or more are accepted of, it is not till then, that the price of the goods is declared; and an additional price is uniformly laid on, to compensate for the supposed defect in the quality of the money. Trade is stagnated—produce cheap—and merchants find it difficult to lay in assortments of foreign manufactures. I have lately heard, that if a lady purchases a dress in the city of Cincinnati, she has to call at almost all the shops in town, before she can procure trimmings of the suitable colours. . . .

Agriculture languishes—farmers cannot find profit in hiring labourers. The increase of produce in the United States is greater than any increase of consumpt[ion] that may be pointed out elsewhere. To increase the quantity of provisions, then, without enlarging the numbers of those who eat them, will be only diminishing the price farther. . . .

Labourers and mechanics are in want of employment. I think that I have seen upwards of 1500 men in quest of work within eleven months past, and many of these declared, that they had no money. Newspapers and private letters agree in stating, that wages are so low as eighteen and three-fourths cents (about ten-pence) per day, with board, at Philadelphia, and some other places. Great numbers of strangers lately camped in the open field near Baltimore, depending on the contributions of the charitable for subsistence. You have no doubt heard of emigrants returning to Europe without finding the prospect of a livelihood in America. Some who have come out to this part of the country do not succeed well. Labourers' wages are at present a dollar and an eighth part per day. Board costs them two three-fourths or three dollars per week, and washing three-fourths of a dollar for a dozen of pieces. On these terms, it is plain that they cannot live two days by the labour of one, with the other deductions which are to be taken from their wages. Clothing, for example, will cost about three times its price in Britain: and the poor labourer is almost certain of being paid in depreciated money; perhaps from thirty to fifty per cent. under par. I have seen several men turned out of boarding houses, where their money would not be taken. They had no other resource left but to lodge in the woods, without any covering except their clothes. They set fire to a decayed log, spread some boards alongside of it for a bed, laid a block of timber across for a pillow, and pursued their labour by day as usual. A still greater misfortune than being paid with bad money is to be guarded against, namely, that of not being paid at all. Public improvements are frequently executed by subscription, and subscribers do not in every case consider themselves dishonoured by non-payment of the sum they engage for. I could point out an interesting work, where a tenth part of the amount on the subscription book cannot now be realized. The treasurer of a company so circumstanced, has only to tell undertakers or labourers, that he cannot pay them. I have heard of a treasurer who applied the funds entrusted to him to his own use, and who refused to give any satisfaction for his conduct. . . . Employers are also in the habit of deceiving their workmen, by telling them that it is not convenient to pay wages in money, and that they run accounts with the storekeeper, the tailor, and the shoemaker, and that from them they may have all the necessaries they want very cheap. The workman who consents to this mode of payment, procures orders from the employer, on one or more of these citizens, and is charged a higher price for the goods than the employer actually pays for them. This is called *paying in trade.*

You have often heard that extreme poverty does not exist in the United States. For some time after my arrival in the country supposed to be exempt from abject misery, I never heard the term poor, (a word, by the by, not often used,) without imagining that it applied to a class in moderate circumstances, who had it not in their power to live in fine houses, indulge in foreign luxuries, and wear expensive clothing; and on seeing a person whose external appearance would have denoted a beggar in Britain, I concluded that the unfortunate must have been improvident or dissipated, or perhaps possessed of both of these qualities. My conjectures may have on two or three occasions been just, as people of a depressed appearance are very rarely to be seen, but I now see the propriety of divesting myself of such a hasty and ungenerous opinion. Last winter a Cincinnati newspaper advertised a place where old clothes were received for the poor, and another where cast shoes were collected for children who could not, for want of them, attend Sunday schools. The charitable measure of supplying the poor with public meals, has lately been resorted to at Baltimore; but there is reason to believe, that most of the people who are relieved in this way, are Europeans recently come into America. In the western country, poor rates are raised in the form of a county tax. They are, however, so moderate as to be scarcely felt. Contracts for boarding the permanently poor are advertised, and let to the lowest bidder, who has a right to employ the pauper in any light work suited to the age or ability of the object of charity. They are said to be well treated. This sort of public exposure must create a repugnance against becoming a pauper. In the Eastern States, work houses are established. It is to be wished that those who follow this plan will not lose sight of the example of England. The operations of bankers, and the recent decline in trade, have been effective causes of poverty; and it seems probable that the introduction of manufacturing industry, and a reduction of base paper, would soon give effectual relief. . . .

27 | Shooting Pigeons

James Fenimore Cooper (1789–1851), born in upstate New York, was an extremely prolific writer. His most significant works are the Leather-stocking Tales, a series of five novels about life on the American frontier. The series takes its name from its hero, a woodsman who is variously called Natty Bumppo, Deerslayer, Hawkeye, Pathfinder, Leather-stocking, and the "trapper."

This excerpt, set in the 1780s, is taken from Pioneers (1823), the first novel in the series to be published. Here Cooper describes a pigeon hunt. The passage furnishes one of the earliest lessons in environmentalism to be found in American literature. It was remarkable that one of the most popular writers of the era perceived the limits of the seemingly inexhaustible American landscape in an era of reckless exploitation of natural resources.

If the heavens were alive with pigeons, the whole village seemed equally in motion, with men, women, and children. Every species of fire-arms, from the French ducking-gun with a barrel near six feet in length, to the common horseman's pistol, was to be seen in the hands of the men and boys; while bows and arrows, some made of the simple stick of a walnut sapling, and others in a rude imitation of the ancient cross-bows, were carried by many of the latter.

The houses and the signs of life apparent in the village, drove the alarmed birds from the direct line of their flight, toward the mountains, along the sides and near the bases of which they were glancing in dense masses, equally wonderful by the rapidity of their motion, and their incredible numbers.

We have already said, that across the inclined plane which fell from the steep ascent of the mountain to the banks of the Susquehanna, ran the highway, on either side of which a clearing of many acres had been made at a very early day. Over those clearings, and up the eastern mountain, and along the dangerous path that was cut into its side, the different individuals posted themselves, and in a few moments that attack commenced.

Among the sportsmen was the tall, gaunt form of Leather-stocking,

James Fenimore Cooper, The Pioneers, or the Sources of the Susquehanna, *Volume Two. (New York, Charles Wiley, 1823.), pp. 41–50.*

walking over the field, with his rifle hanging on his arm, his dogs at his heels; the latter now scenting the dead or wounded birds, that were beginning to tumble from the flocks, and then crouching under the legs of their master, as if they participated in his feelings at this wasteful and unsportsmanlike execution.

The reports of the fire-arms became rapid, whole volleys rising from the plain, as flocks of more than ordinary numbers darted over the opening, shadowing the field like a cloud; and then the light smoke of a single piece would issue from among the leafless bushes on the mountain, as death was hurled on the retreat of the affrighted birds, who were rising from a volley, in a vain effort to escape. Arrows, and missiles of every kind, were in the midst of the flocks; and so numerous were the birds, and so low did they take their flight, that even long poles, in the hands of those on the sides of the mountain, were used to strike them to the earth.

During all this time, Mr. Jones, who disdained the humble and ordinary means of destruction used by his companions, was busily occupied, aided by Benjamin, in making arrangements for an assault of more than ordinarily fatal character. Among the relics of the old military excursions, that occasionally are discoverd throughout the different districts of the western part of New-York, there had been found in Templeton, at its settlement, a small swivel, which would carry a ball of a pound weight. It was thought to have been deserted by a war-party of the whites, in one of their inroads into the Indian settlements, when, perhaps, convenience or their necessity induced them to leave such an incumbrance behind them in the woods. This miniature cannon had been released from the rust, and being mounted on little wheels, was now in a state for actual service. For several years it was the sole organ for extraordinary rejoicings used in those mountains. On the mornings of the Fourths of July, it would be heard ringing among the hills; and even Captain Hollister, who was the highest authority in that part of the country on all such occasions, affirmed that, considering its dimensions, it was no despicable gun for a salute. It was somewhat the worse for the service it had performed, it is true, there being but a trifling difference in size between the touch-hole and the muzzle. Still, the grand conceptions of Richard had suggested the importance of such an instrument in hurling death at his nimble enemies. The swivel was dragged by a horse into a part of the open space that the Sheriff thought most eligible for planting a battery of the kind, and Mr. Pump proceeded to load it. Several handfuls of duck-shot were placed on top of the powder, and the major-domo announced that his piece was ready for service.

The sight of such an implement collected all the idle spectators to the spot, who, being mostly boys, filled the air with cries of exultation and delight. The gun was pointed high, and Richard, holding a coal of fire in a pair of tongs, patiently took his seat on a stump, awaiting the appearance of a flock worthy of his notice.

So prodigious was the number of the birds, that the scattering fire of the guns, with the hurling of missiles, and the cries of the boys, had no other effect than to break off small flocks from the immense masses that continued to dart along the valley, as if the whole of the feathered tribe were pouring through that one pass. None pretended to collect the game, which lay scattered over the fields in such profusion as to cover the very ground with the fluttering victims.

Leather-stocking was a silent, but uneasy spectator of all these proceedings, but was able to keep his sentiments to himself until he saw the introduction of the swivel into the sports.

"This comes of settling a country!" he said—"here have I known the pigeons to fly for forty long years, and, till you made your clearings, there was nobody to skear or to hurt them. I loved to see them come into the woods, for they were company to a body; hurting nothing; being, as it was, as harmless as a garter-snake. But now it gives me sore thoughts when I hear the frighty things whizzing through the air, for I know it's only a motion to bring out all the brats in the village. Well! the Lord won't see the waste of his creatures for nothing, and right will be done to the pigeons, as well as others, by-and-by.—There's Mr. Oliver, as bad as the rest of them, firing into the flocks, as if he was shooting down nothing but Mingo warriors."

Among the sportsmen was Billy Kirby, who, armed with an old musket, was loading and without even looking into the air, was firing and shouting as his victims fell even on his own person. He heard the speech of Natty, and took upon himself to reply—

"What! old Leather-stocking," he cried, "grumbling at the loss of a few pigeons! If you had to sow your wheat twice, and three times, as I have done, you wouldn't be so massyfully feeling'd toward the devils. "Hurrah, boys! scatter the feathers. This is better than shooting at a turkey's head and neck, old fellow."

"It's better for you, maybe, Billy Kirby," replied the indignant old hunter, "and all them that don't know how to put a ball down a rifle barrel, or how to bring it up again with a true aim; but it's wicked to be shooting into flocks in this wasty manner; and none do it, who know how to knock over a single bird. If a body has a craving for pigeon's flesh, why, it's made the same as all other creatures, for man's eating; but not to kill twenty and eat one. When I want such a thing I go into the woods till I find one to my liking, and then I shoot him off the branches, without touching the feather of another, though there might be a hundred on the same tree. You couldn't do such a thing, Billy Kirby—you couldn't do it, if you tried."

/   /   /

The fire from the distant part of the field had driven a single pigeon below the flock to which it belonged, and, frightened with the constant reports of the muskets, it was approaching the spot where the disputants stood, darting first from one side and then to the other, cutting the air with the swiftness of lightning, and making a noise with its wings not unlike the rushing of a bullet. Unfortunately for the wood-chopper, notwithstanding his vaunt, he did not see this bird until it was too late to fire as it approached, and he pulled his trigger at the unlucky moment when it was darting immediately over his head. The bird continued its course with the usual velocity.

Natty [Leather-stocking] lowered the rifle from his arm when the challenge was made, and waiting a moment, until the terrified victim had got in a line with his eye, and had dropped near the bank of the lake, he raised it again with uncommon rapidity, and fired. It might have been chance, or it might have been skill, that produced the result; it was probably a union of both; but the pigeon whirled over in the air, and fell into the lake, with a broken wing. At the sound of his rifle, both his dogs started from his feet, and in a few minutes the "slut" brought out the bird, still alive.

The wonderful exploit of Leather-stocking was noised through the field with great rapidity, and the sportsmen gathered in, to learn the truth of the report.

"What!" said young Edwards, "have you really killed a pigeon on the wing, Natty, with a single ball?"

"Haven't I killed loons before now, lad, that dive at the flash?" returned the hunter. "It's much better to kill only such as you want, without wasting your powder and lead, than to be firing into God's creatures in this wicked manner. But I came out for a bird, and you know the reason why I like small game, Mr. Oliver, and now I have got one I will go home, for I don't relish to see these wasty ways that you are all practysing as if the least thing wasn't made for use, and not to destroy."

"Thou sayest well, Leather-stocking," cried Marmaduke, "and I begin to think it time to put an end to this work of destruction."

"Put an ind, Judge, to your clearings. An't the woods his work as well as the pigeons? Use, but don't waste. Wasn't the woods made for the beasts and birds to harbor in? and when man wanted their flesh, their skins, or their feathers, there's the place to seek them. But I'll go to the hut with my own game, for I wouldn't touch one of the harmless things that cover the ground here, looking up with their eyes on me, as if they only wanted tongues to say their thoughts."

With this sentiment in his mouth, Leather-stocking threw his rifle over his arm, and followed by his dogs, stepped across the clearing with great caution, taking care not to tread on one of the wounded birds in his path. He soon entered the bushes on the margin of the lake, and was hid from view.

Whatever impression the morality of Natty made on the Judge, it was utterly lost on Richard. He availed himself of the gathering of the sportsmen, to lay a plan for one "fell swoop" of destruction. The musket men were drawn up in battle array, in a line extending on each side of his artillery, with orders to await the signal of firing from himself.

"Stand by, my lads," said Benjamin, who acted as an aide-de-camp on this occasion; "stand by, my hearties, and when Squite Dickens heaves out the signal to begin firing, d'ye see, you may open upon them in a broadside. Take care and fire low, boys, and you'll be sure to hull the flock."

"Fire low!" shouted Kirby—"hear the old fool! If we fire low, we may hit the stumps, but not ruffle a pigeon."

"How should you know, you lubber?" cried Benjamin, with a very unbecoming heat for an officer on the eve of battle—"how should you know, you grampus? Haven't I sailed aboard of the Boadishy for five years? and wasn't it a standing order to fire low, and to hull your enemy? Keep silence at your guns, boys, and mind the order that is passed."

The loud laughs of the musket men were silenced by the more authoritative voice of Richard, who called for attention and obedience to his signals.

Some millions of pigeons were supposed to have already passed, that morning, over the valley of Templeton; but nothing like the flock that was now approaching had been seen before. It extended from mountain to mountain in one solid blue mass, and the eye looked in vain, over the southern hills, to find its termination. The front of this living column was distinctly marked by a line but very slightly indented, so regular and even was the flight. Even Marmaduke forgot the morality of Leather-stocking as it approached, and, in common with the rest, brought his musket to a poise.

"Fire!" cried the Sheriff, clapping a coal to the priming of the cannon. As half of Benjamin's charge escaped through the touch-hole, the whole volley of the musketry preceded the report of the swivel. On receiving this united discharge of small-arms, the front of the flock darted upward, while, at the same instant, myriads of those in the rear rushed with amazing rapidity into their places, so that when the column of white smoke gushed from the mouth of the little cannon, an accumulated mass of objects was gliding over its point of direction. The roar of the gun echoed along the mountains, and died away to the north, like distant thunder, while the whole flock of alarmed birds seemed, for a moment, thrown into one disorderly and agitated mass. The air was filled with their irregular flight, layer rising about layer, far above the tops of the highest pines, none daring to advance beyond the dangerous pass; when, suddenly, some of the leaders of the feathered tribe shot across the valley, taking their flight directly over the village, and hundreds of thousands in their rear followed the example, deserting the eastern side of the plain to their persecutors and the slain.

"Victory!" shouted Richard, "victory! we have driven the enemy from the field."

"No so, Dickon," said Marmaduke: "the field is coverd with them; and, like the Leather-stocking, I see nothing but eyes, in every direction, as the innocent sufferers turn their heads in terror. Full one-half of those that have fallen are yet alive; and I think it is time to end the sport, if sport it be."

"Sport!" cried the Sheriff; "it is princely sport! There are some thousands of the blue-coated boys on the ground, so that every old woman in the village may have a pot-pie for the asking."

"Well, we have happily frightened the birds from this side of the valley," said Marmaduke, "and the carnage must of necessity end, for the present.—Boys, I will give you six-pence a hundred for the pigeons' heads only; so go to work and bring them into the village."

This expedient produced the desired effect, for every urchin on the ground went industriously to work to wring the necks of the wounded birds. Judge Temple retired toward his dwelling with that kind of feeling that many a man has experienced before him, who discovers, after the excitement of the moment has passed, that he has purchased pleasure at the price of misery to others. Horses were loaded with the dead; and, after this first burst of sporting, the shooting of pigeons became a business, with a few idlers, for the remainder of the season. Richard, however, boasted for many a year, of his shot with the "cricket;" and Benjamin gravely asserted, that he thought they killed nearly as many pigeons on that day, as there were Frenchmen destroyed on the memorable occasion [in 1782] of [British Admiral] Rodney's victory.

28 | The Lowell Textile Workers

As a young girl in the 1830s, Harriet Hanson Robinson worked in the new textile mills in Lowell, Massachusetts. More than sixty years later, in 1898, Robinson published a book, Loom and Spindle, *which tells of her experiences.*

When the mills first opened, the owners adopted a paternal attitude to encourage respectable girls to work in the factories. Reasonable wages and working conditions combined with carefully chaperoned boarding houses and the encouragement of literary journals to create a genteel atmosphere. But as Robinson makes clear, within a few years the pressure of business competition led to changes. Deeply troubled by the harsh conditions under which many young women labored, Robinson herself later became active in the women's suffrage movement. Robinson lived into the early twentieth century.

CHAPTER II. CHILD-LIFE IN THE LOWELL COTTON-MILLS

In 1831, under the shadow of a great sorrow, which had made her four children fatherless,—the oldest but seven years of age,—my mother was left to struggle alone; and, although she tried hard to earn bread enough to fill our hungry mouths, she could not do it, even with the help of kind friends. And so it happened that one of her more wealthy neighbors, who had looked with longing eyes on the one little daughter of the family, offered to adopt me. But my mother, who had had a hard experience in her youth in living amongst strangers, said, "No; while I have one meal of victuals a day, I will not part with my children." I always remembered this speech because of the word "victuals," and I wondered for a long time what this good old Bible word meant.

/   /   /

That was a hard, cold winter; and for warmth's sake my mother and her four children all slept in one bed, two at the foot and three at the head,—but her richer neighbor could not get the little daughter; and, contrary to all the modern notions about hygiene, we were a healthful and a robust brood.

Harriet Hanson Robinson, Loom and Spindle or Life Among the Early Mill Girls. *(New York, T.Y. Crowell, 1898), pp. 16–22, 37–43, 51–53. From a 1976 reprint by Press Pacifica.*

/   /   /

Shortly after this my mother's widowed sister, Mrs. Angeline Cudworth, who kept a factory boarding-house in Lowell, advised her to come to that city.

/   /   /

I had been to school constantly until I was about ten years of age, when my mother, feeling obliged to have help in her work besides what I could give, and also needing the money which I could earn, allowed me, at my urgent request (for I wanted to earn *money* like the other little girls), to go to work in the mill. I worked first in the spinning-room as a "doffer." The doffers were the very youngest girls, whose work was to doff, or take off, the full bobbins, and replace them with the empty ones.

/   /   /

Some of us learned to embroider in crewels, and I still have a lamb worked on cloth, a relic of those early days, when I was first taught to improve my time in the good old New England fashion. When not doffing, we were often allowed to go home, for a time, and thus we were able to help our mothers in their housework. We were paid two dollars a week; and how proud I was when my turn came to stand up on the bobbin-box, and write my name in the paymaster's book, and how indignant I was when he asked me if I could "write." "Of course I can," said I, and he smiled as he looked down on me.

The working-hours of all the girls extended from five o'clock in the morning until seven in the evening, with one-half hour for breakfast and for dinner. Even the doffers were forced to be on duty nearly fourteen hours a day, and this was the greatest hardship in the lives of these children. For it was not until 1842 that the hours of labor for children under twelve years of age were limited to ten per day; but the "ten-hour law" itself was not passed until long after some of these little doffers were old enough to appear before the legislative committee on the subject, and plead, by their presence, for a reduction of the hours of labor.

I do not recall any particular hardship connected with this life, except getting up so early in the morning, and to this habit, I never was, and never shall be, reconciled, for it has taken nearly a lifetime for me to make up the sleep lost at that early age. But in every other respect it was a pleasant life. We were not hurried any more than was for our good, and no more work was required of us than we were able easily to do.

Most of us children lived at home, and we were well fed, drinking both tea and coffee, and eating substantial meals (besides luncheons) three times a day. We had very happy hours with the older girls, many of whom treated us like babies, or talked in a motherly way, and so had a good influence over us. And in the long winter evenings, when we could not run home between the doffings, we gathered in groups and told each other stories, and sung the old-time songs our mothers had sung, such as "Barbara Allen," "Lord Lovell," "Captain Kid," "Hull's Victory," and sometimes a hymn.

Among the ghost stories I remember some that would delight the hearts of the "Society for Psychical Research." The more imaginative ones told of what they had read in fairy books, or related tales of old castles and distressed maidens; and the scene of their adventures was sometimes laid among the foundation stones of the new mill, just building.

And we told each other of our little hopes and desires, and what we meant to do when we grew up. For we had our aspirations; and one of us, who danced the "shawl dance," as she called it, in the spinning-room alley, for the amusement of her admiring companions, discussed seriously with another little girl the scheme of their running away to-gether, and joining the circus.

/   /   /

I cannot tell how it happened that some of us knew about the En-glish factory children, who, it was said, were treated so badly, and were even whipped by their cruel overseers. But we did know of it, and used to sing, to a doleful little tune, some verses called, "The Factory Girl's Last Day." I do not remember it well enough to quote it as written, but have refreshed my memory by reading it lately in Robert Dale Owen's writings:—

"The Factory Girl's Last Day."

"'Twas on a winter morning,
    The weather wet and wild,
Two hours before the dawning
    The father roused his child,
Her daily morsel bringing,
    The darksome room he paced,
And cried, 'The bell is ringing—
    My hapless darling, haste!'

The overlooker met her
    As to her frame she crept;
And with his thong he beat her,
    And cursed her when she wept.

> It seemed as she grew weaker,
> The threads the oftener broke,
> The rapid wheels ran quicker,
> And heavier fell the stroke.''

The song goes on to tell the sad story of her death while her ''pitying comrades'' were carrying her home to die, and ends:—

> ''That night a chariot passed her,
> While on the ground she lay;
> The daughters of her master,
> An evening visit pay.
> Their tender hearts were sighing,
> As negroes' wrongs were told,
> While the white slave was dying
> Who gained her father's gold.''

In contrast with this sad picture, we thought of ourselves as well off, in our cosey corner of the mill, enjoying ourselves in our own way, with our good mothers and our warm suppers awaiting us when the going-out bell should ring.

/   /   /

CHAPTER IV. THE CHARACTERISTICS OF THE EARLY FACTORY GIRLS.

When I look back into the factory life of fifty or sixty years ago, I do not see what is called ''a class'' of young men and women going to and from their daily work, like so many ants that cannot be distinguished one from another; I see them as individuals, with personalities of their own. This one has about her the atmosphere of her early home. That one is impelled by a strong and noble purpose. The other,—what she is, has been an influence for good to me and to all womankind.

Yet they were a class of factory operatives, and were spoken of (as the same class is spoken of now) as a set of persons who earned their daily bread, whose condition was fixed, and who must continue to spin and to weave to the end of their natural existence. Nothing but this was expected of them, and they were not supposed to be capable of social or mental improvement. That they could be educated and developed into something more than mere work-people, was an idea that had not yet entered the public mind. So little does one class of persons really know about the thoughts and aspirations of another! It was the good fortune of these early mill-girls to teach the people of that time that this sort of labor is not degrading; that the operative is not only ''capable of virtue,'' but also capable of self-cultivation.

At the time the Lowell cotton-mills were started, the factory girl was the lowest among women. In England, and in France particularly, great injustice had been done to her real character; she was represented as subjected to influences that could not fail to destroy her purity and self-respect. In the eyes of her overseer she was but a brute, a slave, to be beaten, pinched, and pushed about. It was to overcome this prejudice that such high wages had been offered to women that they might be induced to become mill-girls, in spite of the opprobrium that still clung to this "degrading occupation." At first only a few came; for, though tempted by the high wages to be regularly paid in "cash," there were many who still preferred to go on working at some more *genteel* employment at seventy-five cents a week and their board.

But in a short time the prejudice against factory labor wore away, and the Lowell mills became filled with blooming and energetic New England women.

/   /   /

In 1831 Lowell was little more than a factory village. Several corporations were started, and the cotton-mills belonging to them were building. Help was in great demand; and stories were told all over the country of the new factory town, and the high wages that were offered to all classes of work-people,—stories that reached the ears of mechanics' and farmers' sons, and gave new life to lonely and dependent women in distant towns and farmhouses. Into this Yankee El Dorado, these needy people began to pour by the various modes of travel known to those slow old days. The stage-coach and the canalboat came every day, always filled with new recruits for this army of useful people. The mechanic and machinist came, each with his home-made chest of tools, and often-times his wife and little ones. The widow came with her little flock and her scanty housekeeping goods to open a boarding-house or variety store, and so provided a home for her fatherless children. Many farmers' daughters came to earn money to complete their wedding outfit, or buy the bride's share of housekeeping articles.

Women with past histories came, to hide their griefs and their identity, and to earn an honest living in the "sweat of their brow." Single young men came, full of hope and life, to get money for an education, or to lift the mortgage from the home-farm. Troops of young girls came by stages and baggage-wagons, men often being employed to go to other States and to Canada, to collect them at so much a head, and deliver them at the factories.

/   /   /

[The] country girls had queer names, which added to the singularity of their appearance. Samantha, Triphena, Plumy, Kezia, Aseneth, Elgardy, Leafy, Ruhamah, Lovey, Almaretta, Sarepta, and Florilla were among them.

Their dialect was also very peculiar. On the broken English and Scotch of their ancestors was ingrafted the nasal Yankee twang; so that many of them, when they had just come *daown*, spoke a language almost unintelligible. But the severe discipline and ridicule which met them was as good as a school education, and they were soon taught the "city way of speaking."

Their dress was also peculiar, and was of the plainest of homespun, cut in such an old-fashioned style that each young girl looked as if she had borrowed her grandmother's gown. Their only head-covering was a shawl, which was pinned under the chin; but after the first payday, a "shaker" (or "scooter") sunbonnet usually replaced this primitive head-gear of their rural life.

But the early factory girls were not all country girls. There were others also, who had been taught that "work is no disgrace." There were some who came to Lowell solely on account of the social or literary advantages to be found there. They lived in secluded parts of New England, where books were scarce, and there was no cultivated society. They had comfortable homes, and did not perhaps need the *money* they would earn; but they longed to see this new "City of Spindles," . . .

The laws relating to women were such, that a husband could claim his wife wherever he found her, and also the children she was trying to shield from his influence; and I have seen more than one poor woman skulk behind her loom or her frame when visitors were approaching the end of the aisle where she worked. Some of these were known under assumed names, to prevent their husbands from trusteeing their wages. It was a very common thing for a male person of a certain kind to do this, thus depriving his wife of *all* her wages, perhaps, month after month. The wages of minor children could be trusteed, unless the children (being fourteen years of age) were given their time. Women's wages were also trusteed for the debts of their husbands, and children's for the debts of their parents.

/   /   /

It must be remembered that at this date woman had no property rights. A widow could be left without her share of her husband's (or the family) property, a legal "incumbrance" to his estate. A father could make his will without reference to his daughter's share of the inheritance. He usually left her a home on the farm as long as she remained single. A woman was not supposed to be capable of spending her own or of using other people's money. In Massachusetts, before 1840, a woman could not legally be treasurer of her own sewing-society, unless some man were responsible for her.

The law took no cognizance of woman as a money-spender. She

was a ward, an appendage, a relict. Thus it happened, that if a woman did not choose to marry, or, when left a widow, to re-marry, she had no choice but to enter one of the few employments open to her, or to become a burden on the charity of some relative.

In almost every New England home could be found one or more of these women, sometimes welcome, more often unwelcome, and leading joyless, and in many instances unsatisfactory, lives. The cotton-factory was a great opening to these lonely and dependent women. From a condition approaching pauperism they were at once placed above want; they could earn money, and spend it as they pleased; and could gratify their tastes and desires without restraint, and without rendering an account to anybody . . .

Among the older women who sought this new employment were very many lonely and dependent ones, such as used to be mentioned in old wills as "incumbrances" and "relicts," and to whom a chance of earning money was indeed a new revelation. How well I remember some of these solitary ones! As a child of eleven years, I often made fun of them—for children do not see the pathetic side of human life—and imitated their limp carriage and inelastic gait. I can see them now, even after sixty years, just as they looked,—depressed, modest, mincing, hardly daring to look one in the face, so shy and sylvan had been their lives. But after the first pay-day came, and they felt the jingle of silver in their pockets, and had begun to feel its mercurial influence, their bowed heads were lifted, their necks seemed braced with steel, they looked you in the face, sang blithely among their looms or frames, and walked with elastic step to and from their work. And when Sunday came, homespun was no longer their only wear; and how sedately gay in their new attire they walked to church, and how proudly they dropped their silver fourpences into the contribution-box! It seemed as if a great hope impelled them,—the harbinger of the new era that was about to dawn for them and for all women-kind.

/   /   /

CHAPTER V. CHARACTERISTICS (CONTINUED).

One of the first strikes of cotton-factory operatives that ever took place in this country was that in Lowell, in October, 1836. When it was announced that the wages were to be cut down, great indignation was felt, and it was decided to strike, *en masse*. This was done. The mills were shut down, and the girls went in procession from their several corporations to the "grove" on Chapel Hill, and listened to "incendiary" speeches from early labor reformers.

One of the girls stood on a pump, and gave vent to the feelings of her companions in a neat speech, declaring that it was their duty to resist all attempts at cutting down the wages. This was the first time a woman had spoken in public in Lowell, and the event caused surprise and consternation among her audience.

Cutting down the wages was not their only grievance, nor the only cause of this strike. Hitherto the corporations had paid twenty-five cents a week towards the board of each operative, and now it was their purpose to have the girls pay the sum; and this, in addition to the cut in wages, would make a difference of at least one dollar a week. It was estimated that as many as twelve or fifteen hundred girls turned out, and walked in procession through the streets. They had neither flags nor music, but sang songs, a favorite (but rather inappropriate) one being a parody on "I won't be a nun."

> "Oh! isn't it a pity, such a pretty girl as I—
> Should be sent to the factory to pine away and die?
> Oh! I cannot be a slave,
> I will not be a slave,
> For I'm so fond of liberty
> That I cannot be a slave."

My own recollection of this first strike (or "turn out" as it was called) is very vivid. I worked in a lower room, where I had heard the proposed strike fully, if not vehemently, discussed; I had been an ardent listener to what was said against this attempt at "oppression" on the part of the corporation, and naturally I took sides with the strikers. When the day came on which the girls were to turn out, those in the upper rooms started first, and so many of them left that our mill was at once shut down. Then, when the girls in my room stood irresolute, uncertain what to do, asking each other, "Would you?" or "Shall we turn out?" and not one of them having the courage to lead off, I, who began to think they would not go out, after all their talk, became impatient, and started on ahead, saying, with childish bravado, "I don't care what you do, *I* am going to turn out, whether any one else does or not;" and I marched out, and was followed by the others.[1]

As I looked back at the long line that followed me, I was more proud than I have ever been since at any success I may have achieved, and more proud than I shall ever be again until my own beloved State gives to its women citizens the right of suffrage.

The agent of the corporation where I then worked took some small revenges on the supposed ringleaders; on the principle of sending the weaker to the wall, my mother was turned away from her boarding-house, that functionary saying, "Mrs. Hanson, you could not prevent the older girls from turning out, but your daughter is a child, and *her* you could control."

---

1. I was then eleven years and eight months old. H.H.R.

It is hardly necessary to say that so far as results were concerned this strike did no good. The dissatisfaction of the operatives subsided, or burned itself out, and though the authorities did not accede to their demands, the majority returned to their work, and the corporation went on cutting down the wages.

And after a time, as the wages became more and more reduced, the best portion of the girls left and went to their homes, or to the other employments that were fast opening to women, until there were very few of the old guard left; and thus the *status* of the factory population of New England gradually became what we know it to be to-day.

/   /   /

29 | *A Journey by Covered Wagon*

*In the spring of 1847 Jane Voorhees Lewis was twenty-three years old and re-
cently married when she, her husband, and her family moved from Hopewell,
New Jersey, to White Hall, Illinois, lured by the favorable accounts of some
former neighbors. Jane kept this simple journal of the journey, presumably to
send to a friend back in New Jersey. The Voorhees completed their trip of about
a thousand miles in forty-four days. Jane's journal offers a representative account of the experiences of nineteenth-century pioneering families.*

April 29th 1847 we started and went by Trenton there crossed the
Delaware took dinner on the Pensylvania shore then went 9 miles to a
beautiful village called Milford where we staid all night   we staid under
a shed   we all slept in the wagons and did not feel afraid   April 30th
started this morning before sunrise and come 3 miles when we stopt
and took breakfast   we have a good road and passed the finest farms
and buildings I ever saw   arived in Philadelphia at 3 oclock and came 4
miles this side and stopped for the night in a woods   the wind blows
hard and it is not very pleasant as the people are passing continualy   I
do not feel like sleeping so I sit writing   all the rest have gone to bed
and I sit on the bed with my paper on the pillow and the candle hangs
by a wire from the hoops   May 1st we got our breakfast by sunrise and
started   we have come 27 miles today   the roads are fine   we keep off
the pike to save the toll   the roads are very hilly   every thing looks a
month earlier than in Jersey   the grain looks fine and the blossoms is
all out . . . I am writing in the wagon by candle light   David and Uriah
have gone to a village about a mile back to look for old tag   he staid
behind   May 2nd   they come back last night without hearing of the dog
but just after we got up he came to us   we heard they had locked him
up and he broke out   it commenced raining about daylight and rained
all day sometimes very fast   we have tried to travel but had to put up
often on account of the rain our covers do not leak a bit   I have not been

"The Journal of Jane Vorhees Lewis," *In* Proceedings of the New Jersey Historical Society.
*(April 1947) Vol. 65: 83–91. Reprinted by Courtesy of the New Jersey Historical Society, Newark,
N.J.*

in a house since we started until today we went in a tavern awhile
Mother cant stand the cold but I can stand cold better than heat the
stove made me sick took breakfast in a blacksmith shop this morning
May 3rd Slept in a tavern last night and took breakfast there it was a
verry nice place we have come 20 miles today through fine country
they build very fine barns the buildings are all stone or brick and fence
7 or 8 rails high I could content myself here if we owned one of those
farms May 4th We have a very good place to stay tonight and clever
people to deal with we have found clever people yet all along they
look as if they are rich here they are many of them dutch [German] and
we can hardly understand them . . . the susquehana river goes through
here this river is the largest I ever saw it has a courious bridge and
heavy toll our toll was I dol 25 cts for both wagons . . . we have come
135 miles and are not sorry we started we all enjoy good health I am
tired at night and sleep sound Mother says she is not as tired as she
was before she started but she sleeps better we all have good appetites
I eat more in one meal than I did in two May 5th Come 25 miles today it is unpleasant traveling . . . we begin to have bad roads and the
water poor the water is all hard and Mother and my hands are almost
black our horses stand the journey well May 6th We have crossed
some large hills today we crossed south mountain the road is cut
along the side of it and looks dangerous saw some beautiful flowers
some trees of wild flowers look like peach blossons only prettier I gathered some we keep off the pike all we can the toll is high and the
road is laid with small stones and it does not ride very good in these
wagons it is a continual jar we cannot walk much the horses walk so
fast we cannot keep up to them Mother and me tried to walk today
crossing these mountains for we was afraid to ride it made my head
turn to look down but the sun shone so hot and could get no air we had
to ride May 7th We got over the mountains last night and put up
in a wood Mother wrote a letter to Jersey and put it in the ofice at
Hagerstown it looks better around this town we get on the national
road here the road is good the toll is high we have stopped for the
night along Cumberland mountain it is lonesome here among the
pines and the owls screaming continually May 8th Come through a
poor mountainous country nothing but log houses and the people look
rough land poor it is difficult to get food for our horses our provisions
is getting scarse and have a great trouble to get more here we came
acrost a family going to Ohio they had two wagons and 16 people children and all we soon left them for we did not care about their company May 10th I did not write yesterday I was taken in the night
sick at my stomach with head ache and tooth ache and sick all day yesterday i was discouraged for the wagon jolted so I could not lay and I
was not able to sit up but is am most well again today the water does
not agree with father and me the rest do not complain of it we have
been 3 or 4 days crossing mountains some higher than I have ever

thought could be crossed but the road is smooth and winds around it anyone that has never seen these mountains cant think how they look so very high   when we got to the top I did not dare look down   I think we are higher than the clouds   we got over the mountains and came to Cumberland a business doing place   their is a railroad here . . . May 11th   We have came to the alleganies   they are not as steep as the Cumberland mountains but longer it has stormed all day   the roads are muddy on the top but the mud cant get deep   the road is full of stages and cart wagons and droves of fat cattle and hogs   they drive them from the west to Baltimore 3 and 400 in a drove   May 12th   Come only 14 miles today Father's horses are both foundered and are very stiff   their came a drover along and bled them in their feet and they are better we cannot hardly sleep nights on account of the stages   they run all night 6 and 7 together with 4 horses to each of them   May 15th   We come through several towns today and have put up for the night at Hilsborough   the wagons stand out in the street and I would rather sleep in the woods for there is a singing school over the way and it makes me feel lonesome   it makes me think more about Jersey to hear the old tunes sung we used to sing their every thing is getting cheaper than it was   we have all been sick of the water   David has been the sickest   he was been sick for two or three days   i forgot to say any thing about the aleganies   they are very tedious but they are not as bad as we expected there is several vilages on them it looks verry backward on them   the trees are not out yet   it is 60 miles over them   we have lost our pails   one we left standing at a spring on the mountain and one got stole out of the feed box . . . May 17th   We come 20 miles today through a beautiful country   we have stopped for the night along a brook a beautiful place on the green grass under the large elm trees   the corn is up so high you can see it over the fields and things in the gardens look almost fit to eat   there is a buttonwood tree along this brook cut down it is hollow Jaques can stand straight in it 6 feet from the bottom   it looks like a house inside   we talk of putting our horses in for a stable   there is coal mines in abundance along this road   we have traveled in Pennsylvania, Virginia and Marlyand . . . Father has traded brown for a 4 year old colt and gave 25 dls to boot   he made a good trade for brown was lame and stiff   she could not get up alone in the morning and the colt is as fat as she can be   he would have been glad to have made as good a trade in Jersey old pompey is better than he looks he stands the journey well   he has a smart team   our horses stand the journey well   May 18th We arrived in Wheeling this morning and waited till this afternoon for a boat but the water is low and there was no boats there large enough to take us   we crossed the Ohio on a flat   we got across very good   mother did not know the boat was moving until we got half over   Wheeling is a large town but it is not pleasant it is under a hill along the river they all burn coal and it is black of the smoke   there is a great business done here   I was glad to set my feet on the shores of Ohio   I could hardly believe it when we got there . . . May 20th   We have come 28 miles today   the roads are fine but heavy toll 25 cts every 10 miles each wagon   the land looks poor and hilly   some of it   the buildings poor   came through several towns that look very well   the grain looks bad here we bought eggs for 4 cts a dozen butter 10 cts a pound oats and corn 30 cts potatoes 25 cts per bushel   May 22nd   It rained yesterday and all night but cleared this morning   every thing was suffering for rain   we staid all night at Eatna at a house kept to accommodate movers   we took a room and got our breakfast there   it went very good to sit and eat instead of standing   the state looks better here   the land is very good   fine timber good buildings   land is worth 12 to 20 dollars per acre   it is thick settled and not so many log houses   May 23rd   I am sitting on a log in the thick woods writing   there is wood each side of the road as far as you can see and the road is as strait as it can be   it is a beautiful evening   our horses are turned out   the pasture is good   they do not go far from the wagons and if they hear a noise they all come running back   we look like an indian camp with our furnace smoking   our dogs lay as if they are dead they are so tired   Jaques bought a violin at Philadelphia and he is playing on that and the rest sits on the logs doing nothing   we would rather sleep in a woods than a house   we crossed the muskingum river at Zanesville   it is a large town and very pretty   yesterday we come through Columbus the capital of Ohio there is not a prettier town in Jersey there is some of the finest building in this town I ever saw   we see movers every day many going and some coming back   May 24th   Come through springfield   there is a railroad here and every thing high   there is a pike goes from here to Dayton we kept the national road   there was no toll on that and they said the movers go that way   we went 6 mile and then we come to an end   their was a top Bridge used for a barn and nothing but a foot path but there was a road laid across to the pike and that ended the National road   May 25th   Come through Dayton a large town and a canal through it   the country here beats all Jersey   rye and wheat is out in head and stands as high as the fence the land is straight we pay 18 cts toll every 28 mile   the buildings are log and brick   the people here seem more like our kind than they did in Pennsylvania land near dayton brings 40 to 50 dollars per Acre   May 26th   Today we crossed the line and now are in Indiana and came through Richmond a beautiful village it is very wet here and the roads bad   we did not stick fast but many did   it beats every thing to see the movers   every time we stop there has been some there before us sometimes there is a large fire burning against a log   we meet some coming back and they look very pittiful and try to persuade us to go back but we would have to hear more than we have to sicken us for it looks better yet than we expected   the buildings are finer than I expected   we do not see as many log houses as we did in Pennsylvania   Mother and me walked 5 mile yesterday   I have walked no more since we crossed three brooks without bridges one came up to the body of the wagon   the land is a little hilly here   May 28th   We got off the turnpike at Richmond on the National road   it is not finished but it is a good road only the wet places they are laid with logs and that is rough enough   their is no toll we can live good   every thing is cheap eggs 3 cts a dozen fresh beef 2½ cts a pound sweet potatoes as good as in the fall 12½ cents a peck the best of bread from 4 to 6 cents a loaf they keep a large stock fat horses and fine carriages   the roads are better   we crossed the blue river   some ride it and some are ferried over   we rode it and it did not come to the Body of the wagon we have a fine place to stay all night in a beech wood on the green grass   we built a fire against a stump stones for andirons   dog chains for trammels and a table stands here for people to eat off   it is a great stopping place for movers   May 31st   It was a very rainy day yesterday   we were caught in a hard dash and could not get the wagons under shelter but at night we got the horses and wagons in a barn and we staid in the house   they was a very clever family   we felt ourselves at home while there and had radishes as thick as my wrist for breakfast this morning   if the people in Jersey was to have every thing to look as well in the spring they would be almost scared and they say it is a backward spring here   I like Indiana better than Ohio so far   June 1st Came through Indianapolis the Capitol   there is a fine state house here and they are building a lunatic asylum   it is very large masons wages are 1½ dol a day and boarded   we turned off the national road to go by Clinton   The national road goes to Terre Haute   we have to put up before night along walnut creek it is so high we cannot cross it will swim a horse and runs swift   they are fixing the bodies of the wagons on blocks to cross in the morning   June 2nd   We got over the creek very well Mother was so afraid she laid on the bed she said if she must drown she would not look   I sat up on the bed and looked out   I could not feel afraid for laughing to see her. June 3rd   Today we crossed the wabash river at Clinton in a ferry boat I was more afraid than I have been at all   the river is deep and was very high and an old concern of a Boat we had no trouble to find Uncle Wicoffs   they live in the town and are doing well   June 6th   we staid their from wednesday until Saturday and baked and cooked enough to last us till we come through . . . we have come on the praries this afternoon and have to stay here all night the nearest house a quarter of a mile from the road   the man of that house come down and invited us to come there to be by the wood and water but we did not go   June 7th   we got off that prairie and come through woodland and beautiful places   we are now in Illinois   we got in yesterday   we have come to another Prairie and have to stay on it all night it is 14 miles the nearest way over   their is nothing to be seen but the sky and ground not a tree or bush or house as far as you can see and as level as a floor   it is very green grass and beautiful flowers but we cannot get any water for ourselves or horses in the morning   we hardly know which way to go we are so turned around   the road does very well some bad wet places and hen very good again   the broadest Prairie we crossed is 16 miles and not a house to be seen   June 8th we have good roads now and pleasant country   the prairies are smaller and

all settled   their is not many log houses and fine peach and apple orchards   their is nothing wanting here but wood   there is plenty of
game here   they shot two duck today and had a good dinner on them
we see plenty of deer and turkeys and geese and Prairie chickens but
have not shot any we had not time to stop long enough to shoot   Jaques
and Uriah takes a turn every day with their guns but it does not amount
to much   I beat them all   I Catched a rabbit in my hands yesterday but
I let it go   June 9th   we come through Springfield Today   it was some
out of our way but we wanted to see the place   it is a beautiful place
and fine buidings   it is on a Prairie   The State house is very fine   It is
built of Cut stone looks like Marble   The bank and Court House is Built
the same   there is a great many stores   The Streets are wide and very
shady large locust trees around the house there is very fine farms
around Springfield   the largest fields I have ever seen with corn knee
high   Some are breaking up the Prairie and planting corn   we saw one
man plowing with 4 yoke of oxen today and they drop the corn in the
furrow and cover the plough   they do not do any thing to it the first
year and raise 25 bushel to the acre   June 10th   we expect to get to
Manchester today   we like this part of the State the best it is better divided with timber and prairie   the grain looks well   the people are very
Clever   we get a great deal give to us milk and radishes and lettuce
some try to take advantage of movers and charge high   June 11th   we
arrived at William Strykers the one that wrote to us to come and was
received with a hearty welcome   they are very fine people and appear
like relation   we feel very much at home here   it is a pretty place   they
are very well off and they have told us to make their house our home
untill we can suit ourselves better   Now I will close my Journal   I expect you will think it is not worth the postage   I think so myself but I
have had a great deal of trouble to get it as good as it is   if I had of
known what a trouble it would be and what little time I would have to
write I should never have promised to send it   I had to write nights
after all the rest had gone to bed and then in that warm wagon and
nothing to set on and so tired and sleepy I did not know sometimes
what I did write   but I tried to tell you as near as I could what passed
on our journey . . .

30 | The Pony Express

The Pony Express was in existence for only eighteen months—from April 1860 to October 1861—but it left a lasting mark on American history and legend. Overcoming the tyranny of distance was a major dream of nineteenth-century Americans. The short-lived success of the Pony Express showed the lengths to which the riders might go to conquer incredible distances and harsh conditions. The discovery of gold in California was naturally followed by a swift increase in the region's population. But much of the Great Plains and Rocky Mountain territories was still sparsely settled. The transcontinental railroad had not yet been built, nor was there coast-to-coast telegraph service. To provide for reliable, year-round communication between Missouri (and the East) and California, the firm of Russell, Majors & Waddell organized the Pony Express, which used horses in relays. The service ran from St. Joseph, Missouri, to Sacramento, California, passing through Cheyenne, Salt Lake City, and Carson City. Its success convinced many Americans of the practicality of a transcontinental railroad. This reading comes from the Memoirs *of Alexander Majors, published in 1893.*

CHAPTER XXII. THE PONY EXPRESS AND ITS BRAVE RIDERS.

During the winter of 1859, Mr. W. H. Russell, of our firm, while in Washington, D. C., met and became acquainted with Senator Gwin of California. . . .

Knowing that Russell, Majors & Waddell were running a daily stage between the Missouri River and Salt Lake City, and that they were also heavily engaged in the transportation of Government stores on the same line, [the Senator] Mr. Russell if his company could not be induced to start a pony express, to run over its stage line to Salt Lake City, and from thence to Sacramento; his object being to test the practicality of

Colonel Prentiss Ingraham (editor), Seventy Years of the Frontier: Alexander Major's Memoirs of a Lifetime on the Border. (*Columbus, Lang's College Book Company, 1950*), pp. 182–185, 187–193.

crossing the Sierra Nevadas, as well as the Rocky Mountains, with a daily line of communication.

After various consultations between these gentlemen, from time to time, the Senator urging the great necessity of such an experiment, Mr. Russell consented to take hold of the enterprise, provided he could get his partners, Mr. Waddell and myself, to join him. . . .

After listening to all Mr. Russell had to say upon the subject, we concluded to sustain him in the undertaking, and immediately went to work to organize what has since been known as "The Pony Express." . . .

Within sixty days or thereabouts from the time we agreed to undertake the enterprise, we were ready to start ponies, one from St. Joseph, Mo., and the other from Sacramento, Cal., on the same day. At that time there was telegraphic communication between the East and St. Joseph, Mo., and between San Francisco and Sacramento, Cal.

The quickest time that had ever been made with any message between San Francisco and New York, over the Butterfield line, which was the southern route, was twenty-one days. Our Pony Express shortened the time to ten days, which was our schedule time, without a single failure, being a difference of eleven days.

To do the work of the Pony Express required between four hundred and five hundred horses, about one hundred and ninety stations, two hundred men for station-keepers, and eighty riders; riders made an average ride of thirty-three and one-third miles. In doing this each man rode three ponies on his part of the route; some of the riders, however, rode much greater distances in times of emergency.

The Pony Express carried messages written on tissue paper, weighing one-half ounce, a charge of $5 being made for each dispatch carried.

As anticipated, the amount of business transacted over this line was not sufficient to pay one-tenth of the expenses, to say nothing about the amount of capital invested. In this, however, we were not disappointed, for we knew, . . . that it could not be made a paying institution, and was undertaken solely to prove that the route over which it ran could be made a permanent thoroughfare for travel at all seasons of the year, proving, as far as the paramount object was concerned, a complete success.

Two important events transpired during the term of the Pony's existence; one was the carrying of President Buchanan's last message to Congress, in December, 1860, from the Missouri River to Sacramento, a distance of two thousand miles, in eight days and some hours. The other was the carrying of President Lincoln's inaugural address of March 4, 1861, over the same route in seven days and, I think, seventeen hours, being the quickest time, taking the distance into consideration, on record in this or any other country, as far as I know. . . .

In the spring of 1860 Bolivar Roberts, superintendent of the Western Division of the Pony Express, came to Carson City, Nev., which was then in St. Mary's County, Utah, to engage riders and station men . . .

route about to be established across the great plains by Russell, Majors
& Waddell. In a few days fifty or sixty men were engaged, and started
out across the Great American Desert to establish stations, etc. Among
that number the writer can recall to memory the following; Bob Haslam
("Pony Bob"), Jay G. Kelley . . .

J. G. Kelley has had a varied experience, and is now fifty-four years
of age, an eminent mining engineer and mineralogist, residing in Den-
ver, Colo. In recalling many reminiscences of the plains in the early
days, I will let him tell the story in his own language:

"Yes," he said, "I was a pony express rider in 1860, and went out
with Bol Roberts (one of the best men that ever lived), and I tell you
it was no picnic. No amount of money could tempt me to repeat my
experience of those days. To begin with, we had to build willow roads
(corduroy fashion) across many places along the Carson River, carrying
bundles of willows two and three hundred yards in our arms, while the
mosquitoes were so thick it was difficult to discern whether the man
was white or black, so thickly were they piled on his neck, face, and
hands.

"Arriving at the Sink of the Carson River, we began the erection of a
fort to protect us from the Indians. As there were no rocks or logs in that vicinity, the fort was built of adobes, made from the mud on the shores of the
lake. To mix this mud and get it the proper consistency to mold into adobes
(dried brick), we tramped around all day in it in our bare feet. This we did
for a week or more, and the mud being strongly impregnated with alkali
(carbonate of soda), you can imagine the condition of our feet. They were
much swollen, and resembled hams. Before that time I wore No. 6 boots,
but ever since then No. 9s fit me snugly.

/   /   /

I was assigned to duty as assistant station-keeper, under Jim Mc-
Naughton. The war against the Piute Indians was then at its height, and
we were in the middle of the Piute country, which made it necessary for
us to keep a standing guard night and day. The Indians were often seen
skulking around, but none of them ever came near enough for us to get
a shot at them, till one dark night, when I was on guard, I noticed one
of our horses prick up his ears and stare. I looked in the direction indi-
cated and saw an Indian's head projecting above the wall.

"My instructions were to shoot if I saw an Indian within shooting
distance, as that would wake the boys quicker than anything else; so I
fired and missed my man.

"Later on we saw the Indian camp-fires on the mountain, and in
the morning saw many tracks. They evidently intended to stampede our
horses, and if necessary kill us. The next day one of our riders, a Mexi-
can, rode into camp with a bullet hole through him from the left to the
right side, having been shot by Indians while coming down Edwards

Creek, in the Quakenasp bottom. This he told us as we assisted him off his horse. He was tenderly cared for, but died before surgical aid could reach him.

/   /   /

"One of my rides was the longest on the route. I refer to the road between Cold Springs and Sand Springs, thirty-seven miles, and not a drop of water. It was on this ride that I made a trip which possibly gave to our company the contract for carrying the mail by stage-coach across the plains, a contract that was largely subsidized by Congress. . . .

"As I look back on those times I often wonder that we were not all killed. A short time before, Major Ormsby of Carson City, in command of seventy-five or eighty men, went to Pyramid Lake to give battle to the Piutes, who had been killing emigrants and prospectors by the wholesale. Nearly all the command were killed in a running fight of sixteen miles. In the fight Major Ormsby and the lamented Harry Meredith were killed. Another regiment of about seven hundred men, under the command of Col. Daniel E. Hungerford and Jack Hayes, the noted Texas ranger, was raised. Hungerford was the beau ideal of a soldier, the hero of three wars, and one of the best tacticians of his time. This command drove the Indians pell-mell for three miles to Mud Lake, killing and wounding them at every jump. Colonel Hungerford and Jack Hayes received, and were entitled to, great praise, for at the close of the war terms were made which have kept the Indians peaceable ever since. Jack Hayes died several years since in Alameda, Cal. Colonel Hungerford, at the ripe age of seventy years, is hale and hearty, enjoying life and resting on his laurels in Italy, where he resides with his granddaughter, the Princess Colona.

"As previously stated, it is marvelous that the pony boys were not all killed. There were only four men at each station, and the Indians, who were then hostile, roamed all over the country in bands of 30 to 100.

"What I consider my most narrow escape from death was being shot at one night by a lot of fool emigrants, who, when I took them to task about it on my return trip, excused themselves by saying, 'We thought you was an Indian.'

/   /   /

"The Pony Express was a great undertaking at the time, and was the foundation of the mail-coach and railroad that quickly followed."

/   /   /

Questions for Part III

1 Describe Lewis and Clark's role as representatives of the United States government to the Indians. How effective do you think their diplomacy was? How would you describe their attitude toward Indians?

2 Describe the schoolmaster in Bingham's satire. Would he make a good teacher? What are Bingham's views on classroom discipline? Are they commonly accepted today? What are Bingham's views on teacher salaries?

3 Cartwright describes the religious "camp-meeting" very vividly. Do we have anything like that today? What are the "jerks"?

4 What led Black Hawk and his followers to side with the British?

5 What is paper money? Why does Flint blame most of the economic troubles on it? Who regulates our currency today? What does Flint think of the American character?

6 In the excerpt by Cooper, what is Leather-stocking's viewpoint? How is it "modern"? What is Billy Kirby's? Who do you think is speaking for Cooper?

7 Describe the changes at Lowell related by Robinson as they affected the workers. How did the workers attempt to fight back? Were they successful?

8 What difficulties did Jane Voorhees Lewis and her family encounter on their westward journey? Compare them with what the early colonists faced.

9 How long did it take the Pony Express to convey messages from Missouri to California? How long does it take for information to travel the same distance today? Discuss the significance of these differences.

PART IV | REFORM, SLAVERY, CIVIL WAR, AND RECONSTRUCTION

Movement from the nationalism of the earlier nineteenth century to antebellum sectionalism dominated the thirty years leading to the Civil War. Both Northerners and Southerners resolutely proceeded westward, but the rapidly growing Southwest, including Alabama, Mississippi, and Louisiana, developed an economy and a society different from those of the new Northwest, which included Ohio, Illinois, and Wisconsin. One region was plantation, the other farm; one slave labor, the other free; one produced agrarian aristocrats, the other cities, entrepreneurs, and lawyers; one grew fundamentalist and fearful of change while the other spawned liberal religions and reform. Beneath it all was a basic— and national—antipathy to the black race that made Southerners fearful of the abolition of slavery and Northerners committed to halting its expansion into their own society.

All of the readings in this section reflect in one way or another the crisis the nation faced. We see the lives of slaves in their letters to each other, in the account of Nat Turner's rebellion, in Frederick Douglass's classic autobiography, and in Henry Bibb's letters to his former master. An excerpt from John Pendleton Kennedy's Swallow Barn presents a Southern view of slavery. The account of Harriet Tubman's life indicates the heroism required for blacks to resist slavery.

Sojourner Truth and Elizabeth Cady Stanton both provide insight into the reform ferment of the Northern states before the Civil War, as it involved the abolition of slavery, the expansion of women's rights, and improved practices of child care.

The armed conflicts in Kansas in the late 1850s were a prelude to the war itself. The impact of war may be seen both in Small's memoirs of a prisoner of war and in the account of the devastation wrought by William T. Sherman's march through Georgia.

We see the first painful and difficult reactions to the close of the Civil War as black and white Southerners react to Reconstruction. The revolution in race relations carried with it striking changes in the most important forms of property and economic relations: ownership of the land and the crops planted on it. By the 1880s, sharecropping had emerged as a replacement for slavery and the hierarchical relations that were a part of slavery. Victory for the Union did not end the crisis of the place of black men and women in American life. Three new amendments to the Constitution had initiated a revolution that, more than a century later, is far from completed.

31 | Reminiscences

From 1848 until her death in 1902, Elizabeth Cady Stanton was among the most influential leaders of the movement for women's rights. Recounted in the second of two selections from her autobiography are the circumstances of her organizing the first women's rights convention at Seneca Falls on July 19 and 20, 1848.

Stanton was also famous as a lecturer on family life and child rearing, issues—as she argues—inextricably linked to women's rights. With her husband, Henry B. Stanton, she supported a broad range of reform movements including abolitionism, temperance, and the reform of marriage and women's property laws. Her discussion of child rearing in the first selection gives a good insight into why Stanton assumed the responsibility for reforming long established traditions and ideas.

I

The puzzling questions of theology and poverty that had occupied so much of my thoughts, now gave place to the practical one, "what to do with a baby." Though motherhood is the most important of all the professions,—requiring more knowledge than any other department in human affairs,—yet there is not sufficient attention given to the preparation for this office. If we buy a plant of a horticulturist we ask him many questions as to its needs, whether it thrives best in sunshine or in shade, whether it needs much or little water, what degrees of heat or cold; but when we hold in our arms for the first time, a being of infinite possibilities, in whose wisdom may rest the destiny of a nation, we take it for granted that the laws governing its life, health, and happiness are intuitively understood, that there is nothing new to be learned in regard to it. Yet here is a science to which philosophers have, as yet, given but little attention. An important fact has only been discovered and acted upon within the last ten years, that children come into the world tired, and not hungry, exhausted with the perilous journey. Instead of being

Stanton, Elizabeth Cady. Eighty Years and More (1815-1897): Reminescences of Elizabeth Cady Stanton. *(London: T. Fisher Unwin, 1898.)*

thoroughly bathed and dressed, and kept on the rack while the nurse makes a prolonged toilet and feeds it some nostrum supposed to have much needed medicinal influence, the child's face, eyes, and mouth should be hastily washed with warm water, and the rest of its body thoroughly oiled, and then it should be slipped into a soft pillow case, wrapped in a blanket, and laid to sleep. Ordinarily, in the proper conditions, with its face uncovered in a cool, pure atmosphere, it will sleep twelve hours. Then it should be bathed, fed, and clothed in a high-necked, long-sleeved silk shirt and a blanket, all of which could be done in five minutes. As babies lie still most of the time the first six weeks, they need no dressing. I think the nurse was a full hour bathing and dressing my firstborn, who protested with a melancholy wail every blessed minutes.

Ignorant myself of the initiative steps on the threshold of time, I supposed this proceeding was approved by the best authorities. However, I had been thinking, reading, observing, and had as little faith in the popular theories in regard to babies as on any other subject. I saw them, on all sides, ill half the time, pale and peevish, dying early, having no joy in life. I heard parents complaining of weary days and sleepless nights, while each child, in turn, ran the gauntlet of red gum, jaundice, whooping cough, chicken-pox, mumps, measles, scarlet fever, and fits. They all seemed to think these inflictions were a part of the eternal plan—that Providence had a kind of Pandora's box, from which he scattered these venerable diseases most liberally among those whom he especially loved. Having gone through the ordeal of bearing a child, I was determined, if possible, to keep him, so I read everything I could find on the subject. But the literature on this subject was as confusing and unsatisfactory as the longer and shorter catechisms and the Thirty-nine Articles of our faith. I had recently visited our dear friends, Theodore and Angelina Grimke-Weld, and they warned me against books on this subject. They had been so misled by one author, who assured them that the stomach of a child could only hold one tablespoonful, that they nearly starved their firstborn to death. Though the child dwindled, day by day, and, at the end of a month, looked like a little old man, yet they still stood by the distinguished author. Fortunately, they both went off, one day, and left the child with Sister "Sarah," who though she would make an experiment and see what a child's stomach could hold, as she had grave doubts about the tablespoonful theory. To her surprise the baby took a pint bottle full of milk, and had the sweetest sleep thereon he had known in his earthly career. After that he was permitted to take what he wanted, and "the author" was informed of his libel on the infantile stomach.

So here, again, I was entirely afloat, launched on the seas of doubt without chart or compass. The life and well-being of the race seemed to hang on the slender thread of such traditions as were handed down by ignorant mothers and nurses. One powerful ray of light illuminated the darkness; it ws the work of Andrew Combe on "Infancy." He had, evidently watched some of the manifestations of man in the first stages of his development, and could tell, at least, as much of babies as naturalists could of beetles and bees. He did give young mothers some hints of what to do, the whys and wherefores of certain lines of procedure during antenatal life, as well as the proper care thereafter. I read several chapters to the nurse. Although, out of her ten children, she had buried five, she still had too much confidence in her own wisdom and experience to pay much attention to any new idea that might be suggested to her. Among other things, Combe said that a child's bath should be regulated by the thermometer, in order to be always of the same temperature. She ridiculed the idea, and said her elbow was better than any thermometer, and, when I insisted on its use, she would invariably, with a smile of derision, put her elbow in first, to show how exactly it tallied with the thermometer. When I insisted that the child should not be bandaged, she rebelled outright, and said she would not take the responsibility of nursing a child without a bandage. I said, "Pray, sit down, dear nurse, and let us reason together. Do not think I am setting up my judgment against yours, with all your experience. I am simply trying to act on the opinions of a distinguished physician, who says there should be no pressure on a child anywhere; that the limbs and body should be free; that it is cruel to bandage an infant from hip to armpit, as is usually done in America; or both body and legs, as is done in Europe; or strap them to boards, as is done by savages on both continents. Can you give me one good reason, nurse, why a child should be bandaged?"

"Yes," she said emphatically, "I can give you a dozen."

"I only asked for one," I replied.

"Well," said she, after much hesitation, "the bones of a newborn infant are soft, like cartilage, and, unless you pin them up snugly, there is danger of their falling apart."

"It seems to me," I replied, "you have given the strongest reason whey they should be carefully guarded against the slightest pressure. It is very remarkable that kittens and puppies should be so well put together that they need no artificial bracing, and the human family be left wholly to the mercy of a bandage. Suppose a child was born where you could not get a bandage, what then? Now I think this child will remain intact without a bandage, and, if I am willing to take the risk, why should you complain?"

"Because," said she, "if the child should die, it would injure my name as a nurse. I therefore wash my hands of all these new-fangled notions."

So she bandaged the child every morning, and I as regularly took it off. It has been fully proved since to be as useless an appendage as the vermiform. She had several cups with various concoctions of herbs standing on the chimney-corner, ready for insomnia, colic, indigestion, etc., etc., all of which were spirited away when she was at her dinner. In vain I told her we were homeopathists, and afraid of everything in the animal, vegetable, or mineral kingdoms lower than the two-hundredth dilution. I tried to explain the Hahnemann system of thera-peutics, the philosophy of the principle *similia similibus curantur,** but she had no capacity for first principles, and did not understand my dis-course. I told her that, if she would wash the baby's mouth with pure cold water morning and night and give it a teaspoonful to drink occa-sionally during the day, there would be no danger of red gum; that if she would keep the blinds open and let in the air and sunshine, keep the temperature of the room at sixty-five degrees, leave the child's head uncovered so that it could breathe freely, stop rocking and trotting it and singing such melancholy hymns as "Hark, from the tombs a doleful sound!" the baby and I would both be able to weather the cape without a bandage. I told her I should nurse the child once in two hours, and that she must not feed it any of her nostrums in the meantime; that a child's stomach, being made on the same general plan as our own, needed intervals of rest as well as ours. She said it would be racked with colic if the stomach was empty any length of time, and that it would surely have rickets if it were kept too still. I told her if the child had no anodynes, nature would regulate its sleep and motions. She said she could not stay in a room with the thermometer at sixty-five degrees, so I told her to sit in the next room and regulate the heat to suit herself; that I would ring a bell when her services were needed.

The reader will wonder, no doubt, that I kept such a cantankerous servant. I could get no other. Dear "Mother Monroe," as wise as she was good, and as tender as she was strong, who had nursed two gener-ations of mothers in our village, was engaged at that time, and I was compelled to take an exotic. I had often watched "Mother Monroe" with admiration, as she turned and twisted my sister's baby. It lay as peacefully in her hands as if they were lined with eider down. She bathed and dressed it by easy stages, turning the child over and over like a pancake. But she was so full of the magnetism of human love, giving the child, all the time, the most consoling assurance that the oper-ation was to be a short one, that the whole proceeding was quite enter-taining to the observer and seemingly agreeable to the child, though it had a rather surprised look as it took a bird's-eye view, in quick succes-sion, of the ceiling and the floor. Still my nurse had her good points. She was very pleasant when she had her own way. She was neat and tidy, and ready to serve me at any time, night or day. She did not wear false teeth that rattled when she talked, nor boots that squeaked when

---

*Like is cured by like, which is a basic principle of homeopathic medicine; A person is cured or strengthened by a minute dose of what, in a healthy person, would produce a symptom of the disease being treated.

she walked. She did not snuff nor chew cloves, nor speak except when spoken to. Our discussions, on various points, went on at intervals, until I succeeded in planting some ideas in her mind, and when she left me, at the end of six weeks, she confessed that she had learned some valuable lessons. As the baby had slept quietly most of the time, had no crying spells, nor colic, and I looked well, she naturally came to the conclusion that pure air, sunshine, proper dressing, and regular feeding were more necessary for babies than herb teas and soothing syrups.

Besides the obstinacy of the nurse, I had the ignorance of physicians to contend with. When the child was four days old we discovered that the collar bone was bent. The physician, wishing to get a pressure on the shoulder, braced the bandage round the wrist. "Leave that," he said, "ten days, and then it will be all right." Soon after he left I noticed that the child's hand was blue, showing that the circulation was impeded. "That will never do," said I; "nurse, take it off." "No, indeed," she answered, "I shall never intefere with the doctor." So I took it off myself, and sent for another doctor, who was said to know more of surgery. He expressed great surprise that the first physician called should have put on so severe a bandage. "That," said he, "would do for a grown man, but ten days of it on a child would make him a cripple." However, he did nearly the same thing, only fastening it round the hand instead of the wrist. I soon saw that the ends of the fingers were all purple, and that to leave that on ten days would be as dangerous as the first. So I took that off.

"What a woman!" exclaimed the nurse. "What do you propose to do?"

"Think out something better, myself; so brace me up with some pillows and give the baby to me."

She looked at me aghast and said, "You'd better trust the doctors, or your child will be a helpless cripple."

"Yes," I replied, "he would be, if we had left either of those bandages on, but I have an idea of something better."

"Now," said I, talking partly to myself and partly to her, "what we want is a little pressure on that bone; that is what both those men aimed at. How can we get it without involving the arm, is the question?"

"I am sure I don't know," said she, rubbing her hands and taking two or three brisk turns round the room.

"Well, bring me three strips of linen, four double." I then folded one, wet in arnica and water, and laid it on the collar bone, put two other bands, like a pair of suspenders, over the shoulders, crossing them both in front and behind, pinning the ends to the diaper, which gave the needed pressure without impeding the circulation anywhere. As I finished she gave me a look of budding confidence, and seemed satisfied that all was well. Several times, night and day, we wet the compress and readjusted the bands, until all appearances of inflammation had subsided.

At the end of ten days the two sons of Æsculapius* appeared and made their examination and said all was right, whereupon I told them how badly their bandages worked and what I had done myself. They smiled at each other, and one said:

"Well, after all, a mother's instinct is better than a man's reason."

"Thank you, gentlemen, there was no instinct about it. I did some hard thinking before I saw how I could get a pressure on the shoulder without impeding the circulation, as you did."

Thus, in the supreme moment of a young mother's life, when I needed tender care and support, I felt the whole responsibility of my child's supervision; but though uncertain at every step of my own knowledge, I learned another lesson in self-reliance. I trusted neither men nor books absolutely after this, either in regard to the heavens above or the earth beneath, but continued to use my "mother's instinct," if "reason" is too dignified a term to apply to woman's thoughts. My advice to every mother is, above all other arts and sciences, study first what relates to babyhood, as there is no department of human action in which there is such lamentable ignorance.

/   /   /

II

In the spring of 1847 we moved to Seneca Falls. Here we spent sixteen years of our married life, and here our other children—two sons and two daughters—were born.

/   /   /

In Seneca Falls my life was comparatively solitary, and the change from Boston was somewhat depressing. There, all my immediate friends were reformers, I had near neighbors, a new home with all the modern conveniences, and well-trained servants. Here our residence was on the outskirts of the town, roads very often muddy and no sidewalks most of the way, Mr. Stanton was frequently from home, I had poor servants, and an increasing number of children. To keep a house and grounds in good order, purchase every article for daily use, keep the wardrobes of half a dozen human beings in proper trim, take the children to dentists, shoemakers, and different schools, or find teachers at home, altogether made sufficient work to keep one brain busy, as well as all the hands I could impress into the service. Then, too, the novelty of housekeeping had passed away, and much that was once attractive in domestic life

*Refers to the Greco- Roman god of medicine. Stanton is being sarcastic here.

was now irksome. I had so many cares that the company I needed for intellectual stimulus was a trial rather than a pleasure. . . .

I now fully understood the practical difficulties most women had to contend with in the isolated household, and the impossibility of woman's best development if in contact, the chief part of her life, with servants and children. Fourier's phalansterie community life* and cooperative households had a new significance for me. Emerson says, "A healthy discontent is the first step to progress." The general discontent I felt with woman's portion as wife, mother, housekeeper, physician, and spiritual guide, the chaotic conditions into which everything fell without her constant supervision, and the wearied, anxious look of the majority of women impressed me with a strong feeling that some active measures should be taken to remedy the wrongs of society in general, and of women in particular. My experience at the World's Anti-slavery Convention, all I had read of the legal status of women, and the oppression I saw everywhere, together swept across my soul, intensified now by many personal experiences. It seemed as if all the elements had conspired to impel me to some onward step. I could not see what to do or where to begin—my only thought was a public meeting for protest and discussion.

In this tempest-tossed condition of mind I received an invitation to spend the day with Lucretia Mott, at Richard Hunt's, in Waterloo. There I met several members of different families of Friends, earnest, thoughtful women. I poured out, that day, the torrent of my long-accumulating discontent, with such vehemence and indignation that I stirred myself, as well as the rest of the party, to do and dare anything. My discontent, according to Emerson, must have been healthy, for it moved us all to prompt action, and we decided, then and there, to call a "Woman's Rights Convention." We wrote the call that evening and published it in the *Seneca Country Courier* the next day, the 14th of July, 1848, giving only five days' notice, as the convention was to be held on the 19th and 20th. The call was inserted without signatures,—in fact it was a mere announcement of a meeting,—but the chief movers and managers were Lucretia Mott, Mary Ann McClintock, Jane Hunt, Martha C. Wright, and myself. The convention, which was held two days in the Methodist Church, was in every way a grand success. The house was crowded at every session, the speaking good, and a religious earnestness dignified all the proceedings.

These were the hasty initiative steps of "the most momentous reform that had yet been launched on the world—the first organized protest against the injustice which had brooded for ages over the character

---

*Refers to cooperative work and living units envisioned by French utopianist Charles Fourier. These "phalanxes" allowed those who labored to receive the largest portion of community earnings.

and destiny of one-half the race." No words could express our astonishment on finding, a few days afterward, that what seemed to us so timely, so rational, and so sacred, should be a subject for sarcasm and ridicule to the entire press of the nation. With our Declaration of Rights and Resolutions for a text, it seemed as if every man who could wield a pen prepared a homily on "woman's sphere." All the journals from Maine to Texas seemed to strive with each other to see which could make our movement appear the most ridiculous. The anti-slavery papers stood by us manfully and so did Frederick Douglass, both in the convention and in his paper, *The North Star,* but so pronounced was the popular voice against us, in the parlor, press, and pulpit, that most of the ladies who had attended the convention and signed the declaration, one by one, withdrew their names and influence and joined our persecutors. Our friends gave us the cold shoulder and felt themselves disgraced by the whole proceeding.

If I had had the slightest premonition of all that was to follow that convention, I fear I should not have had the courage to risk it, and I must confess that it was with fear and trembling that I consented to attend another, one month afterward, in Rochester. Fortunately, the first one seemed to have drawn all the fire, and of the second but little was said. But we had set the ball in motion, and now, in quick succession, conventions were held in Ohio, Indiana, Massachusetts, Pennsylvania, and in the City of New York, and have been kept up nearly every year since. . . .

With these new duties and interests, and a broader outlook on human life, my petty domestic annoyances gradually took a subordinate place. Now I began to write articles for the press, letters to conventions held in other States, and private letters to friends, to arouse them to thought on this question. . . .

In answering all the attacks, we were compelled to study canon and civil law, constitutions, Bibles, science, philosphy, and history, sacred and profane. Now my mind, as well as my hands, was fully occupied, and instead of mourning, as I had done, over what I had lost in leaving Boston, I tried in every way to make the most of life in Seneca Falls. Seeing that elaborate refreshments prevented many social gatherings, I often gave an evening entertainment without any. I told the young people, whenever they wanted a little dance or a merry time, to make our house their rallying point, and I would light up and give them a glass of water and some cake. In that way we had many pleasant informal gatherings. . . .

32 | Letters of Slaves

One of the great efforts of the current generation of American historians has been to capture the black American's experience of slavery directly, rather than from sources generated by whites. As a result of this work a rich harvest of documents has been unearthed, some written by slaves, others dictated to sympathetic whites.

In the letters sampled here we learn about the diverse and complicated relationships among slaves and between slaves and masters. The evidence that slavery was cruel and arbitrary is everywhere abundant, but evident as well is the capacity of human beings to rise above an evil institution, to make lives for themselves and, occasionally, create close interracial relationships. A particularly interesting example of interracial communication is the letter from William Burke to Mary Custis Lee and Robert E. Lee (the Civil War general) who had manumitted slaves and settled several in Liberia.

LETTERS OF SLAVES TO MASTERS

Judith Cocks to James Hillhouse

Marietta, 8th March 1795

Sir

I have been so unhappy at Mrs. Woodbridges that I was obliged to leeve thare by the consent of Mrs. Woodbridge who gave up my Indentures and has offen said that had she known that I was so sickly and expencieve she would not have brought me to this Country but all this is the least of my trouble and I can truly say sir had I nothing else or no one but myself I am sure I should not make any complaint to you But my Little son Jupiter who is now with Mrs. Woodbridge is my greatest care and from what she says and from the useage he meets with there is so trying to me that I am all most distracted therefore if you will be so

Slave Testimony: Two Centuries of Letters, Speeches, Interviews, and Autobiographies, ed. John W. Blassingame and published in 1977 by Louisiana State University Press, pp. 7–8, 13–14, 22–26, 46–47, 95–96, 100–101.

kind as to write me how Long Jupiter is to remain with them as she tells me he is to live with her untill he is twenty five years of age this is something that I had no idea of I all ways thought that he was to return with me to new england or at Longest only ten years these are matters I must beg of you sir to let me know as quick as you can make it convenient I hope you will excuse me of troub Ling you wich I think you will do when you think that I am here in A strange country without one Friend to advise me Mrs. Woodbridge setts out for connecticut and I make no doubt but she will apply to buy Jupiter's time which I beg you will be so good as not to sell to her I had much reather he wold return and Live with you as she allows all her sons to thump and beat him the same as if he was a Dog Mrs. Woodbridge may tell you that I have behaved bad but I call on all the nabours to know wheather I have not behaved well and wheather I was so much to blame She has called me A theif and I denie I have don my duty as well as I could to her and all her family as well as my Strength wold allow of I have not ronged her nor her family the nabours advised me to rite you for the childs sake I went to the Gentlemen of the town for these advise they told me I could get back without any dificulty I entend to return remember me to all your family if you please I thank you for sending me word my dauter was well this is my hand writing I remain the greatest humility[,] you Humble servant

Judith Cocks

please [dont?] show this to Mrs. Woodbridge

Susan Ersey to Beverly Tucker

St. Louis, Oct 24th 1842

Dear Master [Beverley Tucker]—

We, two of your humble Servants have come to the conclusion to write you a few lines upon a subject that has given us much pain, which will be more keenly felt if you will not grant their humble request. We hope and pray that you will not think hard of us in so doing, as we are in much distress, and write the very feelings of our hearts.

About two weeks ago Mr Jones, a neighbour of Mr Bundlett in Texas, called with a letter from Mr Bundlett saying that we must come on with Mr Jones. As we had been here a long time and had become much attached to the place (our Husbands being here) and as we hated the idea of going to Texas, Mr Jones was kind enough to let us remain till March, before which time he expected to hear from you on the subject. Our object in writing dear Master is this: We can't bear to go to Texas with a parcel of strangers—if you were there we should go without saying a word, but to be separated from our husbands forever in this world would make us unhappy for life. We have a great many friends in this place and would rather be sold than go to Texas.

In making this request, dear Master, we do not do it through any disrespect (for you have always been kind to us) but merely because we shall be happier here with our friends and Husbands. We don't think there will be the least difficulty in getting ourselves sold, together with our children from whom we hope you will not separate us. Ersey has six children, the youngest of which is about six weeks old, a fine little Girl. Susan has two Boys, the eldest nearly three years old, and the youngest eight months. We hope dear Master and Mistress that you will not let us go to Texas, but grant us our humble petition.

We are both well, also our children. If you conclude to sell us, please write to any of the following gentlemen, with your terms, with whom you are acquainted. Edward Bates, Andrew Elliott, R. H. Graham or Wm G. Pettus Remember us kindly to Mistress and her children and the Servants & children.   Yours truly
                                                    Susan (Sukey) & Ersey

Usa Payton to Beverly Tucker

                                        St. Louis Mo. Feb. the 23 1851
Dear Master [Beverley Tucker]—
    I now take the oppertunity of writing to you to let you know how I come on I am well and doing well I have 10 child—ren a living & 3 dead I want to hear from you very Bad for you all ways treated Me well & I shall forever like you for it you will please remember me to my old Mistress & tell her I would give any thing in the world to see her My husband is well & doing well I have 4 children with me we are all well please write to me for I want to hear from you very bad Master I wish you would send me a present of Some money if you please for Just at this time I am in particular knead of Some My Mistresses twoo Brothers is dead Both died the Saim Month one of them here at home the other on the Sea I work here I take in washing I get a heep to due & I work very Hard nothing more
    You will please remember me to all of My Coloured friends I want to go to the Farm but I could not gett off when I go I will write to you again Tell Sary Magee her daughters has been living next door to me for more than a year. She is Maried her & her husband belongs to a Sam Dyer.
                                                    Usa Payton

LETTERS FROM SLAVES TO OTHER SLAVES

Sargry Brown to Mores Brown

                                        RICHMOND VA. October 27 1840
DEAR HUSBAND—
    this is the third letter that I have written to you, and have not received any from you; and dont no the reason that I have not received any from you. I think very hard of it. the trader has been here three

times to Look at me. I wish that you would try to see if you can get any one to buy me up there. if you dont come down here this Sunday, perhaps you wont see me any more. give my love to them all, and tell them all that perhaps I shan't see you any more. give my love to your mother in particular, and to mamy wines, and to aunt betsy, and all the children; tell Jane and Mother they must come down a fortnight before christmas. I wish to see you all, but I expect I never shall see you all—never no more.

I remain your Dear and affectionate Wife,

SARGRY BROWN.

James Phillips to Mary Phillips

Richmond, June 20, 1852.

Dear Wife—I will now write to you to inform you where I am and my health. I am well, and I am in hope when you receive this, it may find you well also. I am now in a trader's hands, by the name of Mr. Branton, and he is agoing to start South with a lot of negroes in August. I do not like this country at all, and had almost rather die than to go South. Tell all of the people that if they can do anything for me, now is the time to do it. I can be bought for $900. Do pray, try and get Brant and Mr. Byers and Mr. Weaver to send or come on to buy me, and if they will only buy me back, I will be a faithful man to them so long as I live. Show Mr. Brant and Mr. Weaver this letter, and tell them to come on as soon as they possibly can to buy me. My master is willing to sell me to any gentleman who will be so kind as to come on to buy me. They have got poor James Phillips here with leg irons on to keep him from getting away; and do pray gentlemen, do not feel any hesitation at all, but come on as soon as you can and buy me. Feel for me now or never. If any of you will be so kind as to come on to buy me, inquire for Cochron's Jail. I can be found there, and my master is always at the Jail himself. My master gave me full consent to have this letter written, so do not feel any hesitation to come on and see about poor James Phillips. Dear wife, show it to these men as soon as you get it, and let them write back immediately what they intend to do. Direct your letter to my master William A. Branton, Richmond, Va. Try and do something for me as soon as you can, for I want to get back very bad indeed.—Do not think anything at all of the price, for I am worth twice that amount. I can make it for any person who will buy me, in a short time. I have nothing more to write, only I wish I may be bought and carried back to Harrisburg in a short time. My best love to you, my wife. You may depend I am almost dying to see you and my children. You must do all you can for your husband.

Your husband,
James Phillips.

Letters to Amy Nixon

EDENTON, N.C., Sept. 13, 1835.

My dear daughter—I have for some time had hope of seeing you once more in this world, but now that hope is entirely gone forever. I expect to start next month for Alabama, on the Mississippi river. Perhaps before you get this letter I may be on my way. As I have no opportunity of sending it now I shall leave it with Emily to send.

My dear daughter Amy, if we never meet in this world, I hope we shall meet in heaven where we shall part no more. Although we are absent in body, we can be present in spirit. Then let us pray for each other, and try to hold out faithful to the end.

My master, Mr. Tom Brownrigg, starts the middle of next month, with all the people, except your sister Mary, she is——, and not able to travel. She has five children. Master Richard and family and the Doctor will go on in the spring, and Mary will come with them. Your father and myself came down to see our grand children, brother Simon and all our friends for the last time. I found your children just recovered from the measles. They all send their love to you. We shall try to send you a letter when we get settled in Alabama. Betsey sends her love to you—she expects to go with the Doctor in the spring. Your father, brothers, and sisters, join me in a great deal of love to you and my dear little grand children. Kiss them for their old grand mother.

Farewell, my dear child. I hope the Lord will bless you and your children, and enable you to raise them and be comfortable in life, happy in death, and may we all meet around our Father's throne in heaven, never no more to part. Farewell, my dear child.

From your affectionate Mother,   PHEBE BROWNRIGG.

EDENTON, N.C., Feb. 12, 1836.

My dear Mother—I heard from you by Eliza Little. The letter which you sent me gave me much pleasure to hear that you and my little sisters were well. Eliza said the letter and bundle you sent were open when she received them. I receied one pair of socks, one small apron and slip, and rather more than half a yard of cotton, for which I thank you kindly. In my last letter to you I felt happy to tell you all about my wedding— but ah! mother, what have I to tell you now? a cloud has settled upon me and produced a change in my prospect, too great for words to express. My husband is torn from me, and carried away by his master. Mr. Winslow, who married Miss Little, although he was offered $800 for him that we might not be parted, he refused it. All our family sympathized with me. Miss Joyce told me to go and see Mr. Winslow myself. I went to see him—tried to prevail on him not to carry my husband away, but to suffer him to be bought for $800, that we might not be separated. But mother—all my entreaties and tears did not soften his hard heart—they availed nothing with him.—He said he would "get his own price for him.'' So in a few short months we had to part. O! mother, what shall I do? A time is fast approaching when I shalt want my husband and mother, and both are gone!

Mother, I hope it may be in your power to come on next month and stay with me until May. I should be so happy to see you; so would mistress and Miss Joyce. They are as kind to me as they can be—they both send their love to you and to my little sisters. My health is tolerable—my brothers and sisters are all well. We have had the measles. Grandfather and grandmother came down to take leave of us. They have gone to Alabama, on the Mississippi river. Grandmother left a letter for you, but I had no opportunity to send it before. Miss Joyce thanks you for the book you sent her, and likes it very much. Grandmother wanted you to send father's hymn book, that that she might have something that was his.

My brothers and sisters join me in tender love to you, my dear mother, and dear sisters.—Farewell. Your affectionate daughter,

Emily.

LETTERS OF FORMER SLAVES TO WHITES

Moses Roper to Thomas Price

London, June 27, 1836

Sir,

Having observed, in the report of the discussion between Mr. George Thompson and the Rev. R. J. Breckinridge, at Glasgow, that Mr. Breckinridge questions the accuracy of a statement made by me in reference to the burning alive of a slave in the United States, I beg to hand you the following particulars of that melancholy event.

It happened where I was then living, at Greenville, in the county of the same name, in South Carolina. This slave was a preacher in the state of Georgia. His master told him, if he continued his preaching to his fellow-slaves, he would for the next offense give him 500 lashes. George (for that was the name of the slave) disregarded his master's threat, and continued to preach to them. Upon his master having discovered the fact, George, being dreadfully alarmed lest the threatened punishment should be carried into effect, fled across the Savannah River, and took shelter in the barn of a Mr. Garrison, about seven miles from Greenville. There he was discovered by Mr. G., who shot at him with a rifle, on his attempting to run away, without effect. He was then pursued by Mr. G., who endeavoured to knock him down with the butt end of the piece, unsuccesfully. George wrenched the rifle out of his hands, and struck his pursuer with it. By this time several persons were collected, George was secured, and put into Greenville jail. The facts having transpired, through the newspaper, his master came to Greenville to claim him as his property, but consented, upon being required to do so, to receive 550 dollars as his value, with which he returned home. Shortly after this, George was burnt alive within one mile of the court-house at Greenville, in the presence of an immense assemblage of slaves, which had been gathered together to witness the horrid spectacle from a district of twenty miles in extent.

The manner in which George was burnt was as follows: a pen of about fifteen feet square was built of pine wood, in the centre of which was a tree, the upper part of which had been sawn off. To this tree George was chained; the chain having been passed round his neck, arms, and legs, to make him secure. The pen was then filled with shavings and pine wood up to his neck. A considerable quantity of tar and turpentine was then poured over his head. The preparations having been completed, the four corners of the pen were fired, and the miserable man perished in the flames. When I was last there, which was about two years before I left America for England, not only was the stump of the tree to which the slave George had been fastened, to be seen, but some of his burnt bones. These facts I am ready to attest in the most solemn manner, if required; and, though I have been a slave, I trust my evidence will be received on matters of fact which have come within the range of my own observation, equally with any statement Mr. B. may offer to the British public.

Mr. Breckinridge adverts to the protection which the law is supposed to extend to the slave's life. I beg to say, that whatever the law may be, no such protection is in reality enjoyed by the slave. In illustration of this, I will mention one or two facts. Near the village of Marianna, in Jackson county, West Florida, resided two planters of the names of Sloane and Mauldin. I believe they were relations, certainly they were on the most intimate terms with each other. A negro belonging to Sloane was discovered early one morning on the premises of Mauldin; the fact is, he had run away from his master. Mauldin saw him and called on him to stop, which he refused to do. He then deliberately aimed his rifle at him, and shot him dead. This having been seen by a white man, Mr. Mauldin was tried, and the result was that he substituted another negro in the place of the one he had shot. That negro I have often conversed with.

Take another case: in the village of Liberty Hill (!) a Mr. Bell (a member of a Methodist church) was in the habit of hiring slaves for the cultivation of cotton. Among those so hired was a negro of the name of Henry, the property of a Miss Massie, who had been a favorite slave of her late father. This young man, failing to accomplish the task given him to do on a Saturday, and fearing the punishment of a hundred lashes, with which he had been threatened, finished it on Sunday morning. His labour on the Sabbath was discovered by his master, and on the following day his master, as he said, "for violating the Sabbath," tied him to a tree, and flogged him with his own hand, at intervals from eight in the morning until five o'clock in the evening. About six o'clock two white men, in the employ of Mr. Bell, pitying his wretched condition, untied him, and assisted him home on a horse, a distance of about a mile. He was at this time in a state of great suffering and exhaustion. A short time after they had placed him in the kitchen they heard him groan heavily; Bell also heard him, and said, "I will go out and see what is the matter with the nigger." He went, and found him breathing his last, the victim of his brutal treatment.

This case was brought to trial; my then master, Mr. Gooch, was on the jury. The evidence of the two white men was taken, and Bell was adjudged to pay the value of the slave he had destroyed. This he was unable to do, and a Mr. Connighim, a wealthy and extensive planter in the neighbourhood, paid it for him, on condition of Bell's becoming a driver on one of his estates. To this arrangement he consented, and the matter was settled.

These are the only two instances which I recollect of planters being tried for the murder of slaves. I could report a multitude of cases in which slaves have been murdered, and no account has been taken of them; and on some future day I shall trouble you again on the subject.

I am, Sir,

Yours respectfully,

Moses Roper.

Liberia, Africa,

Aug. 20th, 1854.

Dear Madam and Sir [Mary C. and Robert E. Lee]:—It is with much pleasure, that I take my pen in hand to acknowledge the receipt of your two letters, which gave both Rosabella and myself great comfort to hear from you all.

We receive very few letters from our colored friends and relations. We have been here eight months, and we have all been very sick, with the fever, but I am happy to be able to say that we are still alive and enjoying as good health, as we might expect. For four or five months after we arrived in Africa, my children looked better than I think I ever saw them, they were so fond of palm oil and rice, and eat so much of it, that they fattened very fast. Myself and Rosabella also, enjoyed very good health for four or five months of our residence in Liberia. I must now try to tell you something in regard to how we are getting on, up to this time; as I have no doubt, you will like to hear. You inquire in your letter, what I brought out, and if they were the right sort of articles. When I arrived in Baltimore, preparatory to sailing, I had, with what you gave me, a little over one hundred dollars, but after paying board for two weeks, and buying some things necessary for house keeping, and paying off all my accounts for moving, and getting a few things to the amount of $10, I found, that when I got on board of Ship, I had only

$33 left. When I arrived, I spent two months at Monrovia, which is a very expensive place to live in, having to pay for your wood and water. I found *this* would never do for me, so I got the favor of the agent to allow me a room, up the St. Pauls' river, were I was to settle for the balance of the six months. When I was moved, I had only $3 in cash. The health of myself and family being quite good at that time, I went to work to cut down my lot and clear a spot for a house, not knowing at that time how I should go about it, having no means. Many persons however advised me to go to *shoemaking*, as it would not do for me to be out from eight till four o'clock. I took their advice, and when the six months were out, I had a house of my own to live in. It is 22 by 13 feet and though very rough, yet it is very comfortable. I have found my trade to be very valuable to me indeed. I do not know what I should have done without it. The greatest drawback, is the want of *leather*.

If the Lord continues to bless me with health, I have no doubt that my hands can administer to all my temporal wants. Everything in this country, as I suppose is the case in all new countries, is very high and very hard and inconvenient to get. A little money here, can do but little with regard to farming, and this is certainly the surest and best avenue to wealth, ease and comfort. The only farmers here who are making anything for sale, are those who come to this country with money. Farming is more difficult now than it has been, as all the land on the St. Paul's river has been bought and the emigrants now, have to go back in the forest, some two, three and four miles, and whatever they may plant, is destroyed by the wild hog, the wild cow and many other wild animals. We hope, however, that the time will soon come, when persons will venture to settle a little back from the river, and beasts of burden will be brought into use. At present, there is not one of any kind. In telling you about my house, you might think I was in debt for the whole. It cost from 80 to $100, and I owe about $12 on the whole. I hope soon to be able to live much cheaper than I do at this time, having now everything to buy. I have commenced gardening, raising fowls, Xc., and hope soon to be independent, in the way of chickens, vegetables, and bread stuffs. Great has been the sufferings and mortality among the emigrants, who came out with us. There are many causes for it, which may not be interesting to you to know, nor my business to write. I could write a pamphlet of considerable size of what perhaps might interest you, but as writing is not good for me, passing through the fever, I must conclude for the present. I am very much obliged to you for your corrections in my writing—please correct me always, as I am a self-taught writer. Please present our kindest remembrances to the young ladies and gentlemen and the children. Please write to us by every opportunity and let our friends and relations at Arlington hear from us, when you write to them.

William C. Burke

JOHN PENDLETON KENNEDY

33 | A Southern View of Slavery

*Frank Meriwether, master of the imaginary Virginia plantation Swallow Barn,
is John Pendleton Kennedy's spokesperson for the southern point of view. Like
the author of this pioneering Southern novel, originally published in 1832, Meriwether sees slavery as an obligation that history has placed upon Southern men
of honor. Conceding its inefficiency and its morally dubious character—a view
held by some but by no means all slave apologists—Meriwether sees no choice,
given his views of the capacity of blacks, but to maintain the institution and to
treat slaves as humanely as possible. This view, common in the revolutionary
generation, was losing sway in the South even as Kennedy wrote. Under pressure from Northern antislavery opinion, some Southerners were beginning to
defend slavery as morally correct. Historians still argue about the extent to
which Southerners maintained Meriwether's view of slavery as a necessary evil
in contrast to the more strident and unapologetic proslavery view that emerged
in the decades before the Civil War.*

Having despatched these important matters at the stable, we left our
horses in charge of the servants, and walked towards the cabins, which
were not more than a few hundred paces distant. These hovels, with
their appurtenances, formed an exceedingly picturesque landscape.
They were scattered, without order, over the slope of a gentle hill; and
many of them were embowered under old and majestic trees. The rude-
ness of their construction rather enhanced the attractiveness of the
scene. Some few were built after the fashion of the better sort of cot-
tages; but age had stamped its heavy traces upon their exterior: the
green moss had gathered upon the roofs, and the course weatherboard-
ing had broken, here and there, into chinks. But the more lowly of these
structures, and the most numerous, were nothing more than plain
log-cabins, compacted pretty much on the model by which boys built
patridge-traps; being composed of the trunks of trees, still clothed with
their bark, and knit together at the corners with so little regard to neat-

John Pendleton Kennedy, Swallow Barn, or A Sojourn in the Old Dominion, *Revised Edition.*
(New York, George P. Putnam, 1851), pp. 449–459.

ness that the timbers, being of unequal lengths, jutted beyond each other, sometimes to the length of a foot. Perhaps, none of these latter sort were more than twelve feet square, and not above seven in height. A door swung upon wooden hinges, and a small window of two narrow panes of glass were, in general, the only openings in the front. The intervals between the logs were filled with clay; and the roof, which was constructed of smaller timbers, laid lengthwise along it and projecting two or three feet beyond the side or gable walls, heightened, in a very marked degree, the rustic effect. The chimneys communicated even a droll expression to these habitations. They were, oddly enough, built of billets of wood, having a broad foundation of stone, and growing narrower as they rose, each receding gradually from the house to which it was attached, until it reached the height of the roof. These combustible materials were saved from the access of the fire by a thick coating of mud; and the whole structure, from its tapering form, might be said to bear some resemblance to the spout of a tea kettle; indeed, this domestic implement would furnish no unapt type of the complete cabin.

From this description, which may serve to illustrate a whole species of habitations very common in Virginia, it will be seen, that on the score of accommodation, the inmates of these dwellings were furnished according to a very primitive notion of comfort. Still, however, there were little garden-patches attached to each, where cymblings, cucumbers, sweet potatoes, water-melons and cabbages flourished in unrestrained luxuriance. Add to this, that there was abundance of poultry domesticated about the premises, and it may be perceived that, whatever might be the inconveniences of shelter, there was no want of what, in all countries, would be considered a reasonable supply of luxuries.

Nothing more attracted my observation than the swarms of little negroes that basked on the sunny sides of these cabins, and congregated to gaze at us as we surveyed their haunts. They were nearly all in that costume of the golden age which I have heretofore described; and showed their slim shanks and long heels in all varieties of their grotesque natures. Their predominant love of sunshine, and their lazy, listless postures, and apparent content to be silently looking abroad, might well afford a comparison to a set of terrapins luxuriating in the genial warmth of summer, on the logs of a mill-pond.

And there, too, were the prolific mothers of this redundant brood,—a number of stout negro-women who thronged the doors of the huts, full of idle curiosity to see us. And, when to these are added a few reverend, wrinkled, decrepit old men, with faces shortened as if with drawing-strings, noses that seemed to have run all to nostril, and with feet of the configuration of a mattock, my reader will have a tolerably correct idea of this negro-quarter, its population, buildings, external appearance, situation and extent.

Meriwether, I have said before, is a kind and considerate master. It is his custom frequently to visit his slaves, in order to inspect their con-

dition, and, where it may be necessary, to add to their comforts or relieve their wants. His coming amongst them, therefore, is always hailed
with pleasure. He has constituted himself into a high court of appeal,
and makes it a rule to give all their petitions a patient hearing, and to do
justice in the premises. This, he tells me, he considers as indispensably
necessary;—he says, that no overseer is entirely to be trusted: that there
are few men who have the temper to administer wholesome laws to any
population, however small, without some omissions or irregularities;
and that this is more emphatically true of those who administer them
entirely at their own will. On the present occasion, in almost every
house where Frank entered, there was some boon to be asked; and I
observed, that in every case, the petitioner was either gratified or refused in such a tone as left no occasion or disposition to murmur. Most
of the women had some bargains to offer, of fowls or eggs or other commodities of household use, and Meriwether generally referred them to
his wife, who, I found, relied almost entirely on this resource, for the
supply of such commodities; the negroes being regularly paid for whatever was offered in this way.

One old fellow had a special favour to ask,—a little money to get a
new padding for his saddle, which, he said, "galled his cretur's back."
Frank, after a few jocular passages with the veteran, gave him what he
desired, and sent him off rejoicing.

"That, sir," said Meriwether, "is no less a personage than Jupiter.
He is an old bachelor, and has his cabin here on the hill. He is now near
seventy, and is a kind of King of the Quarter. He has a horse, which he
extorted from me last Christmas; and I seldom come here without finding myself involved in some new demand, as a consequence of my do-
nation. Now he wants a pair of spurs which, I suppose, I must give
him. He is a preposterous coxcomb, and Ned has administered to his
vanity by a present of a *chapeau de bras*—a relic of my military era, which
he wears on Sundays with a conceit that has brought upon him as much
envy as admiration—the usual condition of greatness."

The air of contentment and good humor and kind family attachment, which was apparent throughout this little community, and the
familiar relations existing between them and the proprietor struck me
very pleasantly. I came here a stranger, in great degree, to the negro
character, knowing but little of the domestic history of these people,
their duties, habits or temper, and somewhat disposed, indeed, from
preposessions, to look upon them as severely dealt with, and expecting
to have my sympathies excited towards them as objects of commisera-
tion. I have had, therefore, rather a special interest in observing them.
The contrast between my preconceptions of their condition and the reality which I have witnessed, has brought me a most aggreable surprise.
I will not say that, in a high state of cultivation and of such self-
dependence as they might possibly attain in a separate national existence, they might not become a more respectable people; but I am quite

sure they never could become a happier people than I find them here. Perhaps they are destined, ultimately, to that national existence, in the clime from which they derive their origin—that this is a transition state in which we see them in Virginia. If it be so, no tribe of people have ever passed from barbarism to civilization whose middle stage of progress has been more secure from harm, more genial to their character, or better supplied with mild and beneficient guardianship, adapted to the actual state of their intellectual feebleness, than the negroes of Swallow Barn. And, from what I can gather, it is pretty much the same on the other estates in this region. I hear of an unpleasant exception to this remark now and then; but under such conditions as warrant the opinion that the unfavorable case is not more common than that which may be found in a survey of any other department of society. The oppression of apprentices, of seamen, of soldiers, of subordinates, indeed, in every relation, may furnish elements for a bead-roll of social grievances quite as striking, if they were diligently noted and brought to view.

What the negro is finally capable of, in the way of civilization, I am not philosopher enough to determine. In the present stage of his existence, he presents himself to my mind as essentially parasitical in his nature. I mean that he is, in his moral constitution, a dependant upon the white race; dependant for guidance and direction even to the procurement of his most indispensable necessaries. Apart from this protection he has the helplessness of a child,—without foresight, without faculty of contrivance, without thrift of any kind. We have instances, in the neighborhood of this estate, of individuals of the tribe falling into the most deplorable destitution from the want of that constant supervision which the race seems to require. This helplessness may be the due and natural impression which two centuries of servitude have stamped upon the tribe. But it is not the less a present and insurmountable impediment to that most cruel of all projects—the direct, broad emancipation of these people;—an act of legislation in comparison with which the revocation of the edict of Nantes would be entitled to be ranked among political benefactions. Taking instruction from history, all organized slavery is inevitably but a temporary phase of human condition. Interest, necessity and instinct, all work to give progression to the relations of mankind, and finally to elevate each tribe or race to its maximum of refinement and power. We have no reason to suppose that the negro will be an exception to this law.

At present, I have said, he is parasitical. He grows upward, only as the vine to which nature has supplied the sturdy tree as a support. He is extravagantly imitative. The older negroes here have—with some spice of comic mixture in it—that formal, grave and ostentatious style of manners, which belonged to the gentlemen of former days; they are profuse of bows and compliments, and very aristocratic in their way. The younger ones are equally to be remarked for aping the style of the present time, and especially for such tags of dandyism in dress as come within their reach. Their fondness for music and dancing is a predominant passion. I never meet a negro man—unless he is quite old—that he is not whistling; and the women sing from morning till night. And as to dancing, the hardest day's work does not restrain their desire to indulge in such pastime. During the harvest, when their toil is pushed to its utmost—the time being one of recognized privileges—they dance almost the whole night. They are great sportsmen, too. They angle and haul the seine, and hunt and tend their traps, with a zest that never grows weary. Their gayety of heart is constitutional and perennial, and when they are together they are as voluble and noisy as so many blackbirds. In short, I think them the most good-natured, careless, light-hearted, and happily-constructed human beings I have ever seen. Having but few and simple wants, they seem to me to be provided with every comfort which falls within the ordinary compass of their wishes; and, I might say, that they find even more enjoyment,—as that word may be applied to express positive pleasures scattered through the course of daily occupation—than any other laboring people I am acquainted with.

I took occasion to express these opinions to Meriwether, and to tell him how much I was struck by the mild and kindly aspect of this society at the Quarter.

This, as I expected, brought him into a discourse.

"The world," said he, "has begun very seriously to discuss the evils of slavery, and the debate has sometimes, unfortunately, been levelled to the comprehension of our negroes, and pains have even been taken that it should reach them. I believe there are but few men who may not be persuaded that they suffer some wrong in the organization of society—for society has many wrongs, both accidental and contrived, in its structure. Extreme poverty is, perhaps, always a wrong done to the individual upon whom it is cast. Society can have no honest excuse for starving a human being. I dare say you can follow out that train of thought and find numerous evils to complain of. Ingenious men, some of them not very honest, have found in these topics themes for agitation and popular appeal in all ages. How likely are they to find, in this question of slavery, a theme for the highest excitement; and, especially, how easy is it to inflame the passions of these untutored and unreckoning people, our black population, with this subject! For slavery, as an original question, is wholly without justification or defence. It is theoretically and morally wrong—and fanatical and one-sided thinkers will call its continuance, even for a day, a wrong, under any modification of it. But, surely, if these people are consigned to our care by the accident, or, what is worse, the premeditated policy which has put them upon our commonwealth, the great duty that is left to us is, to shape our conduct, in reference to them, by a wise and beneficent consideration of the case as it exists, and to administer wholesome laws for their government, making their servitude as tolerable to them as we can consistently with our own safety and their ultimate good. We should not be justified in taking the hazard of internal convulsions to get rid of them; nor have we a right, in the desire to free ourselves, to whelm them in greater evils than their present bondage. A violent removal of them, or a general emancipation, would assuredly produce one or the other of these calamities. Has any sensible man, who takes a different view of this subject, ever reflected upon the consequences of committing two or three millions of persons, born and bred in a state so completely dependent as that of slavery—so unfurnished, so unintellectual, so utterly helpless, I may say—to all the responsibilities, cares and labors of a state of freedom? Must he not acknowledge, that the utmost we could give them would be but a nominal freedom, in doing which we should be guilty of a cruel desertion of our trust—inevitably leading them to progressive debasement, penury, oppression, and finally to extermination? I would not argue with that man whose bigotry to a sentiment was so blind and so fatal as to insist on this expedient. When the time comes, as I apprehend it will come,—and all the sooner, if it be not delayed by these efforts to arouse something like a vindictive feeling between the disputants on both sides—in which the roots of slavery will begin to lose their hold in our soil; and when we shall have the means for providing these people a proper asylum, I shall be glad to see the State devote her thoughts to that enterprise, and, if I am alive, will cheerfully and gratefully assist in it. In the mean time, we owe it to justice and humanity to treat these people with the most considerate kindness. As to what are ordinarily imagined to be the evils or sufferings of their condition, I do not believe in them. The evil is generally felt on the side of the master. Less work is exacted of them than voluntary laborers choose to perform: they have as many privileges as are compatible with the nature of their occupations: they are subsisted, in general, as comfortably—nay, in their estimation of comforts, more comfortably, than the rural population of other countries. And as to the severities that are alleged to be practised upon them, there is much more malice or invention than truth in the accusation. The slaveholders in this region are, in the main, men of kind and humane tempers—as pliant to the touch of compassion, and as sensible of its duties, as the best men in any community, and as little disposed to inflict injury upon their dependents. Indeed, the owner of slaves is less apt to be harsh in his requisitions of labor than those who toil much themselves. I suspect it is invariably characteristic of those who are in the habit of severely tasking themselves, that they are inclined to regulate their demands upon others by their own standard. Our slaves are punished for misdemeanors, pretty much as disorderly persons are punished in all societies; and I am quite of opinion that our statistics of crime and punishment will compare favorably with those of any other population. But the punishment, on our side, is remarked as the personal act of the master; whilst, elsewhere, it goes free of ill-natured comment, because it is set down to the course of justice. We, therefore, suffer a reproach which other polities escape, and the conclusion is made an item of complaint against slavery.

"It has not escaped the attention of our legislation to provide against the ill-treatment of our negro population. I heartily concur in all effective laws to punish cruelty in masters. Public opinion on that subject, however, is even stronger than law, and no man can hold up his head in this community who is chargeable with mal-treatment of his slaves.

"One thing I desire you specially to note: the question of emancipation is exclusively our own, and every intermeddling with it from abroad will but mar its chance of success. We cannot but regard such interference as an unwarrantable and mischievous design to do us injury, and, therefore, we resent it—sometimes, I am sorry to say, even to the point of involving the innocent negro in the rigor which it provokes. We think, and, indeed, we know, that we alone are able to deal properly with the subject; all others are misled by the feeling which the natural sentiment against slavery, in the abstract, excites. They act under imperfect knowledge and impulsive prejudices which are totally incompatible with wise action on any subject. We, on the contrary, have every motive to calm and prudent counsel. Our lives, fortunes, families—our commonwealth itself, are put at the hazard of this resolve. You gentlemen of the North greatly misapprehend us, if you suppose that we are in love with this slave institution—or that, for the most part, we even deem it profitable to us. There are amongst us, it is true, some persons who are inclined to be fanatical on this side of the question, and who bring themselves to adopt some bold dogmas tending to these extreme views—and it is not out of the course of events that the violence of the agitations against us may lead ultimately to a wide adoption of these dogmas amongst the slaveholding States. It is in the nature of men to recalcitrate against continual assault, and, through the zeal of such opposition, to run into ultraisms which cannot be defended. But at present, I am sure the Southern sentiment on this question is temperate and wise, and that we neither regard slavery as a good, nor account it, except in some favorable conditions, as profitable. The most we can say of it is that, as matters stand, it is the best auxiliary within our reach.

"Without troubling you with further reflections upon a dull subject, my conclusion is that the real friends of humanity should conspire to allay the ferments on this question, and, even at some cost, to endeavor to encourage the natural contentment of the slave himself, by arguments to reconcile him to a present destiny, which is, in fact, more free from sorrow and want than that of almost any other class of men occupying the same field of labor."

Meriwether was about to finish his discourse at this point, when a new vein of thought struck him:

"It has sometimes occurred to me," he continued, "that we might elevate our slave population, very advantageously to them and to us, by some reforms in our code. I think we are justly liable to reproach, for the neglect or omission of our laws to recognize and regulate marriages, and the relation of family amongst the negroes. We owe it to humanity and to the sacred obligation of Christian ordinances, to respect and secure the bonds of husband and wife, and parent and child. I am ashamed to acknowledge that I have no answer to make, in the way of justification of this neglect. We have no right to put man and wife asunder. The law should declare this, and forbid the separation under any contingency, except of crime. It should be equally peremptory in forbidding the coercive separation of children from the mother—at least during that period when the one requires the care of the other. A disregard of these attachments has brought more odium upon the conditions of servitude than all the rest of its imputed hardships; and a suitable provision for them would tend greatly to gratify the feelings of benevolent and conscientious slaveholders, whilst it would disarm all considerate and fair-minded men, of what they deem the strongest objection to the existing relations of master and slave.

"I have also another reform to propose," said Meriwether, smiling. "It is, to establish by law, an upper or privileged class of slaves—selecting them from the most deserving, above the age of forty-five years. These I would endue with something of a feudal character. They should be entitled to hold small tracts of land under their masters, rendering for it a certain rent, payable either in personal service or money. They should be elevated into this class through some order of court, founded on certificates of good conduct, and showing the assent of the master. And I think I would create legal jurisdictions, giving the masters or stewards civil and criminal judicial authority. I have some dream of a project of this kind in my head," he continued, "which I have not fully matured as yet. You will think, Mr. Littleton, that I am a man of schemes, if I go on much longer—but there is something in this notion which may be improved to advantage, and I should like, myself, to begin the experiment. Jupiter, here, shall be my first feudatory—my tenant in socage—my old villain!"

"I suspect," said I, "Jupiter considers that his dignity is not to be enhanced by any enlargement of privilege, as long as he is allowed to walk about in his military hat as King of the Quarter."

"Perhaps not," replied Meriwether, laughing; "then I shall be forced to make my commencement upon Carey."

"Carey," interrupted Hazard, "would think it small promotion to be allowed to hold land under you!"

"Faith! I shall be without a feudatory to begin with," said Meriwether.

/   /   /

34 | *A Slave Insurrection*

Slaveowners, especially those in states with large slave populations, lived in dread of slave uprisings. The most sensational rebellion was led in 1831 by Nat Turner, a slave in Southampton County, Virginia. Turner's rebellion lasted only five days (August 21–25), but it claimed the lives of fifty-one whites and terrified the South. In addition to leading to a general tightening of restrictions on slaves—in matters like education, marriage, and the right to assemble—the rebellion dealt a serious blow to the chance that the South would voluntarily emancipate its slaves.

The Confessions of Nat Turner *was published in 1832 by Thomas R. Gray, who interviewed Turner shortly before he was tried and executed. How much of the language of these confessions is Turner's and how much is Gray's is impossible to determine. Gray's account was widely read throughout the South.*

Agreeable to his own appointment, on the evening he was committed to prison, with permission of the jailer, I visited Nat on Tuesday the first of November, when, without being questioned at all, he commenced his narrative in the following words:
Sir,

You have asked me to give a history of the motives which induced me to undertake the late insurrection, as you call it. To do so I must go back to the days of my infancy, and even before I was born. I was thirty-one years of age the second of October last, and born the property of Benjamin Turner, of this county. In my childhood a circumstance occurred which made an indelible impression on my mind, and laid the groundwork of that enthusiasm which has terminated so fatally to many both white and black, and for which I am about to atone at the gallows. It is here necessary to relate this circumstance—trifling as it may seem, it was the commencement of that belief which has grown with time, and even now, sir, in this dungeon, helpless and forsaken as I am, I cannot divest myself of. Being at play with other children, when three or four

The Confessions of Nat Turner, Leader of the Late Insurrection in Southampton, Virginia, as Fully and Voluntarily made to Thomas C. Gray. *(Richmond, Virginia, 1832). Reprinted, New York, 1964, pp. 5–17.*

years old, I was telling them something, which my mother overhearing, said it had happened before I was born. I stuck to my story, however, and related some things which went in her opinion to confirm it. Others being called on were greatly astonished, knowing that these things had happened, and caused them to say in my hearing, I surely would be a prophet, as the Lord had shown me things that had happened before my birth. And my father and mother strengthened me in this my first impression, saying in my presence, I was intended for some great purpose, which they had always thought from certain marks on my head and breast.

My grandmother, who was very religious, and to whom I was much attached—my master, who belonged to the church, and other religious persons who visited the house, and whom I often saw at prayers, noticing the singularity of my manners, I suppose, and my uncommon intelligence for a child, remarked I had too much sense to be raised—and if I was, I would never be of any service to any one—as a slave. The manner in which I learned to read and write, not only had great influence on my own mind, as I acquired it with the most perfect ease, so much so that I have no recollection whatever of learning the alphabet—but to the astonishment of the family, one day, when a book was shown me to keep me from crying, I began spelling the names of different objects— this was a source of wonder to all in the neighborhood, particularly the blacks—and this learning was constantly improved at all opportunities. When I got large enough to go to work, while employed, I was reflecting on many things that would present themselves to my imagination. I was not addicted to stealing in my youth, nor have never been. Yet such was the confidence of the Negroes in the neighborhood, even at this early period of my life, in my superior judgment, that they would often carry me with them when they were going on any roguery, to plan for them. Growing up among them, with this confidence in my superior judgment, and when this, in their opinions, was perfected by divine inspiration, from the circumstances already alluded to in my infancy, and which belief was ever afterward zealously inculcated by the austerity of my life and manners, which became the subject of remark by white and black. By this time, having arrived to man's estate, and hearing the Scriptures commented on at meetings, I was struck with that particular passage which says: "Seek ye the kingdom of Heaven and all things shall be added unto you." I reflected much on this passage, and prayed daily for light on this subject. As I was praying one day at my plough, the spirit spoke to me, saying "Seek ye the kingdom of Heaven and all things shall be added unto you." *Question*—What do you mean by the Spirit. *Answer*—The Spirit that spoke to the prophets in former days— and I was greatly astonished, and for two years prayed continually, whenever my duty would permit—and then again I had the same revelation, which fully confirmed me in the impresson that I was ordained for some great purpose in the hands of the Almighty. Several years rolled round, in which many events occurred to strengthen me in this my belief. At this time I reverted in my mind to the remarks made of me in my childhood, and the things that had been shown me. And as it had been said of me in my childhood by those whom I had been taught to pray, both white and black, and in whom I had the greatest confidence, that I had too much sense to be raised, and if I was I would never be of any use to anyone as a slave. Now finding I had arrived to man's estate, and was a slave, and these revelations being made known to me, I began to direct my attention to this great object, to fulfill the purpose for which, by this time, I felt assured I was intended. Knowing the influence I had obtained over the minds of my fellow servants, (not by the means of conjuring and such like tricks—for to them I always spoke of such things with contempt) but by the communion of the Spirit whose revelations I often communicated to them, and they believed and said my wisdom came from God.

And on the twelfth of May 1828, I heard a loud noise in the heavens, and the Spirit instantly appeared to me and said the Serpent was loosened, and Christ had laid down the yoke he had borne for the sins of men, and that I should take it on and fight against the Serpent, for the time was fast approaching, when the first should be last and the last should be first. *Question*—Do you not find yourself mistaken now? *Answer*—Was not Christ crucified? And by signs in the heavens that it would make known to me when I should commence the great work— and until the first sign appeared, I should conceal it from the knowledge of men—and on the appearance of the sign (the eclipse of the sun last February), I should arise and prepare myself, and slay my enemies with their own weapons. And immediately on the sign appearing in the heavens, the seal was removed from my lips, and I communicated the great work laid out for me to do, to four in whom I had the greatest confidence (Henry, Hark, Nelson, and Sam). It was intended by us to have begun the work of death on the fourth of July last. Many were the plans formed and rejected by us, and it affected my mind to such a degree that I fell sick, and the time passed without our coming to any determination how to commence—still forming new schemes and reject- ing them when the sign appeared again, which determined me not to wait longer.

Since the commencement of 1830, I had been living with Mr. Joseph Travis, who was to me a kind master, and placed the greatest confidence in me; in fact, I had no cause to complain of his treatment to me. On Saturday evening, the twentieth of August, it was agreed between Henry, Hark, and myself to prepare a dinner the next day for the men we expected, and then to concert a plan, as we had not yet determined on any. Hark on the following morning brought a pig, and Henry brandy, and being joined by Sam, Nelson, Will, and Jack, they prepared in the woods a dinner, where, about three o'clock, I joined them. . . .

I saluted them on coming up, and asked Will how came he there; he answered his life was worth no more than others, and his liberty as dear to him. I asked him if he though to obtain it? He said he would or lose his life. This was enough to put him in full confidence. Jack, I knew, was only a tool in the hands of Hark. It was quickly agreed we should commence at home (Mr. J. Travis') on that night, and until we had armed and equipped ourselves, and gathered sufficient force, neither age nor sex was to be spared (which was invariably adhered to). We remained at the feast until about two hours in the night, when we went to the house and found Austin; they all went to the cider press and drank, except myself. On returning to the house, Hark went to the door with an ax, for the purpose of breaking it open, as we knew we were strong enough to murder the family, if they were awakened by the noise; but reflecting that it might create an alarm in the neighborhood, we determined to enter the house secretly, and murder them while sleeping. Hark got a ladder and set it against the chimney, on which I ascended, and hoisting a window, entered and came down stairs, unbarred the door, and removed the guns from their places. It was then observed that I must spill the first blood. On which armed with a hatchet, and accompanied by Will, I entered my master's chamber; it being dark, I could not give a death blow, the hatchet glanced from his head, he sprang from the bed and called his wife, it was his last word. Will laid him dead, with a blow of his ax, and Mrs. Travis shared the same fate, as she lay in bed. The murder of this family, five in number, was the work of a moment, not one of them awoke; there was a little infant sleeping in a cradle, that was forgotten, until we had left the house and gone some distance, when Henry and Will returned and killed it. We got here four guns that would shoot, and several old muskets, with a pound or two of powder. We remained some time at the barn, where we paraded; I formed them in a line as soldiers, and after carrying them through all the maneuvers I was master of, marched them off to Mr. Salathul Francis', about six hundred yards distant. Sam and Will went to the door and knocked. Mr. Francis asked who was there, Sam replied it was him, and he had a letter for him, on which he got up and came to the door; they immediately seized him, and dragging him out a little from the door, he was dispatched by repeated blows on the head; there was no other white person in the family. We started from there for Mrs. Reese's, maintaining the most perfect silence on our march, where finding the door unlocked, we entered, and murdered Mrs. Reese in her bed, while sleeping; her son awoke, but it was only to sleep the sleep of death, he had only time to say who is that, and he was no more. From Mrs. Reese's we went to Mrs. Turner's, a mile distant, which we reached about sunrise on Monday morning. Henry, Austin, and Sam went to the still, where, finding Mr. Peebles, Austin shot him, and the rest of us went to the house; as we approached, the family discovered us, and shut the door. Vain hope! Will, with one stroke of his ax, opened it, and we entered and found Mrs. Turner and Mrs. Newsome in the middle of a room almost frightened to death. Will immediately killed Mrs. Turner, with one blow of his ax. I took Mrs. Newsome by the hand, and with the sword I had when I was apprehended, I struck her several blows over the head, but not being able to kill her, as the sword was dull. Will turning around and discovering it, dispatched her also. A general destruction of property and search for money and ammunition always succeeded the murders. By this time my company amounted to fifteen, and nine men mounted, who started for Mrs. Whitehead's (the other six were to go through a byway to Mr. Bryant's and rejoin us at Mrs. Whitehead's), standing in the cotton patch, near the lane fence; we called him over into the lane, and Will, the executioner, was near at hand with his fatal ax, to send him to an untimely grave. As we pushed on to the house, I discovered someone running round the garden, and thinking it was some of the white family, I pursued them, but finding it was a servant girl belonging to the house, I returned to commence the work of death, but they whom I left had not been idle; all the family were already murdered, but Mrs. Whitehead and her daughter Margaret. As I came round to the door I saw Will pulling Mrs. Whitehead out of the house, and at the step he nearly severed her head from her body, with his broad ax. Miss Margaret, when I discovered her had concealed herself in the corner, formed by the projection of the cellar cap from the house; on my approach she fled, but was soon overtaken, and after repeated blows with a sword, I killed her by a blow on the head with a fence rail. By this time, the six who had gone by Mr. Bryant's rejoined us, and informed me they had done the work of death assigned them. We again divided, part going to Mr. Richard Porter's, and from thence to Nathaniel Francis', the others to Mr. Howell Harris', and Mr. T. Doyle's. On my reaching Mr. Porter's, he had escaped with his family. I understood there that the alarm had already spread.

I proceeded to Mr. Levi Waller's, two or three miles distant. I took my station in the rear, and as it was my object to carry terror and devastation wherever we went, I placed fifteen or twenty of the best armed and most to be relied on in front, who generally approached the houses as fast as their horses could run; this was for two purposes, to prevent their escape and strike terror to the inhabitants—on this account I never got to the houses, after leaving Mrs. Whitehead's, until the murders were committed, except in one case. I sometimes got in sight in time to see the work of death completed, viewed the mangled bodies as they lay, in silent satisfaction, and immediately started in quest of other victims. Having murdered Mrs. Waller and ten children, we started for Mr. William Williams'—having killed him and two little boys that were there; while engaged in this, Mrs. Williams fled and got some distance from the house, but she was pursued, overtaken, and compelled to get up behind one of the company, who brought her back, and after showing her the mangled body of her lifeless husband, she was told to get down and lay by his side, where she was shot dead. I then started for Mr. Jacob Williams', where the family were murdered. Here we found a young man named Drury, who had come on business with Mr. Williams. He was pursued, overtaken, and shot. Mrs. Vaughan's was the next place we visited—and after murdering the family here, I determined on starting for Jerusalem. Our number amounted now to fifty or sixty, all mounted and armed with guns, axes, swords, and clubs. On reaching Mr. James W. Parker's gate, immediately on the road leading to Jerusalem, and about three miles distant, it was proposed to me to call there, but I objected, as I knew he was gone to Jerusalem, and my object was to reach there as soon as possible; but some of the men having relations at Mr. Parker's it was agreed that they might call and get his people. I remained at the gate on the road, with seven or eight; the others going across the field to the house, about half a mile off. After waiting some time for them, I became impatient, and started to the house for them, and on our return we were met by a party of white men, who had pursued our blood-stained track and who had fired on those at the gate and dispersed them, which I knew nothing of, not having been at that time rejoined by any of them. Immediately on discovering the whites, I ordered my men to halt and form, as they appeared to be alarmed. The white men, eighteen in number, approached us in about one hundred yards, when one of them fired.

I then ordered my men to fire and rush on them; the few remaining stood their ground until we approached within fifty yards, when they fired and retreated. We pursued and overtook some of them who we thought we left dead; after pursuing them about two hundred yards, and rising a little hill, I discovered they were met by another party, and had halted, and were reloading their guns, thinking that those who retreated first, and the party who fired on us at fifty or sixty yards distant, had all only fallen back to meet others with ammunition. As I saw them reloading their guns, and more coming up than I saw at first, and several of my bravest men being wounded, the others became panic struck and squandered over the field; the white men pursued and fired on us several times. Hark had his horse shot under him, and I caught another for him as it was running by me; five or six of my men were wounded, but none left on the field; finding myself defeated here I instantly determined to go through a private way, and cross the Nottoway River at the Cypress Bridge, three miles below Jerusalem, and attack that place in the rear, as I expected they would look for me on the other road, and I had a great desire to get there to procure arms and ammunition. After going a short distance in this private way, accompanied by about twenty men, I overtook two or three who told me the others were dispersed in every direction. After trying in vain to collect a sufficient force to proceed to Jerusalem, I determined to return, as I was sure they would make back to their old neighborhood, were they would rejoin me, make new recruits, and come down again. On my way back, I called at Mrs. Thomas's, Mrs. Spencer's, and several other places. The white families having fled, we found no more victims to gratify our thirst for blood, we stopped at Major Ridley's quarter for the night, and being joined by four of his men, with the recruits made since my defeat, we mustered now about forty strong. After placing out sentinels, I laid down to sleep, but was quickly roused by a great racket. Starting up, I found some mounted, and others in great confusion; one of the sentinels having given the alarm that we were about to be attacked, I ordered some to ride round and reconnoiter, and on their return the others being more alarmed, not knowing who they were, fled in different ways, so that I was reduced to about twenty again; with this I determined to attempt to recruit, and proceed on to rally in the neighborhood I had left. Dr. Blunt's was the nearest house, which we reached just before day; on riding up the yard, Hark fired a gun. We expected Dr. Blunt and his family were at Major Ridley's, as I knew there was a company of men there; the gun was fired to ascertain if any of the family were at home; we were immediately fired upon and retreated leaving several of my men. I do not know what became of them, as I never saw them afterward. Pursuing our course back, and coming in sight of Captain Harris's, where we had been the day before, we discovered a party of white men at the house, on which all deserted me but two (Jacob and Nat), we concealed ourselves in the woods until near night, when I sent them in search of Henry, Sam, Nelson, and Hark, and directed them to rally all they could at the place we had had our dinner the Sunday before, where they would find me, and I accordingly returned there as soon as it was dark, and remained until Wednesday evening, when discovering white men riding around the place as though they were looking for someone, and none of my men joining me, I concluded Jacob and Nat had been taken, and compelled to betray me. On this I gave up all hope for the present; and on Thursday night, after having supplied myself with provisions from Mr. Travis's, I scratched a hole under a pile of fence rails in a field, were I concealed myself for six weeks, never leaving my hiding place but for a few minutes in the dead of night to get water, which was very near; thinking by this time I could venture out, I began to go about in the night and eavesdrop the houses in the neighborhood; pursuing this course for about a fortnight and gathering little or no intelligence, afraid of speaking to any human being, and returning every morning to my cave before the dawn of day. I know not how long I might have led this life, if accident had not betrayed me, a dog in the neighborhood passing by my hiding place one night while I was out was attracted by some meat I had in my cave, and crawled in and stole it, and was coming out just as I returned. A few nights after, two Negroes having started to go hunting with the same dog, and passed that way, the dog came again to the place, and having just gone out to walk about, discovered me and barked, on which, thinking myself discovered, I spoke to them to beg concealment. On making myself known, they fled from me. Knowing then they would betray me, I immediately left my hiding place, and was pursued almost incessantly until I was taken a fortnight afterward by Mr. Benjamin Phipps, in a little hole I had dug out with my sword, for the purpose of concealment, under the top of a fallen tree. On Mr. Phipps discovering the place of my conceal-ment, he cocked his gun and aimed at me. I requested him not to shoot, and I would give up, upon which he demanded my sword. I delivered it to him, and he brought me to prison. During the time I was pursued, I had many hair breadth escapes, which your time will not permit you to relate. I am here loaded with chains, and willing to suffer the fate that awaits me.

[Gray:] I here proceeded to make some inquiries of him, after assur-ing him of the certain death that awaited him, and that concealment would only bring destruction on the innocent as well as guilty, of his own color, if he knew of any extensive or concerted plan. His answer was, I do not. When I questioned him as to the insurrection in North Carolina happening about the same time, he denied any knowledge of it.

35 | A Slave's Life

Frederick Douglass was perhaps the first national leader among black Americans. Born a slave around 1817, he escaped from slavery in 1838 and by 1841 had become the leading black abolitionist. After publishing his Narrative of the Life of Frederick Douglass *in 1845 (it was enlarged in 1855 and again in 1892), he had to flee to England until 1847, when money from his lecturing and writing enabled him to purchase his freedom. Settling in Rochester, New York, he edited an abolitionist newspaper, the* North Star. *After the Civil War he became the most important black spokesman for the Republican party and served a number of appointive offices. Douglass died in 1895. An eloquent speaker and writer and an astute politician, Douglass set a high standard of political and intellectual leadership.*

I was born in Tuckahoe, near Hillsborough, and about twelve miles from Easton, in Talbot county, Maryland. I have no accurate knowledge of my age, never having seen any authentic record containing it. By far the larger part of the slaves know as little of their ages as horses know of theirs, and it is the wish of most masters within my knowledge to keep their slaves thus ignorant. I do not remember to have ever met a slave who could tell of his birthday. They seldom come nearer to it than planting-time, harvest-time, cherry-time, spring-time, or fall-time. A want of information concerning my own was a source of unhappiness to me even during childhood. The white children could tell their ages. I could not tell why I ought to be deprived of the same privilege. I was not allowed to make any inquiries of my master concerning it. He deemed all such inquiries on the part of a slave improper and impertinent, and evidence of a restless spirit. The nearest estimate I can give makes me now between twenty-seven and twenty-eight years of age. I come to this, from hearing my master say, some time during 1835, I was about seventeen years old.

My mother was named Harriet Bailey. She was the daughter of Isaac

Douglass, Frederick. Narrative of the Life of Frederick Douglass, An American Slave. *(Boston: Anti-Slavery Office, 1845), pp. 1–5, 12–15, 30–32, 35–37, 114–115.*

and Betsey Bailey, both colored, and quite dark. My mother was of a darker complexion than either my grandmother or grandfather.

My father was a white man. He was admitted to be such by all I ever heard speak of my parentage. The opinion was also whispered that my master was my father; but of the correctness of this opinion, I know nothing; the means of knowing was withheld from me. My mother and I were separated when I was but an infant—before I knew her as my mother. It is a common custom, in the part of Maryland from which I ran away, to part children from their mothers at a very early age. Frequently, before the child has reached its twelfth month, its mother is taken from it, and hired out on some farm a considerable distance off, and the child is placed under the care of an old woman, too old for field labor. For what this separation is done, I do not know, unless it be to hinder the development of the child's affection toward its mother, and to blunt and destroy the natural affection of the mother for the child. This is the inevitable result.

I never saw my mother, to know her as such, more than four or five times in my life; and each of these times was very short in duration, and at night. She was hired by a Mr. Stewart, who lived about twelve miles from my home. She made her journeys to see me in the night, travelling the whole distance on foot, after the performance of her day's work. She was a field hand, and a whipping is the penalty of not being in the field at sunrise, unless a slave has special permission from his or her master to the contrary—a permission which they seldom get, and one that gives to him that gives it the proud name of being a kind master. I do not recollect of ever seeing my mother by the light of day. She was with me in the night. She would lie down with me, and get me to sleep, but long before I waked she was gone. Very little communication ever took place between us. Death soon ended what little we could have while she lived, and with it her hardships and suffering. She died when I was about seven years old, on one of my master's farms, near Lee's Mill. I was not allowed to be present during her illness, at her death, or burial. She was gone long before I knew any thing about it. Never having enjoyed, to any considerable extent, her soothing presence, her tender and watchful care, I received the tidings of her death with much the same emotions I should have probably felt at the death of a stranger.

Called thus suddenly away, she left me without the slightest intimation of who my father was. The whisper that my master was my father, may or may not be true; and, true or false, it is of but little consequence to my purpose whilst the fact remains, in all its glaring odiousness, that slaveholders have ordained, and by law established, that the children of slave women shall in all cases follow the condition of their mothers; and this is done too obviously to administer to their own lusts, and make a gratification of their wicked desires profitable as well as pleasurable; for by this cunning arrangement, the slaveholder, in cases not a few, sustains to his slaves the double relation of master and father.

I know of such cases; and it is worthy of remark that such slaves invariably suffer greater hardships, and have more to contend with, than others. They are, in the first place, a constant offence to their mistress. She is ever disposed to find fault with them; they can seldom do any thing to please her; she is never better pleased than when she sees them under the lash, especially when she suspects her husband of showing to his mulatto children favors which he withholds from his black slaves. The master is frequently compelled to sell this class of his slaves, out of deference to the feelings of his white wife; and, cruel as the deed may strike any one to be, for a man to sell his own children to human flesh-mongers, it is often the dictate of humanity for him to do so; for, unless he does this, he must not only whip them himself, but must stand by and see one white son tie up his brother, of but few shades darker complexion than himself, and ply the gory lash to his naked back; and if he lisp one word of disapproval, it is set down to his parental partiality, and only makes a bad matter worse, both for himself and the slave whom he would protect and defend.

Every year brings with it multitudes of this class of slaves. It was doubtless in consequence of a knowledge of this fact, that one great statesman of the south predicted the downfall of slavery by the inevitable laws of population. Whether this prophecy is ever fulfilled or not, it is nevertheless plain that a very different-looking class of people are springing up at the south, and are now held in slavery, from those originally brought to this country from Africa; and if their increase will do no other good, it will do away the force of the argument, that God cursed Ham, and therefore American slavery is right. If the lineal descendants of Ham are alone to be scripturally enslaved, it is certain that slavery at the south must soon become unscriptural; for thousands are ushered into the world, annually, who, like myself, owe their existence to white fathers, and those fathers most frequently their own masters.

I have had two masters. My first master's name was Anthony. I do not remember his first name. He was generally called Captain Anthony—a title which, I presume, he acquired by sailing a craft on the Chesapeake Bay. He was not considered a rich slaveholder. He owned two or three farms, and about thirty slaves. His farms and slaves were under the care of an overseer. The overseer's name was Plummer. Mr. Plummer was a miserable drunkard, a profane swearer, and a savage monster. He always went armed with a cowskin and a heavy cudgel. I have known him to cut and slash the women's heads so horribly, that even master would be enraged at his cruelty, and would threaten to whip him if he did not mind himself. Master, however, was not a humane slaveholder. It required extraordinary barbarity on the part of an overseer to affect him. He was a cruel man, hardened by a long life of slaveholding. He would at times seem to take great pleasure in whipping a slave. I have often been awakened at the dawn of day by the most heart-rending shrieks of an own aunt of mine, whom he used to tie up to a joist, and whip upon her naked back till she was literally covered with blood. No words, no tears, no prayers, from his gory victim, seemed to move his iron heart from its bloody purpose. The louder she screamed, the harder he whipped; and where the blood ran fastest, there he whipped longest. He would whip her to make her scream, and whip her to make her hush; and not until overcome by fatigue, would he cease to swing the blood-clotted cowskin. I remember the first time I ever witnessed this horrible exhibition. I was quite a child, but I well remember it. I never shall forget it whilst I remember any thing. It was the first of a long series of such outrages, of which I was doomed to be a witness and a participant. It struck me with awful force. It was the blood-stained gate, the entrance to the hell of slavery, through which I was about to pass. It was a most terrible spectacle. I wish I could commit to paper the feelings with which I beheld it. . . .

The home plantation of Colonel Lloyd [the second master] wore the appearance of a country village. All the mechanical operations for all the farms were performed here. The shoemaking and mending, the blacksmithing, cartwrighting, coopering, weaving, and grain-grinding, were all performed by the slaves on the home plantation. The whole place wore a business-like aspect very unlike the neighboring farms. The number of houses, too, conspired to give it advantage over the neighboring farms. It was called by the slaves the *Great House Farm.* Few privileges were esteemed higher, by the slaves of the out-farms, than that of being selected to do errands at the Great House Farm. It was associated in their minds with greatness. A representative could not be prouder of his election to a seat in the American Congress, than a slave on one of the out-farms would be of his election to do errands at the Great House Farm. They regarded it as evidence of great confidence reposed in them by their overseers; and it was on this account, as well as a constant desire to be out of the field from under the driver's lash, that they esteemed it a high privilege, one worth careful living for. He was called the smartest and most trusty fellow, who had this honor conferred upon him the most frequently. The competitors for this office sought as diligently to please their overseers, as the office-seekers in the political parties seek to please and deceive the people. The same traits of character might be seen in Colonel Lloyd's slaves, as are seen in the slaves of the political parties.

The slaves selected to go to the Great House Farm, for the monthly allowance for themselves and their fellow-slaves, were peculiarly enthusiastic. While on their way, they would make the dense old woods, for miles around, reverberate with their wild songs, revealing at once the highest joy and the deepest sadness. They would compose and sing as they went along, consulting neither time nor tune. The thought that came up, came out—if not in the word, in the sound and as frequently in the one as in the other. They would sometimes sing the most pathetic sentiment in the most rapturous tone, and the most rapturous sentiment in the most pathetic tone. Into all of their songs they would manage to weave something of the Great House Farm. Especially would they do this, when leaving home. They would then sing most exultingly the following words:—

> "I am going away to the Great House Farm!
> O, yea! O, yea!, O!"

This they would sing, as a chorus, to words which to many would seem unmeaning jargon, but which, nevertheless, were full of meaning to themselves. I have sometimes thought that the mere hearing of those songs would do more to impress some minds with the horrible character of slavery, than the reading of whole volumes of philosophy on the subject could do.

I did not, when a slave, understand the deep meaning of those rude and apparently incoherent songs. I was myself within the circle; so that I neither saw nor heard as those without might see and hear. They told a tale of woe which was then altogether beyond my feeble comprehension; they were tones loud, long, and deep; they breathed the prayer and complaint of souls boiling over with the bitterest anguish. Every tone was a testimony against slavery, and a prayer to God for deliverance from chains. The hearing of those wild notes always depressed my spirit, and filled me with ineffable sadness. I have frequently found myself in tears while hearing them. The mere recurrence to those songs, even now, afflicts me; and while I am writing these lines, an expression of feeling has already found its way down my cheek. To those songs I trace my first glimmering conception of the dehumanizing character of slavery. I can never get rid of that conception. Those songs still follow me, to deepen my hatred of slavery, and quicken my sympathies for my brethren in bonds. If any one wishes to be impressed with the soul-killing effects of slavery, let him go to Colonel Lloyd's plantation, and, on allowance-day, place himself in the deep pine woods, and there let him, in silence, analyze the sounds that shall pass through the chambers of his soul,—and if he is not thus impressed, it will only be because "there is no flesh in his obdurate heart."

I have often been utterly astonished, since I came to the north, to find persons who could speak of the singing, among slaves, as evidence of their contentment and happiness. It is impossible to conceive of a greater mistake. Slaves sing most when they are most unhappy. The songs of the slave represent the sorrows of his heart; and he is relieved by them, only as an aching heart is relieved by its tears. At least, such is my experience. I have often sung to drown my sorrow, but seldom to express my happiness. Crying for joy, and singing for joy, were alike uncommon to me while in the jaws of slavery. The singing of a man cast away upon a desolate island might be as appropriately considered as evidence of contentment and happiness, as the singing of a slave; the songs of the one and of the other are prompted by the same emotion.

/   /   /

I was probably between seven and eight years old when I left Colonel Lloyd's plantation. I left it with joy. I shall never forget the ecstasy with which I received the intelligence that my old master (Anthony) had determined to let me go to Baltimore, to live with Mr. Hugh Auld, brother to my old master's son-in-law, Captain Thomas Auld. I received this information about three days before my departure. They were three of the happiest days I ever enjoyed. I spent the most part of all these three days in the creek, washing off the plantation scurf, and preparing myself for my departure.

The pride of appearance which this would indicate was not my own. I spent the time in washing, not so much because I wished to, but because Mrs. Lucretia had told me I must get all the dead skin off my feet and knees before I could go to Baltimore; for the people in Baltimore were very cleanly, and would laugh at me if I looked dirty. Besides, she was going to give me a pair of trousers, which I should not put on unless I got all the dirt off me. The thought of owning a pair of trousers was great indeed! It was almost a sufficient motive, not only to make me take off what would be called by pigdrovers the mange, but the skin itself. I went at it in good earnest, working for the first time with the hope of reward.

The ties that ordinarily bind children to their homes were all suspended in my case. I found no severe trial in my departure. My home was charmless; it was not home to me; on parting from it, I could not feel that I was leaving any thing which I could have enjoyed by staying. My mother was dead, my grandmother lived far off, so that I seldom saw her. I had two sisters and one brother, that lived in the same house with me; but the early separation of us from our mother had well nigh blotted the fact of our relationship from our memories. I looked for home elsewhere, and was confident of finding none which I should relish less than the one which I was leaving. If, however, I found in my new home hardship, hunger, whipping, and nakedness, I had the consolation that I should not have escaped any one of them by staying. Having already had more than a taste of them in the house of my old master, and having endured them there, I very naturally inferred my ability to endure them elsewhere, and especially at Baltimore; for I had something of the feeling about Baltimore that is expressed in the proverb, that "being hanged in England is preferable to dying a natural death in Ireland." I had the strongest desire to see Baltimore. Cousin Tom, though not fluent in speech, had inspired me with that desire by his eloquent description of the place. I could never point out any thing at the Great House, no matter how beautiful or powerful, but that he had seen something at Baltimore far exceeding, both in beauty and strength, the object which I pointed out to him. Even the Great House itself, with all its pictures, was far inferior to many buildings in Baltimore. So strong was my desire, that I thought a gratification of it would fully compensate for whatever loss of comforts I should sustain by the exchange. I left without a regret, and with the highest hopes of future happiness.

/   /   /

My new mistress proved to be all she appeared when I first met her at the door,—a woman of the kindest heart and finest feelings. She had never had a slave under her control previously to myself, and prior to her marriage she had been dependent upon her own industry for a living. She was by trade a weaver; and by constant application to her business, she had been in a good degree preserved from the blighting and dehumanizing effects of slavery. I was utterly astonished at her goodness. I scarcely knew how to behave towards her. She was entirely unlike any other white woman I had ever seen. I could not approach her as I was accustomed to approach other white ladies. My early instruction was all out of place. The crouching servility, usually so acceptable a quality in a slave, did not answer when manifested toward her. Her favor was not gained by it; she seemed to be disturbed by it. She did not deem it impudent or unmannerly for a slave to look her in the face. The meanest slave was put fully at ease in her presence, and none left without feeling better for having seen her. Her face was made of heavenly smiles, and her voice of tranquil music.

But, alas! this kind heart had but a short time to remain such. The fatal poison of irresponsible power was already in her hands, and soon commenced its infernal work. That cheerful eye, under the influence of slavery, soon became red with rage; that voice, made all of sweet accord, changed to one of harsh and horrid discord; and that angelic face gave place to that of a demon.

Very soon after I went to live with Mr. and Mrs. Auld, she very kindly commenced to teach me the A, B, C. After I had learned this, she assisted me in learning to spell words of three or four letters. Just at this point of my progress, Mr. Auld found out what was going on, and at once forbade Mrs. Auld to instruct me further, telling her, among other things, that it was unlawful, as well as unsafe, to teach a slave to read. To use his own words, further, he said, "If you give a nigger an inch, he will take an ell. A nigger should know nothing but to obey his master—to do as he is told to do. Learning would *spoil* the best nigger in the world. Now," said he, "if you teach that nigger (speaking of myself) how to read, there would be no keeping him. It would forever unfit him to be a slave. He would at once become unmanageable, and of no value to his master. As to himself, it could do him no good, but a great deal of harm. It would make him discontented and unhappy." These words sank deep into my heart, stirred up sentiments within that lay slumbering, and called into existence an entirely new train of thought. It was a new and special revelation, explaining dark and mysterious things, with which my youthful understanding had struggled, but struggled in vain. I now understood what had been to me a most perplexing difficulty—to wit, the white man's power to enslave the black man. It was a grand achievement, and I prized it highly. From that moment, I understood the pathway from slavery to freedom. It was just what I wanted, and I got it at a time when I the least expected it. Whilst I was saddened by the thought of losing the aid of my kind mistress, I was gladdened by the invaluable instruction which, by the merest accident, I had gained from my master. Though conscious of the difficulty of learning without a teacher, I set out with high hope, and a fixed purpose, at whatever cost of trouble, to learn how to read. The very decided manner with which he spoke, and strove to impress his wife with the evil consequences of giving me instruction, served to convince me that he was deeply sensible of the truths he was uttering. It gave me the best assurance that I might rely with the utmost confidence on the results which, he said, would flow from teaching me to read. What he most dreaded, that I most desired. What he most loved, that I most hated. That which to him was a great evil, to be carefully shunned, was to me a great good, to be diligently sought; and the argument which he so warmly urged, against my learning to read, only served to inspire me with a desire and determination to learn. In learning to read, I owe almost as much to the bitter opposition of my master, as to the kindly aid of my mistress. I acknowledge the benefit of both.

/   /   '   /

AFTER ESCAPING FROM SLAVERY

In about four months after I went to new Bedford, there came a young man to me, and inquired if I did not wish to take the "Liberator." I told him I did; but, just having made my escape from slavery, I remarked that I was unable to pay for it then. I, however, finally became a subscriber to it. The paper came, and I read it from week to week with such feelings as it would be quite idle for me to attempt to describe. The paper became my meat and my drink. My soul was set all on fire. Its sympathy for my brethren in bonds—its scathing denunciations of slaveholders— its faithful exposures of slavery—and its powerful attacks upon the upholders of the institution—sent a thrill of joy through my soul, such as I had never felt before!

I had not long been a reader of the "Liberator," before I got a pretty correct idea of the principles, measures and spirit of the anti-slavery reform. I took right hold of the cause. I could do but little; but what I could, I did with a joyful heart, and never felt happier than when in an anti-slavery meeting. I seldom had much to say at the meetings, because what I wanted to say was said so much better by others. But, while attending an anti-slavery convention at Nantucket, on the 11th of August, 1841, I felt strongly moved to speak, and was at the same time much urged to do so by Mr. William C. Coffin, a gentleman who had heard me speak in the colored people's meeting at New Bedford. It was a severe cross, and I took it up reluctantly. The truth was, I felt myself a slave, and the idea of speaking to white people weighed me down. I spoke but a few moments, when I felt a degree of freedom, and said what I desired with considerable ease. From that time until now, I have been engaged in pleading the cause of my brethren—with what success, and with what devotion, I leave those acquainted with my labors to decide.

36 | Letters from an Abolitionist to His Former Master

Henry Bibb (1815–1854) was a Kentucky slave, born of a white father. He had six different masters before he made his final escape from slavery in 1840. Bibb became an abolitionist important both in the United States and in Canada. He sustained a long correspondence with Albert G. Sibley, trying to persuade Sibley of the conflict between his behavior as a slaveholder and his position as a leader of the Methodist Episcopal Church.

Windsor, Sept. 23, 1852

Mr. ALBERT G. SIBLEY

Sir,

It has now been about sixteen years since we saw each other face to face, and at which time you doubtless considered me inferior to yourself, as you then held me as an article of property, and sold me as such; but my mind soon after became insubordinate to the ungodly relation of master and slave; and the work of self-emancipation commenced and I was made free.

I have long felt inclined to open a correspondence with you upon this subject, but have refrained from doing so, until now, for two reasons; first, I knew not your post office address; and secondly, you then held in bondage several of my mother's children, of which you robbed her when you left the State of Kentucky in 1836. But as those obstacles are now both removed out of the way, I can venture to address you.

For more than twenty years, you have been a member of the Methodist Episcopal Church—a class leader and an exhorter of that denomination, professing to take the *Bible,* as your standard of christian duty. But sir, know ye not that in the light of this book, you have been acting the hypocrite all this while! I feel called upon as a christian to call your attention to a few facts with a regard to it. But before doing so, I am happy to inform you that my brothers, John, Lewis, and Granville, whose legs brought them from your plantation, are now all at my house

Slave Testimony: Two Centuries of Letters, Speeches, Interviews, and Autobiographies, ed. John W. Blassingame, (Louisiana State University Press, 1977), pp. 49–54.

in Canada, with our dear mother, free and doing well on British soil: so you need not give yourself any trouble about advertising or looking for them. They have all served you as slaves for 21 to 30 years without compensation, and have now commenced to act for themselves. Is this incompatible with the character of a Bible christian? And yet I suppose that you, with your man robbing possee, have chased them with your dogs and guns, as if they were sheep-killing wolves upon the huge mountain's brow, for the purpose of re-capturing and dragging them back to a mental graveyard, in the name of law and slaveholding religion. Oh! what harmony there seems to be between these two twin sisters; the Fugitive Slave Law and the Methodist E. Church.—Listen to the language of inspiration: "Feed the hungry, and clothe the naked: "Break every yoke and let the *oppressed go free:*" "All things, whatseover ye would that men should do unto you, do ye even so unto them, for *this* is the law and the prophets."

While on the other hand your church sanctions the buying and selling of men, women, and children: the robbing men of their wives, and parents of their off-spring—the violation of the whole of the decalogue, by permitting the profanation of the Sabbath; committing of theft, murder, incest and adultery, which is constantly done by church members holding slaves and form the very essence of slavery. Now, Sir, allow me with the greatest deference to your intelligence to inform you that you are miserably deceiving yourself, if you believe that you are in the straight and narrow path to heaven, whilst you are practising such abominable violations of the plainest precepts of religion.

The fellowship of no number of professing christians, however extended nor the solemn baptism and silent toleration of all the Reverend time serving ministers in creation, can make you really a christian, or dispense with the binding force of the Gospel of Jesus Christ as the rule of your life and practice; and whilst you continue in such an unhallowed course of conduct, your prayers, your solemn fasts and ordinances are an abomination to the Lord, from which he will turn his face away, in disgust, and will not hear or look upon.

I must here conclude for the present, but as this subject is fraught with such vital importance to your eternal interest, and as I have once maintained an intimate relation to you, I shall feel bound as a christian to interest myself in calling your attention to it again.

Yours with becoming respect,
HENRY BIBB,

October 7, 1852

MR. ALBERT G. SIBLEY:
SIR,

At the close of my last I promised to call your attention to this subject again—and in doing so my object is not merely to convince you that I have acquired the art of communicating my thoughts intelligibly on paper to be read by tyrants, notwithstanding they with yourself have done their best to keep me in perpetual bondage and ignorance—but it is to warn you of the great danger to which you are exposed while standing in the attitude of an incorrigible slave-holder. I mean that you shall know that there is a just God in heaven, who cannot harmonize human slavery with the Christian religion: I mean that you shall know that there is a law which is more binding upon the consciences of slaves than that of Congress, or any other human enactment—and I mean that you shall know that all of your slaves have escaped to Canada, where they are just as free as yourself, and that we have not forgotten the cruel treatment which we received at your hands while in a state of slavery. I have often heard you say that a slave who was well fed, and clothed, was far better off than a "free negro," who had no master to provide for and take care of him.

Now with all candour in answer to this proslavery logic, let me ask who is it that takes care of the slave holders and their families? Who is it that clears up the forest, cultivates the Land, manages the stock, husbands the grain, and prepares it for the table? Who is it that digs from the cotton, sugar, and rice fields the means with which to build southern Cities, Steam boats, School houses and churches? I answer that it is the slaves, that perform this labor, and yet they or their children are not permitted to enjoy any of the benefits of these Institutions: your former slaves who are now British subjects, are about trying the *dangerous experiment* of taking care of themselves—which has so far proved to be a very successful one. Their services are worth to them here upon an average one dollar per day—they are also attending a night School for the purpose of learning to read and write. With the above facts before me, I am led to the conclusion that the slave who can take care of himself and master both can certainly take care of himself alone, if he is only given a fair chance. Oh! tell me not then Sir, that a man is happier and better off in a state of chattel bondage than in a state of freedom. The idea of a man being a slave—of being subjected to the will and power of a master, is revolting to his very nature. Freedom to act for oneself though poorly clad, and fed with a dry crust, is glorious when compared with American slavery, even if it should appear dressed in broad cloth, and fed with all of the luxuries which the human appetite could desire. This right is highly appreciated by the wild beasts of the forest and the fowls of the air. The terrific screeche of the hooting night owl is animating to himself and musical to his kind as he goes through the tall forest, from the hill top, to the valley. Not so, with the miserable little screech owl, while he is tied by the leg, or boxed up in a cage though well fed he is made the sport of children. The startling scream of the wild panther, or the roar of the lion—it is majestic and independent in their native desert. Not so when they are chained in a cage to be fed by a "kind master," on Johnny cake, roast beef, or no beef, just as he chooses. But my illustrations are inadequate to describe the injustice, and my abhorence of slave holding.

Again I call your attention to the moral bearing of the subject as it applies to yourself. You profess to be a christian—a leader in the M. E. Church, and the representative of the Lord Jesus Christ, and yet you sold my mother from her little children, and sent them away to a distant land—you sold my brother George from his wife and dear little ones while he was a worthy member, and Clergyman, of the same church, to which *you belong*. In early life you also compelled me to cheat, lie, and steal from your neighbours. You have often made me drive up sheep and hogs which you knew to be the property of your neighbour [illegible line] and the use of your own table.

The language of Holy writ is that "thou shalt not steal" "let every man have his own wife, and every woman her own husband" and parents are strictly required to train up their children in the fear and admonition of the Lord. Every one of these Holy injunctions you have wickedly and willingly broken. Oh! what hypocrisy is this! A Methodist class leader, separating husbands and wives—a Methodist class leader, stealing and slaughtering his neighbours sheep and hogs. Vain is your religion—base is your hypocrisy. We have no confidence in your sheep stealing and man robbing religion. My brothers Granville, John, and Lewis, all unite in corroborating the above facts: and if you dare to deny a single word of it let us hear from you and we will furnish undoubted proof.

Yours with due respect,
H. BIBB

P.S. If you do not answer this soon you may expect to hear from me again.

/   /   /

37 | A Biography by Her Contemporaries

This reading is based on a series of interviews with Harriet Tubman conducted by various people between 1859 and 1865 and published in 1865. Interviews of this sort were common during the Civil War, but usually we do not know the precise sources. When the Civil War ended, Tubman continued to work for the betterment of her fellow blacks. She went to North Carolina to assist in the education of freed slaves, although she herself was illiterate. She also founded an old age home in Auburn, New York, where she died in 1913.

One of the teachers lately commissioned by the New-England Freedmen's Aid Society is probably the most remarkable woman of this age. That is to say, she has performed more wonderful deeds by the native power of her own spirit against adverse circumstances than any other. She is well known to many by the various names which her eventful life has given her; Harriet Garrison, Gen. Tubman, &c.; but among the slaves she is universally known by her well-earned title of *Moses*,—Moses the deliverer. She is a rare instance, in the midst of high civilization and intellectual culture, of a being of great native powers, working powerfully, and to beneficent ends, entirely unaided by schools or books.

Her maiden name was Araminta Ross. She is the granddaughter of a native African, and has not a drop of white blood in her veins. She was born in 1820 or 1821, on the Eastern Shore of Maryland. Her parents were slaves, but married and faithful to each other, and the family affection is very strong. She claims that she was legally freed by a will of her first master, but his wishes were not carried into effect.

She seldom lived with her owner, but was usually "hired out" to different persons. She once "hired her time," and employed it in rudest farming labors, ploughing, carting, driving the oxen, &c., to so good advantage that she was able in one year to buy a pair of steers worth forty dollars.

When quite young she lived with a very pious mistress; but the slave-

Slave Testimony: Two Centuries of Letters, Speeches, Interviews, and Autobiographies, ed. John W. Blassingame, (Louisiana State University Press, 1977), pp. 457–465.

holder's religion did not prevent her from whipping the young girl for every slight or fancied fault. Araminta found that this was usually a morning exercise; so she prepared for it by putting on all the thick clothes she could procure to protect her skin. She made sufficient outcry, however, to convince her mistress that her blows had full effect; and in the afternoon she would take off her wrappings, and dress as well as she could. When invited into family prayers, she preferred to stay on the landing, and pray for herself; "and I prayed to God," she says "to make me strong and able to fight, and that's what I've allers prayed for ever since." It is in vain to try to persuade her that her prayer was a wrong one. She always maintains it to be sincere and right, and it has certainly been fully answered.

In her youth she received a severe blow on her head from a heavy weight thrown by her master at another slave, but which accidentally hit her. The blow produced a disease of the brain which was severe for a long time, and still makes her very lethargic. She cannot remain quiet fifteen minutes without appearing to fall asleep. It is not refreshing slumber; but a heavy, weary condition which exhausts her. She therefore loves great physical activity, and direct heat of the sun, which keeps her blood actively circulating. She was married about 1844 to a free colored man named John Tubman, but never had any children. Owing to changes in her owner's family, it was determined to sell her and some other slaves; but her health was so much injured, that a purchaser was not easily found. At length she became convinced that she would soon be carried away, and she decided to escape. Her brothers did not agree with in her plans; and she walked off alone, following the guidance of the brooks, which she had observed to run North. The evening before she left, she wished very much to bid her companions farewell, but was afraid of being betrayed, if any one knew of her intentions; so she passed through the street singing,

> Good bye, I'm going to leave you,
> Good bye, I'll meet you in the kingdom,—

and similar snatches of Methodist songs. As she passed on singing, she saw her master, Dr. Thompson, standing at his gate, and her native humor breaking out, she sung yet louder, bowing down to him,—

> Good bye, I'm going for to leave you.

He stopped and looked after her as she passed on; and he afterwards said, that, as her voice came floating back in the evening air it seemed as if—

> A wave of trouble never rolled
> Across her peaceful breast.

Wise judges are we of each other!—She was only quitting home, husband, father, mother, friends, to go out alone, friendless and penniless into the world.

She remained two years in Philadelphia working hard and carefully hoarding her money. Then she hired a room, furnished it as well as she could, bought a nice suit of men's clothes, and went back to Maryland for her husband. But the faithless man had taken to himself another wife. Harriet did not dare venture into her presence, but sent word to her husband where she was. He declined joining her. At first her grief and anger were excessive. She said, "she did not care what massa did to her, she thought she would go right in and make all the trouble she could, she was determined to see her old man once more" but finally she thought "how foolish it was just for temper to make mischief" and that, "if he could do without her, she could without him," and so "he dropped out of her heart," and she determined to give her life to brave deeds. Thus all personal aims died out of her heart; and with her simple brave motto, "I can't die but once," she began the work which has made her Moses,—the deliverer of her people. Seven or eight times she has returned to the neighborhood of her former home, always at the risk of death in the most terrible forms, and each time has brought away a company of fugitive slaves, and led them safely to the free States, or to Canada. Every time she went, the dangers increased. In 1857 she brought away her old parents, and, as they were too feeble to walk, she was obliged to hire a wagon, which added greatly to the perils of the journey. In 1860 she went for the last time, and among her troop was an infant whom they were obliged to keep stupefied with laudanum* to prevent its outcries. This was at the period of great excitement, and Moses was not safe even in New-York State; but her anxious friends insisted upon her taking refuge in Canada. So various and interesting are the incidents of the journeys, that we know not how to select from them. She has shown in them all the characteristics of a great leader; courage, foresight, prudence, self-control, ingenuity, subtle perception, command over others' mind. Her nature is at once profoundly practical and highly imaginative. She is economical as Dr. [Benjamin] Franklin, and as firm in the conviction of supernatural help as Mahomet. A clergyman once said, that her stories convinced you of their truth by their simplicity as do the gospel narratives. She never went to the South to bring away fugitives without being provided with money; money for the most part earned by drudgery in the kitchen, until within the last few years, when friends have aided her. She had to leave her sister's two orphan children in slavery the last time, for the want of thirty dollars. Thirty pieces of silver; an embroidered handkerchief or a silk dress to one, or the price of freedom to two orphan children to another! She would never allow more to join her than she could properly care for, though she often gave others directions by which they succeeded in escaping. She always came in the winter when the nights are long and dark, and people who have homes stay in them. She was never seen

---

*A form of opium—Eds.

on the plantation herself; but appointed a rendezvous for her company eight or ten miles distant, so that if they were discovered at the first start she was not compromised. She started on Saturday night; the slaves at that time being allowed to go away from home to visit their friends,— so that they would not be missed until Monday morning. Even then they were supposed to have loitered on the way, and it would often be late on Monday afternoon before the flight would be certainly known. If by any further delay the advertisement was not sent out before Tuesday morning, she felt secure of keeping ahead of it; but if it were, it required all her ingenuity to escape. She resorted to various devices, she had confidential friends all along the road. She would hire a man to follow the one who put up the notices, and take them down as soon as his back was turned. She crossed creeks on railroad bridges by night, she hid her company in the woods while she herself not being advertised went into the towns in search of information. If met on the road, her face was always to the south, and she was always a very respectable looking darkey, not at all a poor fugitive. She would get into the cars near her pursuers, and manage to hear their plans. By day they lay in the woods; then she pulled out her patchwork, and sewed together little bits, perhaps not more than [an] inch square, which were afterwards made into comforters for the fugitives in Canada.

The expedition was governed by the strictest rules. If any man gave out, he must be shot. "Would you really do that?" she was asked. "Yes," she replied, "if he was weak enough to give out, he'd be weak enough to betray us all, and all who had helped us; and do you think I'd let so many die just for one coward man." "Did you ever have to shoot any one?" was asked. "One time," she said, "a man gave out the second night; his feet were sore and swollen, he couldn't go any further; he'd rather go back and die, if he must." They tried all arguments in vain, bathed his feet, tried to strengthen him, but it was of no use, he would go back. Then she said, "I told the boys to get their guns ready, and shoot him. They'd have done it in a minute; but when he heard that, he jumped right up and went on as well as any body." She can tell the time by the stars, and find her way by natural signs as well as any hunter; and yet she scarcely knows of the existence of England or any other foreign country.

When going on these journeys she often lay alone in the forests all night. He whole soul was filled with awe of the mysterious Unseen Presence, which thrilled her with such depths of emotion, that all other care and fear vanished. Then she seemed to speak with her Maker "as a man talketh with his friend" he child-like petitions had direct answers, and beautiful visions lifted her up above all doubt and anxiety into serene trust and faith. No man can be a hero without this faith in some form; the sense that he walks not in his own strength, but leaning on an almighty arm. Call it fate, destiny, what you will, Moses of old, Moses of to-day, believed it to be Almighty God.

She loves to describe her visions, which are very real to her; but she must tell them word for word as they lie in her untutored mind, with endless repetitions and details; she cannot shorten or condense them, whatever be your haste. She has great dramatic power; the scene rises before you as she saw it, and her voice and language change with her different actors. Often these visions came to her in the midst of her work. She once said, "We'd been carting manure all day, and t'other girl and I were gwine home on the sides of the cart, and another boy was driving, when suddenly I heard such music as filled all the air" and, she saw a vision which she described in language which sounded like the old prophets in its grand flow; interrupted now and then by what t'other girl said, by Massa's coming and calling her to wake up, and her protests that she wasn't asleep.

One of her most characteristic prayers was when on board a steamboat with a party of fugitives. The clerk of the boat declined to give her tickets, and told her to wait. She thought he suspected her, and was at a loss how to save herself and her charge, if he did; so she went alone into the bow of the boat, and she says, "I drew in my breath, and I sent it out to the Lord. and I said, O Lord! you know who I am, and whar I am, and what I want; and that was all I could say; and again I drew in my breath and I sent it out to the Lord, but that was all I could say; and then again the third time, and just then I felt a touch on my shoulder, and looked round, and the clerk said, 'Here's your tickets.'"

Her efforts wre not confined to the escape of slaves. She conducted them to Canada, watched over their welfare, collected clothing, organized them into societies, and was always occupied with plans for their benefit. She first came to Boston in the spring of 1859, to ask aid of the friends of her race to build a house for her aged father and mother. She brought recommendations from Berrit Smith, and at once won many friends who aided her to accomplish her purpose. Her parents are now settled in Auburn, and all that Harriet seems to desire in reward for her labors is the privilege of making their old age comfortable. She has a very affectionate nature, and forms the strongest personal attachments. She has great simplicity of character; she states her wants very freely, and believes you are ready to help her; but if you have nothing to give, or have given to another, she is content. She is not sensitive to indignities to her color in her own person; but knows and claims her rights. She will eat at your table if she sees you really desire it; but she goes as willingly to the kitchen. She is very abstemious in her diet, fruit being the only luxury she cares for. Her personal appearance is very peculiar. She is thoroughly negro, and very plain. She has needed disguise so often, that she seems to have command over her face, and can banish all expression from her features, and look so stupid that nobody would suspect her of knowing enough to be dangerous; but her eye flashes with intelligence and power when she is roused. She has the rich humor and the keen sense of beauty which belong to her race. She would like to dress handsomely. Once an old silk dress was given her among a bundle of clothes, and she was in great delight. "Glory!" she exclaimed; "didn't I say when I sold my silk gown to get money to go after my mother, that I'd have another some day?" She is never left in a room with pictures or statuary that she does not examine them and ask with interest about them.

I wish it were possible to give some of her racy stories; but no report would do them justice. She gives a most vivid description of the rescue of a slave in Troy. She fought and struggled so that her clothes were torn off her; but she was successful at last. Throughout all she shouted out her favorite motto, "Give me liberty or give me death," to which the popular heart never fails to respond. When she was triumphantly bearing the man off, a little boy called out, "Go it, old aunty! you're the best old aunty the fellow ever had." She is perfectly at home in such scenes; she loves action; I think she does not dislike fighting in a good cause; but she loves work too, and scorns none that offers.

She said once, just before the [Civil] war, when slavery was the one theme agitating the country,—"they say the negro has no rights a white man is bound to respect; but it seems to me they send men to Congress, and pay them eight dollars a day, for nothing else but to talk about the negro."

She says, "the blood of her race has called for justice in vain, and now our sons and brothers must be taken from our hearts and homes to bring the call for justice home to our hearts." She described a storm; "but the thunder's from the cannon's mouth, and the drops that fall are drops of blood."

She was deeply interested in John Brown; and it is said, that she was fully acquainted with his plans, and approved them. On the day when his companions were executed, she came to my room. Finding me occupied, she said, "I am not going to sit down, I only want you to give me an address" but her heart was too full, she must talk. "I've been studying and studying upon it," she said, "and its clar to me, it wasn't John Brown that died on that gallows. When I think how he gave up his life for our people, and how he never flinched, but was so brave to the end; its clar to me it wasn't mortal man, it was God in him. When I think of all the groans and tears and prayers I've heard on the plantations, and remember that God is a prayer-hearing God, I feel that his time is drawing near." Then you think, I said, that God's time is near. "God's time is always near," she said; "He gave me my strength, and he set the North star in the heavens; he meant I should be free." She went on in a strain of the most sublime eloquence I ever heard; but I cannot repeat it. Oh how sanguine and visionary it seemd then! but now four little years, and Maryland is free by her own act, and the bells are ringing out the declaration, that slavery is abolished throughout the land; and our Moses may walk, no longer wrapped in darkness, but erect and proud in her native State; and the name of him who was hung on the gallows is a rallying cry for victorious armies, and the stone which the builders rejected has become the head of the corner. What shall we fear whose eyes have seen this salvation?

When the war broke out Harriet was very anxious to go to South Carolina to assist the contrabands. The only condition she made was, that her old parents should be kept from want. It was wonderful to see with what shrewd economy she had planned all their household arrangements. She concluded that thirty dollars would keep them comfortable through the winter. She went to Port Royal, and was employed by Gen. Hunter, in scouting service, and accompanied Col. Montgomery in his expedition up the Combahee river. She was afterwards engaged by Gen. Saxton, to take a number of freed women under her charge, and teach them to do the soldiers' washing. She has also been making herb-medicine for the soldiers, which she gives away gratuitously, feeling it to be impossible to receive money from sick soldiers; and she has made cakes and pies for sale, in the intervals of other work.

She has had no regular support from Government; and she feels that she must have some certain income, which she wishes to apply to her parents' support. This society consider her labors too valuable to the freedmen to be turned elsewhere, and have therefore taken her into their service, paying her the small salary of ten dollars per month that she asks for. She is not adopted by any branch as she could not fulfil the condition of correspondence with them. She says, when the war is over she will learn to read and write, and then will write her own life. The trouble in her head prevents her from applying closely to a book. It is the strong desire of all her friends that she should tell her story in her own way at some future time. We think it affords a very cogent answer to the query, "Can the negro take care of himself?"

38 | Two Speeches

Born as Isabella, a slave, in New York State in 1795, Sojourner Truth became free in 1827 when the state completed its gradual emancipation. She worked for some years as a domestic, then in 1841 experienced the call to testify to the sins against her people and her gender. Assuming the name Sojourner Truth, she became a well-known abolitionist speaker.

In the late 1840's she become closely identified with the women's rights movement. She was particularly effective at answering male critics and hecklers who were often part of the early rights meetings.

Many of the other abolitionists moved from their primary reform into the other reform movements that marked the period from the 1830s to the Civil War. Women's rights, the peace movement, prohibition of alcoholic beverages, support for utopian communities, and a variety of dietary and health reforms were some of the movements that ripped through northern society in those years.

The first speech was given at a women's convention in Akron, Ohio, in 1851; the second was delivered at a women's rights convention in New York City in 1853.

I

Well, children, where there is so much racket there must be something out of kilter. I think that 'twixt the negroes of the South and the women at the North, all talking about rights, the white men will be in a fix pretty soon. But what's all this here talking about?

That man over there says that women need to be helped into carriages, and lifted over ditches, and to have the best place everywhere. Nobody ever helps me into carriages, or over mud-puddles, or gives me any best place! And ain't I a woman? Look at me! Look at my arm! I have ploughed and planted, and gathered into barns, and no man could head me! And ain't I a woman? I could work as much and eat as much as a man—when I could get it—and bear the lash as well! And ain't I a woman? I have borne thirteen children, and seen them most all sold off to slavery, and when I cried out with my mother's grief, none but Jesus heard me! And ain't I a woman?

Then they talk about this thing in the head; what's this they call it? [Intellect, someone whispers.] That's it, honey. What's that got to do with women's rights or negro's rights? If my cup won't hold but a pint, and yours holds a quart, wouldn't you be mean not to let me have my little half-measure full?

Then that little man in black there, he says women can't have as much rights as men, 'cause Christ wasn't a woman! Where did your Christ come from? Where did your Christ come from? From God and a woman! Man had nothing to do with Him.

If the first woman God ever made was strong enough to turn the world upside down all alone, these women together ought to be able to turn it back, and get it right side up again! And now they is asking to do it, the men better let them.

Obliged to you for hearing me, and now old Sojourner ain't got nothing more to say.

II

Is it not good for me to come and draw forth a spirit, to see what kind of spirit people are of? I see that some of you have got the spirit of a goose, and some have got the spirit of a snake. I feel at home here. I come to you, citizens of New York, as I suppose you ought to be. I am a citizen of the State of New York; I was born in it, and I was a slave in the State of New York; and now I am a good citizen of this State. I was born here, and I can tell you I feel at home here. I've been lookin' round and watchin' things, and I know a little mite 'bout Woman's Rights, too. I come forth to speak 'bout Woman's Rights, and want to throw in my little mite, to keep the scales a-movin'. I know that it feels a kind o' hissin' and ticklin' like to see a colored woman get up and tell you about things, and Woman's Rights. We have all been thrown down so low that nobody thought we'd ever get up again; but we have been long enough trodden now; we will come up again, and now I am here.

I was a-thinkin', when I see women contendin' for their rights, I was a-thinkin' what a difference there is now, and what there was in old times. I have only a few minutes to speak; but in the old times the kings of the earth would[n't] hear a woman. There was a king in the Scriptures; and then it was the kings of the earth would kill a woman if she come into their presence; but Queen Esther come forth, for she was oppressed, and felt there was a great wrong, and she said I will die or I will bring my complaint before the king. Should the king of the United States be greater, or more crueler, or more harder? But the king, he raised up his sceptre and said: "Thy request shall be granted unto thee—to the half of my kingdom will I grant it to thee!" Then he said he would hang Haman on the gallows he had made up high. But that is not what women come forward to contend. The women want their rights as Esther. She only wanted to explain her rights. And he was so liberal that he said, "the half of my kingdom shall be granted to thee," and he did not wait for her to ask, he was so liberal with her.

Now, women do not ask half of a kingdom, but their rights, and they don't get 'em. When she comes to demand 'em, don't you hear how sons hiss their mothers like snakes, because they ask for their rights; and can they ask for anything less? The king ordered Haman to be hung on the gallows which he prepared to hang others; but I do not want any man to be killed, but I am sorry to see them so shortminded. But we'll have our rights; see if we don't ; and you can't stop us from them; see if you can. You may hiss as much as you like, but it is comin'. Women don't get half as much rights as they ought to; we want more, and we will have it. Jesus says: "What I say to one, I say to all—watch!" I'm a-watchin'. God says: "Honor your father and your mother." Sons and daughters ought to behave themselves before their mothers, but they do not. I can see them a-laughin', and pointin' at their mothers up here on the stage. They hiss when an aged woman comes forth. If they'd been brought up proper they'd have known better than hissin' like snakes and geese. I'm 'round watchin' these things, and I wanted to come up and say these few things to you, and I'm glad of the hearin' you give me. I wanted to tell you a mite about Woman's Rights, and so I came out and said so. I am sittin' among you to watch; and every once and awhile I will come out and tell you what time of night it is.

JOHN LAWRIE
AND AXALLA JOHN HOOLE

39 | Letters on the Civil War in Kansas

The issue of slavery's expansion into the newly settled territories that would become Western states, closed briefly by the Compromise of 1850, opened afresh when Senator Stephen A. Douglas, Democrat of Illinois, introduced a bill early in 1854 for organizing the Kansas and Nebraska territories. The Kansas-Nebraska Act left the determination of the status of slavery to the territories' inhabitants themselves. "Popular sovereignty," as this was called, turned out to mean that decisions were implemented by rifles.

A civil war raged intermittently in Kansas in the mid and late 1850s between proslavery and antislavery settlers. Proslavery forces sacked Lawrence, Kansas, in 1856; John Brown and his followers retaliated with the cold-blooded murder of Southern settlers on Pottawatomie Creek. Kansas became "Bleeding Kansas." Eventually the antislavery forces, who were in the majority, gained control, and Kansas entered the Union in 1861. The Kansas civil war had direct links to the American Civil War. The authors of the letters reprinted here fought on opposite sides. John Lawrie from Indiana fought for the Union through most of the war; Axalla John Hoole of South Carolina fought in the Confederate Army until his death at Chickamauga in 1863.

A NORTHERNER'S VIEW: A LETTER FROM JOHN LAWRIE

Wolf Mound Farm, White Co., Indiana
Apl. 16th, 1857

Dear Art,*

After an absence of ten months I now find myself again at home, and surrounded by old associations, among which prominently stands my long-neglected correspondence with you. It was my hope on my way home that when I reached it I would find you with Bob and Lizzy

V. E. Gibbons (editor), "Letters on the War in Kansas in 1856," In Kansas Historical Quarterly, 1941, 10: 370–373. Used by permission, Kansas Historical Society.

William Stanley Hoole (editor), "A Southerner's Viewpoint of the Kansas Situation, 1856–1857," In Kansas Historical Quarterly, 1934, 3: 43–45; 64–65; 164–166. Used by permission, Kansas Historical Society.

*Arthur Lawrie, John's brother.

261

and the little ones all living under the Lawrie roof-tree. But as I cannot talk to you face to face, I must talk to you through the mail, and tell you where I have been so long and what I have been about.

When I left home on the fifteenth of last June I had no intention of making a home in Kansas. I intended in case I could find any organization ready to take the field against the Missourians [the proslavery settlers], to use my utmost endeavors to change the attitude of the Free-State [anti-slavery] settlers from a defensive to an offensive warfare. When I reached Leavenworth, I was unable to find any organization of Free-State men, and could only tell one when I met him by his hanging head and subdued tone of voice. While remaining in this place, the *Star of the West* landed at the levee having on board the Chicago boys as prisoners, and fifty men could have released them and put them in possession of their arms, but there were a certain "five-thousand Missourians" who lived somewhere not far off that would be most grievously provoked should a rescue be attempted, and consequently none was attempted.

Hearing that people held up their heads and spoke what they thought in Lawrence, I started for that point and soon found myself at home as far as a hatred of tyranny and a thirst for vengeance for the insult of the 21st of May was concerned. The people had concluded to try whether there was truth in the Border Ruffian assertion *The Damned Yankees won't fight!* There was quite a stir among the young men in the way of target-firing and drilling in order to prepare themselves for any emergency that might arise requiring them *to contend with superior numbers,* the only thing that thus far had held them back. I found that arms were really scarce. I expected to find plenty of improved fire-arms, and it was with the greatest difficulty I succeeded in getting an old condemned musket. I was looked upon with distrust by a great many persons in Lawrence, having the appearance of a spy in their eyes. It was complimentary, for my appearance seemed above my position to them; but it was very disagreeable. The only military company in town (*the Stubbs*) expected to attend the convention at Topeka on the second and third of July and the opening of the [anti-slavery] legislature on the Fourth, when it was expected they would be needed to defend the legislature against the Ruffians and troops of the U. S. I applied for admission into the company and was put off with rather evasive answers. I went up to Topeka, however, resolved to prove myself a true man when the trying time came. I found the people discussing the propriety of defending the legislature against all who might attempt to disperse it. A few goddamned white-livered lawyers succeeded in getting through a resolution that it was the determination of the Free-State men *not to molest or hinder the U. S. troops.* On the fourth of July at an hour before noon the troops charged into town and dispersed the legislature and retired again unmolested.

I went back to the place where I worked near Lawrence, and did nothing but damn and curse lawyers and professional politicians until the sixth of August, when it was decided by some of the boys in town to go down to a block house erected by a company of Georgian robbers in the lower part of the territory and whip the robbers and burn the block house. I succeeded in obtaining permission to accompany the Stubbs on this expedition. We all slept in one place that night so that we might be awakened at an early hour and depart unobserved. We marched from one o'clock in the morning until breakfast time when we camped on Coal creek, where we remained two hours awaiting the arrival of two wagons and our captain. We were here joined by the Waukarusa company and the Coal creek company, making our force some seventy strong. From this camp on we had a chance to ride over smooth going, and we only stopped long enough to bait the horses until we reached Bull ceek right in the heart of the enemy's country, where we camped for the night some three hours after dark, having lost our guide about the middle of the afternoon. When the guard was appointed for the night, I had the honor of being selected for the post on extreme left of the camp for the first mounting. I was tired, sleepy and hungry, but I felt the importance of the trust placed in me and managed to keep awake without making much noise by biting my lips and tongue. Our camp had a deep ravine in the rear and a small ravine on each flank, and was kept perfectly dark and quiet. At about one in the morning of the eighth of August (my birthday) I heard the tramp of horses' feet in the direction we came from, apparently right in our trail. I knew that our guide was out and perhaps it might be him, but then again it might not. I began to get very wide awake indeed. Presently I caught a glimpse of *two* horsemen, which satisfied me it was not the guide returning. I cocked my old musket and when they came within about a rod of me ordered them to halt, but instead of halting they clapped in their spurs and wheeled off to the right as fast as their horses would carry them. As quick as they wheeled I drew a bead on them and pulled, but the old musket didn't go, and before I could get ready again they had made some fifty yards when I let them have the buckshot and of course woke up the camp. Our captain inquired who had fired when I told him what had occurred, which I thought was discredited. In the morning I went out to see if I could find some proof in the shape of some of their arms which in their hurry they might have dropped, but only found a blood trail. When I was returning, I met four of our men who were putting out in the direction the two horsemen had taken in the night, and presently they returned with a saddled horse which had a couple of buckshot in him—one on the right side of his rump and the other on the inside of his off hind leg. My credit raised wonderfully when it was seen I really shot at something, and it rose still more when it was afterward discovered that the two men I had shot at were Capt. Cook of the Bull creek Ruffians and one of his scouts.

After the return of our guide we resumed our march in the direction of the Georgian block house, yet some twenty-five miles distant, and met with no incidents worthy of note until we reached the vicinity of the block house, where we were all rather anxious to see how the boys would behave under fire, many of them never having as yet heard singing lead. The night was rather dark, and the enemy showed no light and made no noise. Our captain (who by the way was an old man of wars man) reconnoitered the ground and concluded to lead us right on to the place and take it by assault as we had no artillery to storm the place with. The battalion was divided into two platoons, and the block house approached from toward its front and left so that in case we found it necessary to fire we could give them a destructive cross-fire. We went up as well as old veterans ever dared to go; and if there was any disorder at all whatever, it was occasioned by some of the boys rushing ahead too fast. The sound of our steady *tramp! tramp!* was too much for the garrison and they incontinently fled. We found about ten hundred pounds of bacon, some meal, several sacks of flour, a barrel of sugar, [and?] various articles recognized by many of our men as having been taken from Lawrence on the 21st of May, besides a number of letters written by Free-State men to their friends in the states which had been mailed in U. S. post offices, and probably had been abstracted in Missouri and forwarded to the Robbers of the Blue Lodge in order to give them whatever information they might possess of the prospects and conditions of their writers. After taking out all the provisions and military stores, we fired the block house and started home again by the light of it. On our return we had a most fatiguing time, but reached Lawrence without any incident occurring worthy of note. . . .

I found all our people well. I shall remain here until the middle of June when I intend returning to Kansas.

Your affectionate brother
John Lawrie

A SOUTHERNER'S VIEW: LETTERS FROM AXALLA
JOHN HOOLE

Kansas City, Missouri, Apl. 3d., 1856
My Dear Brother[1]

It has cost me over $102 to get here, besides about $25 which I have spent for necessaries, &c. We have been quite well since we left—with the exception of one day that I had a headache and fever, caused I guess from losing so much sleep, and the fatigue of travelling. We did not get to Nashville until Sunday evening; we left that place Monday about 12

---

1. Thomas Stanislaus Hoole, b. June 29, 1824; d. January 18, 1905. He served throughout the War Between the States as captain (South Carolina) artillery.

o'clock and went down the Cumberland river on the steamer *City of Huntsville* to Cairo, at the junction of the Mississippi and the Ohio rivers, where we changed boats and went up to St. Louis, Mo., where we arrived Friday morning about 8 o'clock. We remained there about two hours, in which time I purchased a six-shooter for $20, and some other things. We then changed boats and sailed up the Missouri river to this place. The boats travel very slow up this river at this time, as it is very low and swift.

I have seen none of the country except along the banks of the river, which is, with very little exceptions, nothing but lofty, rugged rocks, sometimes two or three hundred feet high. It was quite a sight to me at first, but I got very tired of looking at them. I saw thousands of wild geese in the Missouri river; I shot at them once about 200 yards, and of course missed. I saw duck also in abundance. . . .

The banks of the river were low and I could see for miles, but there were houses scattered all over the prairie. I fell in company with a young man who had just married, from Georgia, who said he was going to Kansas, but there were other families along from Georgia, who were going to Missouri, and when they left the boat about 60 miles from here, he left with them and I was not sorry for it, as I did not fancy him much; neither did I fancy his wife. I would have but little to do with them— one objection I had to him was, he drank liquor—

The Missourians (all of whom I have conversed with, with the exception of one who, by the way, I found out to be an Abolitionist) are very sanguine about Kansas being a slave state & I have heard some of them say it *shall* be. I have met with warm reception from two or three, but generally speaking, I have not met with the reception which I expected. Everyone seems bent on the Almighty Dollar, and as a general thing that seems to be their only thought—There was a large box on one of the boats about a week ago coming up the river, which some of the Missourians thought contained Sharp's Rifles, so they sent a deputation to its destination, which was at this place, to have it opened. When they arrived here the person to whom it was consigned refused to let them open it, where-upon they opened it by force—when lo! it contained nothing but a piano. There was a box containing a cannon which a confounded Yankee opened, but closed it up again before any of them could examine it, saying that it was nothing but some cartwheels. His daughter-in-law told me this this morning, hesitatingly, as if her father-in-law had done a smart trick. If she had been a man, I don't know what I should have said, but she was a pretty young woman.

Well, dear brother, the supper bell has rung, so I must close. Give my love to [the immediate family] and all the Negroes. . . . Excuse bad writing for I am very nervous. I am anxious to hear from home . . . direct to Lawrence City, Kansas Territory, as I shall leave word there for my letters to be forwarded to whatever place I go. Your ever affectionate brother,   Axalla.

Lecompton, K. T., Sept. 12, 1856

My dear Mother*

I must write you a few lines to let you know how I am getting along, though I have but little hopes of your getting this as letters for some time past have been miscarried or stopped on the way—but I will make the venture—

I have been unwell ever since the 9th of July. . . . I thought of going to work in a few days, when the Abolitionists broke out and I have had to stand guard of nights when I ought to have been in bed, took cold which . . . caused diarrhea, but . . . I feel quite well [now]. Betsie** is well—

You perceive from the heading of this that I am now in Lecompton, almost all of the Proslavery party between this place and Lawrence are here. We brought our families here, as we thought that we would be better able to defend ourselves when altogether than if we scattered over the country.

Lane came against us last Friday (a week ago to-day). As it happened we had about 400 men with two cannon—we marched out to meet him, though we were under the impression at the time that we had 1,000 men. We came in gunshot of each other, but the regular soldiers came and interferred, but not before our party had shot some dozen guns, by which it is reported that five of the Abolitionists were killed or wounded. We had strict orders from our commanding officer (Gen'l Marshall) not to fire until they made the attack, but some of our boys would not be restrained. I was a rifleman and one of the skirmishers, but did all that I could to restrain our men though I itched all over to shoot, myself. I drew a bead a dozen times on a big Yankee about 150 yards from me, but did not fire, as I knew if I did, the boys all around me would do the same, and we had orders not to fire until the word was given—We had 400 men and we learned after Lane had drawn off his men that he did not have more than 700; had we known it, the regulars would not have arrived soon enough to have kept us from fighting, but we were acting on the defensive, and did not think it prudent to commence the engagement. I firmly believe that we would have whipped them, though we would have lost a good many men. I did not see a pale face in our whole army, every man seemed keen to fight. I for one, did not feel as nervous as I am when I go to shoot a beef or a turkey.

I was in bed when the news came, and the confusion calling the men to arms awoke me. I sprang up, seized my gun, told Betsie to go with the rest of the ladies where they would be out of danger, and went to my post in line. I was so weak that I could scarcely walk, and after I

*Mrs. Elizabeth Stanley Hoole; wife of James Hoole.
**Elizabeth Brunson Hoole; Axalla's wife.

took my position, I sat down waiting for the word to fire. I believe it helped me, for I have been improving ever since—but enough of this—

Gov. Geary arrived here night before last; he is a fine looking man, six feet two inches high, seems to be about forty years old. He issued his proclamation disbanding all armed bodies in the Ter. I hear that Lane and his men say that he has gone too far to back out now and will resist the U.S. troops. That is just what we want, as by that means we will get rid of all his last recruits at any rate. The Gov. also said in his Proclamation that the laws of the Ter. shall be enforced. I think he is all right— at least I hope so.

But my dear Mother, I must close as the stage has come. You must not be uneasy about me, as I hope our difficulties here will soon end, and we will all get to our work soon—I am more uneasy about making money than I am about being killed by the Yankees, though the times looked pretty squally for the last three weeks. . . . Betsie sends love to you and all the rest of the family. . . . My love to you, my very dear Mother,

Your Affectionate Son.

/ / /

Douglas, K. T., July the 5th., 1857

Dear Sister

I fear, Sister, that coming here will do no good at last, as I begin to think that this will be made a Free State at last. 'Tis true we have elected Proslavery men to draft a state constitution, but I feel pretty certain, if it is put to the vote of the people, it will be rejected, as I feel pretty confident they have a majority here at this time. The South has ceased all efforts, while the North is redoubling her exertions. We nominated a candidate for Congress last Friday—Ex-Gov. Ransom of Michigan. I must confess I have not much faith in him, tho he professes to hate the Abolitionists bitterly, and I have heard him say that Negroes were a great deal better off with Masters. Still, I fear him, but it was the best we could do. If we had nominated a Southern man, he would have been sure to have been beaten, and I doubt whether we can even elect a Northerner who favors our side.

One of our most staunch Proslavery men was killed in Leavensworth a few days ago. It is hard to ascertain the facts in relation to the murder correctly, but as far as I can learn, there was an election for something. The man who was killed (Jas. Lyle) went up to the polls and asked for a ticket. An Abolitionist handed him one which he, Lyle, tore in two. The other asked him why he did that; he replied he did all such tickets that way. The Abolitionist told him he had better not do so again, when Lyle told him if he would give him another he would. It was given him, and he tore it also, at which the Abolitionist drew a bowie knife and stabbed Lyle to the heart, then ran a few paces, drew a revolver, and commenced firing at the dying man. The fellow was taken prisoner and eighty men were sent from Lawrence that night, by Jim Lane, to keep Lyle's friends from hanging him. Gov. Walker put out for Leavensworth on Friday to have the prisoner carried to the fort, in order to keep the Abolitionists from rescuing him, or prevent Lyle's friends from hanging him by mob law.

There was a big ball in Lecompton on the night of the 3d., but they had no celebration there yesterday. The Abolitionists had a barbecue at Bloomington, about 8 miles south of this, but it was a party thing, I hear. There was a big celebration at Tecumseh and all were invited to attend, tho it was given by Proslavery men. Judge Cato was the orator of the day. I celebrated the day by hard work . . . so you may guess I felt like sleeping last night. . . .

You must give my love to all. . . . Tell all the Negroes a hundred Howdies for us. . . .

Your Affectionate Brother, Axalla.

P. S. 6th. Mr. Smith, the man engaged with me in work, was bit by a rattlesnake last night about midnight. He got up to give his child a drink of water, & stepped on the snake on the floor. He drank a pint of whiskey and got drunk. He has the Doctor with him this morning, and I hope he will be up in a day or two.

40 | Memoirs of a Prisoner of War

Major Abner B. Small of the Sixteenth Maine Volunteers fought for the Union from the very beginning of the Civil War and wrote these memoirs twenty years after its conclusion. He fought at Fredericksburg, Chancellorsville, and Gettysburg—the heart of the war for the Army of the Potomac. Near the end of the war he was taken prisoner and resided consecutively in three southern prisons: Libby, Salisbury, and Danville. His modest memoirs offer a realistic glimpse of one often forgotten aspect of the clash.

I

Libby Prison was a large brick building, formerly the warehouse of Libby & Son, ship-chandlers and grocers. It fronted on Cary Street at Twentieth, and was three stories high where it faced Cary Street and four stories high at the rear above a wharf. Twentieth Street sloped past our end of the prison. An empty lot sloped past the other; it was from that end that Colonel Tilden had escaped, through the tunnel planned by Colonel Rose. On the Cary Street level at our end were the prison offices. Our room, next above, was a bare low loft, with barred windows at front and rear and others on the long side overlooking Twentieth Street. I suppose there had once been glass in the windows, but there was none then. No air seemed to come in, and the room was smelly and hot and stifling. I took the place assigned to me on the floor and tried to sleep, but sleep I could not.

My first day there, I seized what chances offered to look out of the windows. The view across Cary Street was not inviting; on the other side of the street was a row of empty lots and dingy buildings, and behind them was a confusion of roofs and chimneys. Across the intersection of Cary and Twentieth streets were the tents of the guard, and beyond were more roofs and chimneys. A dozen blocks away in that direction was the rebel Capitol; I couldn't see it, nor cared to behold the cause of my misfortune. I went to the windows overlooking Twentieth

Harold Adams Small, ed., The Road to Richmond, 'Libby, Salisbury, Danville (Prisons).' © 1939 The Regents of the University of California, pp. 159–179.

Street; nothing there but an empty lot, and then a large brick warehouse like our prison. I went to the rear. The view there was better; close below by the wharf was the quiet water of a dock, and beyond an embankment at the farther side of the dock was the rippling James. I looked across and saw open fields, and away downstream I could discern rolling hills by a distant reach of the river. Across from the prison were some factories, and upstream beyond them was the village of Manchester. Between the village and the city were long, white bridges, the nearest half-hidden by green trees on a little island midway of the stream. A mile farther up was Belle Isle, a bigger island, where many Union soldiers, enlisted men, were held prisoners and died. I think there were only officers at Libby.

Major Turner, the commandant, might possibly have been a gentleman under favorable circumstances. It would be treason to common sense to suggest that Dick Turner, the turnkey, was anything but a scoundrel. I heard, and was willing to believe it, that his proper station in life, which he had ambitiously forsaken, was that of a bootblack. His heart was blacker than any brogans that he may ever have shined with a brush. He took pleasure in tormenting us, in subjecting us to little, stinging annoyances. He lied to us for sheer love of that fascinating vice. His vanity was often wounded, and then he was like a hornet let loose in a camp meeting. We ignored him as much as possible when he showed his ugly face in our room.

Our quarters were kept indifferently clean by negroes, who swept the floors every morning and sloshed them twice a week. James River water was used for washing, drinking, cooking, and bathing. We drew it from a single tap in our kitchen, or let it fill a trough there when we could get a chance. The kitchen was furnished with three old cook-stoves and a limited supply of utensils, for the use of those prisoners who preferred to cook their own food. I was at first surprised at this, but soon I was only too glad to take my turn as kitchen scullion, for human nature rebelled at scant rations of corn-and-cob bread, tough beef boiled dry, and bean soup flavored with rancid bacon and garnished with white worms. . . .

We were so anxious to get war news, even of the rebel variety, that we subscribed for Richmond newspapers. We got little comfort, however, from the colums of the *Enquirer* and the *Dispatch*. Our armies were always defeated there, the rebels always victorious. We discounted that, and looked for the announcement of a general exchange of prisoners; but we never found good news.

On September 29th [1864], troops of Butler's army attacked Fort Harrison, a part of the defenses of Richmond, and carried it by assault. The heavy cannonading and bursting of shells only six miles down the river set us wild with hope, and the stay-at-homes of Richmond wild with terror. From the windows of our prison we saw housetops crowded with men and women looking anxiously in the direction of the firing. Bells rang, the "Long Roll" sounded; there was a general turn-out. We knew that down the streets of Richmond were straggling the last reserves of the capital city, to stop the breach; and we hoped they couldn't stop it. Next day there was more cannonading, which kept us in a fever of excitement. The rebels attempted, as we learned later, to recapture the lost fort, and failed; but they held their line of defense. They decided to send us to a safer place.

At three o'clock in the morning of Sunday, October 2d, in a drizzling rain, we were hustled out of the prison under a strong guard, marched across the James, and herded into cars at Manchester. Army haversacks were issued to us, with rations for three days; three hunks of corn-bread and three smaller ones of meat, hardly sufficient for a lunch. We were not permitted to take our blankets. None of us had more than ordinary clothing, and few had hats. The train started, and the miserable collection of crowded cars went rattling towards the farther South. We stopped for the night at Clover Station.

At every stop of the train, hucksters, both black and white, would crowd around to dicker. One old darkey had four sweet-potato pies in one hand and a peck basket in the other. "What do you want for the basket?" inquired Captain Conley. "Golly, Colonel," answered the black, "reckon couldn't 'spose of dat'ere; brung dat to put de blue greenbacks in." Officers in the car with me sold personal property at fabulous prices in rebel currency. Captain Kinsley sold his meerschaum pipe to the engineer of an up train, crossed at Clover Station. He got two hundred dollars for it, and gave me fifty dollars for our mess if we should be separated.

We rattled on, and at half-past three Tuesday afternoon we reached Greensboro, North Carolina. Our cars were sidetracked to await an up train, which soon rounded a curve and came to a stop close beside us. In a worn passenger car, which was neither better nor worse than the one other car in the train, sat Jefferson Davis, and with him a woman, whom we took to be Mrs. Davis, and an officer who looked like General Beauregard.

No man could have sat for a photograph with a sadder face than that worn by Davis. Apparently oblivious of his surroundings, he was possibly seeking a solution of his difficulties. I wondered if he was moved by any feeling of remorse or regret for his suicidal folly. Whatever he may have felt, it was obvious that he imparted none of his feelings to the woman with him. Placid, comely, and well dressed, she got up and swished out to the platform of the car. Looking us over, she said, "Gentlemen, I am exceedingly glad to see you; I hope to see more of you." Was this sarcasm? Those of us that wore hats raised them without a word. The rebel officer stood near the woman, and fidgeted; his manner was nervous and disagreeable. When she went back into the car again, he followed, turned back a seat, and sat facing her. Their conversation may or may not have been interesting. To me, that car and its occupants appeared like a coach of mourners on the way to a funeral.

/   /   /

II

The stockade at Salisbury enclosed a piece of ground perhaps a dozen acres in extent, surrounding an old cotton factory and several smaller buildings which had served, I suppose, as quarters for negroes. Armed sentries paced a raised walk on the outer side of the stockade, and cannon commanded the main gate and pointed inwards from the corners of the yard. The factory was a brick building of three stories with a narrower fourth story; a dingy, shabby, stinking place. From the beginning of the war it had been used as a sort of slop jar, into which the Confederacy had dumped odd lots of political and military prisoners. When we arrived, perhaps eight hundred of these rogues and victims were confined here, and among them were desperadoes called "Muggers," who seemed to have the white card to beat, rob, and kill the weaker of their fellow prisoners.

How can I describe the horrors of our first night at Salisbury? We were forced up the factory stairway, step by step over nameless filth, to the monitor room under the roof. The fiendish "Muggers" crept in and robbed several of our number before an alarm was given. Two officers, then stationed at the door with billets of wood, will never be held accountable for the skull-crushing blows that beat back a "Mugger" as he attempted to force his way in. He fell backwards with a wild scream, and I heard him bound from stair to stair down, down, into what I hoped was the Bottomless Pit.

Early in the morning, the officer of the day was called and complaints were made to him. He denied responsibility and called the commandant, Major Gee, who came and asked who complained and why. Our ranking officer, General Hayes, ignoring Major Gee's extended hand, pointed in silence to the filth-drenched hall and staircase, and then, with a look that brought the color of shame to the commandant's face, demanded larger and better quarters for officers of the United States Army. The general's courageous words, that "ten thousand fresh prisoners would not bear for another hour such indignities," must have had some effect; for we were transferred to the small outbuildings and were permitted the use of open ground within the stockade. The huts were close quarters for us, and were filled with vermin; yet they were preferable to the factory.

My mess and three others occupied one hut, two messes upstairs and two down. Captain Conley and I bunked together, sleeping under the same dirty quilt and ragged blanket. Someone supplied me with a dipper, fork, and spoon; and I ate as decently as I might what food I could get, though my stomach would not always retain what little I swallowed. The prison rations were insufficient. Once or twice they increased, raising our hopes, but then they dwindled again, and we despaired of keeping our strength. We were often thirsty; there were crowded into the stockade seven thousand prisoners, and all the water available came from two or three ordinary wells. Our suffering became so apparent that two worn shovels were thrown to us and we were told to dig. We dug, and about fifteen feet down we came to water. An old bucket resembling a nail cask, and a rope, were then supplied, and a windlass was quickly made from green firewood. Mud and water were scooped up together. The water was held in dippers till the mud had partly settled, and then was drunk. But this was not enough. More than once I was so thirsty that my ears rang and my tongue swelled in my mouth. We would have dug another well, but an official came with a guard and took away the shovels. The prison authorities were always in a fever of suspicion that we were tunneling our way out; it was perhaps a compliment to us that a well was not excepted from the possibilities of escape.

Miserable as our condition was, that of the enlisted men was far worse. We were separated from them by a dead-line guarded by sentries, but we could see them and their sufferings all too plainly. There was no shelter for them. There was not enough food. They were thinly clad; many had no shoes, few had overcoats, and hundreds had only ragged trousers and shirt to cover their nakedness. There was no stream running through the enclosure to carry away filth. The ground was soon reeking, and the air was sour and heavy with the stench of offal. In that filth-glutted soil men lived, slept, and died. Some burrowed holes to lie in, and some lay on little clay-heaps in the open. When rain fell, the borrowers were flooded out, and the heapers were marooned on mud-banks only a few inches above the water, which floated offal full of maggots and vermin. When the sun shone, it could not lighten the misery of these wretched captives.

I saw men wander back and forth, their heads bowed, their eyes searching the ground for a stray bone or morsel of food dropped from some weaker hand. I saw men with clasped fingers and streaming eyes, praying for their dear ones at home, into whose loving eyes they would never look again. I saw men in delirium beat themselves and curse God. And I saw, shuddering as I looked, the dead-cart on its morning rounds, and in it God's images tiered up like sticks of wood.

Death or desertion were the only sure chances of release for our men. I will not censure those who went over to the rebels at Salisbury, as a life-preserving act. Escape seemed impossible. Bordering the yard, near the stockade, was an imaginary line which the men were forbidden to cross, and between their part of the yard and ours was another. These lines were significant, and all prisoners kept away from them, for the sentries would fire at anyone approaching within ten feet of their beats. On October 16th I saw Lieutenant Davis of the 155th New York shot dead as he stood near the line in the yard.

We planned to deliver all the Northern prisoners. Soon after arriving at Salisbury, we began secretly to organize a corps of two divisions, with a capable officer in command of each division and General Hayes directing the whole. So perfectly was this organization effected that every enlisted man over the line knew who his immediate commander was. Codes of signals were adopted and quickly learned. Orders were written, wrapped around stones, and after dark were tossed high over the heads of the sentries pacing the dead-line in the yard.

An attack on the guard, the gate, the batteries outside, the commissary, the railroad station, and the town, was planned for October 18th. We felt reasonably sure of success; but the afternoon before the attack was to be made, Lieutenant Gardner of the 13th Connecticut, in sending a last message of command, threw his carrier-stone too swiftly, and his message, which was not in code, became detached and fell fluttering at the feet of a sentry. The sentry at once called the corporal of the guard, and he the sergeant, and so on, until the officer of the day came, who, it was said, was the only one of the number who could read.

The officers on one side of the line and the men on the other stood as if paralyzed. Every eye was fastened on that little armed group in the center. Like a flash there came to the minds of hundreds the thought of seizing the rebels, holding them as hostages, taking their guns, and breaking out of the stockade; but the rebel officers shouted: "Turn out the guard! Turn out the camp! Man the guns!" Our moment for action was lost. The parapet bristled with muskets, and the black mouths of cannon grinned at us from the corners of the yard. . . .

We were marched to the station and herded into a train, and at five o'clock in the afternoon of Wednesday, October 19th, we were started back to Virginia. By ten o'clock the following night we were at Danville, a few miles over the state line, and there we were marched into another prison.

III

Our prison at Danville, for officers only, was an old tobacco warehouse, known as Prison No. 3 in order to distinguish it from the prisons for enlisted men. It was a brick building of three stories, with a small yard at the rear. We were quartered on the upper two floors, and Mess No. 6 was glad to be on the top floor, since it was warmer there under the roof than on the floor below. The ground floor was used as a promenade, where limited numbers of prisoners were permitted to exercise in daylight hours. We had the use of the back yard for cooking; and there, too, were our sanitary conveniences, which were limited to a wooden trough for washing and one other institution more deplorable than any army sink. Sentries guarded the prison on all sides, and the ground-floor promenade, and the yard.

Lieutenant-Colonel Smith, the commandant, was almost an improvement over our former keepers. The Libby jailers had been bad, and the Salisbury jailers worse; at Salisbury I had even regretted the Turners, and would have taken any amount of Turner in exchange for Gee. It was difficult to believe that either Major Turner or Major Gee had ever been a soldier. It was our general experience that Southern fighting men were human beings like us, but that Southern prison keepers were meanspirited brutes. Colonel Smith, though by no means inclined to pamper us, did occasionally show that he possessed soldierly qualities and a comprehension that we were prisoners of war. I doubt that he enjoyed keeping us.

We were thankful that water was plentiful. The prison was near the Dan River, and details of prisoners under guard brought water in buckets from the stream. It was possible to have a sponge bath, without the sponge, and on rare occasions a few of us could go under guard to the river and get into water all over. After Salisbury, we certainly needed a cleaning; but it was soon too cold for men in our weakened condition to risk a chill for the sake of satisfactory cleanliness. We couldn't, by any mere washing, have rid ourselves of vermin. This prison, like the others, crawled with them.

Our prison rations were hardly sufficient to sustain life. Corn-and-cob bread was the chief item supplied, to which were added at odd times uncertain portions of salt cod or boiled beef. When we could raise money, we bought flour and rice and helped out our diet with sorghum, a few vegetables or apples, and salt. We had utensils for cooking and eating, but no table or kitchen; Mess No. 6 inventoried six tin plates, ten pewter spoons, two tin dippers, seven case-knives, one fork, three jack-knives, and an old stove-hearth on which we fried our delicious flapjacks. These fritters were made of corn-and-cob bread and river water, and sometimes were flavored with dried-apple juice and pepper. We took turns at cooking. Captain Lord beame an expert. It was humiliating to see an officer of the United States Army, with an old stove-hearth under one arm, a handful of splinters under the other, and a rusty can full of corn mush, starting for the back yard to prepare his dinner. I felt honored, but cried with shame, when an enterprising colonel sent his compliments and requested the loan of our stove-hearth.

/   /   /

Our quarters were so crowded that none of us had more space to himself than he actually occupied, usually a strip of the bare, hard floor, about six feet by two. We lay in long rows, two rows of men with their heads to the side walls and two with their heads together along the center of the room, leaving narrow aisles between the rows of feet. The wall spaces were preferred, because a man could brace his back there and sit out the long day or the longer night. There was a row of posts down the center of the room, but these were too few and too narrow to give much help; I know, because I had a place by one of them.

I remember three officers, one a Yankee from Vermont, one an Irishman from New York, and one a Dutchman from Ohio, who messed together by the wall opposite me. When they came to Danville they were distinct in feature and personality. They became homesick and disheartened. They lost all interest in everything, and would sit in the same attitude hour after hour and day after day, with their backs against the wall and their gaze fixed on the floor at my feet. It grew upon me that they were gradually being merged into one man with three bodies. They looked just alike; truly, I couldn't tell them apart. And they were dying of nostalgia.

It gave me the nightmare to lie down in front of those men, so I resolved to break the spell which held them over the grave. I fortified myself, one morning, with corn-and-cob bread and crust coffee, and took up a position directly facing the trio, and looked from one to another repeatedly. After a while the Dutchman raised his eyes and muttered: "Gott in Himmel! Vot for you shoost look on me?" Paying no attention to that, I concentrated my gaze yet more strongly on the others, until the Vermonter asked what the hell I wanted. This aroused the Irishman, who yelled an interrogation point at me. My medicine was working well. I only feared that my strength would fail before I could effect a cure. I stared and stared, and forced the Vermonter and the Irishman to their feet. The Dutchman was fast sinking back into apathy when I spat full in his face. The insult stung him to action, and I ran for my life around the room with Dutchy after me. He soon gave up the chase, but the warm current of blood which I had started did not stagnate. When the three had cooled off, I made them a morning call and explained matters. Perhaps they didn't believe all I said, but they forgave me, and lived. I don't remember what they did to occupy their minds after that; I only know they quit staring at the floor.

Some of the prisoners played chess, checkers, and backgammon. Captain Conley and I had made a set of checkers in Libby, and we still had them, but the game palled on us. Like the ungodly majority, we killed time and escaped insanity with cards. A few of our associates, pursuing the consolations of religion, found none too much time to study the Scriptures; games had no fascinating power over them. A few others, remembering what they had learned at college, engaged in the study of classical or modern languages. Many tried to read, but reading somehow ceased to be a comfort in prison; at least, that was my experience. Our library, moreover, was a small one; it consisted of a few books and some back numbers of monthlies brought to us by the Reverend Charles K. Hall, a Methodist minister of Danville, who occasionally preached to us.

Many of our comrades developed a wonderful talent at handicraft and made hundreds of ornaments from bone and wood. Crosses, rings, and pins were artistically fashioned and most beautifully chased. Busts were carved from bricks taken from the walls. Checkers with monograms and raised figures were cut from bone and bits of wood. Altogether, there was output enough to stock a respectable museum. These objects were not made wholly in the cause of art, nor to while away the time; they were valuable for barter and exchange.

As our money gave out, we sold things to get more, or swapped articles of value or works of art for necessities. Boots, spurs, watches, rings, jack-knives, buttons, even toothpicks, were commodities of traffic. Boots were a quick commodity and brought high prices in debased rebel currency; but we hated to part with them. Captain Conley's pride in a pair of nice boots lasted until his luxurious habit of smoking demanded a sacrifice. The officer of the guard, an inveterate haggler with the general manner and appearance of a Malay pirate, offered one hundred Confederate dollars and finally a pair of shoes also, for the boots, and the offer was accepted. The cash was paid, and the captain, almost in tears, gave up his fine footwear. After a wait of two weeks there was passed into the prison a package addressed to Captain Conley. "My shoes!" he cried. He tore off the wrapper, and for an hour sat and swore at two old army brogans, of different sizes and both for the same foot. My own boots went for cash the day after Christmas. I fared better than Conley; I got a hundred dollars and a pair of shoes that I could wear.

All sorts of makeshifts were adopted to cover our persons as decency demanded. When I was captured, I was the proud possessor of a new staff uniform ornamented with gold lace. Five months later, my most intimate friends would have failed to recognize me in the ragged tramp who sat naked on the floor at Danville and robbed the ends of his trousers in order to reseat them. It was not till after I was paroled that I took those trousers off; I couldn't have done so before, because, after sewing up the legs while I had them on, I couldn't get my feet through.

Although we all became disreputable in appearance, some of us kept up as best we could our proper relations of mutual respect. I am sorry to say that military rank was soon ignored by the majority of officers in Prison No. 3, and that selfishness and dishonesty added to our cup of humiliation and suffering; yet I know that much should be forgiven in men who had almost lost their natural humanity. Our nerves were worn ragged. The slightest of provocations would cause a quarrel. Two cavalry officers, Captain Harris and Lieutenant McGraw, fought over the possession of a few rusty cans. The captain's shirt was torn to shreds, and since it was the only shirt he had, and the remainder of his wardrobe consisted of a well-ventilated pair of trousers, he was to be pitied.

Happily, I remember some manly acts, and examples of Christian character maintained under the most adverse and depressing influences. General Hayes more than once rebuked severely those who indulged in profane and obscene language. Chaplains Fowler and Emerson, Captain Stewart of the 146th Pennsylvania, and Captain Burrage of the 36th Massachusetts seemed never to forget their Christian and moral obligations. I was not closely acquainted with any of these gentlemen, and was influenced by them only in a general way, but influenced I certainly was, and I have never ceased to feel grateful for their good examples. I believe they saved many from moral collapse; not by preaching, but just by being the men they were.

Freedom was more desired than salvation, more sought after than righteousness. We were no sooner in Danville than a start was made at digging a way out. From our windows overlooking open country, away from the town, we could see near the prison a deep ditch; and the plan was to dig a tunnel from the prison cellar to the ditch, and to escape by it at night. A way was found to enter the cellar, and the digging was carried on every night for two weeks; but the attempt came to nothing. The tunnel approached the surface of the ground too closely, and early one morning a sentry stepped on the undermined spot and fell through. The tunnel was traced, and access to the cellar was thereafter shut off. Some prisoners later escaped while returning under guard from the river, where they had gone for water; but these daring ones were few, and their chances were slim.

/   /   /

Christmas came and went with little hope for us this side of the grave. I fell ill, and dragged through another month uncertainly, living in the flickering hope of an exchange. We heard many rumors of negotiations, but nothing seemed to come of them. With February came letters telling us that we should certainly be exchanged soon; and our hopes revived. On Sunday, February 12th, Dr. Hall preached to us from a text in 2 Timothy, which included the exhortation, "Thou therefore endure hardness, as a good soldier of Jesus Christ." Our endurance was nearly at an end.

Then suddenly the welcome intelligence at last arrived. At dusk of Wednesday, February 15th, Colonel Smith came hurrying in and announced that we were to leave for Richmond on the Friday or Saturday following. We cheered and laughed and wept, and sang "Hard Times Come Again No More" and "Home, Sweet Home." Few of us slept, that night, or the next night, either. Orders were read, and changes of orders, and the plans for our departure were uncertain up to the very moment of our going; but finally, at ten o'clock Friday night, we stumbled out of the prison into a darkness that was glorious with the light of promised freedom. We groped our way to the railroad station, where box-cars awaited us, and at midnight the train started for Richmond.

We arrived in the rebel capital at two o'clock Saturday afternoon, and were quartered once more in Libby Prison. Captain Conley and I had the pleasure of sharing our old space on the second floor near a post. We slept soundly, overcome by excitement and exhaustion. In the morning we enjoyed the luxury of hot coffee with milk and sugar, the first we had drunk in six months. At nine o'clock, corn-bread and corned beef were issued; and we noticed that the ration was smaller than ever. We signed the parole, that day. I believe I would have signed any promise without the least intention of keeping it. Monday, we rested on the raw edges of our nerves. Tuesday, we were told that we were to leave the next day.

At eight o'clock in the morning of Wednesday, February 22d, the door of Libby Prison opened to us for the last time, and we went forth free men. Slowly and painfully we made our way to the steamer awaiting us in the James. I fell to the ground repeatedly, but somehow I got there. The steamer was, I think, the *William Allison*. I found a place by the smokestack, and backed up to the stack for warmth, and fell asleep. When I opened my eyes again, the steamer was heading back to Richmond. I might have jumped overboard, but Captain Lord's happy face changed my thought, and I remembered how crooked the James was.

At ten o'clock we were put ashore on the north bank at Cox's Landing, and headed for Aiken's. Between the two landings we crossed the dividing line between South and North; to us, the border between hell and paradise. At half-past eleven we caught sight of the Stars and Stripes at Aiken's Landing, and soon we boarded the steamer *George Leary* for Annapolis. On the steamer we had a light lunch of ham, white bread, and coffee; also a half-ration of whiskey. I think the whiskey came first, and those who drank the portions refused by others, in addition to their own, had no need of the lunch.

The warm welcome for us at Annapolis, the earnest ministrations for our comfort, and the sweet words of sympathy, filled our eyes with tears. That long, linen-draped, well filled table; shall I ever forget it? We were cautioned to control our appetites, and warned of the fatal consequences of too free indulgence; yet, alas for self-confidence and nonresistance, several of our number were soon dead and buried under the Annapolis sod.

We that survived were quartered and fed properly at Camp Parole, and nursed back to health and strength. When I arrived, I weighed ninety pounds. When I left, I was still thin, but gaining steadily. I had leave to go home; and then, being formally exchanged, I reported again for duty with my regiment. While I had been in prison I had received a signal promotion. From first lieutenant and adjutant I was advanced over all the captains and made major. How I had crept up!

41 | In the Track of Sherman's Army

Sidney Andrews, a Northern journalist, visited the Carolinas and Georgia shortly after the end of the Civil War. His dispatches were published as The South Since the War. *His description of Columbia, South Carolina, provides a dramatic picture of defeat. Ironically, accounts like this succeeded to some extent in arousing sympathy for the suffering South, and made many Northerners hesitate over the vigorous Reconstruction that, however necessary to help the freed blacks seemed hard to impose on the white South.*

Columbia, September 12, 1865.
The war was a long time in reaching South Carolina, but there was vengeance in its very breath when it did come,—wrath that blasted everything it touched, and set Desolation on high as the genius of the State. "A brave people never before made such a mistake as we did," said a little woman who sat near me in the cars while coming up from Charleston; "it mortifies me now, every day I live, to think how well the Yankees fought. We had no idea they could fight half so well." In such humiliation as hers is half the lesson of the war for South Carolina.

Columbia is in the heart of Destruction. Being outside of it, you can only get in through one of the roads built by Ruin. Being in it, you can only get out over one of the roads walled by Desolation. You go north thirty-two miles, and find the end of one railroad; southeast thirty miles, and find the end of another; south forty-five miles, and find the end of a third; southwest fifty miles, and meet a fourth; and northwest twenty-nine miles, and find the end of still another. Sherman came in here, the papers used to say, to break up the railroad system of the seaboard States of the Confederacy. He did his work so thoroughly that half a dozen years will nothing more than begin to repair the damage, even in this regard.

The railway section of the route from Charleston lies mostly either in a pine barren or a pine swamp, though after passing Branchville we came into a more open and rolling country, with occasional signs of life.

Sidney Andrews. The South Since the War: As Shown by Fourteen Weeks of Travel and Observation in Georgia and the Carolinas. *(Boston, Ticknor and Fields, 1866), pp. 28–37.*

Yet we could not anywhere, after we left the immediate vicinity of the city, see much indication of either work or existence. The trim and handsome railway stations of the North, the little towns strung like beads on an iron string, are things unknown here. In the whole seventy-seven miles there are but two towns that make any impression on the mind of a stranger,—Summerville and George's,—and even these are small and unimportant places. Elsewhere we stopped, as it appeared, whenever the train-men pleased,—the "station" sometimes existing only in the consciousness of the engineer and conductor.

Branchville was, however, noticeable because of the place it once occupied in Northern anxiety. There is where Sherman was to meet his fate. Have we forgotten how the Richmond papers of early February spoke? They were not at liberty to mention the preparations, etc., but they might say, etc., and the Yankee nation would have sore cause to remember Branchville, etc. Unfortunately, however, Sherman flanked Branchville, just as he had other places of thrice its importance, and it missed the coveted renown. It is nothing but a railroad junction in a pine barren, with a long, low station-house and cotton warehouse, and three or four miserable dwellings.

I found the railroad in better condition than I supposed that I should. The rails are very much worn, but the roadbed is in fair order for nearly the entire distance. The freight-cars seemed in passably good repair; but the passenger-coaches were the most wretched I ever saw,—old, filthy, and rickety. On our train was one new feature,—a colored man and his wife, whose duty it was to wait on the passengers.

I came up from Orangeburg, forty-five miles, by "stage," to wit, an old spring-covered market-wagon, drawn by three jaded horses and driven by Sam, freedman, late slave,—of the race not able to take care of themselves, yet caring, week in and week out, for the horses and interests of his employer as faithfully and intelligently as any white man could. There were six of us passengers, and we paid ten dollars each passage-money. We left Orangeburg at four, P.M.; drove eight miles; supped by the roadside; drove all night; lunched at sunrise by a muddy brook; and reached Columbia and breakfast at eleven, A.M., thankful that we had not broken down at midnight, and had met only two or three minor accidents. I am quite sure there are more pleasant ways of travelling than by "stage" in South Carolina at the present time. Thirty-two miles of the forty-five lie in such heavy and deep sand that no team can travel faster than at a moderate walk. For the other thirteen miles the road is something better, though even there it is the exception and not the rule to trot your mules. The river here was formerly spanned by an elegant and expensive bridge, but the foolish Rebels burned it; and the crossing of the Congaree is now effected in a ferry, the style and management of which would disgrace any backwoods settlement of the West.

The "Shermanizing process," as an ex-Rebel colonel jocosely called it, has been complete everywhere. To simply say that the people hate that officer is to put a fact in very mild terms. Butler is, in their estimation, an angel when compared to Sherman. They charge the latter with the entire work and waste of the war so far as their State is concerned,— even claim that Columbia was burned by his express orders. They pronounce his spirit "infernal," "atrocious," "cowardly," "devilish," and would unquestionably use stronger terms if they were to be had. I have been told by dozens of men that he couldn't walk up the main street of Columbia in the daytime without being shot; and three different gentlemen, residing in different parts of the State, declare that Wade Hampton expresses a purpose to shoot him at sight whenever and wherever he meets him. Whatever else the South Carolina mothers forget, they do not seem likely in this generation to forget to teach their children to hate Sherman.

Certain bent rails are the first thing one sees to indicate the advent of his army. They are at Branchville. I looked at them with curious interest. "It passes my comprehension to tell what became of our railroads," said a travelling acquaintance; "one week we had passably good roads, on which we could reach almost any part of the State, and the next week they were all gone,—not simply broken up, but gone; some of the material was burned, I know, but miles and miles of iron have actually disappeared, gone out of existence." Branchville, as I have already said, was flanked, and the army did not take it in the line of march, but some of the boys paid it a visit.

At Orangeburg there is ample proof that the army passed that way. About one third of the town was burned. I found much dispute as to the origin of the fire, and while certain fellows of the baser sort loudly assert that it was the work of the Yankee, others of the better class express the belief that it originated with a resident who was angry at the Confederate officers. Thereabouts one finds plenty of railroad iron so bent and twisted that it can never again be used. The genius which our soldiers displayed in destroying railroads seems remarkable. How effectually they did it, when they undertook the work in earnest, no pen can make plain. "We could do something in that line, we thought," said an ex-Confederate captain, "but we were ashamed of ourselves when we saw how your men could do it."

We rode over the road where the army marched. Now and then we found solitary chimneys, but, on the whole, comparatively few houses were burned, and some of those were fired, it is believed, by persons from the Rebel army or from the neighboring locality. The fences did not escape so well, and most of the planters have had these to build during the summer. This was particularly the case near Columbia. Scarcely a tenth of that destroyed appears to have been rebuilt, and thousands of acres of land of much richness lie open as a common.

There is great scarcity of stock of all kinds. What was left by the Rebel conscription officers was freely appropriated by Sherman's army, and the people really find considerable difficulty not less in living than in travelling. Milk, formerly an article much in use, can only be had now in limited quantities: even at the hotels we have more meals without than with it. There are more mules than horses, apparently; and the animals, whether mules or horses, are all in ill condition and give evidence of severe overwork.

Columbia was doubtless once the gem of the State. It is as regularly laid out as a checker-board,—the squares being of uniform length and breadth and the streets of uniform width. What with its broad streets, beautiful shade-trees, handsome lawns, extensive gardens, luxuriant shrubbery, and wealth of flowers, I can easily see that it must have been a delightful place of residence. No South-Carolinian with whom I have spoken hesitates an instant in declaring that it was the most beautiful city on the continent; and, as already mentioned, they charge its destruction directly to General Sherman.

It is now a wilderness of ruins. Its heart is but a mass of blackened chimneys and crumbling walls. Two thirds of the buildings in the place were burned, including, without exception, everything in the business portion. Not a store, office, or shop escaped; and for a distance of three fourths of a mile on each of twelve streets there was not a building left. "They destroyed everything which the most infernal Yankee ingenuity could devise means to destroy," said one gentleman to me; "hands, hearts, fire, gunpowder, and behind everything the spirit of hell, were the agencies which they used." I asked him if he wasn't stating the case rather strongly; and he replied that he would make it stronger if he could. The residence portion generally escaped conflagration, though houses were burned in all sections except the extreme northeastern.

Every public building was destroyed, except the new and unfinished state-house. This is situated on the summit of tableland whereon the city is built, and commands an extensive view of the surrounding country, and must have been the first building seen by the victorious and on-marching Union army. From the summit of the ridge, on the opposite side of the river, a mile and a half away, a few shells were thrown at it, apparently by way of reminder, three or four of which struck it, without doing any particular damage. With this exception, it was unharmed, though the workshops, in which were stored many of the architraves, caps, sills, &c., were burned,—the fire, of course, destroying or seriously damaging their contents. The poverty of this people is so deep that there is no probability that it can be finished, according to the original design, during this generation at least.

The ruin here is neither half so eloquent nor touching as that at Charleston. This is but the work of flame, and might have mostly been brought about in time of peace. Those ghostly and crumbling walls and those long-deserted and grass-grown streets show the prostration of a community,—such prostration as only war could bring.

I find a commendable spirit of enterprise, though, of course, it is enterprise on a small scale, and the enterprise of stern necessity. The work of clearing away the ruins is going on, not rapidly or extensively, to be sure, but something is doing, and many small houses of the cheaper sort are going up. Yet, at the best, this generation will not ever again see the beautiful city of a year ago. Old men and despondent men say it can never be rebuilt. "We shall have to give it up to the Yankees, I reckon," said one of two gentlemen conversing near me this morning. "Give it up!" said the other; "they've already moved in and taken possession without asking our leave." I guess the remark is true. I find some Northern men already here, and I hear of more who are coming.

Of course there is very little business doing yet. The city is, as before said, in the heart of the devastated land. I judge that twenty thousand dollars would buy the whole stock of dry goods, groceries, clothing, &c. in store. The small change of the place is made in shinplasters, printed on most miserable paper, and issued by the various business men, "redeemable in United States currency when presented in sums of two dollars and upwards." "Greenbacks" and national currency notes pass without question in the city, but are looked upon with suspicion by the country people. "Having lost a great deal by one sort of paper, we propose to be careful now," they say. Occasionally one sees a State bank-note, but they pass for only from twenty-five to sixty or sixty-five cents on the dollar. There is none of the Confederate money in circulation; though I judge, from what I hear, that considerable quantities of it are hoarded up in the belief that things will somehow take such a turn as to one day give it value.

There is a certain air of easy dignity observable among the people that I have not found elsewhere in the State,—not even in Charleston itself. Something of this is probably due to the fact that the capital is located here; but more of it, probably, to the existence of Columbia College. It was before the war a very flourishing institution, but has been closed during the last three years. The old but roomy buildings are in part occupied by the military authorities, partly by the professors and officers of the college, and are partly closed. No indication is given as to the time of reopening the school. It is said by residents that the city contained some of the finest private libraries in the South; but these, with one or two exceptions, were burned.

The women who consider it essential to salvation to snub or insult Union officers and soldiers at every possible opportunity do not seem as numerous as they appeared to be in Charleston; and indeed marriages between soldiers and women of the middle class are not by any means the most uncommon things in the world; while I notice, in a quiet, un-observant manner, as even the dullest traveller may, that at least several very elegant ladies do not seem at all averse to the attentions of the gentlemen of shoulderstraps. Can these things be, and not overcome the latent fire of Rebellion?

In coming up from Charleston I learned a great many things by conversation with persons, and by listening to conversation between people; and these are some of the more important facts thus learned.

Thus, one man insisted with much vehemence that cotton is king, and that a resolution on the part of the South not to sell any for a year would bring the North upon its knees.

Another man was very confident that the North depends entirely upon the cotton trade for a living, and that a failure to get at least one million bales before spring will bring a tremendous financial crash.

Another gravely asserted that a state of anarchy prevails in the entire North; that the returned soldiers are plundering and butchering indiscriminately; and that there has recently been a most bloody riot in Boston.

Another, and a man of much apparent intelligence, informed me that the negroes have an organized military force in all sections of the State, and are almost certain to rise and massacre the whites about Christmas time.

Another had heard, and sincerely believed, that General Grant's brother-in-law is an Indian, and is on his staff, and that the President had issued an order permitting the General's son to marry a mulatto girl whom he found in Virginia.

A woman, evidently from the country districts, stated that there had been a rising of the negroes in Maryland; that a great many whites had been killed; and that some considerable portion of Baltimore and many of the plantations had been seized by the negroes.

And, finally, an elderly gentleman who represented himself as a cotton factor, declared that there would be a terrible civil war in the North within two years; that England would compel the repudiation of our National debt and the assumption of the Confederate debt for her guaranty of protection.

The people of the central part of the State are poor, wretchedly poor; for the war not only swept away their stock and the material resources of their plantations, but also all values,—all money, stocks, and bonds,—and generally left nothing that can be sold for money but cotton, and only a small proportion of the landholders have any of that. Therefore there is for most of them nothing but the beginning anew of life, on the strictest personal economy and a small amount of money borrowed in the city. It would be a benefit of hundred of millions of dollars if the North could be made to practise half the economy which poverty forces upon this people.

They are full of ignorance and prejudices, but they want peace and quiet, and seem not badly disposed toward the general government. Individuals there are who rant and rave and feed on fire as in the old days, but another war is a thing beyond the possibilities of time. So far as any fear of that is concerned we may treat this State as we please,— hold it as a conquered province or restore it at once to full communion in the sisterhood of States. The war spirit is gone, and no fury can re-enliven it.

The spirit of oppression still exists, however, and military authority cannot be withdrawn till the relation between employer and employed is put upon a better basis. On the one hand, the negro in the country districts must be made to understand, what he has already been taught in the city, that freedom does not mean idleness. On the other hand, the late master should specially be made to understand that the spirit of slavery must go to the grave with the thing itself. It will not be an easy work to teach either class its chief lesson. We must have patience,—patience, and faith that neither faints nor falters.

42 | Blacks' Reactions to Reconstruction

The Reconstruction period remains a subject of intense historical debate. The Thirteenth, Fourteenth, and Fifteenth Amendments to the U.S. Constitution asserted an equality between the races that was not realized in fact. At first the federal government vigorously supported the Freedman's Bureau and the efforts of Reconstruction governments in southern states to help the freed slaves, but within about a decade those efforts were abandoned as the northern public lost interest.

The social revolution brought about by emancipation caused severe problems for both blacks and whites. Just as the slaves' experiences had varied widely, so the newly freed blacks responded to their new situation in many different ways. Their needs were rarely understood by a public ill-prepared to accept blacks as equals or to support the long-term federal intervention that was required to make freedom an economic and social reality.

FELIX HAYWOOD From San Antonio, Texas. Born in Raleigh, North Carolina. Age at Interview: 88

The end of the war, it come just like that—like you snap your fingers. . . . How did we know it! Hallelujah broke out—

> *Abe Lincoln freed the nigger*
> *With the gun and the trigger;*
> *And I ain't going to get whipped any more.*
> *I got my ticket,*
> *Leaving the thicket,*
> *And I'm a-heading for the Golden Shore!*

Soldiers, all of a sudden, was everywhere—coming in bunches, crossing and walking and riding. Everyone was a-singing. We was all walking on golden clouds. Hallelujah!

Botkin, B.A. (editor), Lay My Burden Down: A Folk History of Slavery. (Chicago, University of Chicago Press, 1945), pp. 65–70, 223–224, 241–242, 246–247. Copyright © 1989 by Curtis Brown, Ltd.

Union forever,
Hurrah, boys, hurrah!
Although I may be poor,
I'll never be a slave—
Shouting the battle cry of freedom.

Everybody went wild. We felt like heroes, and nobody had made us that way but ourselves. We was free. Just like that, we was free. It didn't seem to make the whites mad, either. They went right on giving us food just the same. Nobody took our homes away, but right off colored folks started on the move. They seemed to want to get closer to freedom, so they'd know what it was—like it was a place or a city. Me and my father stuck, stuck close as a lean tick to a sick kitten. The Gudlows started us out on a ranch. My father, he'd round up cattle—unbranded cattle—for the whites. They was cattle that they belonged to, all right; they had gone to find water 'long the San Antonio River and the Guadalupe. Then the whites gave me and my father some cattle for our own. My father had his own brand—7 B)—and we had a herd to start out with of seventy.

We knowed freedom was on us, but we didn't know what was to come with it. We thought we was going to get rich like the white folks. We thought we was going to be richer than the white folks, 'cause we was stronger and knowed how to work, and the whites didn't, and they didn't have us to work for them any more. But it didn't turn out that way. We soon found out that freedom could make folks proud, but it didn't make 'em rich.

Did you ever stop to think that thinking don't do any good when you do it too late? Well, that's how it was with us. If every mother's son of a black had thrown 'way his hoe and took up a gun to fight for his own freedom along with the Yankees, the war'd been over before it began. But we didn't do it. We couldn't help stick to our masters. We couldn't no more shoot 'em than we could fly. My father and me used to talk 'bout it. We decided we was too soft and freedom wasn't going to be much to our good even if we had a education.

/   /   /

WARREN MCKINNEY, From Hazen, Arkansas. Born
in South Carolina. Age at Interview: 85.

I was born in Edgefield County, South Carolina. I am eighty-five years old. I was born a slave of George Strauter. I remembers hearing them say, "Thank God, I's free as a jay bird." My ma was a slave in the field. I was eleven years old when freedom was declared. When I was little, Mr. Strauter whipped my ma. It hurt me bad as it did her. I hated him. She was crying. I chunked him with rocks. He run after me, but he didn't catch me. There was twenty-five or thirty hands that worked in the field. They raised wheat, corn, oats, barley, and cotton. All the children that couldn't work stayed at one house. Aunt Mat kept the babies and small children that couldn't go to the field. He had a gin and a shop. The shop was at the fork of the roads. When the war come on, my papa went to build forts. He quit Ma and took another woman. When the war close, Ma took her four children, bundled 'em up and went to Augusta. The government give out rations there. My ma washed and ironed. People died in piles. I don't know till yet what was the matter. They said it was the change of living. I seen five or six wooden, painted coffins piled up on wagons pass by our house. Loads passed every day like you see cotton pass here. Some said it was cholera and some took consumption. Lots of the colored people nearly starved. Not much to get to do and not much houseroom. Several families had to live in one house. Lots of the colored folks went up North and froze to death. They couldn't stand the cold. They wrote back about them dying. No, they never sent them back. I heard some sent for money to come back. I heard plenty 'bout the Ku Klux. They scared the folks to death. People left Augusta in droves. About a thousand would all meet and walk going to hunt work and new homes. Some of them died. I had a sister and brother lost that way. I had another sister come to Louisiana that way. She wrote back.

I don't think the colored folks looked for a share of land. They never got nothing 'cause the white folks didn't have nothing but barren hills left. About all the mules was wore out hauling provisions in the army. Some folks say they ought to done more for the colored folks when they left, but they say they was broke. Freeing all the slaves left 'em broke.

That reconstruction was a mighty hard pull. Me and Ma couldn't live. A man paid our ways to Carlisle, Arkansas, and we come. We started working for Mr. Emenson. He had a big store, teams, and land. We liked it fine, and I been here fifty-six years now. There was so much wild game, living was not so hard. If a fellow could get a little bread and a place to stay, he was all right. After I come to this state, I voted some. I have farmed and worked at odd jobs. I farmed mostly. Ma went back to her old master. He persuaded her to come back home. Me and her went back and run a farm four or five years before she died. Then I come back here.

/   /   /

LEE GUIDON, From South Carolina. Born in South
Carolina. Age at Interview: 89.

Yes, ma'am, I sure was in the Civil War. I plowed all day, and me and my sister helped take care of the baby at night. It would cry, and me bumping it [in a straight chair, rocking]. Time I git it to the bed where its mama was, it wake up and start crying all over again. I be so sleepy. It was a puny sort of baby. Its papa was off at war. His name was Jim

Cowan, and his wife Miss Margaret Brown 'fore she married him. Miss Lucy Smith give me and my sister to them. Then she married Mr. Abe Moore. Jim Smith was Miss Lucy's boy. He lay out in the woods all time. He say no need in him gitting shot up and killed. He say let the slaves be free. We lived, seemed like, on 'bout the line of York and Union counties. He lay out in the woods over in York County. Mr. Jim say all they fighting 'bout was jealousy. They caught him several times, but every time he got away from 'em. After they come home Mr. Jim say they never win no war. They stole and starved out the South. . . .

After freedom a heap of people say they was going to name their-selves over. They named theirselves big names, then went roaming round like wild, hunting cities. They changed up so it was hard to tell who or where anybody was. Heap of 'em died, and you didn't know when you hear about it if he was your folks hardly. Some of the names was Abraham, and some called theirselves Lincum. Any big name 'cept-ing their master's name. It was the fashion. I heard 'em talking 'bout it one evening, and my pa say, "Fine folks raise us and we gonna hold to our own names." That settled it with all of us. . . .

I reckon I do know 'bout the Ku Kluck. I knowed a man named Alfred Owens. He seemed all right, but he was a Republican. He said he was not afraid. He run a tanyard and kept a heap of guns in a big room. They all loaded. He married a Southern woman. Her husband either died or was killed. She had a son living with them. The Ku Kluck was called Upper League. They get this boy to unload all the guns. Then the white men went there. The white man give up and said, "I ain't got no gun to defend myself with. The guns all unloaded, and I ain't got no powder and shot." But the Ku Kluck shot in the houses and shot him up like lacework. He sold fine harness, saddles, bridles—all sorts of leather things. The Ku Kluck sure run them outen their country. They say they not going to have them round, and they sure run them out, back where they came from. . . .

For them what stayed on like they were, Reconstruction times 'bout like times before that 'cepting the Yankee stole out and tore up a scandalous heap. They tell the black folks to do something, and then come white folks you live with and say Ku Kluck whup you. They say leave, and white folks say better not listen to them old Yankees. They'll git you too far off to come back, and you freeze. They done give you all the use they got for you. How they do? All sorts of ways. Some stayed at their cabins glad to have one to live in and farmed on. Some running round begging, some hunting work for money, and nobody had no money 'cepting the Yankees, and they had no homes or land and mighty little work for you to do. No work to live on. Some going every day to the city. That winter I heard 'bout them starving and freezing by the wagon loads.

I never heard nothing 'bout voting till freedom. I don't think I ever voted till I come to Mississippi. I votes Republican. That's the party of my color, and I stick to them as long as they do right. I don't dabble in white folks' business, and that white folks' voting is their business. If I vote, I go do it and go on home.

I been plowing all my life, and in the hot days I cuts and saws wood. Then when I gets outa cotton-picking, I put each boy on a load of wood and we sell wood. The last years we got $3 a cord. Then we clear land till next spring. I don't find no time to be loafing. I never missed a year farming till I got the Bright's disease [one of several kinds of kidney ailments] and it hurt me to do hard work. Farming is the best life there is when you are able. . . .

When I owned most, I had six head mules and five head horses. I rented 140 acres of land. I bought this house and some other land about. The anthrax killed nearly all my horses and mules. I got one big fine mule yet. Its mate died. I lost my house. My son give me one room, and he paying the debt off now. It's hard for colored folks to keep anything. Somebody gets it from 'em if they don't mind.

The present times is hard. Timber is scarce. Game is about all gone. Prices higher. Old folks cannot work. Times is hard for younger folks too. They go to town too much and go to shows. They going to a tent show now. Circus coming, they say. They spending too much money for foolishness. It's a fast time. Folks too restless. Some of the colored folks work hard as folks ever did. They spends too much. Some folks is lazy. Always been that way.

I signed up to the government, but they ain't give me nothing 'cepting powdered milk and rice what wasn't fit to eat. It cracked up and had black something in it. A lady said she would give me some shirts that was her husband's. I went to get them, but she wasn't home. These heavy shirts give me heat. They won't give me the pension, and I don't know why. It would help me buy my salts and pills and the other medicines like Swamp Root. They won't give it to me.

/   /   /

TOBY JONES, From Madisonville, Texas. Born in South Carolina. Age at Interview: 87.

I worked for Massa 'bout four years after freedom, 'cause he forced me to, said he couldn't 'ford to let me go. His place was near ruint, the fences burnt, and the house would have been, but it was rock. There was a battle fought near his place, and I taken Missy to a hideout in the mountains to where her father was, 'cause there was bullets flying everywhere. When the war was over, Massa come home and says, ''You son of a gun, you's supposed to be free, but you ain't, 'cause I ain't gwine give you freedom.'' So I goes on working for him till I gits the chance to steal a hoss from him. The woman I wanted to marry, Govie, she 'cides to come to Texas with me. Me and Govie, we rides that hoss 'most a hundred miles, then we turned him a-loose and give him a scare back to his house, and come on foot the rest the way to Texas.

All we had to eat was what we could beg, and sometimes we went three days without a bite to eat. Sometimes we'd pick a few berries. When we got cold we'd crawl in a brushpile and hug up close together to keep warm. Once in awhile we'd come to a farmhouse, and the man let us sleep on cottonseed in his barn, but they was far and few between, 'cause they wasn't many houses in the country them days like now.

When we gits to Texas, we gits married, but all they was to our wedding am we just 'grees to live together as man and wife. I settled on some land, and we cut some trees and split them open and stood them on end with the tops together for our house. Then we deadened some trees, and the land was ready to farm. There was some wild cattle and hogs, and that's the way we got our start, caught some of them and tamed them.

I don't know as I'spected nothing from freedom, but they turned us out like a bunch of stray dogs, no homes, no clothing, no nothing, not 'nough food to last us one meal. After we settles on that place, I never seed man or woman, 'cept Govie, for six years, 'cause it was a long ways to anywhere. All we had to farm with was sharp sticks. We'd stick holes and plant corn, and when it come up we'd punch up the dirt round it. We didn't plant cotton, 'cause we couldn't eat that. I made bows and arrows to kill wild game with, and we never went to a store for nothing. We made our clothes out of animal skins.

WHY ADAM KIRK WAS A DEMOCRAT

(House Report no. 262, 43 Cong., 2 Sess., p. 106. Statement of an Alabama Negro. [1874])

A white man raised me. I was raised in the house of old man Billy Kirk. He raised me as a body servant. The class that he belongs to seems nearer to me than the northern white man, and actually, since the war, everything I have got is by their aid and their assistance. They have helped me raise up my family and have stood by me, and whenever I want a doctor, no matter what hour of the day or night, he is called in whether I have got a cent or not. And when I want any assistance I can get it from them. I think they have got better principles and better character than the republicans.

Walter L. Fleming (editor), Documentary History of Reconstruction, *Volume Two. (Gloucester, Massachusetts, Peter Smith, 1960), p. 87.*

43 | White Southerners' Reaction to Reconstruction

The Congressional Joint Committee of Fifteen, assembled to examine Southern representation in Congress, was named in December 1865 and served as the Republican response to President Andrew Johnson's lenient plan of Reconstruction. In 1866, the committee held hearings as part of its effort to develop the Fourteenth Amendment. Congress had already, despite the President's veto, enlarged the scope of the Freedmen's Bureau to care for displaced ex-slaves and to try by military commission those accused of depriving freedmen of civil rights.

The testimony of white Southerners, three samples of which are presented below, indicate how difficult it was for the white South to accept the idea of black equality. Congress's reconstruction policy, more stringent than Johnson's but still cautious, appeared radical, even unthinkable, to most white Southerners and probably to many Northerners. Reading such testimony, one begins to understand why the nation has found it so difficult to carry out the mandate of the Fourteenth and Fifteenth Amendments.

B. R. GRATTAN

Washington, D.C., February 10, 1866

Question: Where do you reside?
Answer: Richmond, Virginia.
Question: Are you a native of Virginia?
Answer: Yes, sir: I was raised in the valley of Virginia.
Question: Do you hold any public position?
Answer: I am a member of the present house of delegates of Virginia.
Question: Is that the only public position you have held?
Answer: I held the office of reporter to the court of appeals since January, 1844.

The Report of the Committees of the House of Representatives Made During the First Session, Thirty-Ninth Congress, 1865–'66. *Volume II. (Washington, D.C., Government Printing Office, 1866), Grattan: pp. 161–164; Forshey: pp. 129–132; Sinclair: 168–171.*

Question: I speak of two classes of people in Virginia for the sake of convenience, not with a view of offending anybody. I speak of secessionists and Union men. By secessionists I mean those who have directly or indirectly favored the rebellion; and by Union men I mean those who opposed the rebellion; and by the rebellion I mean the war which has taken place between the two sections of the country. What is the general feeling among the secessionists of Virginia towards the government of the United States, so far as your observation extends?

Answer: So far as I know, the sentiment is universal that the war has decided the question of secession entirely, that it is no longer an open question, and that we are all prepared to abide by the Union and live under it.

Question: You mean to be understood as saying that they suppose that the sword has settled the abstract right of secession?

Answer: Yes; we consider that we put it to the arbitrament of the sword, and have lost.

Question: What proportion of the legislature of Virginia are original secessionists, have in view the definitions I gave?

Answer: I would suppose that there are few members of the legislature who are less able to judge of that matter than myself, for my acquaintance as a member is very limited; but I should suppose, from the general sentiments of the people of Virginia, that while probably a very large proportion of those who are now members of the legislature were not in favor of secession or a dissolution of the Union originally, yet nearly all of them went with their State when it went out. They went heartily with it.

Question: How have the results of the war affected the feelings of Virginians generally? What is the sentiment left in their hearts in regard to satisfaction or dissatisfaction with the government of the United States—love or hatred, respect or contempt?

Answer: I cannot undertake to say generally; my intercourse is very limited. I would rather suppose, however, that while the feeling against the government was originally very strong, that feeling has been very much modified; it is nothing like as strong as it was, and is gradually declining.

Question: You think that the feeling is gradually changing from dislike to respect?

Answer: Yes, I think so.

Question: Have you any reason to suppose that there are persons in Virginia who still entertain projects of a dissolution of the Union?

Answer: None whatever. I do not believe that there is an intelligent man in the State who does.

/   /   /

Question: What has been, in your judgment, the effect, in the main, of President Johnson's liberality in bestowing pardons and amnesties on rebels?

Answer: I think it has been very favorable; I think President Johnson has commended himself very heartily. There is a very strong feeling of gratitude towards President Johnson.

/   /   /

Question: What, in your judgment, would be the consequences of such an infranchisement: would it produce scenes of violence between the two races?

Answer: I believe it would. I have very great apprehension that an attempt of that sort would lead to their extermination, not immediately, but to their gradual extinction. It would set up really an antagonistic interest, which would probably be used as a power, because I have no doubt that the negro vote would be under the influence of white people. You are to recollect that this is not simply a prejudice between the white and black races. It has grown to be a part of our nature to look upon them as an inferior; just as much a part of our nature as it is a part of the nature of other races to have enmity to each other; for instance, between the Saxon Irish and the Celtic Irish, or between the English and the French. You must change that nature, and it takes a long time to do it. I believe that if you place the negro on a footing of perfect equality with the white, it would actually increase the power of the white race, which would control the negro vote; yet it seems to me that nothing can reconcile the white people to that short of equal political power, and I fear, therefore, very much the consequences of any attempt of that sort upon the black race in Virginia.

Question: Would not that prejudice become modified a great deal in case the blacks should be educated and rendered more intelligent than they are now?

Answer: You would have to change their skin before you can do it. I beg leave to say this, so far from there being any unkind feeling to the negro, I believe that there is, on the part of the white race, towards the negro, no feeling but that of kindness, sympathy, and pity, and that there is every disposition to ameliorate their condition and improve it as much as possible; but it is that difference which has existed so long in their obvious distinction of color and condition—

Question: But suppose the condition of the negro should change?

Answer: The condition is annexed to the color. We are accustomed to see the color in the condition.

/   /   /

Question: Is there a general repugnance on the part of whites to the acquisition and enjoyment of property by the blacks?

Answer: I do not know. I do not think there is. Far from it. We would be very glad to see them all doing well and improving their condition.

Question: Do you find a similar repugnance to the acquisition of knowledge by blacks?

Answer: No, sir; far from it; on the contrary, we are trying, so far as we can, to educate them; but we are too poor ourselves to do much in educating other people, and they are certainly too poor to educate themselves.

Question: You would, then, anticipate a struggle of races in case the right of suffrage was given to the blacks?

Answer: Yes, sir; I think so.

Question: You would not anticipate it in case the blacks should vote in the interests of the white race?

Answer: As I said before, I believe that if the blacks are left to themselves, if all foreign influence were taken away, the whites would control their vote. It is not in that the difficulty lies, but it is in the repugnance which the white race would feel to that sort of political equality. It is the same sort of repugnance which a man feels to a snake. He does not feel any animosity to the snake, but there is a natural shrinking from it; that is my feeling. While I think I have as much sympathy for the black race, and feel as much interest in them as anybody else, while I can treat them kindly and familiarly, still the idea of equality is one which has the same sort of shrinking for me, and is as much a part of my nature, as was the antagonism between Saxon and Celt in Ireland.

Question: You are aware that that state of feeling does not exist in Ireland, England, or Scotland towards the blacks?

Answer: No; because they never had them; because they never saw them in their constant condition. So that difference of alienation between Saxon and Celt does not exist here, but it exists in Ireland. It is where that has been the feeling operating for so long that it has become a part of our nature. It is not a simple prejudice, but it becomes part of the nature of the man. . . .

Question: You have not much reason to expect that the legislature of Virginia will adopt this constitutional amendment in case it shall pass both houses of Congress?

Answer: I cannot speak for others, but for myself I say certainly not. No political power would ever induce me to vote for it. That form is much more objectionable than even a proposition to make them voters. It is giving you all the advantages of numbers, while you are taking that from us which, according to the original constitution, we had—three-fifths of the slave population—and no political power will force me to consent to that.

CALEB G. FORSHEY

Washington, D.C., March 28, 1966

Question: Where do you reside?

Answer: I reside in the State of Texas.

Question: How long have you been a resident of Texas?

Answer: I have resided in Texas and been a citizen of that State for nearly thirteen years.

Question: What opportunities have you had for ascertaining the temper and disposition of the people of Texas towards the government and authority of the United States?

Answer: For ten years I have been superintendent of the Texas Military Institute, as its founder and conductor. I have been in the confederate service in various parts of the confederacy; but chiefly in the trans-Mississippi department, in Louisiana and Texas, as an officer of engineers. I have had occasion to see and know very extensively the condition of affairs in Texas, and also to a considerable extent in Louisiana. I think I am pretty well-informed, as well as anybody, perhaps, of the present state of affairs in Texas.

Question: What are the feelings and views of the people of Texas as to the late rebellion, and the future condition and circumstances of the State, and its relations to the federal government?

Answer: After our army had given up its arms and gone home, the surrender of all matters in controversy was complete, and as nearly universal, perhaps, as anything could be. Assuming the matters in controversy to have been the right to secede, and the right to hold slaves, I think they were given up teetotally, to use a strong Americanism. When you speak of feeling, I should discriminate a little. The feeling was that of any party who had been cast in a suit he had staked all upon. They did not return from feeling, but from a sense of necessity, and from a judgment that it was the only and necessary thing to be done, to give up the contest. But when they gave it up, it was without reservation; with a view to look forward, and not back. That is my impression of the manner in which the thing was done. There was a public expectation that in some very limited time there would be a restoration to former relations; and in such restoration they felt great interest, after the contest was given up. The expectation was, and has been up to the present time, that there would be a speedy and immediate restoration. It was the expectation of the people that, as soon as the State was organized as proposed by the President, they would be restored to their former relations, and things would go on as before.

/   /   /

Question: What is your opinion of a military force under the authority of the federal government to preserve order in Texas and to protect those who have been loyal, both white and black, from the aggressions of those who have been in the rebellion?

Answer: My judgment is well founded on that subject: that wherever such military force is and has been, it has excited the very feeling it was intended to prevent; that so far from being necessary it is very pernicious everywhere, and without exception. The local authorities and public sentiment are ample for protection. I think no occasion would occur, unless some individual case that our laws would not reach. We had an opportunity to test this after the surrender and before any authority was there. The military authorities, or the military officers, declared that we were without laws, and it was a long time before the governor appointed arrived there, and then it was some time before we could effect anything in the way of organization. We were a people without law, order, or anything; and it was a time for violence if it would occur. I think it is a great credit to our civilization that, in that state of affairs, there was nowhere any instance of violence. I am proud of it, for I expected the countrary; I expected that our soldiers on coming home, many of them, would be dissolute, and that many of them would oppress the class of men you speak of; but it did not occur. But afterwards, wherever soldiers have been sent, there have been little troubles, none of them large; but personal collisions between soldiers and citizens.

Question: What is your opinion as to the necessity and advantages of the Freedmen's Bureau, or an agency of that kind, in Texas?

Answer: My opinion is that it is not needed; my opinion is stronger than that—that the effect of it is to irritate, if nothing else. While in New York city recently I had a conversation with some friends from Texas, from five distant points in the State. We met together and compared opinions; and the opinion of each was the same, that the negroes had generally gone to work since January; that except where the Freedmen's Bureau had interfered, or rather encouraged troubles, such as little complaints, especially between negro and negro, the negro's disposition was very good, and they had generally gone to work, a vast majority of them with their former masters. I was very gratified to learn that from districts where I feared the contrary. Still this difference was made, particularly by Mr. Carpenter, from Jefferson, the editor of the Jefferson Herald. He said that in two or three counties where they had not been able to organize the Freedmen's Bureau, there had been no trouble at all; nearly all the negroes had gone to work. The impression in Texas at present is that the negroes under the influence of the Freedmen's Bureau do worse than without it.

I want to state that I believe all our former owners of negroes are the friends of the negroes; and that the antagonism paraded in the papers of the north does not exist at all. I know the fact is the very converse of that; and good feeling always prevails between the masters and the slaves. But the negroes went off and left them in the lurch; my own family was an instance of it. But they came back after a time, saying they had been free enough and wanted a home.

Question: Do you think those who employ the negroes there are willing to make contracts with them, so that they shall have fair wages for their labor?

Answer: I think so; I think they are paid liberally, more than the white men in this country get; the average compensation to negroes there is greater than the average compensation of free laboring white men in this country. It seems to have regulated itself in a great measure by what each neighborhood was doing; the negroes saying, "I can get thus and so at such a place." Men have hired from eight to fifteen dollars per month during the year, and women at about two dollars less a month; house-servants at a great deal more.

Question: Do the men who employ the negroes claim to exercise the right to enforce their contract by physical force?

Answer: Not at all; that is totally abandoned; not a single instance of it has occurred. I think they still chastise children, though. The negro parents often neglect that, and the children are still switched as we switch our own children. I know it is done in my own house; we have little house-servants that we switch just as I do our own little fellows.

Question: What is your opinion as to the respective advantages to the white and black races, of the present free system of labor and the institution of slavery?

Answer: I think freedom is very unfortunate for the negro; I think it is sad; his present helpless condition touches my heart more than anything else I ever contemplated, and I think that is the common sentiment of our slaveholders. I have seen it on the largest plantations, where the negro men had all left, and where only women and children remained, and the owners had to keep them and feed them. The beginning certainly presents a touching and sad spectacle. The poor negro is dying at a rate fearful to relate.

I have some ethnological theories that may perhaps warp my judgment; but my judgment is that the highest condition the black race has ever reached or can reach, is one where he is provided for by a master race. That is the result of a great deal of scientific investigation and observation of the negro character by me ever since I was a man. The labor question had become a most momentous one, and I was studying it. I undertook to investigate the condition of the negro from statistics under various circumstances, to treat it purely as a matter of statistics from the census tables of this country of ours. I found that the free blacks of the north decreased 8 per cent.; the free blacks of the south increased 7 or 8 per cent., while the slaves by their sides increased 34 per cent. I inferred from the doctrines of political economy that the race is in the best condition when it procreates the fastest; that, other things being equal, slavery is of vast advantage to the negro. I will mention one or two things in connexion with this as explanatory of that result. The negro will not take care of his offspring unless required to do it, as compared with the whites. The little children will die; they do die, and hence the necessity of very rigorous regulations on our plantations which we have adopted in our nursery system.

Another cause is that there is no continence among the negroes. All the continence I have ever seen among the negroes has been enforced upon plantations, where it is generally assumed there is none. For the sake of procreation, if nothing else, we compel men to live with their wives. The discipline of the plantation was more rigorous, perhaps, in regard to men staying with their wives, than in regard to anything else; and I think the procreative results, as shown by the census tables, is due in a great measure to that discipline.

I think they are very much better off in having homes than the free blacks are. The free blacks in Louisiana, where we had 34,000, with a great deal of blood of the whites in them, and therefore a great deal of white sense, were nothing like so happy and so well off as our slaves are. My observation for many years leads me to this conclusion.

Question: What is the prevailing inclination among the people of Texas in regard to giving the negroes civil or political rights and privileges?

Answer: I think they are all opposed to it. There are some men—I am not among them—who think that the basis of intelligence might be a good basis for the elective franchise. But a much larger class, perhaps nine-tenths of our people, believe that the distinctions between the races should not be broken down by any such community of interests in the management of the affairs of the State. I think there is a very common sentiment that the negro, even with education, has not a mind capable of appreciating the political institutions of the country to such an extent as would make him a good associate for the white man in the administration of the government. I think if the vote was taken on the question of admitting him to the right of suffrage there would be a very small vote in favor of it—scarcely respectable: that is my judgment.

/   /   /

REVEREND JAMES SINCLAIR

Washington, D.C., January 29, 1866

[James Sinclair, a Scottish born minister who served on the Freedmen's Bureau in 1865, had been living in North Carolina for nine years. Though a slaveholder himself, Sinclair opposed succession. This led to the loss of his church and his eventual arrest during the war. In contrast to the testimony of Caleb Forshey, Sinclair's description of relations between whites and blacks suggests that, in some cases, paternalism has been replaced by outright enmity. An outsider in the South both during and after the conflict, Sinclair offers a point of view that seems the most pessimistic in its assessment of whether the wounds of the war would heal in the near future.]

Question: What is generally the state of feeling among the white people of North Carolina towards the government of the United States?

Answer: That is a difficult question to answer, but I will answer it as far as my own knowledge goes. In my opinion, there is generally among the white people not much love for the government. Though they are willing, and I believe determined, to acquiesce in what is inevitable, yet so far as love and affection for the government is concerned, I do not believe that they have any of it at all, outside of their personal respect and regard for President Johnson.

Question: How do they feel towards the mass of the northern people—that is, the people of what were known formerly as the free States?

Answer: They feel in this way: that they have been ruined by them. You can imagine the feelings of a person towards one whom he regards as having ruined him. They regard the northern people as having destroyed their property or taken it from them, and brought all the calamities of this war upon them.

Question: How do they feel in regard to what is called the right of secession?

Answer: They think that it was right . . . that there was no wrong in it. They are willing now to accept the decision of the question that has been made by the sword, but they are not by any means converted from their old opinion that they had a right to secede. It is true that there have always been Union men in our State, but not Union men without slavery, except perhaps among Quakers. Slavery was the central idea even of the Unionist. The only difference between them and the others upon that question was, that they desired to have that institution under the aegis of the Constitution, and protected by it. The secessionists wanted to get away from the north altogether. When the secessionists precipitated our State into rebellion, the Unionists and secessionists went together, because the great object with both was the preservation of slavery by the preservation of State sovereignty. There was another class of Unionists who did not care anything at all about slavery, but they were driven by the other whites into the rebellion for the purpose of preserving slavery. The poor whites are to-day very much opposed to conferring upon the negro the right of suffrage; as much so as the other classes of the whites. They believe it is the intention of government to give the negro rights at their expense. They cannot see it in any other light than that as the negro is elevated they must proportionately go down. While they are glad that slavery is done away with, they are as bitterly opposed to conferring the right of suffrage on the negro as the most prominent secessionists; but it is for the reason I have stated, that they think rights conferred on the negro must necessarily be taken from them, particularly the ballot, which was the only bulwark guarding their superiority to the negro race.

Question: In your judgment, what proportion of the white people of North Carolina are really, and truly, and cordially attached to the government of the United States?

Answer: Very few, sir; very few.

Question: Judging from what you have observed of the feelings of the people of that State, what would be their course in case of a war between the United States and a foreign government?

Answer: I can only tell you what I have heard young men say there; perhaps it was mere bravado. I have heard them say that they wished to the Lord the United States would get into a war with France or England; they would know where they would be. I asked this question of some of them: If Robert E. Lee was restored to his old position in the army of the United States, and he should call on you to join him to fight for the United Sates and against a foreign enemy, what would you do? They replied, "Wherever old Bob would go we would go with him."

Question: Have you heard such remarks since the war is over, as that they wished the United States would get into a war with England and France?

Answer: Oh, yes, sir; such remarks are very common. I have heard men say, "May my right hand wither and my tongue cleave to the roof of my mouth if I ever lift my arm in favor of the United States."

Question: Did you ever hear such sentiments rebuked by bystanders?

Answer: No, sir; it would be very dangerous to do so.

Question: Is the Freedmen's Bureau acceptable to the great mass of the white people in North Carolina?

Answer: No, sir; I do not think it is; I think the most of the whites wish the bureau to be taken away.

Question: Why do they wish that?

Answer: They think that they can manage the negro for themselves: that they understand him better than northern men do. They say, "Let us understand what you want us to do with the negro—what you desire of us; lay down your conditions for our re-admission into the Union, and then we will know what we have to do, and if you will do that we will enact laws for the government of these negroes. They have lived among us, and they are all with us, and we can manage them better than you can." They think it is intefering with the rights of the State for a bureau, the agent and representative of the federal government, to overslaugh the State entirely, and interfere with the regulations and administration of justice before their courts.

Question: Is there generally a willingness on the part of the whites to allow the freedmen to enjoy the right of acquiring land and personal property?

Answer: I think they are very willing to let them do that, for this reason; to get rid of some portion of the taxes imposed upon their property by the government. For instance, a white man will agree to sell a negro some of his land on condition of his paying so much a year on it, promising to give him a deed of it when the whole payment is made, taking his note in the mean time. This relieves that much of the land from taxes to be paid by the white man. All I am afraid of is, that the negro is too eager to go into this thing; that he will ruin himself, get himself into debt to the white man, and be forever bound to him for the debt and never get the land. I have often warned them to be careful what they did about these things.

Question: There is no repugnance on the part of the whites to the negro owning land and personal property?

Answer: I think not.

Question: Have they any objection to the legal establishment of the domestic relations among the blacks, such as the relation of husband and wife, of parent and child, and the securing by law to the negro the rights of those relations?

Answer: That is a matter of ridicule with the whites. They do not believe the negroes will ever respect those relations more than the brutes. I suppose I have married more than two hundred couples of negroes since the war, but the whites laugh at the very idea of the thing. Under the old laws a slave could not marry a free woman of color; it was made a penal offence in North Carolina for any one to perform such a marriage. But there was in my own family a slave who desired to marry a free woman of color, and I did what I conceived to be my duty, and married them, and I was presented to the grand jury for doing so, but the prosecuting attorney threw out the case and would not try it. In former times the officiating clergyman marrying slaves, could not use the usual formula: "Whom God has joined together let no man put asunder;" you could not say, "According to the ordinance of God I pronounce you man and wife; you are no longer two but one." It was not legal for you to do so.

Question: What, in general, has been the treatment of the blacks by the whites since the close of hostilities?

Answer: It has not generally been of the kindest character, I must say that; I am compelled to say that.

Question: Are you aware of any instance of personal ill treatment towards the blacks by the whites?

Answer: Yes, sir.

Question: Give some instances that have occurred since the war.

Answer: [Sinclair describes the beating of a young woman across her buttocks in graphic detail.]

Question: What was the provocation, if any?

Answer: Something in regard to some work, which is generally the provocation.

Question: Was there no law in North Carolina at that time to punish such an outrage?

Answer: No, sir; only the regulations of the Freedmen's Bureau; we took cognizance of the case. In old times that was quite allowable; it is what was called "paddling."

Question: Did you deal with the master?

Answer: I immediately sent a letter to him to come to my office, but he did not come, and I have never seen him in regard to the matter since. I had no soldiers to enforce compliance, and I was obliged to let the matter drop.

Question: Have you any reason to suppose that such instances of cruelty are frequent in North Carolina at this time—instances of whipping and striking?

Answer: I think they are; it was only a few days before I left that a woman came there with her head all bandaged up, having been cut and bruised by her employer. They think nothing of striking them.

Question: And the negro has practically no redress?

Answer: Only what he an get from the Freedmen's Bureau.

Question: Can you say anything further in regard to the political condition of North Carolina—the feeling of the people towards the government of the United States?

Answer: I for one would not wish to be left there in the hands of those men; I could not live there just now. But perhaps my case is an isolated one from the position I was compelled to take in that State. I was persecuted, arrested, and they tried to get me into their service; they tried everything to accomplish their purpose, and of course I have rendered myself still more obnoxious by accepting an appointment under the Freedmen's Bureau. As for myself I would not be allowed to remain there. I do not want to be handed over to these people. I know it is utterly impossible for any man who was not true to the Confederate States up to the last moment of the existence of the confederacy, to expect any favor of these people as the State is constituted at present.

Question: Suppose the military pressure of the government of the United States should be withdrawn from North Carolina, would northern men and true Unionists be safe in that State?

Answer: A northern man going there would perhaps present nothing obnoxious to the people of the State. But men who were born there, who have been true to the Union, and who have fought against the rebellion, are worse off than northern men. And Governor Holden will never get any place from the people of North Carolina, not even a constable's place.

Question: Why not?

Answer: Because he identified himself with the Union movement all along after the first year of the rebellion. He has been a marked man; his printing office has been gutted, and his life has been threatened by the soldiers of the rebellion. He is killed there politically, and never will get anything from the people of North Carolina, as the right of suffrage exists there at present. I am afraid he would not get even the support of the negro, if they should be allowed to vote, because he did not stand right up for them as he should have done. In my opinion, he would have been a stronger man than ever if he had.

Question: Is it your opinion that the feelings of the great mass of the white people of North Carolina are unfriendly to the government of the United States?

Answer: Yes, sir, it is; they have no love for it. If you mean by loyalty, acquiescence in what has been accomplished, then they are all loyal; if you mean, on the other hand, that love and affection which a child has for its parent even after he brings the rod of correction upon him, then they have not that feeling. It may come in the course of time.

/   /   /

Question: In your judgment, what effect has been produced by the liberality of the President in granting pardons and amnesties to rebels in that State—what effect upon the public mind?

Answer: On my oath I am bound to reply exactly as I believe; that is, that if President Johnson is ever a candidate for re-election he will be supported by the southern States, particularly by North Carolina; but that his liberality to them has drawn them one whit closer to the government than before, I do not believe. It has drawn them to President Johnson personally, and to the democratic party, I suppose.

Question: Has that clemency had any appreciable effect in recovering the real love and affection of that people for the government?

Answer: No, sir; not for the government, considered apart from the person of the Executive.

Question: Has it had the contrary effect?

Answer: I am not prepared to answer that question, from the fact that they regard President Johnson as having done all this because he was a southern man, and not because he was an officer of the government.

/   /   /

44 | *A Sharecrop Contract*

The ending of slavery and the impoverishment of the South in the aftermath of the Civil War seriously disrupted Southern agriculture. Five years after the war's end, Southern cotton production was still only about half of what it had been in the 1850s. The large plantations, no longer tended by gangs of slaves or hired freedmen, were broken up into smaller holdings, but the capital required for profitable agriculture meant that control of farming remained centralized in a limited elite of merchants and larger landholders.

Various mechanisms arose to finance Southern agriculture. Tenants worked on leased land. Small landowners gave liens on their crops to get financing. But the most common method of financing agriculture was sharecropping. Agreements like the Grimes family's sharecrop contract determined the economic life of thousands of poor rural families in the southern United States after the Civil War. Families, black and white, lacking capital for agriculture, were furnished the seed, implements, and a line of credit for food and other necessities to keep them through the growing season. Accounts were settled in the winter after crops were in. Under these conditions a small number of farmers managed to make money and eventually become landowners, and the larger part found themselves in ever deeper debt at the end of the year with no choice but to contract again for the next year.

To every one applying to rent land upon shares, the following conditions must be read, and *agreed to.*

To every 30 or 35 acres, I agree to furnish the team, plow, and farming implements, except cotton planters, and I *do not* agree to furnish a cart to every cropper. The croppers are to have half of the cotton, corn and fodder (and peas and pumpkins and potatoes if any are planted) if the following conditions are complied with, but—if not—they are to have only two fifths ($\frac{2}{5}$). Croppers are to have no part or interest in the cotton seed raised from the crop planted and worked by them. No vine crops of any description, that is, no watermelons, muskmelons, . . . squashes or anything of that kind, except peas and pumpkins, and po-

From the Grimes Family Papers (#3357), 1882. Held in the Southern Historical Collection, University of North Carolina, Chapel Hill.

tatoes, are to be planted in the cotton or corn. All must work under my direction. All plantation work to be done by the croppers. My part of the crop to be *housed* by them, and the fodder and oats to be hauled and put in the house. All the cotton must be topped about 1st August. If any cropper fails from any cause to save all the fodder from his crop, I am to have enough fodder to make it equal to one half of the whole if the whole amount of fodder had been saved.

For every mule or horse furnished by me there must be 1000 good sized rails . . . hauled, and the fence repaired as far as they will go, the fence to be torn down and put up from the bottom if I so direct. All croppers to haul rails and work on fence wherever I may order. Rails to be split when I may say. Each cropper to clean out every ditch in his crop, and where a ditch runs between two croppers, the cleaning out of that ditch is to be divided equally between them. Every ditch bank in the crop must be shrubbed down and cleaned off before the crop is planted and must be cut down every time the land is worked with his hoe and when the crop is "laid by," the ditch banks must be left clean of bushes, weeds, and seeds. The cleaning out of all ditches must be done by the first of October. The rails must be split and the fence repaired before corn is planted.

Each cropper must keep in good repair all bridges in his crop or over ditches that he has to clean out and when a bridge needs repairing that is outside of all their crops, then any one that I call on must repair it.

Fence jams to be done as ditch banks. If any cotton is planted on the land outside of the plantation fence, I am to have *three fourths* of all the cotton made in those patches, that is to say, no cotton must be planted by croppers in their home patches.

All croppers must clean out stables and fill them with straw, and haul straw in front of stables whenever I direct. All the cotton must be manured, and enough fertilizer must be brought to manure each crop highly, the croppers to pay for one half of all manure bought, the quantity to be purchased for each crop must be left to me.

No cropper to work off the plantation when there is any work to be done on the land he has rented, or when his work is needed by me or other croppers. Trees to be cut down on Orchard, House field & Evanson fences, leaving such as I may designate.

Road field to be planted from the *very edge of the ditch to the fence,* and all the land to be planted close up to the ditches and fences. *No stock of any kind* belonging to croppers to run in the plantation after crops are gathered.

If the fence should be blown down, or if trees should fall on the fence outside of the land planted by any of the croppers, any one or all that I may call upon must put it up and repair it. Every cropper must feed, or have fed, the team he works, Saturday nights, Sundays, and every morning before going to work, beginning to feed his team (morning, noon, and night *every day* in the week) on the day he rents and feeding it to and including the 31st day of December. If any cropper shall from any cause fail to repair his fence as far as 1000 rails will go, or shall fail to clean out any part of his ditches, or shall fail to leave his ditch banks, any part of them, well shrubbed and clean when his crop is laid by, or shall fail to clean out stables, fill them up and haul straw in front of them whenever he is told, he shall have only two-fifths ($\frac{2}{5}$) of the cotton, corn, fodder, peas and pumpkins made on the land he cultivates.

If any cropper shall fail to feed his team Saturday nights, all day Sunday and all the rest of the week, morning/noon, and night, for every time he so fails he must pay me five cents.

No corn nor cotton stalks must be burned, but must be cut down, cut up and plowed in. Nothing must be burned off the land except when it is *impossible* to plow it in.

Every cropper must be responsible for all gear and farming implements placed in his hands, and if not returned must be paid for unless it is worn out by use.

Croppers must sow & plow in oats and haul them to the crib, but *must have no part of them*. Nothing to be sold from their crops, nor fodder nor corn to be carried out of the fields until my rent is all paid, and all amounts they owe me and for which I am responsible are paid in full.

I am to gin & pack all the cotton and charge every cropper an eighteenth of his part, the cropper to furnish his part of the bagging, ties, & twine.

The sale of every cropper's part of the cotton to be made by me when and where I choose to sell, and after deducting all they may owe me and all sums that I may be responsible for on their accounts, to pay them their half of the net proceeds. Work of every description, particularly the work on fences and ditches, to be done to my satisfaction, and must be done over until I am satisfied that it is done as it should be.

No wood to burn, nor light wood, nor poles, nor timber for boards, nor wood for any purpose whatever must be gotten above the house occupied by Henry Beasley—nor must any trees be cut down nor any wood used for any purpose, except for firewood, without my permission.

Questions for Part IV

1 What do the letters from slaves tell you about life in slavery? Discuss some of the problems mentioned. How are they similar to or different from what you would expect to find in letters by poor but free people?

2 How does Meriwether's view of the capacity of blacks to direct their own lives compare to what you see in the readings by black slaves and ex-slaves? Why do you think he sees such limits to his slaves' abilities? What does this tell you about the institution of slavery?

3 What inspired Nat Turner to rebel? How would you characterize his personality?

4 What does Douglass say about slave singing? How did he come to learn to read? What passage in Douglass's reading do you find most powerful? Why?

5 What does Bibb say about Christianity and slavery? How do you imagine his former master reacted to his letters?

6 What did Frederick Douglass, Henry Bibb, and Harriet Tubman all have in common? Can you detect anything in their characters that would explain their ''success''?

7 How does being both black and a woman influence Sojourner Truth's view of women's rights?

8 How did Elizabeth Cady Stanton's advocacy of women's rights grow out of her personal situation? How do her views of child-rearing relate to her belief in the need for women to have more power in society?

9 Based on what you have read about ''Bleeding Kansas,'' was ''popular sovereignty'' the way to solve the slavery problem? Why do you think people were willing to fight over the slavery issue?

10 What was the ''Shermanizing process'' as Southerners saw it? Does Andrews's account make you feel sympathetic to the defeated South? Why or why not?

11 Based on the evidence you have read, what were some of the attitudes and expectations among the freedmen after the Civil War?

12 Did Southern whites accept the consequences of the Civil War? Explain.

13 What kind of life would a sharecropping family lead? Give details.